Carnap, Tarski, and Quine at Harvard

 *Publications of the Archive of Scientific Philosophy
Hillman Library, University of Pittsburgh*

Steve Awodey, Editor

EDITORIAL BOARD

John Norton
University of Pittsburgh

Richard Creath
Arizona State University

Michael Friedman
Stanford University

James Lennox
University of Pittsburgh

Wilfried Sieg
Carnegie Mellon University

Gereon Wolters
University of Constance

John Earman
University of Pittsburgh

Gottfried Gabriel
University of Jena

Dana Scott
Carnegie Mellon University

Mark Wilson
University of Pittsburgh

 *Publications of the Archive of Scientific Philosophy
Hillman Library, University of Pittsburgh*

Volume 1.
Frege's Lectures on Logic: Carnap's Student Notes, 1910–1914, edited by Erich H. Reck and Steve Awodey

Volume 2.
Carnap Brought Home: The View From Jena, edited by Steve Awodey and Carsten Klein

Volume 3.
The Concept of Probability in the Mathematical Representation of Reality, by Hans Reichenbach, translated and edited by Frederick Eberhardt and Clark Glymour

Volume 4.
Empiricism at the Crossroads: The Vienna Circle's Protocol-Sentence Debate, by Thomas Uebel

Volume 5.
Carnap, Tarski, and Quine at Harvard: Conversations on Logic, Mathematics, and Science, by Greg Frost-Arnold

Carnap, Tarski, and Quine at Harvard

Conversations on Logic, Mathematics, and Science

Greg Frost-Arnold

Open Court
Chicago, Illinois

Front cover photos of Quine, Tarski, and Carnap are attributed to Carl Hempel. They were provided by the Archives of Scientific Philosophy, University of Pittsburgh, and are used with the permission of Peter Hempel and Miranda Hempel.

To order books from Open Court, call toll-free 1-800-815-2280, or visit our website at www.opencourtbooks.com.

Open Court Publishing Company is a division of Carus Publishing Company, dba ePals Media.

Copyright © 2013 Carus Publishing Company, dba ePals Media.

First printing 2013

All rights reserved. No part of this publication may be reproduced, stored in a retrieval system, or transmitted, in any form or by any means, electronic, mechanical, photocopying, recording, or otherwise, without the prior written permission of the publisher, Open Court Publishing Company, a division of Carus Publishing Company, dba ePals Media, 70 East Lake Street, Suite 800, Chicago, Illinois 60601.

Printed and bound in the United States of America.

Designed by John Grandits.

Typeset in LaTeX by Dirk Schlimm.

Library of Congress Control Number: 2013939108

For my parents

Contents

Preface	xiii
1 Overview and Historical Background	**1**
1.1. Introduction: Setting the Historical Stage	1
1.2. The Main Project: A 'Finitist-Nominalist' Language of Science	3
1.3. Mathematics in a Finitist-Nominalist Language	11
1.4. Pre-history of the 1941 Finitist-Nominalist Project	15
2 Justifications for the Finitist-Nominalist Conditions	**27**
2.1. First Justification: *Verständlichkeit*	27
2.2. Second Justification: Overcoming Metaphysics	37
2.3. Third Justification: Inferential Safety	43
2.4. Fourth Justification: Natural Science	45
2.5. Current Justifications for Nominalism	47
3 Objections to the Finitist-Nominalist Project	**51**
3.1. Why Does Carnap Participate, Given His Reservations?	51
3.2. Higher Mathematics *Is* Meaningful	54
3.3. Are Any Infinities Compatible with the FN Project?	61
3.4. Attacking the FN Conditions	65
3.5. An Objection Not in the Notes	71
4 The Finitist-Nominalist Project and Analyticity	**73**
4.1. Under a Finitist-Nominalist Regime, Arithmetic Is Synthetic	74
4.2. Radicalization of Quine's Critique of Analyticity	81
5 Direct Discussions of Analytic Truth in 1940-41	**89**
5.1. What Is Analyticity, circa 1940?	90
5.2. Tarski's Objections to Analyticity	94
5.3. Quine's Disagreements with Carnap circa 1940	102
6 Overcoming Metaphysics through the Unity of Science	**117**
6.1. Unity of Language, Not Laws	118

6.2.	Overcoming Metaphysics	122
6.3.	A Difficulty: What *Cannot* Be Incorporated into a Language of Science?	133
6.4.	Conclusion: The Origin of the Term 'Unified Science'	136

Appendix A   Translation   139

Appendix B   German Transcription   191

References   243

Index   251

Carnap, Tarski, and Quine at Harvard

Preface

Several years ago, I began combing through the Rudolf Carnap Collection at the University of Pittsburgh's Archives of Scientific Philosophy, searching for material about Alfred Tarski's theory of truth. I fortuitously discovered a folder full of dictation notes Carnap had taken during conversations with Tarski and others during the academic year 1940-41. Although I did not initially fully recognize what I had found, those notes eventually became the originating cause of this book. The first part of this book consists of my attempts to understand those documents, both in terms of their place in the history of analytic philosophy, and their often surprising philosophical content. As the subtitle of this book suggests, I have grouped this content into three interdependent sections: mathematical nominalism (mathematics), analytic truth (logic), and the unity of science. This choice of focus certainly reflects my own interests in the history of analytic philosophy; another, almost entirely different book could probably be written about the same archival material. Because these wide-ranging notes would amply reward such study, an edited version of the archival material itself can be found in the Appendix, along with an English translation.

I do not feel that *I* wrote this book. The final product is very much the result of many people—I just happen to be the person who put the most time into the group's project. My inability to see errors that others spotted, and others' insightful and creative suggestions for new directions of inquiry, truly made this a collaborative effort. Brigitta Arden, at the Archives of Scientific Philosophy, has been very helpful in transcribing Carnap's shorthand notes into German, as well as checking the accuracy of older existing transcriptions. An audience at HOPOS 2004 helped improve the core of what is now the first chapter; Alan Richardson and Chris Pincock, in particular, both provided fruitful suggestions. Participants at HOPOS 2008, and Thomas Uebel in particular, provided valuable suggestions for understanding Quine's development during the 1940s. The audience at the 2004 PSA helped iron out some of the deficiencies of the final chapter; Rick Creath provided especially useful feedback both then and later, as the larger project progressed. His *Dear Carnap, Dear Van* was not only an invaluable research tool for present purposes, but also served as an exemplar for this book. Michael Friedman, Don Howard, and Thomas Ricketts each brought their substantial erudition to bear on various ideas presented here; their ability to see the historical 'big picture' was a very helpful corrective. André Carus gave me very helpful suggestions about the historical big picture as well, and chapter 1 in particular was greatly improved as a result. Marion Ledwig, Greg Lavers, and Jon Tsou each undertook the task of reading the entire manuscript when it was close to completion; their fresh eyes provided insightful new perspective on ideas that had been bouncing around in my head for years. Jon, in particular, engaged with my arguments in detail, and (thankfully!) would not let me get away with inferences that were too hasty. Kerri Mommer, my editor at Open Court, greatly improved the manuscript, and Dirk Schlimm did an enormous amount of work typesetting the final project. I am certain I am leaving out several people who helped me recognize and rectify deficiencies in the claims presented here, only because I've been overeager to discuss this material with anyone who would listen for the last few years. I apologize for those omissions.

I am grateful to the journal *HOPOS* for allowing me to use parts of my article "Quine's Evolution from 'Carnap's Disciple' to the Author of 'Two Dogmas,' " vol. 1 (Fall 2011), ©2011 by the International Society for the History of Philosophy of Science. *Philosophy of Science* also allowed me to draw on parts of "The Large-Scale Structure of Logical Empiricism," originally published in vol. 72 (December 2005), ©2005 by the Philosophy of Science Association, all rights reserved. Finally, I must thank the Quine Papers, Houghton Library, Harvard University, and the Rudolf Carnap Collection. The material in the appendices is quoted by permission of the University of Pittsburgh; all rights reserved.

I have saved this book's greatest intellectual debts for last. First is Paolo Mancosu, who found the records of these conversations at roughly the same time I did, and published the first scholarly treatment of them (Mancosu 2005). Writing about documents that no one has ever seen before is not something for which the usual historical training on Plato or Descartes prepares you. I am very fortunate that a philosopher as able and intellectually generous as Paolo began studying these works as well: his perspective kept me from being completely lost as I attempted to wade through Carnap's notes. Perhaps more than he realizes, Paolo's published work and private comments helped eliminate distortions and misunderstandings in my conception of what is going on in this material. Steve Awodey gave me copious and insightful feedback every step of the way, especially when the project was just beginning: he read rough drafts with more care than they deserved at the time. His substantive comments on underdeveloped ideas were a great boon. Laura Ruetsche's help has been essential throughout the process. She possesses the enviable knack of seeing to the core of an issue whose surface I've only scratched, and her input has improved the final product in several ways. Finally, my wife Karen has not only given me a wonderful life, but has been a fantastic philosophical rudder as well.

Greg Frost-Arnold

Chapter 1
Overview and Historical Background

1.1. Introduction: Setting the Historical Stage

During the academic year 1940-41, several giants of analytic philosophy, both established and budding, congregated at Harvard University. The list of philosophers is impressive. Bertrand Russell, who was only at Harvard during the Fall semester of 1940, originally emigrated from Britain in 1938. During 1940, he was embroiled in his infamous legal battles with the City College of New York. In the fall, he gave the William James Lectures at Harvard, a series of talks that presently became *An Inquiry into Meaning and Truth*.[1] Alfred Tarski arrived in the U.S. from Poland in August 1939 for the Fifth International Congress for the Unity of Science, held at Harvard. On September 1, the Nazis invaded Poland. Tarski received permission to stay in the U.S., though his family was stranded in Poland; he held a number of temporary positions (at Harvard, City College of New York, and the Institute for Advanced Study) over the following years, before becoming a professor at the University of California at Berkeley.[2]

Rudolf Carnap and Carl Hempel had immigrated to the U.S. a few years earlier. In December 1935, Carnap moved from Prague to the University of Chicago, where he was eventually offered a permanent position (Carnap 1963, 34). Carnap was a visiting professor at Harvard during the academic year 1940-41. Hempel crossed the Atlantic after being invited by Carnap in 1937 to serve as his research associate (Carnap 1963, 35); he was with Carnap in Harvard as well. He had only published a few articles by 1940, most of which dealt with philosophical issues in probability theory. W. V. O. Quine had already taken up a position at Harvard (he was appointed to Instructor in 1936 and promoted to Assistant Professor in 1941). In 1940, the first edition of his *Mathematical Logic* was published. Nelson Goodman was awarded his Ph.D. at Harvard in 1941 after completing his dissertation, *A Study of Qualities* (submitted in November 1940), which later became

---

1. Russell had also presented much of this material to a seminar he held at the University of Chicago during Winter Quarter 1939, which Carnap attended.
2. Significant historical work on Tarski's first years in the U.S., as well as the rest of his life, can be found in Feferman and Feferman (2004); especially relevant for the present period under study is chapter 5: "How the 'Unity of Science' Saved Alfred Tarski."

The Structure of Appearance.³ This group of philosophers held meetings under the heading of (what Carnap terms) the 'Logic Group' regularly, and they had smaller, informal conversations as well.

Any student of the philosophy of logic, mathematics, or the natural sciences would like to know what these immensely influential and innovative thinkers discussed during their hours together. Such information would be valuable both for the light it could shed on the historical development of analytic philosophy, as well as for purely philosophical reasons: were interesting or compelling arguments made here that do not appear elsewhere? Fortunately, one can almost be a 'fly on the wall' for many of these conversations, both public and private: Carnap had the lifelong habit of taking very detailed discussion notes, and he often took such notes during his year at Harvard. These documents have been preserved and stored in the Rudolf Carnap Collection (RCC), part of the Archives of Scientific Philosophy at the University of Pittsburgh. The present book focuses on these documents. Most of the notes are records of discussions, but some are Carnap's own contemporaneous reflections on the topics, composed in private. Paolo Mancosu has published an excellent overview of this material (Mancosu 2005); I build on his work here.

Several of the above-named philosophers also took part in a larger collaborative community, which was also founded in the Fall of 1940 at Harvard, called the 'Science of Science' dinner and discussion group. This group included many prominent scientists, including many European émigrés, as well as other philosophers. The Harvard psychologist S. S. Stevens, one of the champions of operationism in psychology, spearheaded the effort, apparently prompted by Carnap (Stevens 1974, 408). The mathematicians George David Birkhoff (and his son Garrett), Richard von Mises, and Saunders MacLane, the sociologist Talcott Parsons, the economists Otto Morgenstern and J. A. Schumpeter, as well as Percy Bridgman, Herbert Feigl, Philipp Frank, and C. I. Lewis were all invited to the first meeting; a total of forty-five invitations were sent. Further details about the Science of Science group, including the text of that invitation and a list of invitees, can be found in Hardcastle (2003). My focus here will be exclusively on the Logic Group and its participants, not the larger Science of Science group.⁴

---

3. Goodman also tells us that both Quine and Carnap "read *A Study of Qualities* with great care and made innumerable invaluable suggestions" (Goodman 1966, x). Also, he mentions that his dissertation was not nominalistic, as *Structure of Appearance* is (Goodman 1966, $xvii$); perhaps (part of) the spur to Goodman's change came from the conversations with Carnap, Tarski, and Quine in 1940-41. (However, his dissertation does discuss nominalism; see for example RCC 102-44-10, -11, which are Carnap's discussion notes for conversations with Goodman about his dissertation.)
4. I have only found one document in the Carnap archives from this time period that mentions the Science of Science group: Carnap alludes briefly to von Mises' presentation, in the Science of Science group, of the Kolmogorov-Doob interpretation of probability (102-63-13). This allusion, however, shows that Hardcastle may be too hasty in concluding that what happened at these meetings "must be left to the historically informed imagination" (Hardcastle 2003, 175).

1.2. The Main Project: A 'Finitist-Nominalist' Language of Science

Carnap's discussion notes from 1940-41 cover a wide range of topics. We have records concerning:

- the relations between metaphysics, magic, and theology (RCC 102-63-09),
- the concept *proposition* (102-63-10, -11),
- the interpretation of the probability calculus (102-63-13),
- transfinite rules of inference (102-63-12),
- non-standard models of Peano arithmetic (102-63-08),
- comparisons of formal languages without types (e.g. set theory) to languages with types (exemplified by *Principia Mathematica*) (090-16-09, -02, -26),
- modality (090-16-09, -25),[5]
- Quine's recently published *Mathematical Logic* (090-16-02, -03, -26),
- the treatment of quotation-marks in formalized languages (090-16-13),
- the possibility of a 'probabilistic' consequence relation (090-16-30),
- the relationship between the notions *state of affairs* and *model* in semantics (090-16-10, -11),

and other topics. Some of these are mentioned only briefly; others receive extended treatment.

However, the plurality of Carnap's discussion notes during the spring semester deal with what he and his collaborators call—most briefly—'finitism.' In these notes, Carnap refers to this enterprise by a number of other names as well. The following are Carnap's section headings for entries related to this topic:

- "On Finitistic Syntax" (090-16-27)
- "Logical Finitism" (-24)
- "On the Formulation of Syntax in Finitistic Language" (-23)
- "Finitistic Language" (-06, -08)
- "The Language of Science, on a Finitistic Basis" (-12)
- "Finitistic Arithmetic" (-16)

---

[5]. An insightful treatment of this portion of the notes can be found in Mancosu (2005, 332-35).

- "Conversation about the Nucleus-Language" (-05)

However, this topic is *not* identical with the cluster of claims philosophers today usually associate with the label 'finitism,' namely, the mathematical project associated with Hilbert and his school. Carnap, Tarski, and Quine believed that Hilbertian finitism was long dead as a research program by the time these conversations began.[6] Unlike Hilbert, they are not dealing with the foundations of mathematical inference (specifically, investigating which proofs in classical mathematics can be re-cast into a finitistically acceptable form). Rather, in these conversations, 'finitism' refers to strict requirements Tarski proposes a language must meet to be *verständlich*, that is, understandable or intelligible.

Tarski's proposal varies somewhat from meeting to meeting. Carnap records the first version of it as follows.

> January 10, 1941.
> *Tarski, Finitism.* Remark in the logic group.
> Tarski: I understand at bottom only a language that fulfills the following conditions:
> 1. *Finite* number of individuals.
> 2. *Reistic* (Kotarbiński): the individuals are physical things.
> 3. *Non-Platonic*: Only variables for individuals (things) occur, not for universals (classes etc.)
> (090-16-28)

Three weeks later, Tarski offers a similar, though not identical, characterization of a language he considers completely understandable.

> *Finitism.*
> *Tarski*: I truly understand only a *finite language* S_1:
> only individual variables, [cf. condition 3. above]
> whose values are things, [2. above]
> whose number is not claimed to be infinite (but perhaps also not the opposite). [modified version of 1.]
> Finitely many descriptive predicates. [new requirement]
> (090-16-25)

Let us describe Tarski's proposed conditions for an intelligible language somewhat anachronistically, using the modern apparatus of model theory. We begin with the standard notion of an interpreted language $\mathcal{L} = \langle L, M, \rho \rangle$. L carries the syntactic information about the language: a list of the symbols of the language, the grammatical category to which each symbol belongs, and which strings of symbols qualify as grammatical formulae and which do not. The semantic scheme ρ determines the truth-values of a compound expression formed using logical connectives, given the truth-values of its constituents. M is an interpretation or model that fixes signification of the nonlogical constants of L. Specifically,

---

6. See Detlefsen (1986) for a modern attempt to resuscitate parts of Hilbert's program.

The Main Project: A 'Finitist-Nominalist' Language of Science

$M = \langle D, f \rangle$, where D is a nonempty set, and f is an interpretation function which assigns members of D to singular terms, assigns sets of ordered n-tuples $\subseteq D_n$ to n-ary relation symbols, and a member of $D_n \mapsto D$ to each n-ary function symbol.

Now let us use this apparatus to rephrase Tarski's idea precisely in modern terminology. Tarski is describing a certain type of (interpreted) language $\mathcal{L}$ that has the following four characteristics, which I will henceforth refer to as Tarski's 'finitist-nominalist' (FN) conditions.

(FN 1) $\mathcal{L}$ is first-order.

In a fully understandable language, variables range over individuals only, so one cannot quantify over properties or relations. One might be tempted to interpret Tarski as claiming that any string that contains (the formalized correlate of) 'For all properties $X,\ldots$' is not a grammatical formula of L, since 'being first-order' is a grammatical property. However, we probably should not view Tarski's proposal as a purely grammatical restriction. For immediately following the quotation above, Tarski explains that he is perfectly willing to derive the consequences of sentences containing higher-order variables according to the rules of a proof calculus, but standardly, ungrammatical strings cannot be operated on by the rules of a proof calculus. Tarski's complaint is that he does not truly understand these higher-order sentences. He says:

> I only 'understand' any other language [i.e., a language that does not meet his restrictions—GF-A] in the way I 'understand' classical mathematics, namely, as a calculus; I know what I can derive from what... With any higher, 'Platonic' statements in a discussion, I interpret them to myself as statements that a fixed sentence is derivable (or derived) from other sentences. (090-16-25)

The notion of full or complete 'understanding,' which a mere 'calculus' alone cannot deliver, will be discussed at length in 2.2 below. But we can see that (FN 1) is not a restriction on which strings are grammatical, since Tarski does not consider "higher, 'Platonic' statements" ungrammatical, for nothing can be derived from an ungrammatical string in a proof calculus.

(FN 2) All elements of D are "physical things."

In Tarski's elaboration and discussion of (FN 2), numbers are specifically disallowed from D. Furthermore, combining this with (FN 1), not even the usual Frege-Russell reconstruction of numbers as classes of classes (or concepts of concepts) is allowed in a finitist-nominalist language.

What, exactly, are the 'physical things' of (FN 2)? In Carnap's notes, the discussants do not show much interest in settling upon a specific interpretation.[7] Tarski never articulates precisely what he thinks the 'physical things' are. Three

---

7. Nelson Goodman, in *The Structure of Appearance* (Goodman 1966, 39) and "A World of Individuals" (Goodman 1956, 17), goes so far as to say that nominalism *per se* places no

options the group considers are: (i.) elementary physical particles, such as electrons etc., (ii.) mereological wholes composed of elementary particles (or quanta of energy) (Quine)[8], so that e.g. the objects referred to by the names 'London' and 'Rudolf Carnap' will qualify as physical objects, and (iii.) spatial and/or temporal intervals (Carnap); this final suggestion is derived from the co-ordinate or position languages of Carnap's *Logical Syntax of Language* (090-16-23). In "On Universals," published six years after these discussions, Quine presents a "logic of limited quantification over classes of concrete individuals," whose variables "admit only concrete objects as values." Quine then asks:

> But concrete objects in what sense? Material objects, let us say, past, present, and future. Point-events, and spatio-temporally scattered totalities of point events. (Quine 1947, 82)

But in 1941, there was no consensus (and no explicit desire for consensus) about what should count as a physical object in condition (FN 2).

(FN 1) and (FN 2) place what we would today call *nominalist* requirements on an intelligible language; let us turn to the properly finitist requirement:

(FN 3_R: restrictive version) D contains a finite number of members;

or

(FN 3_L: liberal version) No assumption is made about the cardinality of D.[9]

Tarski originally proposes the restrictive policy, but in later conversations, he clearly favors the liberal policy (see 090-16-04 and -05). Carnap, in his autobiographical recollections of these discussions, attributes the restrictive version to Quine and the liberal version to Tarski and himself (Carnap 1963, 79).

The last restriction Tarski proposes for a finitist-nominalist language can be couched as follows:

(FN 4) $\mathcal{L}$ contains only finitely many descriptive predicates.

Tarski offers no justification for (FN 4), and the participants never address it directly, so I will not discuss it further. Presumably, these four finitist-nominalist restrictions do not single out a unique language: multiple languages could satisfy (FN 1-4). In what follows, I will call the above four conditions the 'finitist-nominalist (FN) conditions' (the first two are nominalist, the third and fourth finitist), and any language satisfying them a 'finitist-nominalist language.'

In other formulations of the group's project, an additional constraint is placed on the language(s) they are attempting to construct. The discussants aim

---

restrictions on what the individuals countenanced by the nominalist are, so long as they are individuals and not classes.
8. For an account and analysis of Quine's later published remarks on physical objects, see Dalla Chiara and di Francia (1995).
9. In 090-16-04, however, Tarski proposes to exclude interpreted languages whose domain is empty or has uncountably many members.

to generate a finitist-nominalist language rich enough to conduct investigations into the logic of science, including metalinguistic investigations (note "syntactic" and "semantic" below) of classical analysis and set theory (they sometimes call such a language a "nucleus language").

> Jan. 31, 1941
> *Conversation with Tarski and Quine on Finitism*
> ... *We together*: So now a problem: What part S of M [the metalanguage of science and mathematics–G.F.-A.] can we take as a kind of nucleus, so that 1.) S is understood in a definite sense by us, and 2.) S suffices for the formulation of the syntax of all of M, so far as is necessary for science, in order to handle the syntax and semantics of the complete language of science. (090-16-25)

Similar sentiments are expressed a few months later.

> June 18, 1941
> *Final Conversation about the nucleus-language*, with Tarski, Quine, Goodman, and Hempel; June 6 '41
> *Summary of what was said previously*. The nucleus language should serve as the syntax-language for the construction of the complete language of science (including classical mathematics, physics, etc.). The language of science thereby receives a piecewise interpretation, since the n.l. is assumed to be understandable. (090-16-05)

On the one hand, the finitist-nominalist conditions place restrictions on an interpreted language's richness; this condition, on the other, restricts a language's poverty. Carnap, Tarski, and Quine realize it may not be possible to construct a language that simultaneously satisfies this criterion as well as (FN 1-4).[10] For immediately following the first of the two quotations immediately above, we find:

> *1*. It must be investigated, if and how far the *poor nucleus* (i.e. the finite language S_1) is sufficient here. If it is, then that would certainly be the happiest solution. If it is not, then two paths must be investigated:
> *2a*. How can we justify the *rich nucleus* (i.e., infinite arithmetic S_2)? I.e., in what sense can we perhaps say that we really understand it? If we do, then we can certainly set up the rules of the calculus M with it.
> *2b*. If S_1 does not suffice to reach classical mathematics, couldn't one perhaps nevertheless adopt S_1 and perhaps show that classical mathematics is not really necessary for the application of science in life? Perhaps we can set up, on the basis of S_1, a calculus for a fragment of mathematics that suffices for all practical purposes (i.e., not something

---

10. In a lecture dated September 8, 1939, Quine had already suggested this line of thought: "nominalism. Probably can't get classical mathematics. But enough mathematics for physical science? If this could be established, good reason to then consider the problem solved" (quoted in Mancosu 2008b, 32).

just for everyday purposes, but also for the most complicated technological tasks). (090-16-25)

In short, they suspect that a metalinguistic analysis of classical mathematics and physics may require a richer language than what the finitist-nominalist criteria allow. If that suspicion is borne out, then either such a richer language must be shown to be understandable, or the weaker mathematics sanctioned in finitist-nominalist languages must be shown to be sufficient to deal with all sophisticated practical applications.[11] Unfortunately, we are not told whether this new condition trumps the finitist-nominalist conditions or not. That is, if classical mathematics is ultimately not understandable, and the mathematics condoned by the FN conditions is insufficient for practical purposes, then what should be discarded: the demand for a single metalanguage of science, or the finitist-nominalist strictures on intelligibility? Thus it is difficult for us to ascertain the relative importance Carnap, Tarski, and Quine attach to these competing conditions. However, none of the participants assert that we should completely abandon those portions of (e.g.) set theory that fail to meet the four finitist-nominalist criteria. Set theory can progress unimpeded by philosophical scruples, even if parts of it are not fully intelligible: Tarski suggests that set theory then becomes a purely formal (i.e. uninterpreted) calculus that merely indicates which sentences can be derived from others (090-16-28). But that is not a barrier to proving theorems.

A published summary of the finitist-nominalist project undertaken in 1941 by Carnap, Tarski, and Quine appears at the end of Carnap's "Intellectual Autobiography," in the section entitled "The Theoretical Language." Carnap's conception of this project had not changed substantially during the intervening years, though it had shifted subtly.

> We [Carnap, Tarski, Quine, and Goodman] considered especially the question of which form the basic language, i.e., the observation language, must have in order to fulfill the requirement of complete understandability. We agreed that the language must be nominalistic, i.e., its terms must not refer to abstract entities but only to observable objects or events. Nevertheless, we wanted this language to contain at least an elementary form of arithmetic... We further agreed that for the basic language the requirements of finitism and constructivism should be fulfilled in some sense. We examined various forms of finitism. Quine preferred a very strict form; the number of objects was assumed to be

---

11. The second alternative was not usual at the time. Frege stressed the importance of understanding the meaning of number words in everyday contexts. And Wittgenstein followed this lead: "In life a mathematical proposition is never what we want. Rather, we use mathematical propositions only in order to infer sentences which do not belong to mathematics from others, which likewise do not belong to mathematics" (Wittgenstein 1921/1961, 6.211). Carnap held such a viewpoint as well: "The chief function of a logical calculus in its application to science is not to furnish logical theorems...but to guide the deduction of factual conclusions from factual premises" (Carnap 1939, 177).

finite and consequently the numbers appearing in arithmetic could not exceed a certain maximum number. Tarski and I preferred a weaker form of finitism, which left it open whether the number of all objects is finite or infinite... In order to fulfill the requirement of constructivism I proposed to use certain features of my Language I in my *Logical Syntax*. We planned to have the basic language serve, in addition, as an elementary syntax language for the formulation of the basic syntactical rules of the total language. The latter language was intended to be comprehensive enough to contain the whole of classical mathematics and physics, represented as syntactical systems. (Carnap 1963, 79)

Several features mentioned earlier re-appear here: the aim of understandability, the ban on abstract entities, a finite universe of discourse (in both the liberal and restrictive variants), the re-interpretation of arithmetic, and the desire that the basic language should serve as the 'syntax language' (which is part of the 'metalanguage') for the total language of science.

However, there are at least two notable discrepancies between this later description and the actual discussion notes of 1941. First, the term 'constructivism' is not explicitly used in the original formulation of the project, though finitism is standardly taken to be a species of constructivism. Second, in his autobiography, Carnap recalls the basic language being an 'observation language,' i.e., a language whose non-logical terms designate observable entities, properties, and relations. As we saw in the discussion of (FN 2), this is incorrect. There is both a conceptual and a historical mistake here. The conceptual mistake is Carnap's conflation of 'nominalist' with 'observable': the concrete/abstract distinction is not coextensive with the observable/unobservable (or /theoretical) distinction. The nominalist (usually[12]) denies the existence or epistemic accessibility of abstracta, but she is free to believe in concrete unobservable entities. For example, protons are usually considered concrete but unobservable.[13] This conceptual mistake is closely related to Carnap's mis-remembering of the historical episode. The requirement that the nucleus language be an observation language is not discussed in 1940-41. As said before, in the discussion notes the domain of discourse is often (though not exclusively)[14] taken to include the elementary

---

12. Goodman, in his (mature) defense of nominalism, takes a slightly different line. He writes: "the line between what is ordinarily called 'abstract' and what is ordinarily called 'concrete' seems to me vague and capricious. Nominalism for me consists specifically in the refusal to recognize classes" (Goodman 1956, 16); thus a Goodmanian nominalist could allow numbers into her ontology, so long as they are treated as individuals. Goodman offers this as a modification or clarification of the doctrine of the original 1947 nominalism paper co-authored with Quine, in which abstracta were rejected.

13. I am perhaps judging Carnap too harshly here. He may just be using the term 'abstract' for what we today would call 'unobservable' (which could include most abstracta); see his (Carnap 1939, 203-5). Also, in 090-16-12, Carnap writes that in a "finitistic," "understood language," the "individuals" will be "certain *observable* things and their *observable* parts" (my emphasis). But the point remains that this is inconsistent with Tarski and Quine's understanding of 'physical objects' as including electrons and quanta of energy.

14. As Paolo Mancosu pointed out to me, Quine and Goodman favored sense-data predicates as the basic terms for the descriptive part of the language (090-16-05). (Carnap,

particles, entities whose names are not part of an observation language. However, this mistake is certainly understandable, given both the aim of the 1941 discussions, and how Carnap tried to achieve related or analogous aims in his own projects. One of Carnap's standing aims in his logic of science project is securing the meaningfulness of scientific language, and Carnap's strategy for achieving that aim is to connect all scientific claims via deductive inference to observation sentences. This will be discussed at much greater length in 6.2.

Let us summarize and take stock. In these 1940-41 conversations, Carnap, Tarski, and Quine (and occasionally Goodman and Hempel) attempt to construct a formal language that simultaneously meets the stringent finitist-nominalist constraints (FN 1-4) and is rich enough to capture (at least the bulk of scientifically necessary) mathematics, and to serve as a metalanguage for science. Since these two conditions pull in opposite directions, this is a difficult goal to achieve. I will postpone discussion of detailed objections to the project until chapter 3, but will note here that Carnap, virtually from beginning to end, is highly suspicious of (FN 1-4), and he criticizes the finitist-nominalist restrictions on various grounds. Although he is willing and able to play by the rules Tarski lays down in (FN 1-4), Carnap questions these rules repeatedly during the course of 1941.[15] In general, Carnap's objections attempt to show that either the finitist-nominalist restrictions yield unpalatable consequences in the domain of the formal sciences, or that higher mathematics is genuinely meaningful.

1.3. Mathematics in a Finitist-Nominalist Language

Carnap, Tarski, and Quine apparently realize from the outset that one of the most pressing and difficult obstacles facing any attempt to construct a finitist-nominalist language for the analysis of science will be the treatment of mathematics. Can a language simultaneously meet Tarski's criteria for intelligibility and contain (at least a substantial portion of) the claims of classical mathematics? A sizable portion of Carnap's notes on 'finitism' deals with how to answer this question. The discussants focus on a simple type of mathematics, viz. classical arithmetic. A number of potential pitfalls present themselves: first, what is the content of assertions about numbers? Can we assert anything about them at all, given that, in a language meeting Tarski's restrictions, the only entities in

Tarski, and Hempel demurred.) If one follows Quine and Goodman on this, then the finitist-nominalist language will contain no basic terms for unobservable items.

15. Carnap's position is very much like that of John Burgess today: Burgess has developed formal systems satisfying various versions of nominalist criteria, but also writes papers with titles such as "Why I Am Not a Nominalist" (Burgess 1983). Carnap's view of nominalism is probably not quite so dim (due to his principle of tolerance), but like Burgess, he is undertaking a project in which he works within the rules set by the nominalist, without fully accepting those rules *in propria persona*. In his autobiography, Carnap describes how he was happy to speak a "realistic or materialistic" language "with one friend," but "with another friend, I might adapt myself to his idealistic kind of language" (Carnap 1963, 17).

the domain of discourse are physical ones? Second, what should be done with numerals that purportedly refer to numbers that are larger than the number of concrete things in the universe? That is, suppose there are exactly one trillion physical things in the universe; what should we then make of the numeral '1,000,000,000,001' and sentences containing it? Finally, what theorems and proofs of classical arithmetic are lost? I shall deal with each of these questions in turn.

1.3.1 Number

As seen in the previous section, in a Tarskian fully understandable language, names do not denote abstract entities. So in such a language, the numeral '7' cannot name a natural number, if that number is considered as a basic, individual object[16], since the natural numbers are excluded from the domain of discourse. And as mentioned above, since a FN language must also be first-order, the Frege-Russell construal of numerals as denoting classes of classes is forbidden as well. But Tarski, Carnap, and Quine want the language to include, at the very least, portions of arithmetic, so they must re-interpret numerals. How do they do so, in such a restrictive linguistic regime?

Tarski's strategy for introducing ordinal numbers[17] is the following: "Numbers can be used in a finite realm, in that we think of the ordered things, and by the numerals we understand the corresponding things" (090-16-25). A nearly identical proposal[18] proposal is outlined in Carnap's autobiography:

> To reconcile arithmetic with the nominalistic requirement, we considered among others the method of representing natural numbers by the observable objects themselves, which were supposed to be ordered in a sequence; thus no abstract entities would be involved. (Carnap 1963, 79)

Let us illustrate this idea with a concrete example. Suppose, in our domain of 'physical things' that have been 'ordered in a sequence,' Tom is the eighth thing, John is the fourth, and Harry the eleventh. (Assume the numeral '0' is assigned to the first thing.) Then the arithmetical assertion '7 + 3 = 10' is re-interpreted as 'Tom + John = Harry.' Put model-theoretically, the interpretation function f of an interpreted language meeting the finitist-nominalist requirements assigns to the numerals of L objects in D: $f(7) = $ Tom, $f(3) =$ John. (Arithmetical signs such as '+' are defined via the version of Peano Arithmetic for PSI in Carnap's *Logical Syntax*, §14 and §20).)

---

16. This assumes, *contra* the current school of structuralism in philosophy of mathematics, that the natural numbers are treated as individuals, not 'nodes in a structure' or however else the structuralist wishes to characterize numbers.
17. The group discusses cardinal number very briefly in (090-16-25).
18. The only difference is that Carnap claims that the things are "observable." As I have mentioned above, this is almost certainly either a mis-remembering by Carnap, and not part of the original proposal, or a discrepancy between Carnap's terminology and ours (as well as that of Tarski and Quine in 1941).

This heterodox view of ordinal numbers raises a number of pressing questions. First, from whence does the sequential order of the physical objects spring? That is, what determines that Tom is 'greater than' John, and that Harry is 'greater than' them both? Must this ordering somehow reflect the actual spatiotemporal positions of Tom, John, and Harry? And if so, where do we 'start counting,' so to speak? Fortunately, it appears such questions can be avoided for the most part. The ordering is intended to be imposed, it seems, by stipulation: Tarski says "we want the (perhaps finitely many) things of the world ordered in some *arbitrary* way" (090-16-23, my emphasis). We may assign any member of the domain of physical things to the numeral '0', and we may choose any other member of the domain to be its successor, and be assigned to the numeral '1'. The sentence '0+1=0' will come out false under any such stipulation, regardless of which physical objects we choose to 'stand in' for 0 and 1 (assuming more than one thing exists). The relation is a successor of need not reflect anything 'in the order of things,' spatial, temporal, or otherwise. There is no further discussion in the notes of how the order is fixed, but the proposal just suggested would allow Tarski, Quine, and Carnap to avoid entangling themselves in thorny questions, so it is quite possible that they imagined the order fixed by 'arbitrary' stipulation.[19]

There is a second, perhaps more obvious worry about this proposal to interpret numerals under a finitist-nominalist regime. Let us suppose that the sentence 'Tom has brown hair' is true. Then, since the name 'Tom' and the numeral '7' both name the same object (model-theoretically, the interpretation function assigns both 'Tom' and '7' the same value), it appears that the sentence '7 has brown hair' will be true. Whatever else numbers cannot be, they certainly cannot be brunettes. So this finitist-nominalist interpretation of numerals will make true many assertions about numbers that, intuitively, are not arithmetical truths. There is no record of Tarski, Quine, and Carnap considering this problem. Perhaps technical refinements could avoid declaring at least some of these sentences true.[20] Note, however, that an analogous problem appears in set-theoretic

---

19. One might object that the notion of sequence or order *presupposes* some concept of the natural numbers, at least on the standard definition of sequence (where a sequence is any class that can be put in one-one correspondence with the natural numbers). So has Tarski just imported numbers into the system? Perhaps not: perhaps the notion of sequence does not presuppose the concept of the natural numbers, even if our standard definition today makes use of them. (Thanks to James Woodbridge for discussion of this issue.)

20. Hartry Field suggests one such refinement (Field 2001, 214-15). His basic idea, couched in our terms, is the following. Recall that the ordering of physical objects of D is arbitrary, and that alternative orderings of the elements of D are possible that would still respect the truths of classical arithmetic captured in the original model (such as '7 + 3 = 10'). This fact could be finessed to eliminate unwanted truths: while '7' may be assigned to a brunette in one assignment of physical objects to numerals, it will be assigned to a blonde in another, and to various hairless physical objects on other assignments. However, in *all* these assignments, '7+3=10' is true. This suggests the following refinement to Carnap, Tarski, and Quine's proposal to re-interpret numerals in a finitist-nominalist language: a (mathematical) sentence ϕ is true (in $\mathcal{L}$) if and only if ϕ is true for all assignments of physical-object-values to numerals (satisfying certain intuitive conditions: for example, we want to rule out assignments in which all numerals are assigned to a single object in D). This 'supervaluational' characterization is only a rough pass, and I will not dwell on

interpretations of arithmetic, such as Zermelo's and von Neumann's. For example, using von Neumann's set-theoretic construction of the natural numbers, '2 ∈ 3' is true; but that does not match up with ordinary usage of arithmetical language. This example shows that the type of problem Tarski faces is not peculiar to his proposal, but rather is likely to occur in any situation in which some portion of language is given an interpretation in some other part of scientific language.

1.3.2 Interpreting numerals that are 'too large'

Now we come to a problem concerning mathematics expressed in finitist-nominalist languages that Tarski, Quine, and Carnap *did* recognize themselves, and spent a considerable amount of time and energy discussing. Suppose there are only k items in the universe. Carnap poses the question: "How should we interpret" the numerical expressions '$k+1$,' '$k+2$,'..., "for which there is no further thing there?" (090-16-06) Initially, the group considers three options (employing the usual notation, where x' is the successor of x):

(a) $k' = k'' = \ldots = k$

(b) $k' = k'' = \ldots = 0$

(c) $k' = 0, k'' = 0', \ldots$

In each of these three cases, at least one of the Peano axioms is violated, and thus so is one of the axioms of Carnap's Language I (PSI) in *Logical Syntax*. If (a) is adopted, then there exist two numbers (recall that 'number' will be interpreted here as some physical object) that will have the same successor (contravening PSI 10); if (b) or (c) is adopted, then the number assigned to '0' will be a successor of some number (contravening PSI 9) (Carnap 1934/1937, 31).[21]

None of these three options is palatable, since none captures the truths of classical arithmetic substantially better than the others. For example, imag-

---

this possibility further; nonetheless, this line of thought shows that perhaps there is a way to interpret '7' that meets (FN 1-4) and certifies substantial portions of arithmetic as true, without also committing us to the truth of sentences like '7 has brown hair.' Of course, if the number of objects in the physical universe is finite, then this proposal still will not capture all of standard arithmetic. Also note that the proposed refinement will still make '7 is a physical object' true, since that sentence is true on all assignments of physical objects to the numeral '7.' (Someone who endorses (FN1-4) might not consider either of the previous two consequences unfortunate.) One could classify this suggestion as a 'nominalist-structuralist' account of mathematics, for it meshes nicely with Benacerraf's founding statement of structuralism:

> Arithmetic is therefore the science that elaborates the abstract structure that all progressions have merely in virtue of their being progressions. It is not a science concerned with particular objects—the numbers. The search for which independently identifiable particular objects the numbers really are...is a misguided one. (Benacerraf 1965/1983, 291)

21. In 090-16-23, Tarski suggests that, for finitist-nominalist purposes, the axiomatization of full Peano arithmetic should be constructed such that the supposition of infinity is treated as an *axiom*, unlike its treatment in PSI. For then, when the finitist-nominalist omits the axiom of infinity, as little arithmetical power as possible is lost.

ine that there are 1000 physical things in the universe. Then the sentence '600 + 600 = 700 + 700' will come out true under proposals (a) and (b), for it is translatable into '999 = 999' and '0 = 0,' respectively. And under (c), the problem just mentioned will be avoided, but the equally counterintuitive '0 = 1000 = 2000' will be true. The absurd arithmetical consequences will not be different in kind if we take a more realistic (i.e., larger) estimate of the number of objects in the universe. So regimes (a)-(c) all certify as true many equations that are false in classical arithmetic. A surprisingly large portion of the discussion notes is devoted to working through proposed solutions to this problem. Strategies other than (a)-(c) are also considered, such as identifying numbers with *sequences* of objects instead of objects *simpliciter*, so that there is no 'last element' forced upon us.

And making these unpalatable equations true is not the only problem with (a)-(c): as Tarski notes, under these conceptions of number "many propositions of arithmetic cannot be proved in this language, since we do not know how many numbers there are" (090-16-25). Why? Suppose that we do not know how many physical objects there are in the material universe. This ignorance will be formally reflected in a refusal to allow any assumptions about the cardinality of the domain of models of $\mathcal{L}$. Then there will be arithmetical sentences that are provable under classical arithmetic (even in primitive recursive arithmetic), but are unprovable in a finitist-nominalist language. If we do not allow ourselves any assumption about the cardinality of the domain (or just the assumption that at least one object exists, as Tarski suggests), then we cannot even prove '$1 + 1 \neq 0$'. So not only are 'intuitively true' arithmetical sentences declared false in this language, but chunks of previously provable assertions can no longer be proven. This issue will be treated at greater length below, in 3.4.2 and 4.1.

Other suggestions were offered for dealing with numbers that are 'too large' in a finitist-nominalist regime; however, none meet with substantially more approval from the other discussants. Interestingly, they never consider treating 'k'', 'k''', etc. as denotationless, i.e., as analogous to 'Santa Claus' (put model-theoretically: $f(k')$ is undefined). This approach (which we today could carry out using free logic) would avoid certifying '600 + 600 = 700 + 700' and '0 = 1000' as true: both would lack a truth-value in 'neutral' free logics, and would be false in 'negative' and 'positive' free logics(assuming a supervaluational semantics). However, even this strategy would not recapture the classical arithmetical truths about numbers greater than k.

In his private notes at this time, Carnap actually runs some basic calculations on the question of how many physical things there are in our universe (090-16-22). Starting from a conjecture of Eddington's, Carnap computes that the number of particles in the universe is approximately 10^{77}. Then, using Quine's proposed ontology, in which classes of particles are things (since bodies are classes of particles), the maximum number of 'things' in the universe is approximately $2^{10^{77}}$. That Carnap goes to the trouble of actually working out how to apply this finitist-nominalist language to a realistic case shows, I believe, that Carnap did take this project fairly seriously, and that for him it was neither an empty game of wordplay nor a merely technical exercise.

1.4. Pre-history of the 1941 Finitist-Nominalist Project

The next chapter will address the justifications discussed within Carnap's 1941 dictation notes for undertaking the finitist-nominalist project. I wish to consider here a different question: from what historical sources do (FN 1-4) spring? What elements of the intellectual context could make this project compelling to its participants? [22] Tarski himself cites Chwistek (090-16-09) and Kotarbiński (090-16-28) for some of the ideas he presents, so I will first briefly outline the claims of these two Polish philosophers that are most relevant to the finitist-nominalist project. Next, I present possible indirect lines of influence that Russell's ideas may have had on the formation of the 1941 FN project. Finally, I briefly sample contemporaneous skeptical complaints about infinity from Wittgenstein and Neurath.

1.4.1 The Poles: Chwistek, Kotarbiński, Leśniewski

The finitist-nominalist project is originally Tarski's proposal; thus, it is natural to look to the philosophical ideas he was exposed to during his intellectual development in Poland to find his inspiration for the FN conditions. Tarski mentions by name two Polish philosophers, and their characteristic views, in the notes: Leon Chwistek's nominalism and Tadeusz Kotarbiński's reism. Chwistek worked in Krakow, which was not part of the Lvov-Warsaw School to which Tarski, Kotarbiński, and many other prominent Polish philosophers belonged.

CHWISTEK'S 'NOMINALISM'   In May 1940, months before the finitist-nominalist project is proposed and explored, Tarski visited the University of Chicago, where he and Carnap had an extended and wide-ranging discussion. Carnap's notes record that Tarski said

> With the higher types, Platonism begins. The tendencies of Chwistek and others ("Nominalism") to talk only about describable things are healthy. The only problem is finding a good execution. Perhaps roughly of this kind: in the first language, numbers as individuals, as in language I [PSI of *Logical Syntax*–G.F.-A.], but perhaps with unrestricted operators; in the second language, individuals that are identical to or correspond to the sentential functions in the first language, so properties of natural numbers expressible in the first language; in the third language, as individuals those properties expressible in the second lan-

---

22. An excellent account of the historical trajectory of Quine's shifting attitudes toward nominalism can be found in Mancosu (2008b).

guage, and so forth. Then one has in each language only individual variables, though dealing with entities of different types. (090-16-09)

Note that Tarski's proposal here is fundamentally different from the FN project. First, this proposal does allow 'higher types,' and thus would qualify as Platonism both under the criterion mentioned in the first sentence of the above quotation, and under (FN 2), which Tarski labeled the 'non-Platonic' requirement. Also, Tarski's suggestion here to use properties as the individuals in the universe of discourse (*prima facie*) violates the restriction of the universe to physical objects only. So it is not immediately evident (a) in what sense 'nominalism' is meant here, or (b) how this view relates to the later FN conditions.

What does Chwistek mean by the term 'nominalism'? It does not directly correspond to any of Tarski's finitist-nominalist conditions (though Chwistek harbors a suspicion of infinity, as we shall see). Chwistek's nominalism, which Tarski appeals to in the above quotation, corresponds more closely to the predicativism of Poincaré's philosophy of mathematics. Concerning Poincaré's view of mathematical objects, Chwistek writes:

> Poincaré was a decided nominalist and could not be reconciled to the existence of indefinable objects, much less to the existence of infinite classes of such objects. Poincaré regarded his belief as the fundamental postulate of a nominalistic logic. He formulated this postulate as follows: 'Consider only objects which can be defined in a finite number of words.' (Chwistek 1935/1949, 21)

In short, the Chwistekian nominalist follows Poincaré's refusal to countenance the existence of any mathematical object that cannot be finitely defined.[23]

It should be noted that Poincaré does not use the word 'nominalism' in this sense. Rather, he views nominalism negatively, claiming that certain people "have thought that... the whole of science was conventional. This paradoxical doctrine, which is called Nominalism, cannot stand examination" (Poincaré 1902/1905, 138; cf. xxiii, 105). So in Poincaré's mouth, the term 'nominalism' means what we today would call 'conventionalism.' Furthermore, Poincaré calls his own view, which Chwistek dubbed 'nominalist,' by a different label: 'pragmatist.' The pragmatists oppose those Poincaré dubs 'Cantorians'–a label which corresponds, in certain important ways, to the cluster of commitments and attitudes currently associated with Platonism in the philosophy of mathematics. Poincaré writes:

> Why do the Pragmatists refuse to admit objects which could not be defined in a finite number of words? Because they consider that an object exists only when it is thought, and that it is impossible to conceive an object which is thought without a thinking subject... And since a thinking subject is a man, and is therefore a finite being, the infinite can

---

23. Folina (1992) provides more detail on Poincaré's predicativism, especially chapter 7.

have no other sense than the possibility, which has no limits, to create
as many finite objects as one likes. (Bouveresse 2005, 66)

So the appellation of 'nominalist,' in Chwistek's mouth, corresponds to Poincaré's term 'pragmatist'; elements of this view are often called 'constructivism' today. Terminological differences aside, Chwistek unequivocally endorses the views just expressed by Poincaré:

Jules Tannery inferred that there must exist real numbers which cannot
be defined in a finite number of words. Such a conclusion is clearly
metaphysical. It presupposes the ideal existence of numbers only some
of which can be known. (Chwistek 1935/1949, 78)

And for Chwistek, like many of his contemporaries, 'metaphysical' is a term of disapprobation. We find fundamentally the same argument in both Chwistek and Poincaré: if we cannot successfully describe a purported mathematical object, then we should not be committed to the existence of that object. And for both men, a description must be finite to succeed—a reasonable requirement, since any describer is a limited creature.[24] Recent work by Jacques Bouveresse demonstrates that this way of dividing up the warring camps in philosophy of mathematics is not unique to Chwistek (and Poincaré) at the beginning of the twentieth century: in that age, "Platonism...is opposed to constructivism. It rests on the assumption that the objects of the (mathematical) theory constitute a given totality" (Bouveresse 2005, 58).

Let us return to Chwistek's conception of nominalism. It goes beyond the inadmissibility of (finitely) indefinable mathematical objects. "The doctrines of the nominalists," Chwistek writes, "depend upon the complete elimination of such objects as concepts and propositions" (Chwistek 1935/1949, 43). Here we find a closer connection to Tarski's finitist-nominalist project, for eliminating higher-order quantification and restricting the domain of discourse to physical objects will rule out any realistic construal of concepts and propositions. How is this stronger claim related to the aforementioned rejection of indescribable objects? Chwistek holds that if one is committed to the existence of indefinable objects, then one is committed to some sort of realism about concepts (*Begriffsrealismus*). This point is argued in detail in Chwistek's "The Nominalist Foundations of Mathematics," published in the issue of *Erkenntnis* immediately following the famous symposium proceedings covering the logicist, intuitionist, and formalist 'foundations of mathematics,' by Carnap, Heyting, and von Neumann respectively; this article was Chwistek's indirect response to that symposium.

In this article, Chwistek proves (within the simple theory of types) that a certain propositional function ϕ exists such "that ϕ is unconstructible [*unkonstruierbar*], so we have proved the existence of an unconstructible function, which is of course a metaphysical result that contradicts nominalism in a radical

---

24. Tarski places logical-philosophical weight on the finitude of human language in his *Wahrheitsbegriff* monograph (Tarski 1983, 253).

way" (Chwistek 1933, 370). Chwistek holds that accepting the existence of such unconstructible entities 'contradicts nominalism' because such an acceptance represents a very strong realism about concepts, at least if propositional functions are (in some sense) independent of us and our cognitive activities of thinking, knowing, and describing. When Chwistek asserts that 'concepts and propositions' must be 'completely eliminated' under a nominalist regime, he presumably means that the nominalist must eliminate concepts and propositions, conceived of as existing independently of our constructive mathematical activities. Without this final qualification, *constructible* functions would qualify as a 'contradiction of nominalism.' But this would be far too strong a result, for Chwistek clearly does not want to declare all of logic and mathematics metaphysical.

In the same article, Chwistek also argues against the existence of propositional functions on more general grounds. He maintains that they are not purely *logical* entities, as Russell and others would have it, for they do not (to put it roughly, and in current terms) stay within the boundaries of syntax alone. He then infers directly from their not belonging to 'pure logic' that they must belong to 'idealistic metaphysics.'

> The axiom of extensionality,[25] despite all the arguments of Wittgenstein, Russell, Carnap et al., has nothing to do with logic, since the metaphysical problem whether propositional functions should count as something different from expressions, or simply as expressions, cannot be decided within logic. From the semantic[26] standpoint the axiom of extensionality is simply false, since e.g. the expression '$\psi x \vee \psi x$' is clearly different from 'ψx', although the equivalence of the two expressions holds for all x. If one nevertheless assumes the axiom of extensionality, then one clearly is not dealing with the foundations of pure logic. One is working much more with a kind of idealistic metaphysics, which I would like to call 'concept-realism,' in analogy with certain medieval theories. (Chwistek 1933, 368–69)

Chwistek's argument is simple: the two propositional functions 'x is thin and x is thin' and 'x is thin' are syntactically different, but Russell et al. hold that they are the same propositional function, because they are extensionally identical– each propositional function is true of exactly the same things. But the symbol-sequences differ between the two, so in Chwistek's idiosyncratic sense of 'pure logic,' the sameness is not purely logical. And if it is not purely logical, Chwistek infers, it must be metaphysics (presumably because it cannot be plausibly construed as empirical). Most philosophers and logicians today, along with many of

---

25. For Chwistek, the axiom of extensionality is: "any two propositional functions that agree in extension are identical" (Chwistek 1935/1949, 133).
26. Chwistek's characterization of semantics is non-standard: for him, semantics is "the study of the structural and constructional properties of expressions (primarily of mathematics)" (Chwistek 1935/1949, 83). This is much closer to what we (and most of Chwistek's contemporaries) would consider *syntax*.

Chwistek's contemporaries, would reject this conception of 'pure logic' as overly impoverished.

Chwistek advances other claims in "The Nominalist Foundations of Mathematics" that are very congenial to Tarski's FN project. For example, Chwistek speaks favorably of Felix Kaufmann's *Das Unendliche in der Mathematik und ihre Ausschaltung* [*The Infinite in Mathematics and its Elimination*], which Chwistek hails as "the renaissance of nominalism in Germany" (Chwistek 1933, 387). "Kaufmann's fundamental idea," Chwistek writes, is "that the meaningful sentences about properties of properties of objects are reducible to sentences about properties of objects" (Chwistek 1933, 385). This would come as welcome philosophical news to any proponent of (FN 1), the view that only first-order sentences are fully meaningful. Elsewhere Chwistek states that if the axioms of infinity and choice (which are necessary to recover certain classical mathematical theorems) are introduced into a logic, then "one must realize that one has obtained certain merely formal relations between sentences, but not contentful results" (Chwistek 1933, 371). This echoes, almost exactly, Tarski's view of higher mathematics under a finitist-nominalist regime, assuming that understandable [*verständlich*] expressions have content [*inhalt*]: namely, higher-order language in mathematics would be characterized as an uninterpreted or empty calculus. In short, Chwistek's influence on Tarski's FN project is perhaps best characterized as indirect, insofar as Tarski shares a basic skepticism about the existence of a mathematical reality independent of the material world and our cognitive practices within it, but he does not adopt Chwistek's specific version of nominalism wholeheartedly.

KOTARBIŃSKI'S REISM   Tarski cites Tadeusz Kotarbiński's 'reism' as the source of (FN 2), the requirement that the domain of discourse must contain only physical objects. Tarski also helped translate one of Kotarbiński's introductory articles on reism into English (Kotarbiński 1935/1955). What is reism? Most simply, it is the view that everything is a *res*, a thing. This is not a terribly informative formulation; recall Quine's answer to 'What is there?' viz., 'Everything' (Quine 1961, 1). More revealingly, Kotarbiński also labels his view 'concretism,' the claim that everything is concrete (so no abstracta exist). He also calls it 'pansomatism': everything is a body. Sometimes Kotarbiński uses 'reism' to designate the weaker view that everything is a *res extensa* or a *res cogitans* (Kotarbiński 1935/1955, 489); but then he adds that his own view, pansomatism, is a particular species of reism, one generated by adding the assumption that "every soul is a body" (Kotarbiński 1935/1955, 495). As mentioned above in 1.2, there is disappointingly little discussion in the Harvard notes of what the participants mean by 'physical thing'; Kotarbiński, fortunately, hints at what he counts as a *res*. He writes: "'Corporeal', in our sense, means the same as 'spatial, temporal, and resistant' "; thus, Kotarbiński counts (e.g.) an electromagnetic field *in vacuo* as a body, since it is spatiotemporal and resists certain charged bodies (Kotarbiński 1935/1955, 489).

Kotarbiński himself recognizes that his pansomatism is closely related to nominalism, for he writes:

> Concretism...joined the current of nominalism, if by nominalism we mean the view that universals do not exist...Not only do properties not exist, but neither do relations, states of things, or events, and the illusion of their existence has its source in the existence of certain nouns, which suggest the erroneous idea of the existence of such objects, in addition to things. (Kotarbiński 1929/1966, 430)

As the end of this quotation makes clear, pansomatism has both an ontological component and a linguistic or semantic one. (Ajdukiewicz's response to Kotarbiński's initial formulations of reism prompted this distinction to be made explicit.) Kotarbiński's idea is that every meaningful sentence containing a grammatical subject or predicate that does not designate any concrete object or objects can be re-phrased, without loss of content, into a sentence in which all grammatical subjects and predicates designate concrete bodies only (Kotarbiński 1935/1955, 490).[27] For example, the reist will transform 'Roundness is a property of spheres' into 'Spheres are round.' What motivates such a transformation or translation? Kotarbiński's answers as follows:

> Generally speaking, if every object is a thing, then we have to reject every utterance containing the words 'property', 'relation', 'fact', or their particularization, which implies the consequence that certain objects are properties, or relations, or facts. (Kotarbiński 1935/1955, 490)

Kotarbiński also explicitly rejects classes (Kotarbiński 1935/1955, 492). Thus we see that (FN 1) and (FN 2) are both consequences of reism. Kotarbiński says that we could declare utterances containing such words either false or nonsensical. Kotarbiński calls 'roundness,' 'property,' etc. 'onomatoids,' that is, merely apparent names, not genuine names. Or, if one chooses to call them 'names,' then they must be thought of as denotationless names, like 'Pegasus.' In places, Kotarbiński suggests that the reist's paraphrase is in fact what was *really* meant all along (Kotarbiński 1929/1966, 432): a hermaneutic reconstruction of everyday language, instead of a revolutionary one, in the terminology of Burgess and Rosen (1996).

To understand Kotarbiński adequately, certain basic views of Tarski's Ph.D. advisor Stanislaw Leśniewski should also be outlined, since Kotarbiński adopts, in service of reism, the formal logic of Leśniewski, who was also a nominalist.[28]

---

27. 'But,' the modern reader may object, 'predicates do not designate concrete bodies. Kotarbiński is guilty of a category mistake (or some other form of nonsense): only singular terms designate individuals.' This modern understanding of predicates is not shared by Kotarbiński, who holds the (ultimately medieval) view that singular terms name a single (concrete) thing, while predicates name several (concrete) things. Interestingly, as Mancosu (2008b) notes, Quine holds this same view in the late 1930s.

28. For more on Tarski's relationship with Leśniewski, see Betti (2008).

Leśniewski rejects the classical set-theoretic conception of classes, replacing it with the notion of a mereological whole (which he nonetheless called a 'class,' for he believed it was the salvageable remainder of the notion Cantor studied). Leśniewski bases his logic on the symbol 'ε,' which is intended to formalize the (ordinary language) copula. 'A ε B' can be given two readings in natural language, both of which are simultaneously possible in Leśniewski's system: 'A is a proper part of, or identical with, B' (the mereological conception) or 'A is one of the Bs.' One might think this latter smuggles in class-membership. However, the idea is that 'B' just names many concrete things—along the lines of the medieval nominalists' view. Interestingly, Quine espouses exactly the same understanding of predicates in a 1937 lecture on nominalism to the Harvard Philosophy Club (Quine papers, folder 2969). Furthermore, Leśniewski takes a pansomatist view of logic itself, as Peter Simons explains:

> expressions, their components and the wholes they constitute are one and all concrete entities: marks on paper, blackboards etc.... Leśniewski does not, as is common metalogical practice, assume there are infinitely many expressions of every category available. A system of logic for him is no less concrete than any other chunk of language. (Simons 1993, 220)[29]

As strange as this view may sound to many modern ears, we will find Tarski and (to a lesser extent) Quine defending this conception of language in the Harvard notes (see 3.4.2); furthermore, Goodman and Quine defend it in their published paper "Steps Toward a Constructive Nominalism."

Finally, there is another, more direct line of influence from Leśniewski to Tarski, which is likely relevant to the Finitist-Nominalist project: intuitionistic finitism. In a 1930 paper, Tarski says that his "personal attitude" concerning the "foundations of mathematics" is "intuitionistic formalism," a view found "in the writings of S. Leśniewski" (Tarski 1983, 62). What is this view? If we follow the reference Tarski provides, we find Leśniewski discussing his proposed sentential logic:

> Having no predilection for various 'mathematical games' that consist in writing out according to one or another conventional rule various more or less picturesque formulae which need not be meaningful or even... which should necessarily be meaningless, I would not have taken the trouble to systematize and to often check quite scrupulously the directives of my system, had I not imputed to its theses a certain specific and completely determined sense, in virtue of which its axioms, definitions, and final directives... have for me an irresistible intuitive validity. I see no contradiction, therefore, in saying that I advocate a rather radical 'formalism' in the construction of my system even though I am an obdurate 'intuitionist'. (Leśniewski 1992, 487)

---

29. See also Simons (2002).

Crucial for present purposes is Leśniewski's demand that the fundamental statements of a logic have a 'meaning' or 'specific and completely determined sense,' instead of being a 'meaningless' 'mathematical game.' The impulse driving Tarski's earlier adherence to intuitionistic formalism may well have expressed itself in 1941 as the desire for an 'intelligible,' 'understandable' language, contrasted (as we saw above in 1.2) with a 'calculus' which simply specifies rules for symbol manipulation. Framed in Leśniewski's terms, the FN conditions guarantee that a language's sentences have a 'certain specific and completely determined sense.'[30] This is only the intuitionist half of 'intuitionistic formalism'; the FN conditions are not completely formalist, for although some of the conditions are formalized (e.g. the prohibition on higher-order quantification), the requirement that the domain D contain only physical objects is not purely formal.

1.4.2 Russellian influences

It may be an understatement to say that Russell towers over logically-informed and logically-inspired philosophy in the twentieth century, especially before 1940. Although he was in residence at Harvard during the fall of 1940, Carnap's notes do not indicate that Russell had sustained involvement in these conversations. Nonetheless, his well-known views about numbers, classes, and abstracta presumably had some effect, even if only indirectly, on Carnap, Quine, and Tarski's discussions. Even if they did not adopt Russell's views completely, at least his output over the previous five decades presumably influenced their conception of which questions are philosophically pressing. In short, what Russell considered philosophically problematic and important partially determined the research horizon for the philosophers who followed in his wake.

In particular, Russell found numbers and classes philosophically troubling. He calls numbers–which, on his preferred analysis, are classes of classes–'fictions of fictions':

> Numbers are classes of classes, and classes are logical fictions, so that numbers are, as it were, fictions at two removes, fictions of fictions. Therefore, you do not have as ultimate constituents of your world, these queer things that you are inclined to call numbers. (Russell 1918/1956, 270)

The fact that the leading philosophical luminary of Carnap, Tarski, and Quine's early careers called classes 'fictions' and declared numbers, the things successfully manipulated by six-year-old children, to be 'queer things' could play some role in inclining Tarski, Quine, and others to consider the refusal to allow numbers into the universe of discourse prima facie plausible or reasonable. Along similar lines, Russell claims that postulating the existence of numbers is 'ad hoc metaphysics.'

---

30. Douglas Patterson's work led me to understand both the content and importance of Tarski's intuitionistic formalism; see Patterson (2012).

[S]o long as the cardinal number is inferred from the collections, not constructed in terms of them, its existence must remain in doubt, unless in virtue of a metaphysical postulate *ad hoc*. By defining the cardinal number of a given collection as the class of all equally numerous collections we avoid the necessity of this metaphysical postulate. (Russell 1918, 156)

This shows that Russell considered taking the existence of numbers as a primitive assumption a metaphysical maneuver. And as we shall see in detail later (2.2 and 3.2), part of the motivation for undertaking the finitist-nominalist project is to demonstrate that (at least a substantive chunk of) mathematics is not metaphysics, but rather cognitively meaningful. Finally, Tarski's requirement that the universe of discourse contains only physical objects can perhaps be seen as a return to the Russellian conception of logic that the *Tractatus* aims to dismantle, namely, that "logic is concerned with the real world just as truly as zoology, though with its more abstract and general features" (Russell 1920, 169). (Carnap considered this Tractarian view a lynchpin of the logical empiricists' epistemology of mathematics. This may explain his strong aversion to the fundamental assumptions of the FN project; chapter 3 will discuss this aversion further.)

However, the logic of *Principia Mathematica* clearly directly violates (FN 1), since it is higher-order. Nonetheless, the axiom of reducibility (roughly) states that all formulae have first-order equivalents, so even in *Principia*, there is a sense in which first-order logic is privileged. The situation is slightly more subtle when it comes to (FN 3). *Principia* adopts an axiom of infinity, but Russell was not happy about the need to do so, and he explicitly considered such an axiom extra-logical. So he would certainly be sympathetic to the motivation behind (FN 3) as well: in *Introduction to Mathematical Philosophy*, he says that we do not know whether the axiom of infinity is true in our world or not, and that physical space and time may be discrete and finite (Russell 1920, 140-41). Also, the fact that Russell considered it worthwhile to eliminate classes from the system of logic in *Principia Mathematica* (the 'no-class' theory) could have conceivably exerted some influence on Tarski's refusal to countenance abstract entities, and on Quine and (to a lesser extent) Carnap's willingness to consider the FN project worth pursuing.[31]

1.4.3 Logical Empiricists skeptical of infinity

Finally, I wish to consider very briefly a few remarks concerning infinity that logical empiricists and their allies made during the first part of the twentieth century. Their attitude towards mathematical infinity is, in general, more hostile than the prevailing sentiments at the beginning of the twenty-first; as a result of this general mood, Tarski's condition that no infinities be presupposed in the

---

31. However, Russell does not assert that classes do not exist; he is an agnostic, instead of an atheist: "we avoid the need of assuming that there are classes without being compelled to make the opposite assumption that there are no classes. We merely abstain from both assumptions" (Russell 1920, 184).

language of science and mathematics (FN 3) would likely appear more reasonable. As just noted, Russell was forced to introduce the axiom of infinity into the logic of the *Principia* in order to capture certain basic results in mathematics, but he found this maneuver philosophically unsatisfying: he considered every proof of a theorem ϕ of classical mathematics that appealed to the axiom of infinity to be better understood as a proof of 'If the axiom of infinity holds, then ϕ.' And Carnap, recalling the heyday of the Vienna Circle, writes: "the constructivist and finitist tendencies of Brouwer's thinking appealed to us greatly" (Carnap 1963, 49).

Wittgenstein, in the *Tractatus*, also rejects the axiom of infinity (5.535). He suggests that in a logically perfect language, each object will have exactly one name; thus, there will be infinitely many objects if and only if there are infinitely many names of objects in a logically perfect language. So the problem with the axiom of infinity, on this line of thought, is that if it is true, then in a logically perfect language what it intends to say is superfluous (though Wittgenstein apparently considers the axiom itself meaningless): the fact that there are infinitely many names already captures ('shows') the infinity of objects. During Wittgenstein's so-called 'middle period,' his antipathy towards the notion of infinity grows stronger. I will not attempt to analyze his complex pronouncements in detail here, but at the most basic level, one worry seems to be that for finite beings who speak a language with a finite vocabulary and rules, the introduction of infinity seems ill-suited. This position bears clear affinities to those of Chwistek and Poincaré described earlier.

Wittgenstein, of course, was not a fully-fledged member of the Vienna Circle, so one might think that the Circle members would view his skepticism about infinity as a mistake, born from Wittgenstein's insufficient knowledge of, and respect for, scientific practice. However, this is not the case. Otto Neurath, who had very little patience for what he called Wittgenstein's 'metaphysics,' was also hesitant to introduce the term 'infinite' and its cognates into the unified language of science. For Neurath, it seems that the problem is not merely that the superficially mathematical/analytic axiom of infinity is extra-logical/synthetic, or even that it is false, but rather that the very concept of infinity is, in some sense, unacceptable for an anti-metaphysical empiricist.

> Perhaps there are theological residues also... in certain applications of the concept of infinity in mathematics. The attempts to make mathematics finite, especially in applications to concrete events, are certainly part of tidying up [the language of science]. Frequently we need only to give a finite meaning to statements with infinitesimal or transfinite expressions. (Neurath 1983, 43)

Similar to the views of Russell just above, Neurath claims the concepts of classical mathematics are 'theological'–a close relative (if not a species) of 'metaphysical.' Note also that the FN project is, in part, an attempt to fulfill the final sentence of Neurath's quotation, for it attempts to confer a finite meaning upon claims of classical mathematics involving infinity. Years later, Neurath articulated his worries about infinity again, when scientific philosophers grew more interested in the concept of probability: "There remains the difficulty to apply a calculus with an infinite collective to empiricist groups of items, to which the expressions 'finite' and 'infinite' can hardly be applied" (Neurath 1946, 81). Neurath does not fully flesh out this objection; I mention this only to show that Neurath's skepticism about infinity continued over several years before and after the Harvard discussions, and stretched across different topics.

In 1940-41, when many of the greatest scientific philosophers of the twentieth century spent a year together, the plurality of their academic collaboration focused on the question: 'What form should an intelligible language adequate for analyzing science take, if the number of physical things in the universe is possibly finite?' And, as a corollary, 'How will this force us to change arithmetic?' In this chapter, I have examined the conditions Tarski proposes a language must meet in order to be intelligible, and how these conditions might be compatible with mathematical discourse. Many twenty-first century students of philosophy may be somewhat surprised that such a question occupies the center of these philosophers' discussions: why did they not instead discuss the issues we today consider more closely related to the core of their published, public views? This sense of surprise might make it appear that the finitist-nominalist endeavor is a peripheral side project for these great minds, fundamentally unrelated to the real areas of research for these philosophers.

However, this appearance is deceiving. For, as we shall see, several topics that are fundamental to scientific philosophers (both pre- and post-1940) are intimately involved in this interrelated set of questions. The most obvious and direct connection is to Quine's (short-lived) and Goodman's (long-lived) nominalism. Second, as we shall see in 3.1, Carnap assimilates the finitist-nominalist endeavor to his work on the semantics of scientific language and relation between observational and theoretical languages, which began explicitly in 1936 with "Testability and Meaning" and continued well after 1941, to "The Methodological Character of Theoretical Concepts" and beyond (Carnap 1956b). But, even more importantly, the 1941 conversations fundamentally concern the relation of mathematics to the natural world, an issue Carnap and other logical empiricists (especially Schlick and Hahn) considered of paramount importance throughout their careers, since the new mathematical logic held the promise of delivering a wider range of truths independent of empirical facts about the world, and thus a tenable (i.e., non-Millian) empiricist view of mathematics appeared possible. For this reason, the finitist-nominalist project involves the notion of analytic truth, the issue that perhaps looms largest in historical hindsight. Closely intertwined with analyticity is the question of the best form for the emerging field of formal semantics, the immediate heir of the logical empiricists' concern with the notion of meaning (and meaningfulness) that often occupied center stage for them during the twenties and thirties. The differences of opinion between Carnap, Tarski, and Quine on this matter are many and varied, so I will not attempt to summarize them now. The admissibility of modal (and other intensional) languages is drawn into the discussion of the finitist-nominalist project, in part because they want to set up the language such that it is *possible* that the number of physical things in the universe is finite, but Tarski and Quine are skeptical of intensional languages. Finally, insofar as the finitist-nominalist project aims to develop a single, unified language for the analysis of all scientific discourse, it is also intertwined with the issue of the unity of science, an idea whose heyday was in the 1930s, but whose conceptual grandchildren live on today in various reductionism debates. In each of the following chapters, I not only present and analyze the details of the 1940-41 discussion notes in their own terms, but will also examine how they relate to the wider themes just canvased.

Chapter 2
Justifications for the Finitist-Nominalist Conditions

The official year of birth for modern Anglophone nominalism is generally taken to be 1947, with Quine and Goodman's *Journal of Symbolic Logic* article "Steps Toward a Constructive Nominalism." In a footnote to that article, the authors acknowledge that the initial impetus and strategy for their nominalist project was proposed in the 1940-41 academic year by Tarski, and discussed with the authors and Carnap (Quine and Goodman 1947, 112). Thus, these discussions at Harvard can be seen as a, if not the, wellspring of current nominalism. The previous chapter set out Tarski's finitist-nominalist criteria (FN 1-4), and explored them in some detail. A crucial question that was not addressed then, but will be in this chapter, is the following: what motivates or justifies these finitist-nominalist criteria? First, I discuss the justifications Tarski, Carnap, and Quine articulate for undertaking the finitist-nominalist project. I discern four kinds of rationales Tarski, Quine, and Carnap consider for a finitist-nominalist project, summarized under the following headings: intelligibility, the anti-metaphysical impulse, inferential safety, and natural science. The first three support (FN 1) and (FN 2), and the fourth supports (FN 3). Finally, I will briefly outline the two primary current justifications for nominalism today, and describe how they relate to those considered by the Harvard discussants.

2.1. First Justification: *Verständlichkeit*

2.1.1 Assertions meeting the FN criteria are *verständlich*

As we have seen above (in 090-16-25 and -28), Tarski claims that a language must meet his finitist-nominalist restrictions in order to qualify as 'fully understandable' or intelligible. We also saw above (1.2) that the only motive for this project Carnap mentions in his autobiography is the aim of understandability. In the 1940-41 notes themselves, Carnap clearly views the FN criteria as purportedly necessary conditions on the understandability of a language as well, for we find him writing the following:

> [L]ogic and arithmetic also remain in a certain... sense finitistic, if they should really be understood. (090-16-24)

Is this talk of sequences whose length is greater than the number of things in the world at peace with the principle of finitism? I.e., is such a sentence understandable for the finitist? (090-16-27)

In both these quotations, which Carnap wrote to himself in private (i.e., they are not part of a conversation with Quine and Tarski), Carnap holds that a finitist considers a language understandable only if it meets the finitistic criteria. (Terminological reminder: Carnap calls someone who accepts all of (FN 1-3), not just (FN 3) alone, a 'finitist'.)

Quine's view of the relation between intelligibility and nominalism is similar to Tarski and Carnap's, but he couches it differently. In December 1940, before Tarski proposed the FN language-construction project, Quine delivered a lecture on the topic of "the universal language of science" (102-63-04). In it, he discussed philosophers' attempts to eliminate certain "problematic universals" from the language of science. "In each case" of eliminating universals, Quine writes, "we do it in order to reduce the obscure to the clearer." This is similar to Tarski and Carnap's view of the aim of the FN restrictions described above, for aversion to universals is a classic characteristic of nominalism, and presumably, the 'obscure' is less understandable than the 'clear.' (However, Quine may intend 'clear' to have primarily epistemological, instead of semantic, force here; I expand on this suggestion below, in 2.1.4.) So, in short: Tarski, Quine, and Carnap all hold that a central rationale for undertaking this language construction project is that such a language would be maximally 'intelligible' or 'clear.'

2.1.2 What does 'understandable' mean in the discussion notes?

The obvious question to ask next is: What do the participants mean by *verständlich*? Unfortunately, the discussion notes record very little. It is frustrating that the notes lack an explanation of intelligibility, since all parties involved acknowledge it as the central motivation for constructing a finitist-nominalist language. More specifically, the notes do not explicitly explain why a language violating any of Tarski's finitist-nominalist criteria is not (fully) understandable; why, for example, would a sentence beginning with 'There exists a property such that...' be as unintelligible as an obviously ungrammatical string of English words, or Heidegger's infamous metaphysical claim "*das Nichts nichtet*"? Furthermore, the participants do not completely agree (though their positions are not mutually exclusive) among themselves about which particular assertions should count, in an intuitive or pre-theoretic way, as fully understandable and which not: Carnap claims, contra Tarski and Quine, that classical, infinite arithmetic *is* intelligible, though he concedes full set theory may not be (090-16-25).[1] The notes from the final day of collaborative work on the finitist-nominalist language highlight how unclear and imprecise the concept of *Verständlichkeit* is for the participants. Carnap writes:

---

1. In the same document, Carnap also says that he considers understandability a matter of degree.

> We agree the language should be as understandable as possible. But perhaps it is not clear what we properly mean by that. Should we perhaps ask children psychological questions, what the child learns first, or most easily?[2] (090-16-05)

So Carnap himself does not know what is meant by *verständlich*, even six months into the project, and the dictation notes show no response to his query from the other participants. However, this quotation does suggest that for Carnap, understandability is a pragmatic (in Carnap's sense) characteristic of a linguistic expression, i.e., a property that depends on the language-user; I shall return to this idea later in the chapter.

Despite these discouraging signs, our interpretive prospects are not hopeless, for *some* material in the discussion notes provides insight into what *verständlich* means for Tarski, Quine, and Carnap. In particular, Tarski contrasts an intelligible language with an uninterpreted formal calculus.

> Tarski: I fundamentally understand only a language that fulfills the following conditions:
> [Here are the three finitist-nominalist conditions–G.F.-A.]
> I only 'understand' any other language in the way I 'understand' classical mathematics, namely, as a calculus; I know what I can derive from what (rather, I have derived; 'derivability' in general is already problematic). With any higher 'Platonic' statements in a discussion, I interpret them to myself as statements that a fixed sentence is derivable (or derived) from certain other sentences. (He actually believes the following: the assertion of a sentence is interpreted as signifying: this sentence holds in the fixed, presupposed system; and this means: it is derivable from certain foundational assumptions.) (090-16-28)

The contrast between fully 'intelligible language' and 'uninterpreted calculus' also appears, albeit more briefly, elsewhere in the discussion notes (090-16-25, -04, -05). Tarski draws the same contrast in *Wahrheitsbegriff*: "we are not interested here in 'formal' languages and sciences in one sense of the word 'formal,' namely sciences to the signs and expressions of which no meaning is attached...We shall always ascribe quite concrete and, for us, intelligible meanings to the signs which occur in the languages we shall consider" (Tarski 1983, 166-67). Quine makes a similar point in 1943's "Notes on Existence and Necessity": "The nominalist, admitting only concrete objects, must either regard classical mathematics as discredited, or, at best, consider it a machine which is useful despite the fact that it uses ideograms of the forms of statements which involve a fictitious ontology" (Quine 1943a, 125). To put the point in the terminology of Carnap's *Logical Syntax*, merely knowing the formation and transformation rules

---

2. Carnap also discusses which languages children can learn in his correspondence with Neurath during the protocol-sentence debate (Uebel 2007, 238).

of a calculus does not constitute genuine understanding.[3] That is, understanding what a sentence *s* means requires more than knowing which sentences are provable from *s* and conversely. Such a viewpoint finds a more recent expression in John Searle's 'Chinese Room' thought-experiment, which purports to show that a computer program cannot understand a language, because the computer's operations are restricted to the realm of syntax (Searle 1980). In short, regardless of what the detailed content of *Verständlichkeit* might be, it at least requires that a language be more than an uninterpreted calculus or 'empty formalism,' in addition to its being a pragmatic notion.

2.1.3 What does 'understandable' or 'intelligible' mean in Carnap's publications?

The contrast between an understood language and an uninterpreted calculus also emerges clearly in Carnap's published remarks during this period. For when Carnap discusses the notion of *understanding*, he repeatedly connects it with *interpretation*. In both *Foundations of Logic and Mathematics* in 1939 and *Introduction to Semantics* in 1942, to 'understand' a sentence is to know how to interpret that sentence—and to interpret a sentence is to assign it truth-conditions via semantic rules. Carnap writes in *Introduction to Semantics*:

> By a **semantical system** (or interpreted system) we understand a system of rules...of such a kind that the rules determine a **truth-condition** for every sentence of the object language... In this way the sentences are interpreted by the rules, i.e. made understandable, because to *understand* a sentence, to know what is asserted by it, is the same as to know under what conditions it would be true. (Carnap 1942, 22; bold in original, my italics)

We find a virtually identical claim three years earlier, in *Foundations of Logic and Mathematics*:

> Therefore, we shall say that we *understand* a language system, or a sign, or an expression, or a sentence in a language system, if we know the semantical rules of the system. We shall also say that the semantical rules give an *interpretation* of the language system. (Carnap 1939, 152-53; my emphasis)

Clearly, Carnap's publications both before and after the Harvard conversations of 1940-41 reveal a conception of understanding that dovetails with the conception he and Tarski articulate during the Harvard conversations: both the published and the unpublished remarks treat uninterpreted calculi as not understood.

We now have the materials needed to make the central point of this section, connecting the notion of *Verständlichkeit* to broader themes in Carnap's work and to twentieth-century philosophy more generally. Since an interpretation of

---

3. Formation rules determine the well-formed formulae or grammatical strings of a calculus; transformation rules are often called 'inference rules' today.

First Justification: *Verständlichkeit*

a grammatical string of symbols gives its truth-condition, and for Carnap (and many others) at this time, a sentence's meaning is captured by its truth-condition, an interpretation supplies meanings to (otherwise meaningless) characters. This is why, in the discussion notes, 'uninterpreted calculus' is contrasted with 'intelligible language': an uninterpreted calculus has no meaning conferred upon it. And, recalling that *verständlich* and its cognates are pragmatic notions, it appears that 'intelligible' is the pragmatic (i.e., language-user-dependent) correlate of the semantic notion 'meaning.' That is, a speaker understands a particular sentence if and only if she knows that sentence's meaning. (Meaningfulness differs from understandability because a sentence can be meaningful, even in my native language, although I do not understand it–for example, I might lack the requisite vocabulary to understand a perfectly meaningful sentence in a contemporary article on biochemistry.) *Verständlichkeit* is thus intimately connected to discussions of meaning and meaningfulness, notions which have occupied center stage in analytic philosophy throughout much of its history.

There is another, derivative sense of 'understanding' that Carnap offers, both at this time and later in his career; to examine it, a brief detour is needed. This second sense does not appear in Carnap's discussions of semantics in general, but rather in his treatment of the semantics of fundamental scientific theories. Carnap's basic idea, put simply, is that incomplete interpretations may provide understanding as well, if certain other conditions (to be spelled out shortly) are also met. In *Foundations of Logic and Mathematics*, Carnap first notes that, as the history of science has progressed, we have less and less "intuitive understanding" of the foundational terms of modern science, such as Maxwell's electromagnetic field and, more strikingly, the wave-function in quantum mechanics (Carnap 1939, 209). (Here, 'intuitive' perhaps carries Kantian overtones, even if it is not intended to match precisely the Kantian characterization of intuition.) Carnap writes that "the physicist... cannot give us a translation into everyday language" of 'ψ' (the symbol for the quantum-mechanical wave-function) (Carnap 1939, 211). Given Carnap's account above, in which understanding is achieved via interpretation, this appears to create a problem: how can modern physical theories be understood on Carnap's account, given that some of the fundamental, i.e. "primitive" (Carnap 1939, 207), terms do not admit of direct interpretation?

Carnap maintains that there is a sense in which a modern physicist "understands the symbol 'ψ' and the laws of quantum mechanics" (Carnap 1939, 211). This seems reasonable: it would be Pickwickian to claim that Stephen Hawking does not understand quantum mechanics. Carnap suggests that a physicist's understanding consists in using a physical theory, including the sentences containing 'unintuitive' terms that cannot be 'translated into ordinary language,' to explain previously observed phenomena and make new predictions. And this sort of understanding can be achieved via a partial or incomplete interpretation of a calculus, provided that the uninterpreted, 'unintuitive' terms are appropriately inferentially connected to the interpreted terms. Carnap writes:

> It is true a theory must not be a "mere calculus" but possess an interpretation, on the basis of which it can be applied to facts of nature. But it is sufficient... to make this interpretation explicit for elementary [roughly: observational–G.F.-A.] terms; the interpretation of the other terms is then indirectly determined by the formulas of the calculus, either definitions or laws, connecting them with the elementary terms... Thus we understand 'E' [the symbol for Maxwell's electric field–G.F.-A.], if "understanding" of an expression, a sentence, or a theory means capability of its use for the description of known facts or the prediction of new facts. An "intuitive understanding"... is neither necessary nor possible. (Carnap 1939, 210-11)

Carnap still maintains this view several years later, in his autobiography. In the course of articulating what is currently called the 'syntactic view of scientific theories,'[4] Carnap writes:

> the interpretation of the theoretical terms supplied by the [semantic] rules is incomplete. But this incomplete interpretation is sufficient for an understanding of the theoretical system, if "understanding" means being able to use in practical applications; this application consists in making predictions of observable events, based on observed data, with the help of the theoretical system. (Carnap 1963, 78)

Carnap's basic picture is clear: a partially interpreted calculus qualifies as understood, provided that such a calculus—including its terms that are not directly interpreted—is inferentially related in a substantive way to the unproblematically understood terms and sentences of 'everyday language' and thus is useable in practical applications, especially explanation and prediction. The terms that are not directly interpreted (i.e., the 'theoretical' ones such as the quantum mechanical wave-function) can be useful 'for making predictions of observable events' only if they are appropriately inferentially connected to the directly interpreted ones.[5] (Note that this liberalized version of 'understanding' includes Carnap's narrower, original version as a degenerate case, in which all the terms of the language belong to the everyday language.) In *Logical Syntax* §84, Carnap also claims that practical application is one means of supplying an interpretation to an abstract calculus—although there, the calculus to be interpreted is drawn from pure mathematics, not natural science. Carnap writes: "the interpretation of

---

4. See Mormann (2007) for a detailed discussion of the logical empiricists' views of scientific theories.
5. Carnap's theory of meaning for scientific language is thus a hybrid of so-called referentialist/representationalist/truth-conditional and inferentialist/conceptual role semantics, or what Fodor and Lepore (1991) call 'Old' and 'New Testament' semantics, respectively. Carnap employs Old Testament semantics at the level of observable or elementary terms, and the New Testament, inferential role semantics is applied to the 'higher' or theoretical reaches of scientific language. Thus, it is misleading to call this account of the content of scientific theories the 'syntactic view,' since it essentially involves directly assigning *semantic* values to at least some of the predicates, viz. the observational terms.

First Justification: *Verständlichkeit* 33

mathematics is effected by means of the rules of application" of pure mathematics to synthetic sentences (Carnap 1934/1937, 327). Carnap's use of partial interpretations will be discussed at greater length below, in 3.1 and 3.2.1.

But what is the *point* of producing such a partial interpretation? What does it achieve? In *Foundations*, Carnap first introduces the issue of the understandability of a physical theory in the following terms: (how) can a layperson understand the content of the theory?

> Suppose that we intend to construct an interpreted system of physics–or the whole of science. We shall first lay down a calculus. Then we have to state semantical rules... For which terms, then, must we give rules, for the elementary or the abstract ones? We can, of course, state a rule for any term, no matter what its degree of abstractness... But suppose we have in mind the following purpose for our syntactical and semantical description of a system of physics: the description of a system shall teach a layman to understand it, i.e., to enable him to apply it to his observations in order to arrive at explanations and predictions. A layman is meant as one who does not know physics but has normal senses and understands a language in which observable properties of things can be described (e.g., a suitable part of everyday non-scientific English). (Carnap 1939, 204)

Here again, we see evidence that Carnap considers the intelligibility of a language to be a pragmatic matter: what is understandable to one language-user (e.g. a particle physicist) will likely be different from what is understandable to another (e.g. an auto mechanic), and vice versa.

To diverge momentarily from the main trajectory of this chapter, this text also points to an interesting historical fact about twentieth-century philosophy of science. The distinction that Carnap draws between 'elementary' and 'abstract' terms is virtually identical to the now-infamous distinction between the observational and theoretical vocabularies. This latter distinction is often said to have been introduced to isolate the 'empirical content' of a scientific theory.[6] But the above quotation shows that, at least in *Foundations*, Carnap does not draw the distinction in order to isolate empirical content, but rather to make a scientific theory understandable to a layperson. These two aims are related, but clearly different. (However, we cannot be thoroughgoing revisionists about the aim of the observational-theoretical distinction: in "Testability and Meaning" (Carnap 1936-37),Carnap endorses the goal traditionally ascribed to him.) Additionally, the purpose Carnap states here dovetails nicely with one of Neurath's goals for the Unified Science movement (and his *Encyclopedia of Unified Science*, of which *Foundations* is an installment): to democratize science by presenting scientific claims in a form everyone can understand.

---

6. For example, van Fraassen attacks the attempt to identify empirical import using this distinction (van Fraassen 1980, 54).

2.1.4 What does 'understandable' or 'intelligible' mean for Quine?

So much for Carnap's published remarks on understandability; how does Quine conceive of *Verständlichkeit*? Quine, to the best of my knowledge, never explicitly affirms or denies Carnap's conception of understanding (circa 1940) as knowledge of truth-conditions. In fact, I have not found an explicit characterization of (much less necessary and sufficient conditions for) intelligibility or understandability anywhere in Quine's published corpus. This absence is conspicuous, given that Quine frames his critique in "Two Dogmas" in terms of analyticity and/or synonymy failing to be "understandable" (Quine 1951, 32) or "intelligible" (Quine 1951, 26). However, two letters he writes to Carnap in the 1940s provide hints about the meaning Quine attaches to 'intelligibility' during this period. In a 1947 letter to Carnap, Quine writes that he considers an 'exclusively concrete ontology' intelligible:

> I am not ready to say, though, that when we fix the basic features of our language... our guiding consideration is normally convenience exclusively. In my own predilection for an exclusively concrete ontology there is something which does not reduce in any obvious way to considerations of mere convenience; viz., some vague but seemingly ultimate standard of intelligibility or clarity. (Creath 1990, 410)

Two points about this quotation are relevant for present purposes. First, for Quine, 'intelligibility' and 'clarity' are (at least roughly) synonymous. This closely echoes the language of Quine's December 1940 lecture, briefly discussed above, in which 'problematic universals are eliminated' in order to 'reduce the more obscure to the clearer.' Carnap does not, as far as I could find, tie intelligibility to clarity. Second, for Quine, the standard of intelligibility is ultimate or fundamental: not only is it irreducible to 'mere convenience,' but it is not reducible to anything else either. A similar sentiment is expressed in Goodman and Quine's "Steps Toward a Constructive Nominalism": "Why do we refuse to admit the abstract objects that mathematics needs? Fundamentally this refusal is based on a philosophical intuition that cannot be justified by appeal to anything more ultimate" (Quine and Goodman 1947, 105). Readers of the 1947 paper have often found this justification (if it can be called a justification) for nominalism unsatisfying (Burgess and Rosen 1996, 205). I propose that we interpret the 'intuition' of 1947 as a (transformed) version of the 1941 demand for intelligibility; this could shed some light on what Goodman and Quine might have had in mind with their cryptic published claim. This exegetical conjecture draws support from the fact that just as *Verständlichkeit* is both the primary motivation for the 1941 project and yet remains unclear and vague to the people using the term, so too the 'intuition' of 1947 is the 'fundamental' impetus for undertaking the nominalist constructions, and yet Goodman and Quine offer no explicit explanation of it. The primary difference between the 1941 and 1947 expressions of nominalism is that the former is primarily, though probably not exclusively, semantic (claims involving abstracta are, at best, meaningless strings), whereas the latter is ontological (abstracta do not exist).

First Justification: *Verständlichkeit* 35

The considerations of the previous paragraph lead one to suspect that Quine holds, at this point in his career, that epistemic virtues are distinct from pragmatic ones, i.e., 'convenience' and simplicity. Such a suspicion is borne out by a letter Quine writes to Carnap in 1943 regarding their Harvard discussions two years earlier.

[T]he program of finitistic construction system on which the four of us talked at intervals in 1941... may indeed be essential to a satisfactory epistemology. The problem of epistemology is far from clear, as you have emphasized; and essential details of the aforementioned program must depend, as we have seen, on some increased clarification as to just what the epistemological question is. I am more hopeful than you of the eventual possibility of such a clarification; i.e., the possibility of eventually reducing to the form of clear questions the particular type of inarticulate intellectual dissatisfaction that once drove you to work out the theory of the *Aufbau*, and Goodman his related theory...

[I]n the course of... discussion it began to appear increasingly that the distinguishing feature of analytic truth, for you, was its epistemological immediacy in some sense... Then we [Tarski and Quine] urged that the only logic to which we could attach any seeming epistemological immediacy would be some sort of finitistic logic. (Creath 1990, 294-95)

First, note the final two sentences of this quotation. Given that in 1941 the stated goal of the finitist-nominalist project was to construct a fully *verständlich* language, it seems reasonable to infer that for Quine *Verständlichkeit* is closely associated with 'epistemological immediacy.' Presumably, whatever is epistemologically immediate does not stand in need of further justification (for such knowledge is not 'mediated'). Quine appears to be expressing some form of epistemological foundationalism. Quine's notion of intelligibility in the above letters differs from that found in Carnap's published remarks. In the latter, intelligibility appears primarily as a semantic-pragmatic concept: a language is understandable to a particular person if that person knows the meaning of its sentences (i.e., can interpret the language's symbols). In 1943, however, Quine apparently thinks the goal of intelligibility (or often 'clarity' in Quine's idiolect) was primarily an non-pragmatic, epistemological concept.[7]

---

7. There is an equivocation here in the term 'pragmatic,' which stems from Carnap's terminology. Following Charles Morris, in discussions of language, Carnap uses 'pragmatic' to refer to those aspects of language that are dependent on individual speakers. On the other hand, when Carnap says that the choice between languages or linguistic frameworks is pragmatic, he means that the decision of which language to use is not made on the grounds of evidence (i.e., there is not one language best supported by the evidence), but rather (at least in part) on the grounds of convenience, simplicity, or utility. Quine's interpretation of 'intelligible' is clearly non-pragmatic in the second sense (for it 'does not reduce to mere convenience'), but it is uncertain whether it is non-pragmatic in the first, i.e., whether it is independent of individual language speakers. In any case, the epistemic vs. semantic distinction between Quine and Carnap holds in 1943.

Why has Quine apparently run together semantics and epistemology? Here is one conjecture. When we survey the various projects of analysis that early twentieth-century philosophers undertake, we can distinguish two distinct types of endeavor: semantic analysis, which aims to uncover the 'real meaning' or logical form of a sentence often 'hidden' beneath the sentence's surface structure, and epistemological analysis, which aims to uncover the grounds for the truth of a claim. These two types of analysis can be tied together; the verification criterion of meaning is one way to achieve that association,[8] and Carnap asserts in the *Aufbau* that a constitution system aims to exhibit not only the epistemic order of our knowledge, but also the meanings of our concepts (Carnap 1928/1963, 246). However, semantic and epistemic analyses can be kept distinct, and there are longstanding precedents in the analytic tradition for doing so: for example, Russell's analysis of definite descriptions is clearly a semantic analysis, not an epistemological one. But given that early analytic philosophers (including Carnap) often conflated semantic and epistemic analyses, it is less surprising that Quine would run them together in his reflections on the finitist-nominalist project of 1941. However, it should be noted that, within Carnap's discussion notes of the time, *Verständlichkeit* is not an explicitly epistemological (as opposed to semantic) concept. The closest *verständlich* comes to assuming an epistemic aspect is in the final conversation, where (as we have seen) Carnap suggests that perhaps the order in which children learn concepts may reflect the order of intelligibility of those concepts.

I would like to draw out two further points from the quotation above. First, it provides evidence that Quine, like Carnap, felt the participants in the Harvard discussions had not clearly fixed the meaning of 'understandable,' and that they recognized this fundamental unclarity. Second, the beginning of the above quotation reveals something interesting about the relative intellectual trajectories of Carnap and Quine. As is well known, Quine recants epistemological foundationalism in his later, post-nominalist work; "Epistemology Naturalized" is a particularly strident example. However, Carnap had already moved, many years before, to a version of the anti-foundationalist epistemological position that Quine later expounds (though Carnap's anti-foundationalism differs from Quine's). It is *Quine* who in 1943 was still "hopeful of the possibility of clarification of the epistemological problem," whereas Carnap was not. Quine, not Carnap, still held in 1943 that there could be some sort of 'epistemologically immediate' material, which could be used as an Archimedean point in the analysis of knowledge. Quine recognized that Carnap is not 'hopeful' about such a project in 1943. Thus, to put the point baldly, Quine's brief history of empiricism found in "Epistemology Naturalized" can perhaps be read as an *autobiographical* history leading up to 1969, instead of as the story of old-fashioned empiricism

---

8. The basic idea survives in the 'liberalized' meaning criteria found in Carnap's later "Testability and Meaning": "Two chief problems of the theory of knowledge are the question of meaning and the question of verification... But, from the point of view of empiricism, there is a... closer connection between the two problems. In a certain sense, there is only one answer to the two questions" (Carnap 1936-37, 419).

from Hume through Carnap, which finds its anti-foundationalist apotheosis in Quine.

In response to the above letter from Quine, Carnap replies that he considers 'the distinguishing feature of analytic truth' unequivocally *not* its epistemological immediacy, but rather its independence from any substantive, contingent facts (Creath 1990, 308). Quine, in reply, concedes the point (Creath 1990, 311, 336). However, Quine could have avoided his mistake if he had paid closer attention to what he had already recognized in the first letter: in 1943, Carnap does not think that there is any clear traditional 'problem of epistemology' to be solved, so Carnap would likely not be interested in attempting to identify 'epistemologically immediate' or otherwise foundational items of knowledge. In sum, though Quine and Carnap disagreed in the 1940s about the possibility of well-posed epistemological questions from the standpoint of scientific philosophy, both agreed that *Verständlichkeit* had not been given an exact characterization, despite the central role that term played in their Harvard discussions. And while Quine (after the fact, at least) treats *Verständlichkeit* as primarily an epistemological concept, Carnap tends to think of it as semantic-pragmatic.

2.2. Second Justification: Overcoming Metaphysics

Another rationale for pursuing the finitist-nominalist project present, both implicitly and explicitly, in the Harvard discussions is the desire to purge (cognitively significant) discourse of metaphysics. It is well known that the logical empiricists and their allies (e.g. Russell and Wittgenstein) held a very negative view of metaphysics. The group of Polish philosophers from which Tarski came, the Lvov-Warsaw School, also shared this anti-metaphysical animus to some degree (Simons 1993), (Wolenski 1993). As a group, however, they tended to be neither as fervently[9] nor as unanimously anti-metaphysical as their Viennese contemporaries. For example, Tarski's slightly more relaxed attitude towards metaphysics around this time appears in a 1936 letter to Neurath: "even if I [Tarski] do not underestimate your battle against metaphysics... I personally do not live in a constant and panic fear of metaphysics" (Mancosu 2008a, 210). The impetus to eliminate metaphysics was shared by many analytic philosophers in the early twentieth century, though it took varying forms; chapter 6 will catalogue some of this variety.

The anti-metaphysical drive is closely connected to the notion of *Verständlichkeit* discussed in the previous section. One characterization of metaphysics widespread among the logical empiricists and their intellectual kin is the following: if a string of symbolic marks x is metaphysical, then x is meaningless.[10] (The

---

9. Chwistek, who exhibits an anti-metaphysical streak (as we saw above in 1.4.1), was not part of the Lvov-Warsaw school.
10. Precisely this characterization is found in Carnap's "Overcoming Metaphysics through the Logical Analysis of Language," but the same idea is clearly set forth in the

converse does not hold: the string '$)yPQ))$', which is meaningless in standard formalizations of predicate logic, is not metaphysics.) And presumably, if a given word or sentence is meaningless, then it is not understandable, since to say that A understands p is to say that A knows the meaning of p. The connection to the finitist-nominalist project is clear: by *modus tollens*, if every word and every sentence in an interpreted language is 'fully understandable,' then there are no metaphysical words or sentences in that language. This argument is never fully articulated in the discussion notes; in particular, the conditional 'If something is meaningless, then it is not understandable' never appears. Nonetheless, given that that conditional seems patently true (for how could one understand nonsense?), it seems reasonable to connect Carnap, Tarski, and Quine's discussions of intelligibility in this way to their shared aversion to metaphysics qua cognitively meaningless utterances and inscriptions. And if the central claim of 2.1.3 above–that in these notes, 'intelligible' should be understood as the pragmatic correlate of 'meaningful'–is correct, then the goal of constructing an intelligible language coincides with the goal of constructing a language free of objectionable metaphysics. In short, given the unintelligibility of meaningless discourse, a fully intelligible language would also be a language free from metaphysical impurities, and it seems likely that such a connection was at least implicit in the minds of the Harvard discussants.

But Carnap's notes from the discussions of 1940-41 contain more than implicit attacks on metaphysics. There are explicit references to noxious metaphysical theses as well. Tarski and Quine hold that adopting (FN 1) and (FN 2) would prevent a pernicious slide into a certain kind of metaphysics, which they call 'Platonism,' after the grandfather of all metaphysicians. Recall that, in the first articulation of his proposal, Tarski labels (FN 1), the requirement that variables be first-order, the 'non-Platonic' requirement (090-16-28). The participants do not offer a detailed or precise characterization of Platonism; but it involves at least higher-order logic and/or (transfinite) set theory.[11] (FN 1) rules out higher-order logic, and adding (FN 2) to it rules out (even first-order) set theory. For example, we find Tarski saying (as we have seen before):

> It would be a wish and a guess that the whole general set theory, as beautiful as it is, will disappear in the future. With the higher types, Platonism begins. The tendencies of Chwistek and others ("nominalism") to talk only about designatable things are healthy. (090-16-09)

And even earlier, in a discussion with Russell and Carnap, Tarski asserts: "A Platonism underlies the higher functional calculus (and so the use of predicate variables, especially higher types)" (102-63-09).

Tractatus, as well as in many of Schlick's and Neurath's writings. Philosophical differences arise in cashing out the content of 'meaningless.'

11. Without specifically addressing Carnap, Tarski, or Quine's conception of Platonism circa 1940, Bouveresse (2005) discusses the shifting meanings of the term 'Platonism' in the early part of the twentieth century.

Second Justification: Overcoming Metaphysics

In a December 1940 lecture at Harvard, before Tarski introduces (FN 1-3) (102-63-04), Quine distinguishes mathematics from logic as follows: "'logic' = theory of joint denial and quantification," while "'mathematics' = (Logic +) theory of ∈." Quine then goes on to say that "mathematics is Platonic, logic is not." Why should the set-membership relation introduce Platonic commitments? Quine explains that "there are no logical predicates," while '∈' is a predicate. He then claims:

> Predicates bring ontological claims (not because they designate, for they are syncategorematic here, since variables never occur for them; rather:) because a predicate takes certain objects as values for the argument variable; so e.g. '∈' demands classes, universals; thus mathematics is Platonic, logic is not. (102-63-04)

That is, if there are any true statements of the form '$P \in Q$,' then there must be at least one class (provided '∈' is given the standard interpretation). For Quine, accepting the existence of at least one class is tantamount to accepting Platonism. This position is stronger than the one he published a year before in "Designation and Existence" Quine (1939), for there Quine asserts that a nominalist could hold '$P \in Q$' to be true, provided the nominalist does not *quantify* (ineliminably) over the Q-position. And later in the same 1940 lecture, Quine asserts that higher mathematics is based on "a myth," for the axioms of set theory are "not univocally determined" by "familiar common sense results for finite classes, parallel to common sense laws about heaps." (Quine's conception of the relationship between 'myth' and 'metaphysics' is not clear; at the very least, 'myth' is not a term of approbation, epistemic or otherwise.) And Quine harbored these suspicions of set theory even before Tarski proposes constructing a finitist-nominalist language. In short, (first-order) set theory is Platonic, along this line of thinking, because it forces us to admit the existence of classes.

So why do Tarski and Quine also suspect higher-order logic of being metaphysics, even when the domain of discourse consists solely of (concrete) individuals? In Quine's May 1943 letter to Carnap, reflecting on the Harvard discussions, we find:

> I argued, supported by Tarski, that there remains a kernel of technical meaning in the old controversy about [the] reality or irreality of universals, and that in this respect we find ourselves on the side of the Platonists insofar as we hold to the full non-finitistic logic. Such an orientation seems unsatisfactory as an end-point in philosophical analysis, given the hard-headed, anti-mystical temper which all of us share;... So here again we found ourselves envisaging a finitistic constitution system. (Creath 1990, 295)

Presumably, the 'kernel of technical meaning in the old controversy' is composed of two decisions: (i) whether, contra (FN 1), to allow non-concrete individuals into the domain of quantification, as discussed in the previous paragraph, and (ii) whether, contra (FN 2), to adopt a higher-order logic. For Quine, by this point in his career, a commitment to higher-order logics brings in its wake a commitment to the 'reality of universals.' Why? In 1939's "Designation and Existence," Quine articulated his famous dictum "To be is to be the value of a variable" (Quine 1939, 708). In that article, he uses this dictum to characterize nominalism within the framework of modern logic: a language is nominalist if its variables do not ineliminably range over any abstracta.[12] And properties and relations, which are quantified over in second-order logics, are (for Quine and many others) paradigmatically abstract entities.[13] In short, a language is metaphysical if it quantifies (ineliminably) over abstract entities; in (first-order) set theory, those abstracta are sets, and in higher-order logic, those abstracta are properties and relations.[14]

Taking a wider historical view, it merits notice that Quine has transformed the old issue of nominalism into a form more congenial to logical empiricists and their allies: "The nominalist... claims that a language adequate to all scientific purposes can be framed in such a way that its variables admit only concrete objects, individuals, as values" (Quine 1939, 708). That is, what was previously seen as a metaphysical question ('Are universals real?') is transformed into a logico-linguistic question: 'Is a certain type of formalized language expressively rich enough to capture the content of scientific discourse?' This shows clearly that whatever differences may have existed between Quine and Carnap at this time, Quine is fully on board with the basic research program Carnap espouses in the *Aufbau*, "Overcoming Metaphysics through the Logical Analysis of Language," *Logical Syntax*, and later works: a central task of modern scientific philosophy is to transform metaphysical (pseudo-)questions into well-posed logico-linguistic ones about the language of science. He and Carnap might disagree on which language forms are preferable or acceptable, but the general strategy for tackling perennial philosophical questions is the same.

Conspicuously absent from both the discussion notes of 1940-41, as well as from other textual sources before and after that time, is an explanation of *why* admitting abstracta as values of variables constitutes objectionable, metaphysical Platonism for Tarski and Quine. A hint about the attractions of nominalism for Quine is found in a lecture from October 1937, where he describes the aims of nominalism:

1) To avoid metaphysical questions as to the connection between the realm of universals and the realm of particulars; how universals enter

---

12. Quine writes: "In realistic languages, variables admit abstract entities as values; in nominalistic languages they do not" (Quine 1939, 708).

13. Quine does not tell us where or how to draw the line between concrete and abstract entities (Quine 1939, 708). Also, in "Designation and Existence," he does not appear to hold that all abstract entities correspond to predicates in a formalized language; that is, Quine appears to leave open the possibility that abstracta could be part of the domain of individuals.

14. For further published remarks on Quine's conception of nominalism, Platonism, classes, and relations, see "On Universals" (Quine 1947) and "Notes on Existence and Necessity" (Quine 1943a), especially §5.

into particulars, or particulars into universals.
2) To provide for reduction to statements ultimately about tangible things, matters of fact. This by way of keeping our feet on the ground–avoiding empty theorizing. (Mancosu 2008b, 28)

The first point, reminiscent of Socratic questions concerning how particulars 'participate' in the universals they instantiate, is clearly a metaphysical question; but it is not obvious that set theory and/or second-order logic engage this hoary issue in any substantive fashion. Quine's second point is not much more enlightening: it simply expresses the suspicion of abstracta and predilection for concreta, which characterize (if not define) the nominalist's position.

Quine and Tarski's silence about why admitting abstracta as values of variables is fundamentally unpalatable grows more troubling when we note that labeling higher-order logic and/or set theory as metaphysics does not mesh well with the conception of metaphysics offered elsewhere by logical empiricists and their fellow travelers. Of course, both the explicatum and the explanandum of the term 'metaphysics' vary over time and between different thinkers. Nonetheless, most logical empiricists and their allies, most of the time, strongly resist classifying large tracts of logic and mathematics as metaphysical. (As a result, special exceptions are made in accounts of meaning and knowledge to account for logic and mathematics. For example, Wittgenstein's distinction in the *Tractatus* between pseudo-propositions that are nonsense [*unsinnig*] and those that are senseless [*sinnlos*] places *unsinnig* metaphysics in a separate category from *sinnlos* logic and mathematics, even though both 'say nothing about the world.') So not only do Tarski and Quine omit an explicit explanation of why classes and relations are objectionably metaphysical, but such a view appears to clash with the view of metaphysics presented by many of their philosophical peers. However, Russell may consititute an exception: recall his talk in 1.4.2 of "these queer things called numbers," which he considers 'fictions of fictions.'

Furthermore, perhaps there is no explanation to give here, and the proponents of this view recognize that fact. As mentioned earlier, in Quine and Goodman's published paper that they acknowledge is an outgrowth of the 1941 discussions, they admit that their "refusal [to countenance abstracta] is based on a philosophical intuition that cannot be justified by appeal to anything more ultimate" (Quine and Goodman 1947, 105). So the rejection of abstracta is not based on any more fundamental (or even articulated) theory of knowledge and/or meaning that declares abstracta unknowable and/or signs for them meaningless. Of course, we should not assume they speak for Tarski as well, but if Tarski did attempt to 'justify' his rejection of abstracta 'by appeal to anything more ultimate,' that justification is not recorded in the Harvard discussion notes, and it did not impress Goodman and Quine enough to include it in their article.

We today, looking back, could impute to them a causal theory of knowledge and/or reference (see 2.5.1 below)–perhaps even just as an implicit, unarticulated assumption–but such an interpretation would be conjectural. Paolo Mancosu has suggested that such a conjecture would be misguided, and that epistemological concerns are not at the heart of Tarski and Quine's predilection for nominalism:

> What is striking about Tarski and Quine in comparison to contemporary nominalism is the fact that the motivation for nominalism is not argued on epistemological grounds. Contemporary nominalism has been, by and large, an attempt to reply to Benacerraf's dilemma on how we can have access to abstract entities. Tarski and Quine['s]... anti-Platonism originates from metaphysical qualms and from methodological commitments favoring paucity of postulated entities. (Mancosu 2008b, 52)

Mancosu is certainly right to stress the near-total absence of epistemological rationales offered by Tarski and Quine, especially in contrast with current nominalists. However, a few qualifications to this claim should be registered. First, as this section has emphasized, Tarski and Quine are somewhat short on explanations for what exactly is objectionable or unacceptable about the 'Platonic metaphysics' they think is embodied in set theory or higher-order logic. If pressed on the issue (e.g., if they were explicitly asked 'What's so horrible about this particular bit of metaphysics?'), they could conceivably fall back on epistemological justifications. Second, as was quoted in the previous section, Quine writes to Carnap in 1943 that he (and Tarski) considered FN languages to enjoy an 'epistemological immediacy,' so issues concerning knowledge are not completely alien to Quine's reasons for favoring nominalism.

Finally, a remark Tarski makes in his *Wahrheitsbegriff* monograph about "the nature of language itself" can be construed as a kind of epistemic justification for finitism. "[L]anguage, which is a product of human activity, necessarily possesses a 'finitistic' character, and cannot serve as an adequate tool for the investigation of facts, or for the construction of concepts, of an eminently 'infinitistic' character" (Tarski 1983, 253). If our investigations are conducted within a finite language, then there is some sort of barrier from our accessing and expressing any truths about the infinite, and it is not unreasonable to think of this barrier as epistemic in character: our tools for inquiry are not adequate for certain tasks.[15] So while Mancosu is right that Tarski and Quine certainly do not emphasize any epistemological justifications for nominalism in or around 1940-41, it may be too strong to say that their motivations lacked *any* epistemic component.

2.3. Third Justification: Inferential Safety

The next justification for the finitist-nominalist restrictions I will discuss does not appear in Carnap's dictation notes. However, Carnap mentions this justification

---

15. Interestingly, many linguists today think that human language does have an infinitistic character: "Infinity is one of the most fundamental properties of human language, maybe the most fundamental one" (Lasnik 2000, 3). For a critical assessment of this view, see Pullum and Scholz (2010).

Third Justification: Inferential Safety

elsewhere, as do Quine and Goodman, so I consider it here. Roughly, the idea is that Russell's paradox reveals that certain logics suffer serious problems, and therefore these logics should be avoided. Differences arise, however, over the size of this class of problematic logics: Quine and Goodman consider the group of suspicious logics to be wider than Carnap does. In the Goodman and Quine paper on nominalism we find an expression of this argument.

> Why do we refuse to admit the abstract objects that mathematics needs?... What seems to be the most natural principle for abstracting classes or properties leads to paradoxes. Escape from these paradoxes can apparently be effected only by recourse to alternative rules whose *artificiality and arbitrariness arouse suspicion that we are lost in a world of make-believe*. (Quine and Goodman 1947, 105; my emphasis)

And presumably, the (supposed) inhabitants of a 'world of make-believe' do not exist. Their argument can, I think, be cast as follows: if we admit quantification over classes and/or properties into our logic, then we can have either a 'natural' logic that leads to inconsistencies, or an 'artificial' logic that avoids inconsistencies in an *ad hoc* manner.[16] But neither a natural but inconsistent logic, nor an artificial but consistent logic, is particularly desirable. So Goodman and Quine recommend we allow neither classes nor properties as the values of variables. A similar idea appears in a letter written to Carnap in 1947, in which Quine suggests that Platonism is likely responsible for the logical paradoxes.

> I agree that the logical antinomies are symptoms of a fundamental unsoundness somewhere, but I suspect that this unsoundness lies in platonism itself–i.e., in the admission of abstract values of bindable variables. (Creath 1990, 409)

Here, again, Quine asserts that the real lesson of Russell's paradox is that we should give up quantifying over abstracta. Quine was not alone: Paul Bernays expounded a comparable view several years earlier.

> Several mathematicians and philosophers interpret the methods of Platonism in the sense of conceptual realism, postulating the existence of a world of ideal objects containing all the objects and relations of mathematics. It is this absolute Platonism which has been shown untenable by the antinomies. (Bernays 1935/1983, 261)

---

16. In "On Universals," Quine reiterates the charge of ad hoc-ness against the type-theoretic formulation of mathematics current at his time:
> It is as clear a formulation of the foundations of mathematics as we have. But it is platonistic. And it is an *ad hoc* structure which pretends to no intuitive basis. If any considerations were originally felt to justify the binding of schematic predicate letters, Russell's paradox was their *reductio ad absurdum*. The subsequent superimposition of a theory of types is an artificial means of restituting the system in its main lines merely as a system, divorced from any consideration of intuitive foundation. (Quine 1947, 80–81)

(It should however be noted that Bernays, unlike the nominalist Quine of 1947, believes that a "moderate Platonism" can survive the paradoxes.)

Though Carnap can muster some sympathy for this impulse, his response to Russell's paradox is not so drastic. One basic lesson Carnap takes from the paradoxes is that, *ceteris paribus*, if one logic's rules of inference and axioms are stronger than a second logic's, then the first is more likely to contain an inconsistency than the second. And for some purposes, inferential safety is of paramount value, trumping inferential and/or expressive power. In his autobiography, Carnap writes: "It is true that certain procedures, e.g. those admitted by constructivism or intuitionism, are safer than others. Therefore it is advisable to apply those procedures as far as possible," though we do lose logical strength by restricting ourselves to those means alone (Carnap 1963, 49). Thus we can interpret Carnap as attempting to discover, in the 1941 discussions, the limits of a language in which only (ultra-)constructivist procedures are applied. But his view is clearly different from Quine and Goodman's. For immediately following the above quotation, Carnap writes:

> However, there are other forms and methods which, though less safe because we do not have a proof of their consistency, appear to be practically indispensable for physics. In such a case there seems to be no good reason for prohibiting these procedures so long as no contradictions have been found. (Carnap 1963, 49)

So whereas for Quine, Russell's paradox casts doubt upon any logic that quantifies over abstracta, Carnap is willing to employ any useful logic that has not been shown inconsistent. For languages constructed to avoid the logical paradoxes, Carnap must either not consider them to be 'artificial' as Quine does, or else he does not consider artificiality a fatal flaw of such languages. In fact, Carnap would likely agree with both disjuncts of the previous statement: Carnap explicitly claims that the type restrictions which prohibit the paradoxes are natural,[17] and his principle of tolerance condones languages that feel intuitively 'artificial.' So in short, Carnap recognizes that weaker languages enjoy the advantage of being safer, insofar as they are less likely to engender contradictions or lead from true premises to false conclusions; but he does not think the logical antinomies cast aspersions on every language that quantifies (ineliminably) over classes or relations, as Quine does. An analogy may be helpful here. When a scientific

---

17. In a discussion with Tarski about the comparative advantages of *Principia Mathematica*-style logics vs. first-order set theory, Carnap says: "The types appear to me completely natural and understandable [*verständlich*]; and to a certain extent, stratification too" (090-16-26). And in his later logic textbook, Carnap writes:

> A language with no type distinctions... seems unnatural with regard to non-logical sentences. For since in such a language a type-differentiation is also omitted for descriptive signs, formulas turn up that can claim admission into the language as meaningful sentences that have verbal counterparts as follows: 'The number 5 is blue,' 'The relation of friendship weighs three pounds.' (Carnap 1954/1958, 84)

theory encounters robust data at odds with that theory's predictions, two options (roughly speaking) present themselves: reject the theory, or make an *ad hoc* modification in order to save it. The anomalous data are analogous to the paradoxes; Quine's response is closer to the first option, Carnap's to the second. This is not necessarily a condemnation of Carnap's view: LeVerrier's discovery of Uranus via data *prima facie* at odds with Newtonian theory shows that introducing a hypothesis to save a theory from potential refutation is not always the wrong response to data at odds with one's theory.

2.4. Fourth Justification: Natural Science

Another justification that Tarski and Quine offer for pursuing the finitist-nominalist project could be called the 'argument from natural science.' The previous rationales all supported (FN 1-2) (viz. the language is first-order and its domain contains only physical objects), which we could consider support for nominalism. The argument from natural science, however, is only a justification for finitism (FN 3). This argument roughly follows one of Hilbert's justifications, in "On the Infinite," for his very different type of finitism (Hilbert 1926/1983). Tarski begins with a reasonable assertion: the number of individuals in our world "is perhaps in fact finite" (090-16-25). If the universe contains only finitely many physical things, and if (FN 1-2) hold, then it follows that the domain D has finitely many members–and this is the restrictive version of (FN 3). If we wish rather to leave open the possibility that an infinite number of physical things exist, and we accept (FN 1-2), then the liberal version of (FN 3) follows. Note that if one does not accept (FN 1-2) then (FN 3) becomes much more contentious. As explained previously, (FN 1-2) prevent the two most common ways of introducing mathematical objects into a language, and mathematical infinities are usually paradigmatic examples of infinite totalities.

Carnap replies to Tarski's claim by suggesting that there are infinities. These come in two varieties: logico-mathematical and physical. The usual mathematical infinities will directly violate the spirit of the nominalist enterprise. As examples of empirical, physical infinities, Carnap suggests space and, with more conviction, time. He claims:

> even if the number of subatomic particles is finite, nonetheless the number of events can be assumed to be infinite (not just the number of temporal instants...but the number of instants a unit distance away from each other, in other words: infinite length of time.) (090-16-24)

Carnap's suggestion to use events or spatiotemporal intervals instead of physical objects for the domain of a language of science obviously violates the letter of the law of (FN 2), but Carnap likely believes it does not violate its spirit–for spatiotemporal events (and intervals between them) are still manifestly part of the natural, physical world, unlike numbers and their ilk.[18] So, Carnap is suggesting, if we expand (FN 2) to allow as elements of the domain not just physical objects or bodies but rather any entity that is (broadly speaking) part of the physical world, then (FN 3) does not force itself upon us, provided there are an infinite number of events or spatiotemporal intervals.

Tarski responds to Carnap's challenge in two related ways. The first engages Carnap on his own terms; the second suggests that Carnap's critique has missed the fundamental point of introducing (FN 3). First, Tarski replies directly to Carnap's suggestion that space and time will provide us with infinities, even if there are only a finite number of physical objects in the universe. Tarski asserts that space and time, contrary to initial appearances, may actually be finite: "perhaps quantum theory will give up continuity and density" for both space and time by quantizing both quantities. Furthermore, Tarski says, time and space could both be circular, in which case there would not be an infinite number of finite spatial or temporal intervals. In short, Tarski claims that developments in quantum and relativistic physics may in fact show that space and time are actually finite. Interestingly, Carnap makes a similar point in "Truth and Confirmation" a few years earlier, when he asks his readers to "contemplate the possibility of a language with a discontinuous spatiotemporal order which might be adopted in a future physics" (Carnap 1936/1949, 126).

Second, Tarski suggests that arguing that there is in fact an infinite quantity somewhere in the actual material world misunderstands one motivation behind (FN 3), at least in its liberal version. Tarski holds that the number of physical things in the world is *prima facie* an empirical matter. Tarski says: "we want to build the structure of the language so that this possibility [viz. that the number of things is finite] is not excluded from the beginning" (090-16-23). The basic idea is simple: the form of the language we use to describe the empirical world should not prejudge the number of entities in the universe, and (the liberal version of) Tarski's scheme leaves this question open, as it should. Put otherwise, 'How many spatial positions (or temporal intervals) are there?' is just as empirical a question as 'How many subatomic particles are there?' If one accepts (FN 2), and if one also wishes to incorporate classical (first-order) arithmetic into one's language (as e.g. Carnap does in Languages I and II in *Logical Syntax*), then one would be committed to an infinite number of physical objects. To put the matter in Carnapian terms: how many entities there are in the universe–as well as the topological structure of (actual) space and time–are intuitively or pretheoretically synthetic matters, and Tarski's (FN 3) prevents them from becoming analytic ones. That is, questions about the number of things in the universe or about the structure of space and time should be determined by the structure of the world, not by the structure of the language used for science.

But, one may ask on Carnap's behalf, how exactly would allowing 'infinite arithmetic' (S_2) exclude the possibility of circular time from the beginning? Why

---

18. Kotarbiński, whom Tarski invokes when he proposes (FN 2), however, explicitly denied that events are acceptable for the reist (Kotarbiński 1929/1966, 432).

can't we have an infinite arithmetic, and simultaneously believe that time and space are circular (or otherwise finite)? If one is committed to the FN project, then this Carnapian challenge can be answered, as follows. If one accepts that

(i) the semantic content of numerals must be physical entities of some sort,

(ii) finite temporal and spatial intervals are a sort of physical entity, and

(iii) the only live candidates for infinite collections of physical entities are the temporal or spatial intervals (so we assume e.g. that there are only finitely many particles),

then admitting infinite arithmetic *does* force one to admit that either time or space cannot be finite. So, if Carnap truly needs non-circular time or non-spherical space in order to make the axiom of infinity true, then positing the axiom of infinity as part of the basic language of science does 'rule out from the beginning' the possibility that both space and time are finite.

2.5. Current Justifications for Nominalism

Current justifications for undertaking nominalist projects usually take one of two forms: an argument from (some version of) a causal theory of knowledge and/or reference, and a desire to refute the so-called 'indispensability argument' for mathematical entities and mathematical truths. The first is a positive argument for nominalism, the second is a negative argument against a popular objection to nominalism.

2.5.1 The positive argument: from a causal theory of knowledge and/or reference

The leading current argument for nominalism can be cast as a simple syllogism, whose major premise is a concise statement of the causal theory of knowledge.

(P1) We can only have knowledge of things causally related (or relatable) to us.

(P2) Numbers and other abstracta are not causally related (or relatable) to us.

Therefore, we cannot have knowledge of numbers or other abstracta.

(This argument is neutral with respect to the ontological question of whether abstracta exist or not.) Both premises have been challenged. More criticism has been leveled at the first, presumably because many philosophers consider a defining feature of an abstract object to be its 'standing outside' the causal order. I will not discuss these objections; an excellent treatment of the dialectic of objections-and-replies can be found in Burgess and Rosen (1996, ch. 1).

Another variant of this syllogism replaces (P1) with a statement of the causal theory of reference:

($P1_R$) We can only *successfully refer to* things causally related (or relatable) to us.

The conclusion is modified accordingly: we cannot successfully refer to abstracta. And presumably we cannot say much of significance about items to which we cannot successfully refer. Causal theories of knowledge and reference did not appear in an explicit, fully-fledged form until the 1960s and 70s, so it is not at all surprising that Carnap's 1940-41 notes do not contain explicit statements of the views expressed in (P1) and ($P1_R$). However, if Tarski et al. were directly asked in 1941, they probably would not explicitly deny that we can only know about or refer to entities that are somehow causally connected or connectible with us. After all, if something is a physical entity, then (with exceptions)[19] it is causally connectible to us; and if something is an abstract entity, then it is not causally connectible to us.[20]

2.5.2 The negative argument: rebutting the indispensibility argument

Shortly after the 1947 Quine-Goodman paper appeared, Quine rejected nominalism. (Goodman did not.) Hilary Putnam and the post-nominalist Quine argued for the existence of mathematical abstracta on the grounds that relinquishing such abstracta would force us to relinquish much of modern science. We should be unwilling to pay that price for maintaining nominalist scruples. Current nominalist projects, such as Hartry Field's seminal *Science without Numbers*, usually consist of 'reconstructive' projects that attempt to rebut this indispensability argument. In such a nominalist project, a certain field of natural science is recast in a form that does not quantify ineliminably over abstract entities. Field claims that if empirical science can be reconstructed nominalistically, then belief in mathematical objects becomes "unjustifiable dogma" (Field 1980, 9). The literature on the indispensability argument is vast, and I will not comment upon the merits of the argument itself. I only wish to stress that one common justification or motivation for undertaking a technical nominalistic project today is to rebut the indispensability argument. By constructing a scientific theory that does not quantify over numbers, the modern nominalist shows that numbers are, in principle if not in practice, dispensable for that theory.

Since the indispensability argument did not appear in its fully-fledged form until around 1970, an explicit desire to rebut it could not have been a motivation for undertaking the 1941 project. However, there is a substantive precursor of the modern indispensability argument in Carnap's notes. We encountered it above in 1.2, when discussing the lower bound on the poverty of a finitist-nominalist language's expressive power; here is the relevant section again:

> If S_1 [the finitist-nominalist language of arithmetic] does not suffice to reach classical mathematics, couldn't one perhaps nevertheless adopt

---

19. For example, the laws of physics prohibit me from being in causal contact with events outside my past and future light cones.
20. Unless, like Penelope Maddy (1990), one holds that we are in causal contact with a set of cardinality 52 when we see a complete pack of playing cards.

S_1 and show that classical mathematics is not really necessary for the application of science to life? Perhaps we can set up, on the basis of S_1, a calculus for a fragment of mathematics that suffices for all practical purposes (i.e. not something just for everyday purposes, but also for the most complicated tasks of technology). (090-16-25)

This is not precisely Hartry Field's program, but it is similar: in both cases, the aim is to show that a proper subset of modern mathematics, which can be made nominalistically acceptable, is sufficient for all applications of mathematics in science. Tarski comes even closer to Field's program in a 1948 letter to Woodger:

> classical mathematics is at present an indispensible tool for scientific research in empirical science. The main problem for me is whether this tool can be interpreted or constructed nominalistically or replaced by another nominalistic tool which should be adequate for the same purposes. (Mancosu 2005, 346)

This prompts an interesting question: what is the relationship between the modern indispensability argument and the Tarski-Carnap-Quine demand that their 'understandable' language be sufficient to express (at least a substantial portion of) mathematics and natural science? To answer this question, we need an explicit statement of the present-day indispensability argument. One current formulation, taken from Mark Colyvan, is the following:

1. We ought to have ontological commitment to all and only those entities that are indispensable to our best scientific theories.

2. Mathematical entities are indispensable to our best scientific theories.

3. Therefore, we ought to have ontological commitment to mathematical entities. (Colyvan 2001, 11)

The 1941 project differs from the modern one primarily in the first premise: there is no normative claim concerning ontological commitments explicitly forwarded in the discussion notes. Nothing in the texts decisively rules out attributing this position to the participants as an implicit belief, but this potentially anachronistic interpretation is certainly not forced upon us, either. Instead, we can view Carnap et al. (or a proper subset of them) as replacing the modern normative-cum-ontological claim with the goal of a unified language of science (see chapter 6). Whether failure of a language to meet that aim automatically disqualifies it in the discussants' eyes is not, as mentioned above in section 1.2, discussed in Carnap's notes. We know that Quine, a decade after the Harvard discussions, opts for disqualification: his rationale for eventually repudiating nominalism is that we lack sufficient mathematics to do science if we abide by nominalist strictures. Carnap's principle of tolerance puts him in a somewhat different position: he would not 'disqualify' any language categorically–rather, he would likely say that a particular language is merely inexpedient for this or that purpose. And the ultimate value of various, potentially conflicting purposes is not something about which there is (or can be) a fact of the matter. Thus one might expect that Carnap would remain agnostic about languages meeting the FN conditions. However, he does not: he resists the fundamental assumptions of the project from beginning to end. An examination of the details of Carnap's resistance form the core of the following chapter.

Chapter 3
Objections to the Finitist-Nominalist Project

3.1. Why Does Carnap Participate, Given His Reservations?

As previous chapters have shown, Carnap is an active participant in the finitist-nominalist project, cooperating with Tarski and Quine throughout the academic year. However, anyone familiar with Carnap's fundamental philosophical views should suspect that he harbors serious reservations about it. This chapter covers Carnap's main objections to the FN conditions, and adds a Carnap/Frege-inspired one of my own. Given that Carnap is not convinced of the merits or value of Tarski's proposed restrictions, and resists accepting them wholeheartedly, it is natural to ask: why does Carnap engage in this project? Carnap's participation appears to be more than politely humoring his respected colleagues. For he not only discusses this topic with them repeatedly and at length, taking notes throughout, but he also works on the problems privately, in his own time, working out the dry details of formal axiom systems that aim to satisfy the FN criteria. I see at least two reasons Carnap would participate in this project, despite his skepticism toward its fundamental assumptions: (i) the principle of tolerance, and (ii) the possibility of assimilating Tarski's FN project to Carnap's own investigations into the relation between observational and theoretical languages, which pre-date the 1941 discussions.

One likely reason Carnap participates in the FN project stems from one of the most far-reaching components of his intellectual stance, namely, the principle of tolerance.[1] The version of the principle most relevant for present purposes is the following: there is no one single correct language (or logic), and as a practical corollary for the working logician, different logics may be developed, and their properties investigated, even if they are incompatible.[2] Carnap puts this abstract principle into practice, for he is willing to investigate, in detail, the construction and consequences of languages whose philosophical motivations or foundational assumptions he does not fully endorse. For example, Carnap's Language I (PSI) in *Logical Syntax* is evidence of this willingness. PSI is intended to capture formally

---

1. Alan Richardson suggests that "the first principle of Carnap interpretation" should be to "take his principle of tolerance seriously" (Richardson 2004, 64).
2. In *Logical Syntax*, Carnap writes: "Everyone is at liberty to build up his own logic, i.e. his own form of language, as he wishes" (Carnap 1934/1937, 52).

an intuitionist stance towards mathematics: PSI "fulfills the fundamental conditions of Intuitionism" (Carnap 1934/1937, 48), a stance that Carnap himself did not fully embrace at the time of publication.[3] Yet he nonetheless devotes a large chunk of *Logical Syntax* to the axiomatic articulation of such a language, and an investigation of its logical properties.[4] I suggest that Carnap, in 1941, is undertaking the same kind of endeavor, and with the same rationale, as he did in *Logical Syntax*. That is, he is again attempting to construct a formal language that meets requirements he does not fully endorse *in propria persona*, and he can justify this activity by appealing, as he did in *Logical Syntax*, to the principle of tolerance. And even at the time of writing his autobiography, Carnap was still officially publicly agnostic about nominalism, on the grounds of tolerance: "the principle that everyone is free to use the language most suited to his purpose has remained the same throughout my life... I still hold it today, e.g. with respect to *the contemporary controversy about a nominalist or Platonist language*" (Carnap 1963, 18).

However, merely citing the principle of tolerance does not explain why Carnap was willing to investigate the particular type of language Tarski proposes. The principle of tolerance merely supplies permission to study formal languages satisfying the FN strictures, but that permission applies equally to an infinite number of other languages that Carnap never investigates. So we would like to find some further rationale for Carnap's engagement in the FN project that explains why, out of the infinitely many languages a tolerant logician of science [*Wissenschaftslogiker*] is permitted to investigate, Carnap chose to devote his energies to this one. A suggestion for such a rationale can be found in the section of his autobiography entitled "The Theoretical Language." There, Carnap closely ties (and perhaps even assimilates) the 1941 FN project to work he had previously begun on the logical relationship between the observational and theoretical parts of a scientific theory. This work has its early roots in the discussions of protocol-sentences in the early 1930s.[5] The general problem of connecting the abstract mathematical structures involved in modern physical theories to observations, especially acute in the age of general relativity and quantum mechanics, exercised several logical positivists, including Schlick and Reichenbach in earlier decades (Friedman 2001). Carnap's project assumes a more familiar and canonical form in 1936-37's "Testability and Meaning" (the first Carnapian text in which the observational/ theoretical distinction explicitly appears and

---

3. In the first half of 1931, when Carnap began the manuscript that eventually became *Logical Syntax*, he "originally, in agreement with the finitist ideas with which we sympathized in the circle, had the intention of constructing only Language I" (Carnap 1963, 56). However, he gave this up when Hahn and Gödel pointed out to him that his PSI could not capture the real numbers. See Awodey and Carus (2007) and Uebel (2007, 145).
4. In the interest of historical completeness, there is probably at least one other reason Carnap discusses PSI at length: it is a language in which its own syntax can be formulated. This feature of PSI both is interesting in itself, and decisively refutes then-current claims to the contrary, advocated by followers of the *Tractatus*. They held that syntax could only be 'shown,' not 'said': "The rules of logical syntax must go without saying" (3.334).
5. For much more on the protocol-sentence debate, see Uebel (2007).

performs significant philosophical work) and 1939's *Foundations*. Here is Carnap's autobiographical, *post facto* explanation of how the 1941 project connects to work he had previously done on the nature of scientific theories.

> In *Foundations of Logic and Mathematics*, I showed how the system of science... can be constructed as a calculus whose axioms represent the laws of the theory in question. This calculus is not directly interpreted. It is rather constructed as a "freely floating system," i.e., as a network of primitive theoretical concepts which are connected with one another by the axioms... Eventually, some of these [theoretical concepts] are closely related to observable properties and can be interpreted by semantical rules which connect them with observables...
>
> In subsequent years I frequently considered the problem of the possible forms of constructing such a system, and I often discussed these problems with friends. I preferred a form of construction in which the total language consists of two parts: the observation language which is presupposed as being completely understood, and the theoretical language...
>
> My thinking on these problems received fruitful stimulation from a series of conversations which I had with Tarski and Quine during the academic year 1940-41...We considered especially the question of which form the basic language...must have in order to fulfill the requirement of complete understandability. (Carnap 1963, 78-79)

For Carnap, the observation language 'is presupposed as being completely understood.' Recall the virtually identical claim in 2.1.3, in the quotation from *Foundations* where Carnap characterizes an 'elementary' or observational language as one which is fully comprehensible to a layperson. Thus when Tarski talks in 1941 about the only kind of languages he 'truly understands,' and tries to build a serviceable scientific language out of such languages, Carnap links this to his own previous work on the connections between theoretical language and observational language developed in "Testability and Meaning." Assuming Carnap's memory of events more than a decade earlier can be trusted in this matter,[6] he viewed Tarski's 1941 project as closely related to a project he himself had already begun. It is plausible that Carnap would have considered the time and effort invested in the finitist-nominalist program worthwhile, if he believed it pursued a line of inquiry he was already researching. If Carnap considered Tarski's proposal a continuation of one of his own investigations, then we can understand why Carnap, by his own lights, is not only permitted (by the principle of tolerance) to work on Tarski's project, but also why he is willing to do so.

---

6. It is possible that Carnap imposes this synthesis of his own observational/theoretical work with Tarski's FN project only much later, since he does not write his intellectual autobiography until more than a decade after the Harvard conversations occurred.

3.2. Higher Mathematics *Is* Meaningful

As noted in 1.2, Tarski maintains that sentences that do not meet the finitist-nominalist conditions are nothing but empty formalism. As such, they are to be treated as part of a mere calculus, which can be manipulated according to a set of rules but never given a genuine, philosophically acceptable interpretation, i.e., a meaning. Parts of classical mathematics are thereby classed as meaningless; the participants usually call such statements 'higher' mathematics, and I will follow their terminology here. Carnap's intuitions, however, run strongly against considering (at least some of) higher mathematics meaningless. (In the discussion notes, after the FN criteria are proposed, there is no record of Quine explicitly siding with Tarski; however, his 1947 paper with Goodman unequivocally endorses Tarski's position.) The discussion notes do not contain much material in which Carnap defends the meaningfulness of higher mathematics, but he does offer at least two brief rebuttals. The first argument for the intelligibility of non-finitist arithmetic appeals to an analogy between claims in higher mathematics and claims in theoretical physics; the second suggests that invoking a potential infinity could render classical arithmetic intelligible.

3.2.1 An analogy between mathematics and physics

As mentioned earlier, Quine gives a wide-ranging lecture in December 1940 entitled "Logic, Mathematics, Science." In it, he claims that higher mathematics is 'Platonic,' and that science more generally is full of "myths" (see 2.3 above). Carnap responds[7] to this as follows (this is the entirety of the document containing Carnap's response):

> Dec. 20, 1940.
> *Quine is discussed.*
> Can we perhaps conceive of the higher, non-finitistic parts of logic (mathematics) thus: its relation to the finitistic parts is analogous to the relation of the higher parts of physics to the observation sentences? Thereby non-finitistic logic (mathematics) would become non-metaphysical (like physics). Perhaps light is also thereby thrown on the question of whether a fundamental difference exists between logic-mathematics and physics. (090-16-29)

What does this quotation, couched in terms of 'metaphysics,' have to do with defending the meaningfulness of mathematics? As mentioned above, for logical empiricists and their allies at this time, the following equivalence holds: an apparently meaningful string of symbols is nonsense (or 'meaningless') if and

---

7. It is unclear whether Carnap's response was public or private. The heading of the note reads "Quine is discussed," but no interlocutors appear in this note of Carnap's. Usually, when recording discussions, Carnap attributes claims to one person or another; ordinarily, the only occasions in these notes in which Carnap does not mention speakers is when he writes private notes for himself.

only if that string qualifies as metaphysics. Furthermore, it seems reasonable to hold that if a given string of symbols is not understandable, then that string is meaningless or nonsense, especially since Tarski declares calculi unintelligible, if they cannot be given a meaningful interpretation, i.e., an interpretation meeting (FN 1-4). Thus if Carnap can show that non-finitistic mathematics is 'non-metaphysical,' he thereby demonstrates that it is meaningful, and hence by *modus tollens* understandable.

So, given this connection between metaphysics, meaningfulness, and intelligibility, what is Carnap's argument for the intelligibility of mathematics? He offers an argument by analogy; in Carnap's words, the analogy is:

observation sentences : *higher parts of physics* ::
finitistic mathematics : *higher, non-finitistic mathematics*

What, concretely, does this express? I take Carnap as conjecturing that the relationship between observation sentences and (e.g.) Einstein's field equations (EFE) is sufficiently similar in the relevant respects (whatever those might be) to the relation between the statements of elementary (finitist) arithmetic and 'higher' Zermelo-Fraenkel set theory, or even classical arithmetic as expressed in Peano's axiomatization. That is,

report from Eddington's eclipse expedition : *EFE* ::
2+5=7 : *Peano arithmetic (or ZF)*

If Carnap's conjectured analogy captures a relevant similarity, then to reach his desired conclusion that higher mathematics is not metaphysics, Carnap only needs the assumption that Einstein's field equations are not metaphysical. What should we make of this argument? First, it is not clear that Quine and/or Tarski would grant that EFE and the other fundamental laws of physics are completely or unequivocally non-metaphysical. For as we saw above, Quine for one claims in his December 1940 lecture that "science is full of myth and hypostasis"; in that declaration, Quine appears to include the laws of fundamental physics.

Second, is the analogy a good one? There are obvious dissimilarities between the two cases. For example: what form of 'finitistic' mathematical statements would be most similar to observation sentences (for relevant purposes)? Is '2+5=7' sufficiently like the report that came back from Eddington's eclipse expedition? The latter makes spatiotemporally specific claims, the former does not: as philosophers since Plato have observed, we do not say '2+5=7 at 3:30 PM EST, January 21 1987.' So might '2+5=7' be more analogous to phenomenological laws of natural science? However, this difference (like several others one could point to)[8] does

---

8. For example, as Carnap points out (102-63-15), to derive an observational prediction from physical laws, initial conditions are necessary; however, there appears to be no analog to initial conditions in the mathematical case, in which particular arithmetic theorems are derived from the Peano axioms. However, I cannot see how this difference would matter, pro or contra, to Carnap's claim that higher mathematics is made meaningful by

not appear relevant to Carnap's claim that higher mathematics is meaningful and hence non-metaphysical. It appears that all that Carnap needs to draw from the case of physics is the following:

(1) Observation sentences are uncontroversially meaningful.

(2) Sentences expressing substantive scientific theories, such as Einstein's field equations, stand in substantive inferential relations (which need not be equivalences, from "Testability and Meaning" on) with these meaningful observation sentences.

(3) These inferential relations render Einstein's field equations 'meaningful by association.' (In general, if a symbolic string s stands in a non-trivial inference relationship with a meaningful sentence, then s is meaningful.)

From these three premises, Carnap infers that the Einstein field equations are meaningful. Then the question is: do analogues of the above three hold in the mathematical case? That is, are each of the following true?

(1′) Sentences like '2+5=7' are uncontroversially meaningful.[9]

(2′) Higher arithmetical statements, such as the Peano axioms or ZF, stand in substantive inferential relations (possibly weaker than equivalence) to finitist ones.

(3′) These relations make the higher, non-finitist statements meaningful by association.

It seems to me that (1′) would be questioned by Tarski and Quine for sufficiently large numerals, that (2′) is obviously true, and that premise (3′) would be contested as well. For (3′) is in tension with Tarski's claims that any sentence not interpreted in accordance with the FN conditions is not intelligible, and is no more than a counter in an empty calculus. And we see virtually the same assertion in the Goodman and Quine paper on nominalism:

> if it $[\forall n(n + n = 2n)]$ cannot be translated into nominalistic language, it will in one sense be meaningless for us. But, taking that formula as a string of marks, we can determine whether it is indeed a proper formula of our object language, and what consequence-relationships it has to other formulas. We can thus handle much of classical logic and mathematics without in any further sense understanding, or granting

---

the meaningfulness of lower mathematics plus the inferential relations between lower and higher mathematics.

9. Where exactly we draw the line between sentences like '2+5=7' and sentences of 'higher mathematics' is not important for the present argument, so long as we draw a line somewhere. (This is analogous to the situation with the observational/theoretical distinction in philosophy of science: many who use the distinction (e.g. Carnap and van Fraassen) admit that it is vague, but allow their interlocutors to draw the boundary within the class of vague cases wherever they like, so long as neither side of the distinction has no members.)

the truth of, the formulas we are dealing with. (Quine and Goodman 1947, 122)

However, despite Tarski, Quine, and Goodman's (implicit) rejection of (3′), it is nonetheless a guiding assumption behind many later logical empiricist attempts at a criterion of meaningfulness (as we shall see in chapter 6). Carnap, from (at latest)[10] *Foundations* in 1939, argues that theoretical physics is meaningful or non-metaphysical on the grounds that it can be given a partial interpretation in an observational language. The exact form of an observational language is left open, but it is assumed to be meaningful (see 2.1.3). Now, one could question Carnap's claim that a partial interpretation confers full meaningfulness or intelligibility on the entire calculus. And it seems that Quine and Tarski must not have accepted Carnap's partial-interpretation view, for if they did, they would not dispute the meaningfulness of higher mathematics.

To fill in the details of the historical context, it should be noted that Carnap is not the only philosopher to suggest an analogy between variable-free formulas of arithmetic and observation reports in natural science.[11] This analogy also appears in Poincaré's *Science and Hypothesis*. He writes:

> We see successively that a theorem is true of the number 1, of the number 2, of the number 3, and so on—the law [which holds for an infinite number of cases] is manifest, we say, and it is so on the same ground that every physical law is true which is based on a very large but limited number of observations.
>
> It cannot escape our notice that here is a striking analogy with the usual [=natural scientific] processes of induction...
>
> No doubt mathematical recurrent reasoning and physical inductive reasoning are based on different foundations, but they move in parallel lines and in the same direction. (Poincaré 1902/1905, 13-14)

Poincaré introduces the analogy to illustrate an important similarity between reasoning in mathematics and in physics. However, Poincaré holds that the justification for the ampliative inference is different in the two cases: in the physical case, we must assume that the physical world will continue to behave in the future as it has in the past, along with the rest of the skeptical worries about induction. In the mathematical case, however, we need only assume that a mathematical operation can be repeated indefinitely. Note that Poincaré is here

---

10. The germ of this idea appears slightly earlier, in "Testability and Meaning." There, Carnap claims that, for empiricists, 'confirmable' is closely tied to '(empirically) meaningful,' and Carnap holds that incompletely confirmable claims should be admitted as scientifically acceptable. That is, we find an epistemological analogue of the semantic thesis of partial interpretation in "Testability and Meaning," plus the view that confirmability and meaningfulness are coextensive for empiricists.
11. Mancosu also discusses historical precursors to this argument (Mancosu 2005, 340). He includes Hilbert's finitistic project as well. See Mancosu (2001) for further details of the general conception attributed to Poincaré in this paragraph and Gödel in the next.

concerned with the discovery and justification of physical and mathematical laws, not (explicitly) with their meaningfulness or intelligibility, as Carnap is.

Gödel, in a conversation with Carnap on March 26, 1948, also suggests that there is a substantive analogy between higher mathematics and theoretical physics.

> He [Gödel] sees a strong analogy between theoretical physics and set theory. Physics is confirmed through sense-impressions; set theory is confirmed through its consequences in elementary arithmetic. The fundamental insights in arithmetic, which cannot be reduced to anything simpler, are analogous to sense-impressions. (088-30-03)

As in Poincaré's case, Gödel is concerned with the justification of set theory and physical theory, not with their meaningfulness. But if an assertion is justifiable, then it must be meaningful (even if neither Poincaré nor Gödel ever explicitly argued for that claim). And as Carnap explicitly states in "Testability and Meaning," for empiricists, the question 'How is a claim confirmed?' is to a first approximation the same as 'What is the meaning of a claim?' Whether Gödel would endorse this tenet of empiricism is another question, most likely to be answered in the negative. Finally, I will leave it for others to speculate on how the brief quotation above relates to Gödel's famous claim that "we do have something like a perception... of the objects of set theory" (Gödel 1963/1983, 483-84). I will merely point out that Gödel here says only that the claims of elementary arithmetic are '*analogous* to sense-impressions'; they are not a type of sense-impressions, and neither do they belong to a genus containing them and sense-impressions, as some of Gödel's other remarks seem to suggest.

3.2.2 Potential infinity to the rescue?

On January 31, 1941, after Tarski has set out his finitist-nominalist criteria for the second time, Carnap directly objects to declaring the sentences of classical arithmetic unintelligible. One rationale Carnap offers for his view relies on the concept of potential infinity.

> I: It seems to me that, in a certain sense, I really understand infinite arithmetic. Let us call it language S_2: variables only for natural numbers, with operators (so also negative universal sentences) for the purpose of recursive definitions. To Tarski and Quine's question, as I take it, if the number of things is perhaps in fact finite:... I do not feel as averse toward the concept of possibility as Tarski and Quine. It seems to me that the possibility always exists of taking another step in forming the number series. Thus a potential, not an actual infinity (Tarski and Quine say: they do not understand this distinction). (090-16-25)

Carnap goes on to say that he is not as convinced of the intelligibility of set theory as he is of higher arithmetic, though the difference is likely one of degree. From the very brief description above, it appears that S_2 is richer than PSI in

Logical Syntax: 'negative universal sentences,' such as '$\neg \forall x \forall y (x = y)$,' are not expressible in PSI. (This is because PSI contains no quantifier symbols; free variables are used to express generality, and '$\neg(x = y)$' in PSI would be equivalent in standard first-order logic to '$\forall x \forall y \neg (x = y)$.') However, S_2 and PSI would both contain theorems that the Tarskian finitist-nominalist would either remain agnostic about or deem false.

How, exactly, is Carnap's invocation of potential infinity intended to demonstrate that classical arithmetic is understandable? Carnap may have something like the following in mind: suppose we begin counting by pointing to objects in the world and 'marking them off,' one number for each object. Further suppose that the number of objects in our world is some finite n, and in the process of our marking off objects, we arrive at the 'final' object. *prima facie*, it appears that we could still count past the number n; i.e., even if we 'run out' of objects, we can continue counting unimpeded. In such a situation, nothing could stop us from proceeding to $n + 1$ and beyond (with our eyes closed, perhaps): to any finite number, we could always add one and produce a new number. Our ability to understand the structure and properties of the natural numbers, on this line of thought, is independent of how many things happen to exist in our world. The intelligible outruns the actual.

Such an idea is intuitively appealing; how might Tarski's viewpoint be defended? First, a finitist-nominalist could suggest that any numerals we generate greater than n should be regarded as similar to 'Pegasus,' 'unicorn,' and other non-denoting words. That is, we are only producing new numerals, not new numbers. Or, even less hospitably to the Carnapian line, numbers greater than the number of things in the world should be considered as inhabiting the same philosophical (i.e. epistemological and/or semantic) boat as God, entelechies, essences, and other traditional topics of metaphysics that are mere pseudo-concepts devoid of meaning on the logical empiricists' view.[12] So a Tarskian could happily grant that we are able to produce numerals intended to pick out a number greater than the number of things in the universe, provided that such numerals are somehow not genuinely meaningful. The ability to generate a concept does not ensure its meaningfulness. So, the bare fact that we can generate such numerals is no guarantee of their meaningfulness or their epistemological respectability, since we can generate (in some sense) noxious metaphysical pseudo-concepts as well. How might Carnap respond? The claims of classical arithmetic, unlike objectionable metaphysical ones, (i) are ineliminably used in science (see especially *Logical Syntax* §84) and (ii) are governed by a set of rules such that there is a standard of 'checkability' for them, and as a result all competent mathematicians will agree on what constitutes sufficient evidence for or against a given arithmetical claim, in contrast with the perennial

---

12. In other words, on this suggestion, Tarski subscribes to the following claim about meaning (part of what is now known as 'Millianism' or 'Direct Reference Theory'): the meaning of a name is exhausted by what it designates, so a name that designates nothing has no meaning, i.e., is meaningless (and therefore, according to logical empiricists, metaphysical).

wrangling of the metaphysicians who repeatedly talk past one another (Carnap 1956a, 218-19).

Let us consider a second finitist response to Carnap's suggestion that the notion of potential infinity will save classical arithmetic. There is a tradition in finitist writings, deriving from Hilbert, of conceiving numbers as inscribed vertical strokes (so | | | is identified with the number three).[13] Tarski, drawing on this idea, could respond to Carnap that it is not true that, to a finite number of inscribed strokes, we can always add another: at some point, if the material of the physical universe is finite, we will run out of 'ink,' i.e., the material necessary to draw the strokes. So if numbers simply are sets of inscribed strokes, and the 'ink' of the universe is finite, then every number no longer has a successor. Carnap would likely answer by denying such a thoroughly 'physicalized' conception of numbers; this will be discussed in detail in 3.4.1 below.

Before moving on to Carnap's other responses to the finitist-nominalist project, two further remarks should be made. First, Carnap offers no explication of the distinction between a potential infinity and an actual one.[14] The distinction between potential [*potentiales*] and actual is perhaps different from the distinction between possible [*möglich*] and actual. Carnap seems to be suggesting that in this world one can always take a further step in the number series, not that there could have been more subatomic particles (or whatever our fundamental entity of choice) than there are in our actual world. However, Carnap's use of the term 'potential' is perhaps just sloppiness, for a few days later (Feb. 17, 090-16-23), he writes (in another diatribe against the Tarskian viewpoint) that "arithmetic...deals with possible, not actual, facts," and as we saw in the quotation from the notes that began the present discussion, Carnap says that he is 'not as averse to the concept of *possibility* as Tarski and Quine'–not the concept of *potentiality*.

Second, Carnap's appeal to possibility in order to appease the finitist-nominalist is an undeniable precursor of one of the major current attempts to reconcile nominalist scruples with modern scientific practice. Carnap's basic idea has been developed extensively, by Chihara (1990) and Hellman (1989) in particular; for an excellent survey of this work, see Burgess and Rosen (1996). Generally speaking, these viewpoints accept nominalist conditions of some kind, and also adopt modal concepts governed by some form of modal logic. Thus, for example, instead of being committed to the assertion that an infinity exists (either as an axiom or a derived theorem), a modal nominalist can content herself with the weaker assertion that it is possible that an infinity exists. Mathematics then studies what is possible. But of course, many philosophers who are sympathetic to the strictures of nominalism are unsympathetic to modal notions, just as Quine and Tarski are in the quotation from 1941 above.

13. See Hilbert (1926/1983, 192) and Tait (1981, 525).
14. Hailperin (1992) has characterized a 'potential-infinite domain' as, roughly and abstractly, a finite set of basic objects and a set of deterministic rules for generating further objects from the basic ones. He explicitly avoids assuming that a set exists that contains all the objects so generated.

3.3. Are Any Infinities Compatible with the FN Project?

Carnap tries repeatedly to resurrect some type of infinity that is compatible with the spirit, if perhaps not the letter, of the finitist-nominalist conditions. Presumably, once such an infinity is at hand, we can satisfy the nominalist without hobbling arithmetic with finitist conditions. We have already seen two instances of this: in the immediately preceding section, we found Carnap suggesting that the notion of a potential or possible infinity could perhaps be compatible with the FN criteria, and serve as a stepping stone to classical mathematics. Second, at the end of chapter 2, we saw Carnap argue that space and time are actually infinite, even if the number of objects in the physical universe is finite. Since spatiotemporal intervals are not usually considered abstract objects–they do seem different from numbers, classes, and properties–this would presumably require a modification to the letter of (FN 2) ('the domain of quantification includes physical *objects* only'), though probably not its fundamental spirit. Tarski appears, in that section of the discussion notes, to allow that spatiotemporal intervals are sufficiently un-abstract to be considered candidates for the nominalist's ontology, but he denies that the number of spatiotemporal intervals must necessarily be infinite; as we have seen, he holds rather that the number of spatiotemporal intervals that exist is a contingent matter.

Carnap offers a third strategy for recovering infinity that attempts to respect the finitist's worry that assuming the existence of an infinite number of individuals is not purely logical. He suggests using *sequences* of physical objects, instead of objects themselves, to construct an *ersatz* infinity and thereby avoid reaching the 'final number.' Then the dubious assumption that there are infinitely many physical things can be avoided. However, Carnap discusses this proposal within the context of a finitist-nominalist treatment of syntax; correspondingly, the particular objects and sequences thereof that Carnap has in mind are *symbols* (of the object language). Thus far, I have focused primarily on the effects of adopting the FN conditions upon mathematics, and upon arithmetic in particular. However, these conditions will require restrictions in other areas as well, including syntax. Carnap, Tarski, and Quine do occasionally discuss the implications of the FN criteria for a theory of syntax. I will first describe the sections of the discussion notes that deal with Carnap's proposal for syntax, and subsequently offer my interpretation of what Carnap is doing in them.

Carnap's proposal for a finitist-nominalist syntax first appears in private reflections on the initial discussion of Tarski's project. He attempts to meet Tarski halfway by relaxing Tarski's restrictions somewhat, while preserving the spirit of the finitist-nominalist program. I here summarize the five main theses of Carnap's proposal (090-16-27 and -23).

(S1) Individual symbols in the object language are concrete things, i.e. tokens; (it is possible that) there are finitely many of them.

(S2) Formulae (and proofs) of the object language are ('non-spatial') sequences of object language symbols. Some formulae are physically instantiated, others are not.

(S3) Formulae that are not physically actualized in object language symbols can be referred to metalinguistically, using sequences of names of the object language symbols.

(S4) Formulae that are not and could never be physically actualized can nonetheless be referred to via abbreviations.[15]

(S5) Such a syntax may suffice to 'build an unrestricted arithmetic.'

This summary of Carnap's proposal for finitistic syntax clearly shows that he is attempting to broker a compromise between Tarski's radical program and his own philosophical sensibilities. In Carnap's proposal for syntax, the basic, component symbols of the object language[16] meet the FN criteria: they are physical things, they are tokens instead of types (and thus need not involve us in properties and/or classes), and they are finite in number. However, under Carnap's proposal, the formulae (and therefore the proofs) in the object-language consist of non-spatial sequences of these symbols, so there are genuine sentences of the object language that do not occur anywhere in the physical universe. (The class of sentences is defined as all those sequences, actualized or not, that satisfy the formation rules for the language.) Nonetheless, we can refer to such non-actual sentences either by their names in the metalanguage, or by using abbreviations for them (S3-4). So, in Carnap's finitist syntax, when we speak of 'all sentences of a language,' we include items that are not concretely realized in the actual world. Furthermore, in certain possible worlds, Carnap's syntax would even admit items that *could not* be concretely actualized: if the amount of material in the world is finite, there will be sentences of the language that are too long to inscribe anywhere.

Stepping back to take a wider historical view, this highlights a substantial difference between Carnap's approach to the philosophical study of language and Quine's. Carnap is very far from both the nominalist Quine of "Steps Toward a Constructive Nominalism," and the behavioral-linguist Quine of *Word and Object*, when Carnap claims that our definition of 'sentence' should include items that are physically impossible to actualize. In both his nominalist and postnominalist phases, Quine holds adamantly to the assumption that our language is part of the same material world we inhabit and our sciences investigate,[17] and

---

15. Whether the abbreviations appear in the object language, metalanguage, or both is not entirely clear. The default assumption is that the abbreviations are in the object language, but in the example Carnap gives, he uses the symbols for the metalinguistic names of object-language symbols.
16. Calling this a 'language' may be contentious: it is not obvious that we are still dealing with a genuine language if linguistic symbols are taken as tokens instead of types.
17. Carnap summarizes this position nicely in (090–16–06): "the world *in* which we write is the same as the world *about* which we write."

should be studied accordingly, viz. using empirical methods. Carnap, on the other hand, studies language primarily as a mathematical subject instead of a natural one;[18] this fact is highlighted by his above characterization of formulae for a finitist-nominalist syntax. For reasons to be discussed later, I believe this difference looms large in the subsequent disputes over analyticity. In brief, Quine thinks that which sentences count as analytic is an empirical (i.e. synthetic) matter, whereas Carnap thinks that which sentences count as analytic (in a formalized language) is itself an analytic question, and thus need not be accountable to the particular facts of the matter in our actual world.[19] As we will see below in 5.3.1, one fundamental difference separating Quine and Carnap in 1941 is that Quine believes linguistic concepts (such as analyticity) should be treated as empirical, descriptive concepts, whereas Carnap treats them as logico-mathematical. Further discussion of Carnap's syntax will appear in 3.4.2 below.

Let us return to February 17, 1941, and specifically to Carnap's claim that his proposal will allow us to 'build up an unrestricted arithmetic.' Carnap is arguing that one could admit that there are only a finite number of things (and hence symbols) in the world, but nonetheless maintain that this group of things could be used to construct an infinite sequence in the metalanguage, though not in a physically actual sense of 'construct.' As an extreme example to make Carnap's idea vivid and simple, make the Parmenidean assumption that there is only one thing a in the physical universe. If this thing has a name in the physical universe, then we must assume that a serves as its own name (like the language proposed by the professors of Lagado in *Gulliver's Travels*), since there is only one thing in the universe. Carnap's suggestion appears to be that we could still generate (though not with 'pencil and paper,' so to speak, in that same Parmenidean universe) an infinite sequence: $\langle a \rangle, \langle a, a \rangle, \langle a, a, a \rangle \ldots$ This infinite sequence of finite sequences would serve as the interpretation of the natural numbers, instead of things themselves (rather, in this extreme example, 'the thing itself'). The natural numbers would then have the usual properties ascribed to them in classical arithmetic. (This example is unrepresentative in that no real mathematical language can be set up within this object language, since there is only one symbol in the object language.)

Carnap recognizes that, in a universe with a finite number of objects, we will reach a sequence length after which we cannot physically write down any further elements. In the extreme example just presented, we reach that length immediately. Carnap's response (as we have seen above) is that we can use abbreviations, such as $10^{3,000,000}$, to refer to such sequences that cannot be inscribed. But while the abbreviational strategy will give us expressions for more numbers than would be available without abbreviations, it seems that we will nonetheless eventually run up against a 'ceiling.' Introducing abbreviations will raise that ceiling con-

---

18. Carnap makes similar claims in his autobiography: "only the structural pattern, not the physical properties of the ink marks, [are] relevant for the function of language" (Carnap 1963, 29).
19. This idea is presented and explored in Ricketts (1982).

siderably, but there will still be gigantic numbers that we could not express with our limited material for symbol-tokens. (I am assuming that we cannot introduce an abbreviation for transfinite numbers, since Carnap never mentions this, and it would obviously and blatantly violate the FN criteria.) In short, appealing to abbreviations appears to postpone the problem without solving it.

However, one might wonder whether this is a serious problem: what is the ultimate significance of our inability to write down a symbol for something in a given language? There are many familiar results concerning the inexpressibility of various concepts in a given language: Tarski's theorem about the indefinability of truth (in certain types of languages) is perhaps the most famous; the proof that there are indefinable real numbers is another example. In neither of these two cases is the result normally taken to mean that there is no such thing as truth-in-$\mathcal{L}$, or that undefinable real numbers somehow do not exist (*pace* 1.4.1 above). In both cases, the moral usually drawn concerns the limitations of the *language* in question, not about the things it is used to discuss. However, it should be noted that the inexpressibility in the FN case is quite different from that of Tarski's theorems about truth and real numbers. In the case Carnap discusses, the inexpressibility is quite clearly a *physical* limitation (we run out of 'ink' at some point), whereas the other results are logico-mathematical limitations: even if there were an infinite amount of physical ink in our universe, truth-in-$\mathcal{L}$ still could not be defined within $\mathcal{L}$, provided $\mathcal{L}$ meets certain conditions.[20]

Niceties concerning the number of physical symbols aside, Carnap's proposal to use sequences in place of objects apparently violates the spirit of nominalism in an obvious way, which may have already occurred to the reader: sequences, as customarily understood, are simply classes with further mathematical structure,[21] and classes are paradigmatic *entia non grata* (to borrow Quine's phrase) for the modern nominalist in general and a proponent of Tarski's FN project in particular. To be precise, merely allowing expressions for classes into one's language would not contravene either (FN 1) (no higher-order variables) or (FN 2) (only physical objects in D). For example, the truth of '$a \in \{a, b, c\}$' is compatible with all the finitist-nominalist conditions; furthermore, so is the truth of '$\exists x (x \in \{a, b, c\})$,' provided that a, b, c are physical objects. However, '$\exists x (a \in x)$' could never be true in a language satisfying (FN 2) (assuming the standard interpretation for the symbols), because if it were true, the universe of discourse would

---

20. Kripke and Woodruff's fixed-point theory of truth as well as Gupta's revision theory of truth do define truth-in-$\mathcal{L}$ within $\mathcal{L}$; in both cases, certain classical assumptions about the structure of language are modified, and the resulting logic is non-classical (e.g. bivalence fails).

21. Specifically, a sequence is usually defined as a class plus a function that takes the members of that class to the first n natural numbers. Tarski uses this definition (Tarski 1983, 121). Carnap himself characterizes sequences in *Introduction to Semantics* as follows. "A sequence with n members is, so to speak, an enumeration of the objects (at most n); it can be represented in two different ways: (1) by a predicate of degree 2 which designates a one-many relation between the objects and the ordinal numbers up to n, (2) by an argument expression containing n terms (in this case, the argument expression and the sequence designated are said to be of degree n)" (Carnap 1942, 18). These definitions, which presuppose the natural numbers, would presumably have to be rejected by a finitist-nominalist.

have to include a set. Quine sees the situation clearly in his response to Carnap's proposal to replace physical things with sequences in a FN theory of syntax:

> *Quine*: The decisive question here is whether we introduce variables for these sequences. We must do so in order to make an unrestricted arithmetic. But then we are thereby making an ontological assumption, namely about the existence of sequences. But if we do this, then we can *in the same way also assume classes, classes of classes etc.*; with that we also obtain an unrestricted arithmetic. But with that we would give up reistic finitism. (090-16-23)

In order to violate (FN 2), it is not sufficient simply to allow expressions for classes (or sequences) into the language; there must be circumstances under which variables may be substituted for class- or sequence-terms. Quine's response is the obvious reply to Carnap's proposal, given the ground rules governing a finitist-nominalist language. The more interesting or difficult question is: given that sequences are so conceptually close to classes, what was Carnap thinking when he made this proposal to use sequences? I see at least three viable possibilities. First, he might think that sequences are relevantly different from classes and other abstracta; however, there is no evidence in the notes that he did (and I have not found any evidence elsewhere). Second, he might disagree with the second sentence in the quotation from Quine: Carnap might believe we can recapture classical arithmetic without introducing variables. Third, he may have recalled that Tarski introduced the assumption, discussed above in 1.3.2, that "numbers can be used in a finite realm, in that we think of the ordered things, and by the numerals we understand the corresponding things" (090-16-25). Thus, if Tarski allows that sequence, perhaps he would allow others. However, there is a clear difference between the sequence Tarski introduces and the one Carnap suggests: all the items ordered in Tarski's case are concrete, whereas Carnap generates a sequence of sequences. Unfortunately for us, Carnap's notes do not contain a direct reply to Quine, nor does the other surrounding text make it clear which of these three (if any) is closest to what Carnap was thinking. In any case, none of Carnap's three attempts to reintroduce infinity into a finitist-nominalist language–by spatiotemporal intervals, by potential or possible infinity, or by sequences of concrete symbols–meet with approval from his interlocutors.

3.4. Attacking the FN Conditions

Thus far in this chapter, we have examined Carnap's attempts to defend classical arithmetic, by arguing that a finitist-nominalist could either countenance higher arithmetic as meaningful, or accommodate some kind of infinity. However, Carnap does not merely defend his own viewpoint from Tarski and Quine's criticisms; he also takes the offensive, attacking the finitist-nominalist conditions directly. Carnap's two primary criticisms are, first, that Tarski's view of numbers as physical objects rests upon a 'mistaken conception of arithmetic,' and second, that adopting the finitist-nominalist viewpoint in syntax will lead to unacceptable consequences for logic. Before turning to those two relatively well-developed criticisms, I will mention a very brief remark Carnap makes about Tarski's general idea, even before Tarski explicitly lays out his three conditions for an understandable language. On March 4, 1940, Tarski gives a lecture at the University of Chicago on the semantic conception of truth. During this visit, he and Carnap privately discuss several topics in logic and philosophy, including what form a formalized language for the purposes of science should take. Tarski suggests (roughly) that such languages should be predicative. Carnap responds to Tarski as follows:

> I: This restriction... corresponds to finitism and intuitionism; the tendency (since [Poincaré]) of this restriction is healthy and sympathetic; but didn't it turn out that *mathematics is thereby complicated intolerably, and that the restriction is arbitrary*? (090-16-09, my emphasis)

Carnap objects to revisions of mathematics that create unnecessary complications, and he believes that the system Tarski is describing would do so. This sentiment is not an isolated occurrence: Carnap makes basically the same point in his autobiographical essay (Carnap 1963, 49). Tarski, immediately thereafter, agrees with Carnap that intuitionist mathematics is problematic, but suggests that even though the intuitionists have failed thus far to construct an elegant system of mathematics, we need not conclude that nothing of the sort can be done.

3.4.1 Arithmetic is distorted

Carnap thinks the FN conditions distort the nature of arithmetic. Near the conclusion of a long conversation with Tarski and Quine, Carnap writes (with what might be exasperation):

> It seems to me that the entire proposal suffers from a mistaken conception of arithmetic: the numbers are reified; arithmetic is made dependent on contingent facts, while in reality it deals with conceptual connections; if one likes: with possible, not with actual facts. (090-16-23)

As this quotation makes clear, Carnap feels there is something fundamentally wrong with Tarski's proposal to interpret numerals as denoting physical objects, and its corollary that some of arithmetic becomes empirical and contingent. But what sort of mistake is this? What, exactly, does Carnap believe is fundamentally wrong here? Presumably, it cannot be that Tarski's proposal fails to capture the essence of number, for Carnap is constitutionally opposed to questions of essence. Carnap's resistance to the FN conditions appears even more problematic given that, in 1941, Carnap has been explicitly committed to his principle of tolerance for several years.[22] According to this principle, "Everyone is at liberty to build up... his own form of language as he wishes" (Carnap 1934/1937, 52). *Prima facie*, Carnap's attack on the FN conditions seems intolerant: why not give Tarski the liberty to construct a language that meets his criteria? The same point can be put in slightly different terms. One formulation of the principle of tolerance is: which sentences are analytic is itself an analytic matter, i.e. there is no fact of the matter concerning which sentences are really analytic.[23] Thus, analyticity is always language-relative, and what is analytic in one language need not be in another. The apparent problem raised by Carnap's criticism of the FN project can now be phrased as follows: Carnap appears to be pushing the view that arithmetic is analytic *simpliciter*, as opposed to analytic with respect to particular languages.

So our question now is: what fault, exactly, does Carnap find with Tarski's basic idea—and (how) is this fault-finding compatible with Carnap's commitment to the principle of tolerance and his aversion to questions of essence? The error Carnap sees in Tarski's ways, I will argue, can be conceived of as one of explication;[24] that is, Carnap thinks Tarski's explicatum (taking numbers to be physical objects) misses the target explicandum (arithmetic of the natural numbers). Carnap does not articulate this explicitly in the discussion notes, but his attitude comes through fairly clearly in *Foundations*, which is roughly contemporaneous. There, Carnap writes:

> For any given calculus there are, in general, many different possibilities of a true interpretation.[25] The practical situation, however, is such that for almost every calculus which is actually interpreted and applied in science, there is a certain interpretation or a certain kind of interpretation used in the great majority of cases of its practical application. This we will call the customary interpretation (or kind of interpretation) for the calculus... The customary interpretation of the logical and mathematical calculi is a logical, L-determinate interpretation; that of the geometrical and physical calculi is descriptive and factual. (Carnap 1939, 171)

Carnap's basic ideas are clear: (i) every formal calculus intended to model inferences in the sciences has a particular interpretation (or family of interpretations), called the 'customary interpretation,' associated with it. Carnap apparently believes that this interpretation is somehow specified by 'practical application.'

---

22. However, as we shall see shortly, Carnap's tolerance takes a more moderate form from 1939 onward.
23. This explains why Carnap believed Quine's indeterminacy of translation thesis vindicates his own views (Creath 1990, 41).
24. Carus (2007) provides a detailed exploration of Carnap's concept of explication.
25. 'True interpretation' corresponds *very* roughly to 'model' in modern terminology. More specifically, Carnap defines a true interpretation S of a calculus C as an interpretation that fulfills the following three conditions: (i) if the proof calculus C permits the derivation of B from A, then either A is false in S or B is true in S; (ii) if there is a proof of A in C, then A is true in S; and (iii) if there is a proof of $\neg A$ in C, then A is false in S (Carnap 1939, 163).

(Carnap does not explain how scientific practice fixes meanings; the question of how use can fix meaning is still debated.) (ii) Interpretations can be logico-mathematical or descriptive: for example, an interpretation that takes the universe of discourse to be the natural numbers or the set-theoretic hierarchy is logico-mathematical, while an interpretation whose universe of discourse contains all and only the US presidents (or any other set of physical objects) will be descriptive. (iii) The customary interpretation for the arithmetical calculus is a logico-mathematical one.[26]

This understanding of Carnap (viz., he believes Tarski misses his target explicandum) also shows why Carnap has not violated his principle of tolerance: one can be tolerant and still point out errors in explication. A tolerant stance requires Carnap to let Tarski set up whatever formal language he wishes; however, tolerance does not require every formal language to model every natural language equally well. Such a view is madness. In fact, Carnap makes this point explicit in *Foundations*: his answer to the question 'Is logic conventional?' is 'It depends upon the method one chooses for constructing a logic.' If one begins by laying out the proof calculus purely formally, i.e., without regard for the meanings of the marks used, then of course one may lay down any rules whatsoever, and logic is conventional (and thus arbitrary) in a very strong sense. However, if one begins not purely formally, but with marks having meaning–i.e., with genuine words–then one cannot set up any calculus whatsoever, assuming the calculus is intended as a formalized version of the original, meaningful language. Under this second method, logic is not completely conventional, for the meanings of the words impose constraints upon the rules of the proof calculus (though Carnap acknowledges that there could be more than one proof calculus adequate to an interpreted language, so that a logical calculus still has a conventional element, even under the second method) (Carnap 1939, 168-71). This is a moderated kind of tolerance. For example, if we take '$\vee$' to have the meaning 'or' usually has in English (as opposed to treating it as solely and completely defined certain rules of inference), then any calculus that allows one to infer A from $A \vee B$ alone is a very poor one–at least as a model (or even refinement) of English. Similarly, applying this principle to the FN project, any arithmetical calculus in which we cannot infer the existence of a (new and distinct) number $n + 1$ from the existence of the

---

26. Carnap makes basically the same point a few pages later:
> The question is frequently discussed whether arithmetic and geometry... have the same nature or not... [T]he answer depends upon whether the calculi or the interpreted systems are meant. There is no fundamental difference between arithmetic and geometry as calculi, nor with respect to their possible interpretations; for either calculus there are both logical and descriptive interpretations. If, however, we take the systems with their customary interpretation–arithmetic as the theory of numbers and geometry as the theory of physical space–then we find an important difference: the propositions of arithmetic are logical, L-true, and without factual content; those of geometry are descriptive, factual, and empirical. (Carnap 1939, 198)

number n is a rather poor calculus for the usual meanings given to '+', '1', and the other marks that appear in arithmetical writings.

Tarski, of course, could respond that his aim is not to interpret arithmetic as it is currently practiced; his point, however, is to change it fundamentally.[27] That is, his goal is not to capture as much of usual arithmetic as possible, but rather to determine how much of usual arithmetic can be saved, given what he considers a philosophically and scientifically sane conception of what exists.[28] On this view, Tarski sees himself as rescuing arithmetic from the clutches of a dubious Platonism. In modern terms, his proposal could be viewed as a scientific revolution in something like the Kuhnian sense, in which many older, customary ideas are discarded. Specifically, a proponent of the FN conditions could argue that the axiom of infinity in Peano arithmetic should be considered analogous to the parallel postulate in Euclidean geometry. (To be clear, this suggestion is not explicitly raised in the notes.) We say that (e.g.) the Pythagorean theorem is mathematically true in Euclidean geometry, but the theorem is empirically false of physical space, since (on a physical interpretation of the calculus, in which straight lines are identified with freely falling massive bodies and light rays) one of its axioms fails to hold in the physical world. Could we perhaps analogously maintain that 'There exist infinitely many odd numbers' is mathematically true in classical (Peano) arithmetic, but empirically false? Carnap stresses, throughout his writings, Einstein's distinction between physical and mathematical geometry. Could there perhaps be a similar distinction drawn between physical and mathematical arithmetic? We have seen Carnap assert above that there could be an empirical/descriptive interpretation of the arithmetical calculus, but that the customary interpretation of arithmetic involves only logical objects. But, we may then query Carnap, how is the applicability of arithmetic secured?

Carnap could respond to a Tarskian proposal for revolution as follows: one may propose any revision of arithmetic (or any other set of concepts and/or claims) one chooses; however, if one revises too much, then it is no longer clear one is still doing arithmetic at all. And without some requirement that the target explicandum be captured to some degree, we are engaged in an enterprise without

---

27. In Burgess and Rosen's terms, on this interpretation, Tarski takes the FN project to be attempting a "revolutionary" re-conceptualization of arithmetic, instead of a merely "hermeneutic" task, in which the re-conceptualization "is taken to be an analysis of what really 'deep down' the words of current theories have meant all along" (Burgess and Rosen 1996, 6). Mancosu agrees that Quine and Tarski's "approach lies squarely in the revolutionary tradition" (Mancosu 2008b, 51).

28. Steve Awodey reminded me that Carnap thinks explicata can be 'revisionary' instead of 'hermaneutic' as well (Carus 2007, 278), so that cannot be the essential difference between him and Tarski on this matter. But Carnap's allowed revisions are different in kind from those envisaged by the finitist-nominalist project: Carnap's revisions tend to be formal/linguistic in character. Carnap's explicata make a vague explicandum precise, distinguish separate senses for ambiguous terms (e.g., two senses of probability), and remove inconsistencies in usage (e.g. reforming the use of 'true' in everyday language). Carnap, in general, attempts to preserve as much scientific content as possible, while 'sanitizing' the language in the above three ways. Tarski is apparently not concerned with content preservation as much as Carnap is; and therein lies the fundamental difference between them.

substantive standards for success. Furthermore, in the case of revolutions in the natural sciences, radical revisions that appear to 'change the subject' can be justified on the grounds that they lead to better predictive success. It does not appear that Tarski's proposal could improve our predictive powers, though I would not wish to rule out creative scientists finding a way to do so in the future. Euclidean geometry is 'shown empirically false' by *inter alia* identifying 'straight line' in the mathematical vocabulary with light rays and freely falling masses in the world. Without this identification or one like it, it would make no sense to say that the parallel postulate has been 'empirically disproved,' because the geometry would not connect to the empirical world in an significant way.[29] In the formal sciences, however, standards are somewhat different: no one would have accepted Frege's notion of a concept-script if it failed to preserve standard mathematical inferences. Similarly, Weierstrass's revision of the concept of limit would have been rejected if it had not sufficiently matched the usage in previous theorems involving limits. In short, an appeal to view Tarski's proposal as a revision or revolution comes to a plea for exemption from a primary standard of success for projects of his type, viz., conformity with existing results and usage (the other primary standards in formal-mathematical explication being simplicity or elegance and consistency).

3.4.2 Problems with proofs

We now return to the topic of finitist-nominalist syntax, introduced above in 3.3. In Goodman and Quine's 1947 "Steps Toward a Constructive Nominalism," the issue of a finitistic syntax is front and center. They explain the problem facing the finitist-nominalist, which Carnap had raised years before, quite clearly:

> Classical syntax, like classical arithmetic, presupposes an infinite realm of objects; for it assumes that the expressions it treats of admit concatenation to form longer expressions without end. But if expressions must, like everything else, be found in the concrete world, then a limitless realm of expressions cannot be assumed. Indeed, expressions construed in the customary way, as abstract typographical shapes, do not exist at all in the concrete world; the language elements in the concrete world are rather inscriptions or marks, the shaped objects rather than the shapes... Consequently, *we cannot say that in general, given any two inscriptions, there is an inscription long enough to be the concatenation of the two.* (Quine and Goodman 1947, 106; my emphasis)

Serious limitations follow for proofs. Recall the standard textbook definition of a proof of ϕ (in a calculus C): a sequence $\langle \phi_1, \phi_2, \ldots \phi_n \rangle$ of formulas (in C) such that ϕ_n is ϕ, and for each $i \leq n$, either ϕ_i is an axiom or ϕ_i follows from some of the preceding members of the sequence using a rule of inference of C. Now, suppose all the 'ink' in the physical universe is exhausted in writing down the formulas $\langle \phi_1, \ldots \phi_{n-1} \rangle$. We then cannot give a proof of the conclusion ϕ_n even

---

29. For an extended and insightful development of related ideas, see Friedman (2001).

if it intuitively follows from the previous $n-1$ formulas, since there will not be any material left to write down the final formula. As a result, all our usual rules of inference will admit exceptions, and would thereby no longer be 'rules' in the usual sense. For example, we are no longer guaranteed that from A and B one can infer $A \wedge B$, since for large enough A and B, there will not be enough material (in a finite universe) to write down the conjunction of both, after writing down the first two. Similar reasoning holds for other rules of inference. Such a finitistic proof calculus would be radically semantically incomplete: every model that satisfies A and satisfies B will also satisfy $A \wedge B$, but the proof calculus will not be able to prove $A \wedge B$ from A, B. Prospects for finitist syntax will be even dimmer if we take Tarski's original suggestion that "we ought to take as expressions, sentences, and proofs only actually written down items" (090-16-27). For, if that restriction is adopted, we could only infer sentences that are inscribed somewhere (or spoken sometime, etc.). As we saw in 3.3, Carnap recognized these problems, and considered them to be a serious defect in the FN conditions.

3.5. An Objection Not in the Notes

Before concluding this chapter, I would like to consider a final objection to the FN project that does not appear in the notes. There are, of course, many criticisms one might level against the finitist-nominalist viewpoint that are not raised in Carnap's discussion notes; generations of anti-nominalist and anti-finitist philosophers have generated a small library of them. However, I will present only this objection, because (i) it is not one of the usual objections to nominalism in general, (ii) it is based on a thesis that apparently enjoys some consensus among philosophers, and because (iii) I believe it is Carnapian in spirit (though I will not argue for that final point). The crux of the objection is this: an answer to the question 'What counts as an individual?' (or '...as a unit,' or '...as a thing'), which determines in part how many 'things' there are, is not the kind of claim about which there is a fact of the matter. In Carnap's terms, it is an analytic issue, not a synthetic one; it is perhaps analogous to a choice of co-ordinate system in physics.

Something similar to this idea appears in *Republic* VII: Plato claims the unit is intelligible, not sensible. More importantly in the present context, it also appears in Frege's *Grundlagen*: Frege asks us to consider a complete pack of playing cards. If someone points to the pack and asks you 'How many (things) are there?', the correct answer will be 'It depends': if the questioner is asking about the number of suits, the answer is four, if about cards, the answer is fifty-two, and if about molecules, the answer is much larger. Thus the question 'How many (things) are there?' is not well posed, because it admits of more than one answer, depending on further specifications. And what holds for the pack of cards also holds, presumably, for the entire material universe: there is no fact of the matter about how many things there are. Of course, once one specifies what is to count as an individual (e.g. spades), then it becomes a well-posed question with a univocal answer (thirteen). Without such a further specification, there is no fact of the matter about how many things there are in the natural world.

How might a Tarskian respond to this challenge? Here is one straightforward reply: no matter what is taken as a unit (i.e., no matter what are taken to be the elements of the domain of quantification), whether it be quarks, spatiotemporal intervals, quanta of energy, etc., if the domain is restricted to physical entities, then one will always come out with a (possibly) finite number of things. (Obviously, allowing variables to range over the natural numbers, the real numbers, or the set-theoretic hierarchy would automatically yield an infinity.) Thus, the initial lack of a well-posed formulation is rendered innocuous: the Tarskian will let you turn it into a well-posed formulation in whichever way you please, so long as the only things the variables range over are physical in one way or another.

In the end, none of Carnap's criticisms of the finitist-nominalist project made much headway with Tarski or Quine. In conclusion, I wish to stress that Carnap's failure to win converts is, in many cases, not necessarily indicative of the quality of Carnap's arguments, but rather of the differing fundamental philosophical stances Tarski and Quine bring to the table in 1941. First, if Tarski and Quine had accepted Carnap's suggestion that a partially-interpreted calculus should also count as meaningful or intelligible *simpliciter*, then they would have been strongly inclined to view Peano arithmetic, and perhaps even set theory, as intelligible too. Second, if Quine and Tarski were not so averse to modal notions, perhaps they would have accepted Carnap's proposal to use the notion of a potential or possible infinity in lieu of an actual infinity in order to build up classical mathematics. Carnap's willingness to allow for modal idioms explains why, for him, the understandable outruns the actual. Finally, if Tarski and Quine did not consider the study of language to be strictly about physical, empirical language, they might be more deeply worried about the very real problems Carnap points out that arise with syntax and proof under a finitist-nominalist regime. But if syntax only studies empirical language, and thus only the physically possible inscriptions, then consequences that strike Carnap as intolerable (e.g. given two expressions, one cannot always form their conjunction) appear tolerable, if not quite desirable. The differences between Carnap's conception of the logical/descriptive distinction, and the competing conceptions of Tarski and Quine, are the subject of the following two chapters.

Chapter 4
The Finitist-Nominalist Project and Analyticity

If a philosopher today is engaged in a free-association session, and the prompt is 'Carnap and Quine,' then the response will almost certainly be 'the analytic/synthetic distinction' or a cognate expression. Quine's attack on the notion of analytic truth is, by most philosophers' standards, one of the most influential and widely adopted 'big ideas' of twentieth-century Anglophone philosophy. Among scholars working in the history of analytic philosophy, the disagreement between Quine and Carnap over the analytic/synthetic distinction is one of the most studied episodes. Thus, one might hope that during Carnap and Quine's academic year together, they would discuss their conflicting viewpoints on this issue at length and in detail. Quine, in his autobiography, leads the reader to believe as much:

> The fall term of 1940 is graven in my memory for more than just the writing of *Elementary Logic*. Russell, Carnap, and Tarski were all at hand... My misgivings over meaning had by this time issued in explicit doubts about the notion, crucial to Carnap's philosophy, of an analytic sentence: a sentence true purely by virtue of the meanings of its words. I voiced these doubts, joined by Tarski, before Carnap had finished reading us his first page [of his manuscript for *Introduction to Semantics*]. The controversy continued through subsequent sessions and without progress in the reading of Carnap's manuscript. (Quine 1985, 149–50)

Unfortunately, this tantalizing claim is misleading. First, it misleads us in a small way: Quine's claim that the group did not advance past the first page of Carnap's manuscript is demonstrably false. Carnap's notes record a discussion of the adequacy of a particular definition that appears in chapter 17 of the manuscript of *Introduction to Semantics* (090-16-03),[1] which becomes definition 18-1 in the published version. Quine's representation of the situation in the above quotation is inaccurate in a second, more significant way. Although there are several scattered remarks in Carnap's dictation notes dealing with analyticity (or, in his preferred terminology at the time, with 'L-truth'), there are disappointingly few

---

1. This documentary evidence does not show that Tarski and Quine read all of the manuscript up to the seventeenth chapter, but it does show that they did discuss more than the first page, *contra* Quine's quoted claim to the contrary.

sustained discussions of the issue. Of course, it is possible that there were many more such conversations on the topic of analyticity, but Carnap failed to record them. I know of no evidence for such a supposition beyond Quine's claim above; and as we have just seen, Quine's reminisces about this time period are not always veridical. Interestingly, the discussant who manifests the most sustained and direct animosity toward analyticity is not Quine but Tarski.

Fortunately, we need not despair that the 1940-41 notes shed no light on the vexed concept of analyticity. Not only are there scattered instances in which the group does directly discuss analytic truth and kindred concepts, but the finitist-nominalist project also bears a clear (albeit indirect) relation to analyticity. This relationship is the focal point of the present chapter; the discussion notes directly addressing analyticity are taken up in the following chapter. This chapter has two parts: first, I flesh out the conceptual relationship between finitism-nominalism and analyticity by sketching which portions of arithmetic would become synthetic under a Tarskian regime; in order to do this, a digression through Carnap's conception of semantics circa 1940 is necessary. Second, I offer a historical conjecture about the radicalization of Quine's attack on analytic truth.

4.1. Under a Finitist-Nominalist Regime, Arithmetic Is Synthetic

Though Carnap, Tarski, and Quine do not directly discuss analyticity a great deal during their academic year together, the finitist-nominalist project, which does occupy a large portion of their time and energy, bears indirectly on the notion of analytic truth. How? As Carnap unhappily notes, under Tarski's regime "arithmetic is made dependent on contingent facts," i.e., it becomes a synthetic enterprise (090-16-23). This would be disappointing for Carnap, for he thinks one of the genuine intellectual advances made by the logical empiricists consisted in showing that arithmetic is both analytic (contra Kant and Poincaré) and a priori (contra Mill) without lapsing into some form of Platonic metaphysics. Tarski's proposal would appear to Carnap as regressing to a Millian, empiricist view of mathematics.[2]

Given that Carnap considers arithmetic to be synthetic under the finitist-nominalist restrictions, we can ask the further question: which parts, exactly, become synthetic? The answer is: less than one might initially imagine. I will justify that answer presently, but first we must clarify what is meant by 'synthetic' here. First, 'synthetic' does not mean 'neither logically true nor logically false' in the modern sense, i.e. 'false in at least one model, but not in all'–for if it did, classical first-order Peano arithmetic would be synthetic, since its postulates are only true in some models but not in all. Second, one might attempt to cash out 'arithmetic becomes synthetic' via Carnap's distinction between descriptive interpretations and logical ones (discussed in 3.4.1). A descriptive interpretation

---

2. Albert Casullo (1988) argues that experience could disconfirm arithmetic, though not on finitist-nominalist grounds. For a critical discussion of his proposal, see Wilson (2000).

of a set of sentences takes as its domain empirical objects, while the domain of a logical interpretation of a set of sentences consists of logical objects, so Tarski's conditions turn mathematical language into a descriptive language. However, although Carnap (as seen in previous chapters) thinks interpreting mathematical language as descriptive is a mistake, simply assigning the numerals to physical objects instead of numbers (considered either as individuals or in the Frege-Russell way) does not, by itself, make arithmetic synthetic. For then 'Rushmore = Rushmore,' 'Carnap wrote *Principia Mathematica* or Carnap did not write *Principia Mathematica*,' and any other instance of a logical truth containing descriptive terms would count as synthetic—another unpalatable consequence for Carnap. Put otherwise: though Carnap claims that every sentence given a logical interpretation is analytically true or false, he does not hold the converse (Carnap 1939, 180). So what *is* the sense of 'synthetic' here? At this stage in Carnap's career, a sentence is analytic in an interpreted language if and only if the semantic rules of that language determine the truth-value of that sentence. If the semantic rules do not suffice to determine a sentence's truth-value, then that sentence is synthetic or factual (and conversely).[3] So, if Carnap is correct that arithmetic becomes factual under Tarski's restrictions, it must be the case that there are arithmetical claims whose truth-value is determined by the semantic rules of classical arithmetic, but whose truth-value is left indeterminate by the semantic rules of finitist-nominalist arithmetic.

In order to determine which arithmetical sentences become synthetic, we must answer the question: how does Carnap conceive of semantic rules in 1941? His conception is, in some ways, close to modern formal semantics, but there are clear differences as well. The fundamental unit of study for semantics for Carnap is the semantical system, which he defines as "a system of rules, formulated in a metalanguage and referring to an object-language, of such a kind that the rules determine a truth condition for every sentence of the object language...the rules determine the meaning or sense of the sentences" (Carnap 1942, 22). A semantic system consists of three kinds of rules: rules of formation, rules of designation, and rules of truth. (In Carnap's estimation, a fundamental achievement of Tarski's *Wahrheitsbegriff* consists in showing that the third can be defined given the first two.) The rules of formation provide a recursive definition of 'sentence of L.' Rules of designation provide designata for the (non-logical) signs.[4] Specifically, it consists of sentences of the form 'b designates c,' where (i) if b is a

---

3. In *Foundations*, Carnap writes:
> We call a sentence of semantical system S (logically true or) L-true if it is true in such a way that the semantical rules of S suffice for establishing its truth...If a sentence is either L-true or L-false, it is called L-determinate, otherwise (L-indeterminate or) factual. (The terms 'L-true', 'L-false', and 'factual' correspond to the terms 'analytic,' 'contradictory,' and 'synthetic', as they are used in traditional terminology.) (Carnap 1939, 155)

Essentially identical claims are found in *Introduction to Semantics* (Carnap 1942, 140–42).
4. The distinction between logical and non-logical signs is part of the semantic system, according to Carnap. We can think of it as part of the rules of formation, or as a separate, fourth set of rules associated with the semantic system (Carnap 1942, 24).

name (i.e. individual constant), then c is an object, and (ii) if b is a predicate (or relation letter), then c is a property (or relation). As an example of the first kind, Carnap offers (where German is the object-language and English the metalanguage) "'Mond' designates the moon," and as an example of the second, "'kalt' designates the property of being cold" (Carnap 1939, 151). Note that Carnap treats predicate letters as referring to properties and relations, unlike modern models, which instead assign sets of n-tuples n-ary predicates. What is the status of these rules, according to Carnap? "[T]he rules of designation do not make factual assertions as to what are the designata of certain signs. There are no factual assertions in pure semantics" (Carnap 1942, 25). In short, the rules of designation and the rules of truth are analytic, if we are not engaged in empirical, descriptive linguistics.

The rules of truth are almost identical to the ones familiar to us today: the truth-values of sentences containing logical connectives are given by the usual truth-tables, and the rule for the universal quantifier is more-or-less identical to the one current today. The only substantive difference of formulation between Carnapian rules of truth and modern ones appears at the level of atomic sentences, and results from Carnap's interpreting predicates as properties instead of sets. Carnap writes (where the 'n' subscript means the expression is in the grammatical category of noun, and the 'p' subscript indicates a predicate): "A sentence of the form '$\ldots_n$ ist $-_p$' is true if and only if the thing designated by '$\ldots_n$' has the property designated by '$-_p$'" (Carnap 1939, 151). In modern model theory, a model assigns to each n-ary predicate a set of n-tuples, not a property (some people construe properties as extensions of predicates, but Carnap, like many, does not). For Carnap at this time, a property is an extension in every state of affairs; that is, a first-order monadic property is a function that assigns a set of individuals to every possible world. This is identical to what is standardly called an *intension* today. Lastly, if the language under consideration contains variables, Carnap says we must introduce rule(s) of values, which specify a range of values for each kind of variable in the language, as well as (what we today would call) rules of satisfaction for open formulas. (Rules of values are analogous to rules of designation, and rules of satisfaction are analogous to the rules of truth.) The rule of values, which specifies the universe of discourse for a language, is also analytic in Carnap's view (Carnap 1939, 174). The domain can be specified via simple enumeration, or by specifying a condition something must meet to be a member of the set; Carnap's own examples include "all space-time points, or all physical things, or all events, or all human beings in general" (Carnap 1942, 44). Variables themselves, however, can be either logical signs or descriptive signs, depending on whether the variables only range over logical objects or not (Carnap 1942, 59).

With this characterization of Carnapian semantics in hand, we can better understand one of Carnap's claims that sounds strange to modern ears. In his autobiography, in a discussion of the axioms of infinity and of choice, Carnap writes:

we [the Vienna Circle members] realized that either a way of interpreting them as analytic must be found, or, if they are interpreted as non-analytic, they cannot be regarded as principles of mathematics. I was inclined towards analytic interpretations... I found several possible interpretations of the axiom of infinity, different from Russell's interpretation, of such a kind that they make this axiom analytic. The result is achieved, e.g., if not things but positions are taken as individuals. (Carnap 1963, 47-48)

The idea that an interpretation can make an axiom analytic is perplexing for a modern reader. For we today characterize logical truth as truth under all interpretations, i.e., all models. If we recognize that Carnap holds analytic truths to be logical truths (during this period, he calls analytic truth 'L-truth,' i.e., logical truth), then it seems that analytic truths should be true under all interpretations, contra Carnap's suggestion above. This difficulty is solved by recognizing that Carnap does not characterize analytic truth as truth-in-all-interpretations. Analytic truth for Carnap, as we have seen, is truth in virtue of the semantic rules; and one of the semantic rules specifies the universe of discourse. Thus if the domain is taken to be an uncontrovertibly infinite collection such as the natural numbers, then the semantic rules alone will determine the truth-value of the axiom of infinity to be true. Of course, there will be other interpretations under which the axiom of infinity becomes analytically false (e.g., let $D = \{0, 1, 2\}$), and others under which it becomes synthetic (e.g., $D = \{x : x \text{ is a physical object}\}$).[5]

But then the modern reader might worry: if we are allowed to include that much information about the language to determine which sentences are 'true in virtue of meaning,' then will there be any sentences that are *not* true in virtue of meaning? For example, looking at the matter from the modern perspective, suppose we are given an interpreted language, in which 't' is an individual constant and 'P' a monadic predicate, and that the interpretation function f of this language is such that $f(`t') = a$ and $f(`P') = \{a, b, c\}$. Then the truth-value of 'Pt' is determined by the information about the interpreted language alone, i.e., no empirical tests need to be run to determine its truth-value (since we don't need to make any observations to ascertain that $a \in \{a, b, c\}$ is true). Every atomic sentence then appears to be analytic; this is an obviously unacceptable consequence, especially to Carnap. What has happened? Carnapian semantics would not allow $f(`P') = \{a, b, c\}$ as a semantic rule of the language. Instead, the semantic rule for predicates take the form: $f(`P') = $ the property (of being) X.

---

5. At this point, someone might object as follows (especially if she is sympathetic to Tarski's finitist-nominalist program). First, it seems that mathematics is thereby forced to take a specific subject matter; in Carnap's case, this would be positions. So it is no longer clear that we can legitimately apply these 'mathematical truths' to any and all physical objects, since we have restricted the domain of quantification to positions. But Carnap does think mathematical theorems can be used to infer one factual statement about physical objects from another, and not just statements about positions. Second, by analogous reasoning, 'Less than 100 things exist' can be made analytic, if living U.S. presidents are taken as the individuals in the domain. That appears to be a nearly worthless kind of analyticity.

And thus the language alone would not (in general) determine the truth-value of an atomic sentence 'Pt,' for (on Carnap's picture) it is an empirical question whether the object denoted by 't' in fact has the property designated by 'P' in the actual world. During his semantic phase, Carnap identifies "extension" (contrasted with intension) with "*contingent* reference or denotation" (Carnap 1963, 63; my emphasis). That is, in order to determine the extension of a word (unlike its intension), empirical, factual information is necessary.

To put the point roughly, whereas the modern conception takes 'logically true in $\mathcal{L}$' to be truth in all $M = \langle D, f \rangle$ of $\mathcal{L}$, Carnap (to put the matter in modern terminology) fixes D, and then takes analytic truth to be 'true for almost all f'. The 'almost' must be included, because Carnap places certain restrictions on the interpretation function.[6] For example: if, for a particular f, the object-language predicate corresponding to the property of being a horse is assigned set S, then in that same f, the set assigned to the predicate corresponding to the property of being a stallion must be a proper subset of S.[7] It is in this sense that 'All bachelors are unmarried' is an analytic truth, for its truth is fixed by the language in which it is couched. This basic idea also appears in *Logical Syntax* §34c-d (though without the 'almost,' and with different terminology, since Carnap has not yet entered his semantic period), in the definition of 'analytic-in-language-II.' There, Carnap specifies the elements of D once and for all (as the class of accented expressions, i.e. $0, 0', 0'' \ldots$), but then sets up the definition of analyticity so that a sentence will be analytic *simpliciter* if it is true[8] for all grammatically appropriate assignments of values to its variables and non-logical constants.

Now we can ask: what semantic rules govern arithmetical language–and more specifically, arithmetical language meeting the finitist-nominalist conditions? Since there is no list of such rules in Carnap's discussion notes, the following proposal must be somewhat conjectural.[9] First, the maximal allowable domain is the set of all physical objects. Perhaps we should include, as allowable domains, all (non-empty) proper subsets thereof: Tarski remarks, as we saw in 1.2, that he would like to construct an arithmetic that makes no assumption about the

---

6. The notation here is anachronistic, but the underlying idea is in Carnap's *Introduction to Semantics* §19.
7. This is assuming that the language contains primitive predicate letters corresponding to 'horse' and 'stallion.' Interestingly, this situation is one of the primary reasons Carnap considered the transition from syntax to semantics to be necessary: he believes the syntactic conception of language cannot correctly capture this relation between 'horse' and 'stallion' (Carnap 1942, 87).
8. In *Logical Syntax*, Carnap eschews the notion of truth; so this actually reads 'analytic.'
9. In *Foundations*, Carnap describes what a (true) interpretation of the Peano postulates would be:

> We have... to choose any infinite class, to select one of its elements as the beginning member of a sequence, and to state a rule determining for any given member of a sequence its immediate successor.... '[0]' designates the beginning member of the sequence; if '...' designates a member of the sequence, then '...'' designates its immediate successor; 'N' designates the class of all members of the sequence that can be reached from the beginning member in a finite number of steps. (Carnap 1939, 181)

number of things in the world. For arithmetic to get off the ground, the elements of D must be arranged in a sequence; Tarski suggests that we impose the order arbitrarily upon the physical objects, but it does not fundamentally matter what the source of this ordering is. The semantic rules for designation must be such that the first n numerals (starting from '0') designate the first n objects in the sequence. That is, where '$S(x)$' means 'successor of x,' $S(a) = b$ if and only if b immediately follows a in the sequence of physical objects. However, it does not matter which object is the beginning member of the sequence, or which objects come where in the sequence. Setting up our semantic rules such that a single sequence is picked out once and for all will lead us to the problem that some numbers will be brunettes, discussed in 1.3.1. Thus I propose that we do not include in our semantic rules any one particular interpretation of the numerals, but rather just make all admissible interpretations subject to the above constraint.

Finally, we need rules of designation to deal with a numeral whose intended referent outstrips the number of physical objects in the world. Recall from 1.3.2 that Carnap records three proposals for interpreting such numerals. Assuming that 'k' is the name of the 'final' physical object in the universe, the three proposals are:

(a) $k' = k'' = \ldots = k$

(b) $k' = k'' = \ldots = 0$

(c) $k' = 0, k'' = 0', \ldots$

(There are $k + 1$ total physical objects in such a universe, since the first object is assigned to '0'.) The first two both follow the spirit of Frege's 'chosen object' proposal for handling non-denoting expressions; they differ from one another in that (a) makes the 'final' object in the universe the chosen one,[10] whereas in (b) it is the first object (i.e., the one assigned to '0').[11] Option (c) can be intuitively conceived as a circle whose circumference one can trace an indefinite number of times as one writes down the numerals: two numerals are assigned to the same object if and only if the numbers they are intended to denote are identical modulo $k + 1$. In each of these three cases, at least one of the Peano axioms is violated. If (a) is adopted, then two distinct 'numbers'–those are scare-quotes, since numbers are understood as physical objects here–will have the same successor (namely, the objects denoted by '$k - 1$' and by 'k'). (Though of course, under all three proposals, if the domain is finite, there will be cases in which two numerals, such that one is an ancestral-numeral of the other, denote the same object.) If (b) or

---

10. Graham Priest has defended such a picture of the natural numbers (Priest 1994); he has also explored generalizing models of arithmetic that have the other forms Carnap, Tarski, and Quine consider (Priest 1997). However, Priest studies these models within the context of the paraconsistent logic *LP*, unlike the Harvard discussants, who wish to retain classical logic.

11. Russell considers a similar proposal in *Introduction to Mathematical Philosophy* (Russell 1920, 132).

(c) is adopted, then the object designated by '0' will be the successor of some number.

Now we are in a position to ask: which arithmetical claims are classically analytic, but synthetic under Tarski's restricted arithmetic? First, any sentence of the language that asserts (or denies) that there exist at least n distinct numbers will become synthetic, since 'There exist n distinct physical things' is synthetic. What about variable-free formulae of arithmetic, such as '$2 + 3 = 5$': do they maintain their analytic status under a finitist-nominalist regime? Some do, and some do not. The sentence '$2 + 3 = 5$' will be true regardless of the cardinality of the domain, and this is the case under any of (a)–(c), so it is analytically true in all three semantics. And '$2 + 3 \neq 5$' will be false in any domain under (a)–(c), so it can be considered analytically false. However, the same cannot be said of '$1000 = 2000$' or '$2 + 3 \neq 7$': each of these will be false in certain domains but true in others. Under rule (a) or (b), '$1000 = 2000$' will be true for domains with cardinality less than or equal to 1001, false otherwise. Under rule (c), this sentence is true for domains in which $1000 = 2000 \bmod k + 1$ ($k + 1$, as before, is the number of elements in the domain), false otherwise. For similar reasons, in certain domains the classically true '$2 + 3 \neq 7$' will be false. The preceding can be generalized as follows: for all variable-free arithmetical sentences, all atomic sentences or their negations (i.e., those of the form $n = m$ or $n \neq m$) that are analytically true in classical arithmetic will be analytically true under a Tarskian regime, assuming we adopt one of (a)–(c). However, atomic sentences that are analytically false in classical arithmetic become synthetic under the finitist-nominalist reconstrual (e.g. '$1000 = 2000$'), as do their negations (e.g. '$2 + 3 \neq 7$'). In short: though all the classically analytically true variable-free arithmetical literals[12] are analytically true under the finitist-nominalist setting as well, the classically analytically false arithmetical literals become synthetic, with the exception of logical falsehoods such as '$5 \neq 5$.'[13]

Which other sentences become synthetic depends upon which particular semantic rules are adopted. What further sentences that are classically analytic become synthetic under (a)? If we adopt the 'liberal' version of (FN 3), so that we allow as a possibility that the number of physical objects in the universe is infinite, then the assertion (or denial) of 'No two numbers have the same successor' becomes synthetic, along with all the sentences that imply it. The same holds for 'No number is its own successor.' Both of these are false if the domain is finite, but not if the domain is infinite; thus the semantic rules alone do not determine the truth-values of these sentences. If, however, we endorse the stricter version of (FN 3), and claim that the number of physical objects in the universe is finite, then the truth-value of both of these sentences (and those that entail them) can be computed from the semantic rules–though here they become analytically false, unlike the classical case. Under the (b) and (c) semantics, these two sentences would be analytically true, if we allowed ourselves, among our semantic rules,

---

12. A literal is an atomic sentence or the negation of an atomic sentence.
13. Greg Lavers helped me to see that final point correctly.

the anti-Parmenidean assumption that the universe does not contain exactly one thing; without it, these two sentences will be synthetic under (b) and (c) as well. I do not see any reason why this anti-Parmenidean assumption should be considered a semantic rule: although it is pretty clearly false that our universe contains only one physical object, the kinds of reasons adduced to support that conclusion are presumably empirical in character. (We could stipulate the anti-Parmenidean assumption as a semantic rule, but that would be unmotivated by the language we actually speak and are attempting to model: such a stipulation would be analogous to declaring 'Adolf Hitler died in 1945' a semantic rule.)

Which other classically analytic arithmetical sentences become synthetic under the semantic rules (b) and (c)? The situation parallels that of (a) above: if we adopt the liberal version of (FN 3), then any assertion that implies the sentence '0 is not the successor of any number' or its denial will become synthetic. The truth-value of this sentence cannot be calculated from the semantic rules, since it will be false if the domain is finite, but could be true under an infinite domain. Similarly, if we adopt the strict version of (FN 3), then we can calculate the truth-value of this sentence (and all those which imply it) from the semantic rules. However, unlike the classical case, it would be evaluated *false*. And if the domain of discourse is allowed to contain only one individual, then this sentence is synthetic under semantic rule (a).[14]

4.2. Radicalization of Quine's Critique of Analyticity

4.2.1 "Truth by Convention" is less radical than "Two Dogmas"

Richard Creath has argued that Quine's 1936 "Truth by Convention" should not be read as a full frontal assault on the intelligibility, applicability, or usefulness of the notion of analytic truth.[15] He argues that such a reading is anachronistic,

---

14. The question of how to formulate a theory of arithmetic in finite models is still being investigated today by Krynicki and Zdanowski (2005) and Mostowski (2001). The question of what happens to first-order logic when we restrict ourselves to *finite* models is a vibrant research area as well; see Rosen (2002) for an overview.

15. Quine has a battery of arguments concerning analyticity, in part because there are several different ways to characterize analytic truth. To summarize Quine's multifarious critiques: if a characterization of analyticity can meet the epistemological demands of Carnap and other logical empiricists (viz., it underwrites the a prioricity of mathematics and logic), then Quine thinks it is obscure and/or trivial and/or uninstantiated. For example, 'true in all logically possible worlds' is more obscure than 'analytic,' 'can be held true come what may' is true of every sentence, and 'is held true come what may' is uninstantiated. On the other hand, after "Two Dogmas," Quine countenances certain notions of analyticity. He proposes a definition of 'stimulus analyticity' in *Word and Object*, and another account in terms of language learning in *Roots of Reference* (Quine 1974, 80). "However," Quine says of such a characterization of analyticity, "I see little use for it in epistemology or methodology of science" (Quine 1986, 95). Peter Hylton has stressed this as the core of Quine's critique of analyticity: Quine "rejects the idea that there is a defensible distinction *which will play the role that Carnap allotted it*" (Hylton 2007, 53). In short, Quine's later view of analyticity is that any intelligible explication of it cannot carry the epistemological weight Carnap places on the notion.

and arises from the temptation to read the radical criticism of analyticity found in "Two Dogmas" into an article written fifteen years earlier. On Creath's interpretation, "Truth by Convention" is better viewed as "more nearly a request for clarification than an attack" (Creath 1987, 487) on Carnap's notion of analytic truth.

Creath marshals published and unpublished textual support for the view that Quine was not convinced that analyticity and kindred concepts are fundamentally incoherent until several years after "Truth by Convention." He first points out that "Truth by Convention" grew out of three lectures Quine gave to the Harvard Society of Fellows in 1934, and these lectures praise Carnapian views almost unequivocally.[16] Quine himself later describes these three lectures on Carnap as "abjectly sequacious" (Quine 1991, 266).[17] So, Creath reasons, if the document that "Truth by Convention" grew out of was extremely sympathetic to Carnap's position, then Quine's position in "Truth by Convention" itself is probably not diametrically opposed to Carnap's position. But this evidence is not conclusive, since Quine could have rejected Carnapian analyticity after his 1934 lectures but before writing "Truth by Convention," despite surface similarities between the two documents. Thus Creath offers a second piece of evidence: at the 1937 American Philosophical Association meeting, Quine presented a lecture entitled "Is Logic a Matter of Words?" In it, Quine argues for what he later calls the 'linguistic doctrine of logical truth,' which Quine considers to be part of Carnap's position. So there is evidence of Quine defending Carnap's views both shortly before and immediately after he wrote "Truth by Convention."

Consider a third batch of textual evidence for Creath's view. During the greater part of the 1940's, in Quine's published (Quine 1943a, 120) and unpublished writings (Creath 1990, 298 and 332), his attitude toward analyticity is one of growing skepticism, but not the dismissal that we find in "Two Dogmas." For example, in "The Problem of Interpreting Modal Logic," Quine claims to give an "interpretation of pre-quantificational modal logic" in terms of analyticity, viz., "The result of prefixing 'Necessarily' to any statement is true if and only if the statement is analytic' (Quine 1943b, 45). Presumably, one would not give an interpretation of modality in terms of analyticity if one considered analyticity to be thoroughly incomprehensible. And in the same article, Quine calls the suggestion (which he attributes to Goodman) that the analytic/synthetic distinction is merely a matter of degree a "dismal possibility" (Quine 1943b, fn.4). Thus, it seems that Quine had not yet abandoned all hope for an epistemically powerful notion of analyticity at this stage, even if he believed it had not yet received a satisfactory explanation. And a similar attitude is echoed in a 1947 letter from Quine to Morton White: "It's bad that we have no criterion of intensional synonymy; still, this frankly and visibly defective basis of discussion offers far more hope of

16. For further analysis of these lectures, see Hylton (2001).
17. Yemima Ben-Menahem has suggested, however, that important seeds of Quine's later critiques can be found in the 1934 lectures: "What seems to have happened between 'Lectures' and 'Truth by Convention' is not so much a philosophical about-face on Quine's part as a consolidation of already incipient ideas" (Ben-Menahem 2006, 229).

clarity and progress, far less danger of mediaeval futility, than does the appeal to attributes, propositions, and meanings" (White 1999, 339-40). This hypothesis finds further confirmation in a December 1946 lecture of Quine's:

> The ideas which I have offered... this hour have been mainly negative: the obscurity of our conception of analytic [*sic*], and the difficulty of doing anything about it... But I want to say in closing that my attitude is not one of defeatism, nor one of dismissing the problem as illusory. We have real problems here, meaningful problems worth working on. My feeling is... that we should recognize that we have not been doing very well, but not that we should give up trying. (Quine 2008, 35)

Clearly, Quine had not yet admitted defeat in his attempts to draw the analytic/synthetic distinction at this point in time. And furthermore, he believed it a 'real' and 'meaningful' task worth undertaking. In short, even into the later 1940s, Quine showed a reluctance to accept and endorse any notion of analyticity found in Carnap's contemporaneous writings, but he had not yet reached the view we find in "Two Dogmas."

A final piece of historical evidence for viewing Quine's critique in "Truth by Convention" as less radical than that of "Two Dogmas," which Creath does not mention, is particularly telling. It provides a clue as to when and where Quine gave up Carnap's notion of analytic truth. In "Homage to Carnap," his eulogy for Carnap at the 1970 Philosophy of Science Association meeting, Quine says he first contacted Carnap "in Prague 38 years ago," which would be Fall 1932, and that he, Quine, "was very much Carnap's disciple for six years" (Quine 1976, 41). This implies that "Truth by Convention" was composed during the period of Quine's life in which he considered himself a disciple of Carnap; thus "Truth by Convention" probably should not be viewed as fundamentally rejecting one of Carnap's most cherished ideas.

I shall proceed on the assumption that these pieces of evidence above are conclusive: that is, I will assume that "Truth by Convention" presents a less radical challenge to analytic truth than "Two Dogmas." That is, Quine has not completely rejected something like the notion of analyticity that Carnap hopes for in 1936. And this is reflected in the differing views expressed in "Truth by Convention" and "Two Dogmas": "Two Dogmas," unlike "Truth by Convention," makes the radical claim that no intelligible, non-empty explication of analytic truth can be found. Furthermore, "Two Dogmas," unlike "Truth by Convention," suggests the radical thesis that even mathematics and logic are not analytic. If this difference between "Two Dogmas" and "Truth by Convention" is genuine, then this immediately prompts a historical question: what, if anything, prompted the radicalization of Quine's attack on analyticity–*why* did Quine's view change from the more moderate one found in "Truth by Convention" to the more radical view of "Two Dogmas"? I will argue that two partial causes are found in the 1940-41 academic year. First, in Tarski's finitist-nominalist system, certain statements of arithmetic, a discipline usually considered analytic since Frege, turn out to be synthetic. But the notion that apparently analytic sentences could be synthetic foreshadows a central claim found in "Two Dogmas" but not "Truth by Convention": no assertion is forever immune from revision, even the intuitively analytic statements of logic and arithmetic. Second, in section 5.3.4, we shall see that during these discussions, Quine saw clearly that Carnap had begun to conceive of analytic truth (and other logico-linguistic concepts) in intensional and semantic terms, instead of the extensional and syntactic framework endorsed in 1934's *Logical Syntax*. Quine, however, strongly espoused the extensional approach to analysis his entire career, and preferred syntactic analyses to semantic ones. Finally, 5.3.5 presents a further virtue of this picture of Quine's development: it can be used to resolve a dispute between two leading commentators concerning when, precisely, Quine reached the radical view of analyticity expressed in "Two Dogmas."

4.2.2 Influence on Quine's attack on analyticity, I: contracting the class of analytic truths

One might think that Quine's transformation is just the result of time and reflection: all the conceptual ingredients for his rejection of Carnapian analytic truth are present in "Truth by Convention." They simply needed time to 'ferment' or mature in Quine's mind to produce a final, decisive break fifteen years later; Creath hints at such a picture (Creath 1990, 31), and Ben-Menahem expresses this view more explicitly (Ben-Menahem 2006, 229). Although (as I shall describe presently) at least some crucial ingredients of the later break are undoubtedly present in "Truth by Convention," there is good reason to question this account. A revealing sign is found in the quotation from Quine's "Homage to Carnap" just above: Quine says he was Carnap's disciple 'for six years.' This probably means the years 1933-38 inclusive, which obviously includes "Truth by Convention," published in 1936. Now the natural question to ask next is: what happened in 1939 that could end a six-year discipleship? A few paragraphs later in the "Homage," Quine writes:

> In 1939 Carnap came to Harvard as visiting professor. These were historic months: Russell, Carnap, and Tarski were here together. Then it was that Tarski and I argued long with Carnap against his idea of analyticity. (Creath 1990, 466)

Quine's memory is obviously not entirely accurate here. The academic year in which Carnap, Tarski, and Russell visited Harvard was of course 1940-41, not 1939-40. Despite this minor misremembering on Quine's part, it is reasonable to suspect that this 'historic' clash of philosophical titans marks the end of Quine's discipleship under Carnap—especially since Quine recalls, more than three decades later, arguing about analyticity with Carnap at that time. Quine makes similar remarks in his autobiography (though he recalls the dates correctly there), as we saw in the first paragraph of this chapter.

In "Truth by Convention," one way Quine questions the analytic/ synthetic distinction is the following. The truths of logic are rendered conventional by assuming every instance of certain sentence-forms involving the words 'and,' 'not,' and 'all' to be true by "linguistic fiat." Quine then asks: if we are allowed to declare certain sentences true simply by linguistic fiat, why couldn't we continue expanding this list of conventional truths, and include (for example) Einstein's field equations in our list of sentences true by convention as well? And there is no reason to stop with fundamental physical laws: as long as we can declare any sentence true we like, we could include 'The Earth is larger than 15,000 kilometers in diameter.'

> If in describing logic and mathematics as true by convention what is meant is that the primitives can be circumscribed in such a fashion as to generate all and only the truths of logic and mathematics, the characterization is empty... the same might be said of any other body of doctrine as well.[18] (Quine 1976, 102)

In effect, Quine questions the existence of a reasonable and motivated cut-off point for statements considered true by convention that would prevent an indefinite expansion of such truths beyond the realm of logic and perhaps mathematics.[19] He cannot see any special quality that the terms 'or' and 'not' possess that (e.g.) 'mass-energy density' lacks, such that sentences essentially involving the former but not the latter can legitimately be simply stipulated to be true. In short, we can read Quine as making a slippery slope argument: once we permit one sentence to be true by linguistic fiat, there is no principled ground for stopping the unlimited inflation of such truths. This line of thought takes a more exact form in an article that Quine penned jointly with Goodman in 1940: "Elimination of Extra-logical Postulates." This article provides a formal procedure for converting any system of postulates framed in a formal language into a postulate-free language that has, in an important sense, the same content as the original postulate system. The basic idea is to transform the postulates, which could be intuitively synthetic (hence the 'Extra-logical' in the title), into definitions in the language, which are considered paradigmatically analytic by proponents of analyticity. Quine improved this formal recipe in "Implicit Definition Sustained."[20]

---

18. A few years later, Quine will not even allow that the truths of mathematics can be so circumscribed. He takes Gödel's incompleteness results to show that we "can't even formulate adequate, usable conv'ns afterward," since no logical system captures all the logico-mathematical truths (Quine Papers, Folder 3144).

19. A few years later, Quine will not even allow that the truths of mathematics can be so circumscribed. He takes Gödel's incompleteness results to show that we "can't even formulate adequate, usable conv'ns afterward," since no single logical system captures all the logico-mathematical truths (MS storage 299, Box 12, folder: Phil. 20m-1940).

20. There, Quine writes:
> Briefly, the point is that there is a mechanical routine whereby, given an assortment of interpreted undefined predicates 'F_1'...'F_n', governed by a true axiom or a finite list of such, we can switch to a new and equally economical set of undefined predicates and define 'F_1'...'F_n' in terms of them, plus auxiliary arithmetical notations, in such a way that the old axioms become true by arithmetic. (Quine 1976, 133–34)

In the finitist-nominalist conversations of 1940-41, Quine is presented with the converse possibility. Instead of expanding the conventional, and thus analytic, truths from logic and mathematics into natural science, Tarski presents a philosophically motivated language-form in which the number of supposedly analytic, conventional truths is contracted. When Quine sees that arithmetical assertions can become synthetic under certain conditions, this shows him concretely that the boundary between the analytic and the synthetic can be considered porous in *both* directions.[21] In "Truth by Convention," only one of the directions is considered, and the analytic status of logic and mathematics is not in doubt.[22] After suggesting that the behavioristic sign of analyticity is being held true come what may, Quine writes:

> There are statements that we choose to surrender last, if at all, in the course of revamping our sciences in the face of new discoveries; and among these there are some which we will not surrender at all, so basic are they to our whole conceptual scheme. *Among the latter are to be counted the so-called truths of logic and mathematics*, regardless of what further we may have to say of their status in the course of a subsequent sophisticated philosophy. (Quine 1976, 102; my emphasis)

That is, in "Truth by Convention," Quine still considers the theorems of logic and mathematics analytic, because we will not give them up–his worries instead involve understanding analyticity as truth by linguistic fiat. However, in "Two Dogmas," we see Quine question even the analytic status of logic, because logical truths can be surrendered in the course of empirical investigation:

> Even a statement very close to the periphery can be held true in the face of recalcitrant experience by pleading hallucination or by amending certain statements of the kind called logical laws.... Revision even of the logical law of the excluded middle has been proposed as a means of simplifying quantum mechanics. (Quine 1951, 40)

That is, Quine believes that certain developments in the empirical enterprise of quantum physics could lead to changes in the logical laws, and therefore, even logic can be considered partly synthetic, since it is responsive to new discoveries about the empirical world.[23] Quine's suggestion is that the class of paradigmati-

---

21. It should be noted that the earlier revolution in geometry, beginning with the development of non-Euclidean geometries and culminating in the General Theory of Relativity, might provide an another case in which sentences that at least some people considered analytic (most importantly, the parallel postulate) became empirical. I must thank an anonymous referee for this point.

22. In a footnote to *Word and Object*, Quine says that "Truth by Convention" did not claim that there are no analytic truths (Quine 1960, 65n.).

23. Because I draw a distinction between inflating and contracting the class of analytic truths, I demur from Mancosu's assertion that making certain apparently empirical sentences "unrevisable despite all observations [inflation]... is just the other side of the coin of claiming that logical propositions might be just as revisable as the physical ones [contraction]" (Mancosu 2005, 330). The phrase 'The other side of the coin' is of course metaphorical, so Mancosu may not intend to say they are very similar; but 'Every synthetic

cally analytic sentences can be contracted, a suggestion we see clearly in Tarski's FN project. However, in "Two Dogmas," the contraction appears even more severe than in the finitistic language construction project. However, it is not stronger than Tarski's 1935 claim, made in conversation, that "he had never uttered a sentence which he had not considered to be revisable" (Mancosu 2005, 331). Tarski makes similar claims in a 1944 letter to Morton White:

> I am ready to reject certain logical premises (axioms) of our science in exactly the same circumstances in which I am ready to reject empirical premises... certain new experiences of a very fundamental nature may make us inclined to change just some axioms of logic. And certain new developments in quantum mechanics seem clearly to indicate this possibility. (White 1987, 31-32)

And it seems likely that Tarski voiced those views about logic in Quine's presence at some point during their year together at Harvard.

I am not claiming that Quine's willingness in "Two Dogmas" to renounce the supposed analyticity of logic and mathematics definitely stems from the 1940-41 finitist-nominalist project, in which certain arithmetical claims become synthetic. However, these conversations with Tarski and Carnap, in which certain portions of arithmetic are considered dependent on empirical facts about the world, certainly could have planted the idea in his head, or perhaps more likely, cultivated the germ of an idea he had already entertained. Additionally, I am not suggesting this radicalization of Quine's critique of analyticity (namely, from 'The corpus of analytic truths can be indefinitely expanded'[24] to 'The corpus of analytic truths can be indefinitely expanded *or contracted*') is the only conceptual step needed to move from the Quine of 1936 to the Quine of 1950. In particular, Quine is not yet profoundly skeptical of synonymy in "Truth by Convention" or (as we shall see) in the 1940-41 discussions with Tarski and Carnap, where Quine, apparently without hesitation or compunction, defines analytic truth using the notion of synonymy. And "Two Dogmas," of course, contains a sustained attack on the notion of synonymous expressions. This section has only presented part of Quine's intellectual journey from "Truth by Convention" to "Two Dogmas." Another, perhaps more important, will be described in the next chapter, where we see how Quine's (antecendent) antipathy towards intensional languages is transformed into a criticism of Carnapian analyticity and Carnap's characterization of synonymy in the early 1940s.

---

sentence can be unrevisable' and 'Every analytic sentence can be revisable' are not equivalent (they are opposite directions of a conditional, if we make the standard identification of 'synthetic' and 'not analytic').

24. Actually, in "Truth by Convention," Quine apparently only applies his indefinite-expansion argument to analyticity conceived as 'true by linguistic fiat,' not necessarily to Quine's preferred behavioristic conception of analyticity.

Chapter 5
Direct Discussions of Analytic Truth in 1940-41

This chapter is an exposition and analysis of the characterizations of analytic truth, and the arguments concerning analyticity, that appear in the 1940-41 discussion notes. First, I outline each primary participant's preferred characterization of logico-linguistic concepts in general, and of analyticity in particular. I then briefly compare some of the relative merits of each approach before examining Tarski and Quine's objections in the notes to Carnap's notion of analyticity. Tarski's two most well-developed objections to the analytic/synthetic distinction are reconstructed and evaluated. The first, a version of the 'Any sentence may be held true come what may' argument familiar from "Two Dogmas," either misunderstands Carnap's position, or does not conflict with it. Tarski's second objection, which is not as familiar from public debates over analyticity, is based upon Gödel's incompleteness results. This argument does not tell decisively against the analytic/synthetic distinction either, unless we characterize language and meaning fundamentally proof-theoretically.

Quine, unlike Tarski, does not articulate complete arguments against Carnapian analyticity in the notes; rather, he simply voices disagreement with two of Carnap's core commitments. Nonetheless, Quine's points of contention do allow us to characterize the philosophical differences between the two cleanly, and thereby better understand the historical grounds and development of Quine's critique of analyticity. The first difference between the two is that Carnap holds sentences of the form 'p is analytic' to be themselves analytic, whereas Quine considers them synthetic. Second, Quine considers Carnap's characterization of analyticity in modal terms fundamentally unclear. Motivations and arguments for each side are reconstructed, drawing on published work when possible. Finally, this material suggests another historical conjecture concerning the radicalization of Quine's critique of analyticity. In *Logical Syntax*, Carnap is explicitly committed to analyzing logico-linguistic concepts in syntactic and extensional terms, which is the method Quine preferred his entire philosophical career. In the mid-thirties, however, Carnap shifts toward semantic and intensional treatments of certain key linguistic concepts, but Quine does not follow him. Thus Quine's break with Carnap is not simply a matter of Quine changing his views, but of Carnap's views changing as well.

5.1. What Is Analyticity, circa 1940?

The aim of this chapter is to examine and analyze the treatment of analyticity in the 1940-41 discussion notes and related texts. Before proceeding, a potential terminological difficulty must be dispelled. Neither the word '*analytisch*' nor its cognates appear in Carnap's discussion notes of 1940-41. The phrase that does appear, and which corresponds for Carnap at this time to what we today call 'analytic', is 'logically true' (abbreviated as 'L-true'). Carnap explicitly states in print that his notion of L-truth is intended to be a modern, scientific version of the older, traditional philosophical notion of analyticity. What makes this terminology somewhat unfortunate for us is that the currently dominant notion of logical truth (a sentence true in all models) is not identical to analytic truth. For the later Quine, the notion of logical truth is intelligible, whereas analyticity traditionally conceived is not. Thus Quine will not maintain that logical truths are analytic, at least in the Carnapian sense of 'true in virtue of the meanings of the sentences alone.' To complicate matters further, Quine finds certain empirical characterizations of analyticity acceptable at various points in his career; e.g., *Word and Object* and *Roots of Reference* both propose reformed, empirical usages for 'analytic' (see 5.3.1).

Thus, despite initial appearances, 'L-truth' in 1941 should be interpreted into our modern idiom not as 'logical truth' but rather as 'analyticity,' in the full-blooded Carnapian sense of 'truth in virtue of language, independently of any empirical matters of fact.' (Carnap regards this sense of L-true/analytic as rough: it is the explicandum, not the explicans.) This notion, not modern logical truth, is both Carnap's grail and the later Quine's target.[1] In the 1941 notes, Quine proposes "a criterion for logically-true: either logically provable or transformable through synonyms into a logically-provable sentence" (102-63-03). The first disjunct corresponds to the notion of theorem (a notion Quine never abandons), whereas the second disjunct is precisely the notion of Frege-analyticity Quine later attacks in "Two Dogmas." This quotation shows that 'logically true' or 'L-true' in these notes should not be taken in the sense of 'theorem of a proof calculus,' 'truth in virtue of logical form,' or as 'true in all models,' but rather as 'analytic.'

Before plunging into the details of Tarski, Quine, and Carnap's differing conceptions of analyticity, a rough schema of their approaches may help us see the forest before examining the trees. Carnap thinks analyticity should be treated as fundamentally semantic and intensional, Tarski agrees with Carnap that it is semantic, but holds that our account of it should be couched in extensional language (as in his *Wahrheitsbegriff*), while Quine holds that the concept of analyticity should be cashed out extensionally, and would prefer it to be syntactically explicated. Each of the three chooses his approach not because of any particular view he has about analyticity, but because of more general views he holds on

---

1. See Creath (1990, 303), where Carnap spells out clearly the terminological differences between himself and Quine.

the proper way to analyze language scientifically. That is, Carnap (by the late thirties) considers semantics a powerful philosophical tool and has no aversion to intensional languages, as *Meaning and Necessity* makes abundantly clear; Tarski is a great apostle of semantic methods, but all his important work is done using extensional languages, as he himself stresses to Carnap (090-16-09); and Quine tells us that he developed a very strong preference for extensional languages even before he finished college. So, in a very general way, each of the three philosophers attempts to analyze 'analytic' during 1940-41 along roughly the same lines he would analyze any other logico-linguistic term in scientific philosophy.

Let us now examine Carnap's notion of analytic truth in more detail, before turning to the critiques of Tarski and Quine. Carnap's basic conception of analyticity in the early forties has already been outlined in 4.1: a sentence s of language L is analytic-in-L if and only if the semantic rules of L determine the truth-value of s. This characterization appears in the discussion notes (090-16-11, 102-63-03), though it marks a shift from the characterization in 1939's *Foundations of Logic and Mathematics*: "In the Encyclopedia article [*Foundations*], I took 'L-true' to be 'true on the basis of the meaning of logical signs alone.' In the new MS [*Introduction to Semantics*]: on the basis of all signs" (102-62-03). This generalization is necessary for 'All mares are horses' to count as analytically true in English, a consequence Carnap considers desirable. This characterization of analyticity or L-truth is not intended as a formal definition. In *Meaning and Necessity*, Carnap calls this characterization in terms of semantic rules a "convention," "an informal formulation of a condition which any proposed definition of L-truth must fulfill in order to be adequate as an explication of our explicandum" (Carnap 1956a, 10). And in *Introduction to Semantics*, Carnap points out that 'truth in virtue of semantic rules' cannot be a metalinguistic characterization of L-truth, on the grounds that '... is a semantic rule' belongs to the metametalanguage.

Carnap presents another characterization of analyticity in the discussion notes (090-16-11), and in roughly contemporaneous print. Carnap (apparently in his own voice) considers the following two definitions of analytic truth (where 'S' abbreviates 'semantic system' and 'C' abbreviates 'formal calculus'):

a_i is L-true $=_{df}$ $\begin{cases} 1. a_i \text{ is true in every state of affairs in S.} \\ 2. a_i \text{ is true for each model of C.} \end{cases}$

What does each of these two definitions amount to? Let us examine them in order. We have already seen (in 4.1) what a semantic system S is: essentially, an assignment of individuals to names, of properties and relations to predicates and relation letters, and the usual rules for logical connectives familiar from the recursive clauses of Tarski's definition of truth. But what is a 'state of affairs' for Carnap at this time? In the notes, he writes:

> *state* = assignment of primitive descriptive predicates of the corresponding language to the individuals (of the universe of discourse of the language). Then each $\mathfrak{pr}^1$ [monadic predicate] is coordinated with a class of

individuals, each pr^2 [binary relation letter] is coordinated with a class of ordered pairs of individuals. (090-16-11)

In order for such a set of values assigned to linguistic expressions to qualify as a full-blown state of affairs, the assignment must be complete, in the sense that every n-ary relation letter must be assigned a class of ordered n-tuples *etc.* The intuitive justification for allowing these assignments to vary within a single semantic system is presumably that any 'bare' (i.e., property-less) individual can bear any logically possible property or relation. (And in a Carnapian semantic system, individuals are 'bare' in this sense: the only information the semantic system provides specifically about them is their names.)

Additional conditions are imposed on object languages whose primitive predicates express properties that are not 'logically independent,' so that not all assignments are allowed as genuine states of affairs. For example, in any particular state of affairs, the class assigned to the predicate 'mare' must be a subset of the class assigned to the predicate 'horse,' since the property of being a mare is only instantiated by entities also having the property of being a horse. When all the primitive predicates of the object language designate 'logically independent' properties, however, there are no such additional constraints (090-16-11). This mirrors the characterization of L-state in *Introduction to Semantics* §19K-L. Also, Carnap uses this framework to characterize a notion of synonymy: two predicates are synonymous if they "have the same extension not only in the actual world, but rather in every possible world, thus in every total-state ('state' in Semantics (I) [*Introduction to Semantics*])" (102-63-07). Finally, the characterization of 'L-true' as 'true in all states of affairs' shows, more perspicuously than the 'true in virtue of the semantic rules' formulation, why Carnap held L-truth to be identical to necessary truth (090-16-25).

Now let us consider the second definition of L-truth above, which uses the concept *model* instead of *state of affairs*, and *calculus* instead of *semantic system*. This definition of L-truth corresponds to the current model-theoretic notion of logical truth. Tarski introduces and uses this framework, which he characterizes thus:

> *Models. Tarski* apparently refers to a partially interpreted calculus, namely, all logical symbols are interpreted; for the usual signs, it is only determined that they are descriptive; but their interpretation is left open. A model for this system = a sequence of n entities, which are coordinated (as designata) to n descriptive signs. (090-16-11)

This is similar, if not identical, to the framework for semantics that Tarski uses in his *Wahrheitsbegriff* monograph and "On the Concept of Logical Consequence" (Tarski 1983, 416-17). Tarski's notion of models is also close to Carnap's notion of states of affairs for a semantic system. The primary difference is that Tarski does not first interpret predicates and relation letters as properties and relations, whereas Carnap's semantic system does. As a result, the 'additional conditions' imposed upon states of affairs involving logically dependent properties (such as *mare* and *horse*) are not imposed on the models: under the model/calculus framework, 'All mares are horses' will not come out as L-true. Actually, this requires qualification: it holds only if 'mare' and 'horse' are (treated as) primitive predicates in the language. In "On the Concept of Logical Consequence," Tarski makes provision for non-logical constants that are defined; thus if we have, as a part of the specification of our language, the definition 'mare $=_{df}$ female horse,' then 'All mares are horses' will be L-true, provided we demand that all defined constants be eliminated before applying the test for L-truth (Tarski 1983, 415). There is still a difference between Carnap and Tarski, though, since Carnap would want 'All mares are horses' to be analytic even if the object language did not explicitly contain a definition of 'mare' (Creath 1990, 305). However, as Carnap notes, as long as all the properties designated by terms in a semantic system are logically independent, the states of affairs/semantic system and the model/calculus one will agree on the class of L-true sentences. And if, within the Tarskian model/calculus framework, we have appropriate definitions for all the predicates expressing logically dependent properties, then any substantive difference between the two approaches also disappears.

Carnap's discussion notes record little of Tarski's own positive view of L-truth. It is not clear from the notes whether it is Tarski or Carnap who first raises the possibility of defining analyticity in terms of models; however, Tarski had already given this definition in print in 1936: "a class of sentences can be called *analytical* if every sequence of objects is a model of it" (Tarski 1983, 418).[2] The only two direct statements that Tarski makes about L-truth in the notes are the following: "Tarski: We only want to apply 'logically true' and 'logical consequence' when it holds for every meaning of the non-logical constants" (102-63-12). (Again, Tarski may mean here 'every meaning of the primitive non-logical constants.') This formulation is not especially interesting or novel, but it does highlight one fact worth noticing: Tarski considers logical truth to be best cashed out as a matter of meaning, i.e. of semantics, not primarily a syntactic affair. In this, he differs from Quine's preferences of even 1940, as we shall see in the following subsection.

The second comment Tarski makes about L-truth occurs in a discussion about how to introduce a term 'T' representing temperature into their regimented language for science. (The sentence '$T(t, x_0, y_0, z_0, t_0)$' formally expresses the assertion that the temperature at space-time point (x_0, y_0, z_0, t_0) is t.)

---

2. There is a substantial body of research discussing how much Tarski's concept of logical consequence differs from our current one. In particular, there is disagreement over whether Tarski operates with a varying or fixed domain conception of model in his 1936 paper on logical consequence. Etchemendy (1988) first suggested that Tarski was working with a fixed-domain notion, instead of the modern, variable one. There have been a number of rebuttals to Etchemendy's view, culminating in Gomez-Torrente (1996). Bays (2001) and Mancosu (2006) defend the fixed-domain view; Mancosu shows that Tarski still holds this conception of model in 1940, by drawing on unpublished material from that year.

> Just as we define 'descriptive' through an ultimately arbitrary enumeration, in the same way we also define the further concepts ('L-true$_2$' or whatever) through an enumeration of sentences in S [the language] involving T, so that the logical consequences ('L-implies$_1$') are taken as L-true$_2$. These sentences signify, for example: [1] T only takes quintuples, and [2] for true quintuples of real numbers, no 2 quintuples differ only in their first element, and [3] that for every quadruple, there is a quintuple with a unique first element; but furthermore also: [4] the function should be continuous, should have a first derivative, perhaps also a second etc. (090-16-10)

Note how different this is from any model-theoretic proposal to characterize L-truth and L-implication. By merely stipulating (in the metametalanguage) which sentences containing 'T' are L-true, Tarski's proposal can completely bypass the intensional notions of state of affairs and logical possibility, as Quine happily notes immediately following Tarski's claim.

5.2. Tarski's Objections to Analyticity

When philosophers today think of critics of Carnap's notion of analyticity, Quine springs to mind first. However, when Carnap mentions criticisms of analyticity in print, they are often attributed to Tarski. For example, in *Introduction to Semantics*, Carnap writes: "Tarski expresses, however, some doubt whether the distinction between... L- and F-truth is objective or more or less arbitrary" (Carnap 1942, 87; cf. vii). We find Carnap stressing Tarski's role in his autobiography as well: "my emphasis on the fundamental distinction between logical and non-logical knowledge,... which I share with many contemporary philosophers, differs from that of some logicians like Tarski and Quine" (Carnap 1963, 13; cf. 30, 36, 62, 64). (Carnap's choice of words is perhaps telling: those who agree with him on this fundamentally philosophical issue are 'philosophers,' while those who disagree are 'logicians.') This likely stems from Carnap's claim that Tarski and Quine's position is the result of their working almost exclusively on formal languages intended to model mathematics and logic, instead of natural science (Carnap 1963, 932).

Tarski gave a talk at the University of Chicago at the end of spring term 1940, and on June 3, he and Carnap had an extended private discussion on topics of shared interest (090-16-09). One of the issues they discussed at length is Tarski's suspicion, voiced at the end of 1936's "On the Concept of Logical Consequence," that the logical/descriptive distinction is somehow vague, unprincipled, or perhaps even arbitrary. In that article, Tarski writes:

> Underlying our whole construction [of the definition of consequence] is the division of all terms of the language discussed into logical and extra-logical. This division is certainly not quite arbitrary. If, for exam-

ple, we were to include among the extra-logical signs the implication sign, or the universal quantifier, then our definition of the concept of consequence would lead us to results that obviously contradict ordinary usage. On the other hand, no grounds are known to me which permit us to draw a sharp boundary between the two groups of terms. It seems to be possible to include among logical terms some which are usually regarded by logicians as extra-logical without running into consequences which stand in sharp contrast to everyday usage. (Tarski 1983, 418-19)

In short, the standard that must be satisfied by any division of terms into logical and extra-logical is conformity with existing 'everyday usage,' and this is why the division is 'not quite arbitrary.' But Tarski thinks equally good levels of conformity can be reached by different choices for the division between logical and extra-logical terms. In other words, the logical/extra-logical division is underdetermined by the available linguistic evidence; in 'ordinary usage,' the logical/descriptive boundary is vague. From this supposition that different choices of the boundary could capture the relevant linguistic phenomena equally well, Tarski concludes:

Perhaps it will be possible to find important objective arguments which will enable us to justify the traditional boundary between logical and extra-logical expressions. But I also consider it to be quite possible that investigations will bring no positive results in this direction, so that we shall be compelled to regard such concepts as 'logical consequence,' 'analytical statement,' and 'tautology' as relative concepts which must, on each occasion, be related to a definite, although in greater or less degree arbitrary, division of terms into logical and extra-logical. The fluctuation in the common usage of the concept of consequence would–in part at least–be quite naturally reflected in such a compulsory situation. (Tarski 1983, 420)

In short, the truth-values of sentences of the form 'A is a logical consequence of B' and 'C is analytic' are relative to a more or less arbitrary distinction between logical and non-logical terms.

But this sounds very similar to Carnap's principle of tolerance, since specifying which terms are logical (and hence are given a fixed meaning) is an essential part of specifying a language for him. If, contra Tarski's suspicions, it were completely non-arbitrary which terms are logical and which not (and assuming the meanings of the logical terms are also determinate), then there would be One Correct Logic, which is anathema to the tolerant Carnap. The primary difference is that Carnapian tolerance is not especially beholden to ordinary linguistic usage, and thus Tarski's position here is actually less 'tolerant' than Carnap's at the time. Given the similarity between Tarski and Carnap's viewpoints, it may seem surprising that Carnap considered Tarski one of his greatest opponents on the issue of analyticity. In order to reduce this perplexity, in this section I examine Tarski's two primary arguments against the notion of analyticity in June 1940, as well as Carnap's replies. Since this discussion pre-dates those on finitism, it is not tightly linked to the later project undertaken at Harvard. We shall see that in certain ways, Tarski misunderstands or talks past Carnap; nonetheless, genuine differences between the two can also be formulated.

5.2.1 Tarski's first objection: *any* sign can be logical

To begin their conversation concerning the tenability of the logical/descriptive distinction, Carnap proposes to distinguish logical terms from non-logical ones as follows: "indicate the simplest logical constants in the customary systems, and declare that everything definable from them is also logical." Tarski replies that he "has no such intuition; for one could equally well reckon 'temperature' as a logical term as well," as follows: simply fix the truth-values of all the atomic sentences involving the predicate 'Temp' (representing temperature), and maintain that assignment "in the face of all observations." In this way, any atomic statement could be stipulated to have the value *true* by a semantic rule. Note that this is a stronger claim than that found in Tarski's paper on logical consequence: in the discussion notes, he makes no mention of the 1936 requirement that the division into logical and descriptive signs must respect existing usage. Tarski's objection appears to be a version of the often-heard claim (which supposedly challenges Carnap's position on analyticity) that which assertions are taken as unrevisable is arbitrary: the truth-value of 'The temperature at spacetime point p_0 is t_0' could, for some investigator and/or in some language, remain the same 'in the face of all observations,' i.e., held true come what may, to echo "Two Dogmas." We encountered a form of this objection in the earlier discussion of "Truth by Convention" (4.2): which sentences, exactly, are we allowed to declare true by convention, and which not? I say this 'supposedly' challenges Carnap's position because one form of the principle of tolerance is just that the choice of assertions taken as analytic is arbitrary;[3] different choices yield different languages.

Furthermore, as is becoming more fully recognized among current philosophers,[4] Carnap clearly holds that a statement's being held true 'come what may' neither implies nor is implied by that statement's being analytic: "the concept of an analytic statement which I take as an explicandum is not adequately characterized as 'held true come what may' " (Carnap 1963, 921). Analytic sentences need not be held true come what may, for the language we are speaking can change; Car-

---

3. For an explanation of why this follows the usual formulation of the principle of tolerance, see Friedman (1999, 202) and Ricketts (1994).
4. Stathis Psillos puts the point clearly:
> A common criticism against analyticity, made by both Quine and Hempel, is that there is no point in distinguishing between analytic and synthetic statements, because all statements in empirical science are revisable... But since, as Hempel said, there are no such truths... there is no point in characterizing analyticity. However, such criticisms have always misfired against Carnap. Carnap never thought analyticity was about inviolable truth, 'sacrosanct statements,' unrevisability or the like... Already in [*Logical Syntax*], Carnap noted that no statements (not even mathematical ones) were unrevisable. Anything can go in the light of recalcitrant evidence. (Psillos 2000, 154)

nap thinks that this is exactly what happened when the scientific community made the transition from the Newtonian view of space and time to the relativistic one.[5] As a result of this language change, the metric tensor changed from a logical sign to a descriptive one. Conversely, a sentence can be held true come what may and remain synthetic: someone need only be dogmatic enough about what is actually the case, without asserting that what is the case is true in virtue of the meanings of the words she is using (for example, consider a theist of absolutely unshakeable convictions). So where did the notion that analytic statements are exactly those held true 'come what may' originate, if not with Carnap? It is Quine who uses unrevisability as a criterion of analyticity in "Truth by Convention" (quoted at length in 5.3.1 below), and reiterates it in "Two Dogmas," as a 'behavioristic' correlate of the old philosophical notion of analyticity.[6] His fundamental challenge appears to be that Carnap's notion of analyticity is insufficiently empirical, and thus fails to be a scientifically respectable concept. Ricketts (1982) provides the seminal work exploring this line of thought; others, including Creath (2004) and George (2000), understand Quine's challenge in basically the same way.

Carnap responds to Tarski that, in a language where the truth-values of atomic sentences containing 'Temp' are all fixed (via semantic rules), 'Temp(t, p)' would be a "mathematical function, a logical sign, and not the physical concept of temperature." Here Carnap apparently grants Tarski that one can make any term in a constructed language a logico-mathematical one,[7] but Carnap then states that such a term would become a non-descriptive, non-factual term in the constructed language, even if it is homophonic or homographic with a factual term of natural language. If we decide, on practical grounds, that the language we are constructing should respect the logical/descriptive distinction (to the extent that it exists) in everyday language, then we cannot construct a language of physics that includes Tarski's imagined 'Temp' predicate as the formal correlate of 'temperature' in the practicing scientist's parlance. In either case, there is no pressing problem for Carnap's view: if we are not required to re-capture everyday language within our artificial language, then it does not matter that 'Temp' (or any other term) becomes logico-mathematical. On the other hand, if we do require our artificial language to save the linguistic phenomena of extant usage to some degree, then we cannot stipulate the truth-values of atomic sentences attributing temperatures to spatiotemporal points. Carnap claims the crucial difference between logical and physical terms is shown as follows: for

---

5. For an excellent discussion of this Carnapian view, see Friedman (1999).
6. Whence Quine's view that a priori (and thus, for him and the logical empiricists, analytic) claims can be thought of as claims that can be held true come what may? Interestingly, this phrase echoes C. I. Lewis, Quine's erstwhile graduate school teacher and later colleague: "that is a priori which we can maintain in the face of all experience, come what will" (Lewis 1929, 231). See Baldwin (2007) for more on Lewis's influence on Quine; Baldwin quotes an interview with Donald Davidson, in which Davidson suggests that Quine's epistemology is Lewis's minus the analytic/synthetic distinction.
7. However, as we saw in 3.4.1, Carnap is clear in *Foundations* that if we are trying to model an extant language formally, then we cannot assign an arbitrary meaning to every term, for then our formal language would not be an accurate model of our target language.

closed sentences containing the physical temperature predicate (as opposed to Tarski's un-empirical predicate), "we cannot find the truth-value through mere calculation." Thus, as seen earlier, a sentence is analytic in L if its truth-value can be arrived at via calculation. In particular, during Carnap's semantic period, this means calculation ultimately from the semantic rules of L, as we shall see in the following subsection.

5.2.2 Tarski's second objection: Gödel sentences

Tarski seizes upon Carnap's characterization of analyticity in terms of calculability to lodge a second objection against the logical/descriptive distinction. Tarski immediately retorts to Carnap's quoted statement above that 'Temp' would qualify as a logico-mathematical term on Tarski's construal: "That proves nothing, since that is often not the case for mathematical functions either, since there are undecidable sentences" in mathematics. That is, in sufficiently rich formalizations of arithmetic, there are mathematical claims, such as the Gödel sentence, which cannot be proved or disproved via the axioms and rules of inference of that calculus. From the fact of undecidability, Tarski immediately concludes that there is "no fundamental difference between mathematical but undecidable sentences and factual sentences." This argument is enthymatic, so any detailed reconstruction requires some conjecture. Here is one attempt to spell out Tarski's argument:

(P1) If a sentence ϕ in a (formal) language L is logico-mathematical, then ϕ or $\neg \phi$ can be justified via mere calculation.

(P2) If a sentence ϕ of L can be justified via mere calculation, then the axioms and inference rules of L suffice to prove ϕ.

(GT) If a Gödel sentence G is expressible in L, then neither G nor $\neg G$ can be proved from the axioms and inference rules of L, if L is consistent.

(C1) Thus, if L is consistent, then neither G nor $\neg G$ can be justified via mere calculation, so G is not logico-mathematical.

(P3) But G is logico-mathematical.

Since premises (C1) and (P3) are contradictory, at least one of (P1-P3) must be false. Tarski places the blame on (P1): mere calculability fails to separate the mathematical sentences from the descriptive ones. Then, in order to reach his stronger, final conclusion that there is 'no difference between undecidable mathematical sentences and empirical ones,' Tarski will need a premise in the neighborhood of the following:

(P4) No criteria besides calculability can effectively separate logico-mathematical sentences from factual ones.

That is, if mere calculability is the only viable or plausible candidate for drawing a sharp distinction between logico-mathematical truths and factual ones, and the above argument from (P1-3) shows that calculability cannot draw the distinction in the (intuitively) correct place, then there is no criterion to underwrite or support the distinction.

Immediately following Tarski's claim that there is no fundamental difference between the Gödel sentence and factual sentences, Carnap merely replies "[i]t seems to me that there is" such a difference, and the conversation ends there. Although we do not have an articulated rebuttal from Carnap here, we can infer a more complete response with some confidence from his published writings. Carnap would most likely reject (P2) and maintain (P1). The Carnap of the semantic period would replace (P2) above with

(P2$_{Semantics}$) If a sentence ϕ can be justified via mere calculation, then the semantic rules of L suffice to determine that ϕ is true.

Put otherwise, calculability is identified with analyticity. But even the pre-semantic Carnap of *Logical Syntax* would reject (P2) as too narrow a notion of calculation: there, Carnap allows calculation to include an infinite hierarchy of metalanguages, with transfinite rules of inference, associated with a given object language. In the terminology of *Logical Syntax*, c-rules (for 'consequence'), not d-rules (for 'derivation,' answering to what we now call 'rules of proof'), are used to determine whether a sentence is analytic or not. And in these stronger languages, sentences that cannot be proved in the object language *can* be proved—including, in particular, a Gödel sentence of the lowest-level language, since the c-rules include the infinitary ω-rule, which completes Peano Arithmetic (Tennant 2008, 102). On either option—appealing to semantic rules or to the hierarchy of metalanguages of *Logical Syntax*—the inference to (C1) is blocked, and Tarski's argument would be defused.

Thus, this dispute between Tarski and Carnap, as I have reconstructed it, reduces to the question of whether Carnap is entitled to this wider notion of calculation or not: is the replacement of (P2) with (P2$_{Semantics}$) legitimate? This question—'What is calculation?'—has a normative component, like virtually all philosophically interesting questions of conceptual explication. Thus, an indisputable answer is not to be expected. With that caveat stated, we can appropriate one argument for Carnap from *Logical Syntax*: "The [Gödel] sentence, which is analytic but irresoluble in language II, is thus in II$_d$ [the language "which results from II by limitation to the d-rules"] an indeterminate sentence." And "sentences that are indeterminate" are "designated by us as descriptive, although they are interpreted by their authors as logical" in such cases. Carnap says that the same holds for the language of *Principia Mathematica*. And further, he writes: "the universal operator... is a proper universal operator in languages I and II, but in the usual languages—for instance, in [*Princ. Math.*]—it is an improper one..., because these languages contain only d-rules." Thus Carnap comes to the surprising conclusion that "the universal operator in both *Principia Mathematica* and II$_d$ is not logical but descriptive" (Carnap 1934/1937, 231).[8] In short: Carnap holds that a language with only d-rules makes certain 'apparently' logico-mathematical terms (including '$\forall x$') and sentences (such as the Gödel sentence) descriptive or synthetic,[9] but a language with appropriate c-rules as well can classify such terms and sentences as logical or analytic. Carnap's case for a Gödel sentence being synthetic in proof-theoretically characterized languages is straightforward: neither it nor its negation is provable in the formal language. So, Carnap could argue that his wider notion of calculation draws the line between logical and desciptive in the intuitively correct place, since it does not class the universal quantifier and the Gödel sentence as synthetic or descriptive.

After Carnap's syntax period, c-rules are replaced by semantic rules, which play essentially the same role that c-rules did earlier. In a sufficiently rich formalization of arithmetic, a Gödel sentence that intuitively asserts 'This sentence is unprovable' is true in the standard model or intended intereptation of the language in which it is expressed (if the formalization is consistent)–and for Carnap, semantic rules fix a model or interpretation (Carnap 1939, 182). There are non-standard models in which this sentence is false, but in such models the term 'provable' is assigned an interpretation in which it does not correspond to our usual notion of proof. Since Carnap's specification of a language during his semantic period includes fixing the intended interpretation, he can hold that the truth value of a Gödel sentence is determined by the specification of the language in which it is stated, i.e. it is analytic. In sum, in favor of his wider notion of calculation, Carnap could say that an explication that makes the Gödel sentence synthetic fails to match up with the intuitive distinction between mathematical and empirical claims–though Tarski may deny that any such 'intuitive' boundary separates the Gödel sentence from the claims of physical theory.

I do not know of any sections of the Tarskian corpus that could be marshaled to support the narrower, proof-theoretic notion of calculability that Tarski (in the above reconstruction) endorses. Nonetheless, one can adduce arguments in favor of (P2). The current, widely-accepted notion of computability is closer to the narrower conception of calculability, though modern computability is perhaps too narrow even to be a plausible candidate for distinguishing logical from descriptive sentences. But the fact that there is a convergent and almost universally accepted explication of computability may count in favor of understanding calculation as computation, for at least the latter is sufficiently clear by virtually everyone's standards. A second consideration that might be introduced to support the Tarskian viewpoint is subtler, but likely not one Tarski himself would have articulated–in part because it is not, I will argue, compelling in the last analysis.

Consider the following rough but natural line of thought: every genuine, meaningful sentence is couched in some language. Without some form of lan-

---

8. Incidentally, this shows Creath's claim that Carnap would not allow any of the standard logical vocabulary to be descriptive (Creath 1996, 261) is false.
9. Neil Tennant has suggested that the Gödel sentence of a formal theory could be thought of as synthetic, for very similar reasons (Tennant 1997, 294), though he does not fully embrace this suggestion *in propria persona*.

guage to speak or write in, communication and assertion as we know it would be impossible. But any non-trivial[10] language has a consequence relation: given that some set of well-formed formulae are true, the consequence relation indicates which formulae of that language are also true. Part of what makes a given language the particular language it is and not another is its consequence relation: the difference between the language of the intuitionist and that of the classical logician can be clearly seen in their different consequence relations. Both languages contain grammatical strings of the form 'not-not-p,' but only in classical logic is p a consequence of this string. Logically-minded students of language can codify this relation in the form of rules of inference and axioms. We can formulate this basic point within the context of natural language users, as well: if someone makes an assertion in a natural language l, she must in some sense be committed, perhaps only tacitly, to the consequence relation of l[11] (or at least that portion of the consequence relation that bears on that assertion), otherwise she would not make the assertion she does in fact make, but a different one; that is, she would not be speaking l. For example, someone who asserts 'Bob has no siblings' in English also commits herself to asserting that Bob has no brothers, or else she's either contradicting herself or not really speaking English. If someone speaks or writes in l, that person is thereby committed implicitly or explicitly to the sentences that are consequences in l of her utterances—otherwise she would be speaking or writing in some other language. And if one makes an assertion in the logician's proof-theoretic formalization of l (call it l^*), then one is committed at least to the theorems provable from the rules of inference and axioms of l^*.

Now, these sentences made true by the consequence relation of l are not justified in the same way that other assertions couched in l (or l^*) are justified:[12] the theorems and their natural language correlates are 'taken on board' by the very expression of a proposition in l or its formalization. The fact that I express my assertions in l^* constitutes the ultimate justification for the theorems of l^* – though speaking of 'justification' here is misleading, since it is very different from offering evidence. A claim in l^* would not express what it does in fact express, if the theorems of l^* did not hold. This is one way of explaining why, for Carnap and other logical empiricists, mathematics and logic are not susceptible of empirical justification: their warrant comes from being an unavoidable concomitant of the language we use to express anything about the world. In Ian Hacking's apt phrase, describing this fundamentally Tractarian idea, the theorems are 'by-products' of the language we use (Hacking 1979).

Now we have reached the point where a Tarskian can lodge a complaint against Carnap's wider notion of calculability; the complaint will be clearer if applied to the Carnap of *Logical Syntax*, so he will be the immediate target. There,

---

10. A language in which no sentence is a consequence of any other sentence is possible, but trivial.
11. This way of thinking about language in terms of assertion and commitment is ably represented today by Brandom (1994).
12. More fully: they are not justified in the same way, unless Quine's later views on the empirical justification of logic and mathematics are correct.

as mentioned above, Carnap does not identify the analytic truths (i.e., the truths in virtue of calculation) with the sentences provable from the inference rules and axioms of l^*, but rather from the inference rules and axioms of a stronger metalanguage (and metametalanguage, etc.). The previous rationale for sentences we consider 'true by calculation' thereby disappears, for we express ourselves in the object language, not the metalanguage. If we confined ourselves to the inference rules and axioms of the object language l^*, then the only sentences 'true in virtue of calculation' will be the theorems of the object language–which is exactly Tarski's contention. For if a Gödel sentence can be constructed in l^*, then it is of course not a theorem of l^* (assuming l^* is consistent).

However, we can forward a forceful rejoinder on Carnap's behalf. The treatment of sentences 'made true by the consequence relation' in the previous paragraphs had to be presented in a somewhat misleading way in order to make the argument for Tarski's viewpoint. Consequence is standardly taken to be a thoroughly *semantic* notion: 'A is a consequence of B' is usually taken to mean that A is true in every case where B is true. However, consequence was not treated semantically above, since 'sentence true in virtue of the consequence relation' was treated as equivalent to 'theorem'; but this is an inadequate characterization of consequence for any incomplete proof calculus. Now, if we consider the language that we use not merely as a formal proof system, but as endowed with semantic properties, then Carnap's wider characterization of 'true in virtue of calculation' falls out of using a meaningful language ('calculation' may not be the most apposite term, but that is immaterial). Put in terms of language users, if an l-user is entitled or committed to the sentences true in virtue of the consequence relation of l simply by uttering a sentence in l, then the l-speaker is entitled to more than the natural-language correlates of the theorems of that language, if the proof calculus is incomplete. And allowing the l-speaker to draw on that semantic information corresponds to allowing Carnap's wider notion of calculation, viz. truth in virtue of the semantic rules of the language, not Tarski's narrower one. Now, at this point Quine's indeterminacy of translation thesis is salient: for he there denies that such semantic rules should be allowed as a part of the scientifically respectable picture of the world. If he is right, then this Carnapian rebuttal to Tarski is unacceptable. However, if Quine is right about semantic rules' unscientific status, then Tarski's complaint based on the Gödel sentence is the least of Carnap's problems.

5.3. Quine's Disagreements with Carnap circa 1940

5.3.1 Analyticity is an empirical concept, not a logical one

As suggested above (in 4.2), Quine's criticisms of Carnap most likely had not reached fully mature form by 1940. Nonetheless, the seeds had been planted, and the fault lines between the two philosophers began to show. The first public appearance of significant differences between Quine and Carnap is "Truth by

Convention." One of its main arguments, as described earlier, is that the domain of stipulated (conventional, analytic) truths can be expanded indefinitely, with no precise and principled cut-off point. But there is another suggestion, very briefly mentioned in "Truth by Convention," that reappears in a slightly different form in the Harvard discussion notes. This suggestion is developed at greater length in "Two Dogmas", though it is still somewhat inchoate there, and reaches its fully-fledged form in *Word and Object*. Here is the original passage from "Truth by Convention":

> there is the apparent contrast between logico-mathematical truths and others that the former are a priori, the latter a posteriori;... Viewed behavioristically and without reference to a metaphysical system, this contrast retains reality as a contrast between more and less firmly accepted statements; and it obtains antecedently to any *post facto* fashioning of conventions. (Quine 1976, 102)

Quine here claims that if we lack empirical (specifically, 'behavioristic') criteria for identifying the a priori (and thus analytic) sentences, then 'a priori' and 'analytic' are metaphysical terms. That is, analyticity must be cashed out in empirical (synthetic) terms, or else it is just as semantically and epistemically objectionable as God, souls, obscure Heideggerian dicta, and other bits of philosophy that the logical empiricists wished to avoid. That explains why Quine characterizes analytic truths in "Two Dogmas" as claims 'held true come what may': he considers language users' acceptance of claims susceptible to empirical investigation.

Recent commentators have suggested that Quine and Carnap 'talked past' one another a great deal in their debate over analytic truth (George 2000), (Richardson 2003). For example, as just mentioned, Carnap never accepts characterizing the class of analytic truths as the class of sentences held true come what may; thus it is natural to suggest that Carnap and Quine are just operating with divergent definitions, and thus are bound to 'talk past' each other. However, in the Harvard discussion notes, we find a clear statement distinguishing Quine's position from Carnap's along the lines just discussed. The basic distinction can be stated as follows: consider a sentence of the form 'p is analytic.' Carnap thinks such sentences are analytic, while Quine believes they are synthetic, so their truth-value must be determined by empirical/observational means.[13] This appears in the context of the group's attempt to develop a notion of L-truth suitable not just for mathematics, but for empirical science as well. As an example of an empirical term, they use 'T' to refer to temperature (at a spacetime point).

> *Tarski*: The physicist chooses certain sentences as conditions that a proposed claim about T must satisfy, in order to be assumed as (logically) correct, before experiments about the truth are made. [Such sentences include: 'every atomic sentence involving 'T' must have exactly five

---

13. Thus what follows is further evidence for the view attributed to Ricketts above in 5.2.1. It is also partial evidence against Robert Hudson's heterodox view that Carnap draws the analytic/synthetic distinction partly on empirical grounds (Hudson 2010).

arguments' (four spacetime coordinates and one scalar for the temperature)]

Quine: It is then the task of a behavioristic investigation to determine what conditions of this kind physicists set up.

I: No, that would give only the corresponding pragmatic concept. As with all other semantic (and syntactic) concepts, here also the pragmatic concept gives only a suggestion, and is not determined univocally. (090-16-10)

This quotation shows that Quine considered the question 'Which claims are analytic?' to belong to empirical investigation (specifically, a 'behaviorist' study).

This, in turn, shows why Quine pursues accounts of analyticity and synonymy in *Word and Object* and elsewhere, a fact that might otherwise appear perplexing, given Quine's reputation as the hero who has slain the analytic/synthetic distinction. The point illustrated by the above quotation clears up this potential perplexity: the Quinean notions of 'stimulus synonymy' and 'stimulus analyticity' in *Word and Object*, and the definition of 'analytic' in terms of language learning in *Roots of Reference*, are explicitly and thoroughly *empirical* notions–thus they are scientifically respectable and intelligible. As Quine writes a few years after the Harvard discussions:

> the meaning of an expression is the class of all the expressions synonymous with it... The relation of synonymity, in turn, calls for a definition or a criterion in psychological and linguistic terms. Such a definition, which up to the present has perhaps never even been sketched, would be a fundamental contribution at once to philology and philosophy. (Quine 1943a, 120)

Exactly such a psycho-linguistic criterion is, of course, spelled out at length in *Word and Object*. Quine expresses a similar sentiment a few years later:

> Synonymy, like other linguistic concepts, involves parameters of times and persons, suppressible in idealized treatment: the expression x is synonymous with the expression y for person z at time t. *A satisfactory definition of this tetradic relation would no doubt be couched, like those of other general concepts of general linguistics, in behavioristic terms.*.. So long, however, as we persist in speaking of expressions as alike or unlike in meaning (and regardless of whether we countenance meanings themselves in any detached sense), we must suppose that there is an eventually formulable criterion of synonymy in some reasonable sense of the term. (Quine 1943b, 44; my emphasis)

Here again, we see that Quine thinks synonymy must be at bottom (in non-'idealized' cases) given a behavioristic account, just like other linguistic concepts.

A final note about this difference between Carnap and Quine: Quine held Carnap's view in his 1934 "Lectures on Carnap": "Analytic propositions are true by linguistic convention. But... it is likewise a matter of linguistic convention which propositions we are to make analytic and which not" (Creath 1990, 64). So for a time in the mid-thirties, presumably ending with "Truth by Convention" at the latest, Quine thought it perfectly acceptable to consider a sentence of the form 'p is analytic' (i.e., p is true by convention) to be itself analytic (true by convention). In short, Quine's view on this matter was once Carnap's.

While we now have a clear formulation of one difference between Quine and Carnap–a difference that persisted, it appears, for the rest of their careers–it is much less clear whether there is a well-posed question in the vicinity of this disagreement over whether 'p is analytic' is itself analytic or not. Why? To put the point in a Carnapian manner, it may be analogous to asking: 'Which is correct: pure geometry or applied geometry?' However, the Quinean could presumably respond to this characterization of the question as follows: 'A given mathematical system wouldn't deserve the name "geometry" at all, if it did not admit of an interpretation involving spatiotemporal magnitudes in the empirical world.' Perhaps the best we can do here is to indicate possible reasons motivating each view. As a rationale for Carnap's view that analyticity should be treated as an analytic concept, we can point to most people's willingness to adopt the formalizations of other syntactic and semantic concepts. That is, Gödel showed how to formalize the predicate 'provable' within number theory, thereby showing that the concept of provability is just as logico-mathematical as addition, conjunction, etc. Analyticity is of course not in general co-extensive with provability, but, to put the point in Carnap's terminology, every statement provable in a formal calculus is analytic in any interpretation that makes the axioms of the calculus true and its rules of inference truth-preserving. Furthermore, for Carnap, and especially the Carnap of *Logical Syntax*, the concept of analyticity is an generalization of the notion of theorem. Thus, since 'provable' is a logico-mathematical predicate, and analyticity is intended as a generalization of provability, this strongly suggests 'analytic' is a logico-mathematical predicate as well. This conclusion would be bolstered by Tarski's demonstrating how to define 'true in L' in a purely logico-mathematical way, given the expressions of L and names for the expressions of L.[14] (For one might wonder whether, even if provability is a logico-mathematical notion, truth might not be.) Since analytic truth is a species of truth, Tarski's work lends further plausibility to notion that analyticity, like truth, can be treated as a logical concept by scientifically-minded philosophers.

What motivates Quine's view that analyticity should be considered an empirical concept? One rationale appears in the quotation from "Truth by Convention" at the beginning of this subsection: the actual pattern of human acceptance of claims 'obtains antecedently to any *post facto* fashioning of conventions.' The same idea appears in the "Lectures on Carnap" as follows: "in any case, there are more and less firmly accepted sentences prior to any sophisticated system of thoroughgoing definition" (Creath 1990, 65). If 'antecedently' and 'prior to' are construed temporally, then this is obviously true, since a theory always

---

14. See Frost-Arnold (2004) for evidence that Tarski considers his analysis of truth to be logico-mathematical instead of empirical or 'physicalist,' as Hartry Field (1972) suggests.

post-dates its subject: the physical behavior of falling apples and the Earth's tides occurred long before Newton proposed his law of universal gravitation. Thus Quine presumably has something akin to conceptual precedence or priority in mind. Conceptual priority can be a thorny notion; however, we can locate the sense Quine attaches to this notion. In both "Lectures on Carnap" and "Truth by Convention," Quine appeals to the explanatory fiction of having a list of all sentences currently accepted as true in front of us. The sentences on this list that we accept so firmly that we would not reject them under any circumstances, Quine says, are those that can or should be declared true by convention (Creath 1990, 65). The way we select which sentences to elevate to analytic status via stipulation, for Quine, is by finding exactly those sentences that would never be abandoned. So the sense of conceptual priority at issue comes at least to this: if there are no irrevocable sentences, then there are no analytic sentences. And Quine suggests, in the closing section of "Two Dogmas" (though not in "Truth by Convention") that the antecedent of the preceding conditional is true. As mentioned earlier, Carnap denies Quine's claim that all analytic sentences are irrevocable; during a scientific revolution such as the transition from Newtonian to relativistic physics, the analytic truths of the language of physics change (put otherwise, the language of physics changes): the theorems of Euclidean geometry that make ineliminable use of the parallel postulate switch from being analytic to synthetic.

Elsewhere in Quine's writings, the conceptual priority of firmness of acceptance over analyticity is couched in even stronger terms. Quine declares the notion of Carnapian analyticity to be considered artificial, in a pejorative sense. In "The Problem of Interpreting Modal Logic," when explaining how 'No spinster is married' can be taken as analytic, on the grounds that it is a definitional abbreviation of a logical truth, Quine writes:

> I should prefer not to rest analyticity thus on an *unrealistic fiction* of there being standard definitions of extra-logical expressions in terms of a standard set of extra-logical primitives. What is rather in point, I think, is a relation of synonymy, or sameness of meaning, which holds between expressions of *real* language though there be no standard hierarchy of definitions. (Quine 1943b, 44; my emphasis)

Quine had already privately made a similar point in a 1943 letter to Carnap:

> A common answer... is to say that 'No spinster is married' is a definitional abbreviation of a logical truth, 'No woman not married is married.' *Here we come to the root of the difficulty: the assumption of a thoroughgoing constitution system*, with fixed primitives and fixed definitions of all other expressions, *despite the fact that no such constitution system exists.* (Creath 1990, 296; my emphasis)

In the letter he writes in reply, Carnap responds directly to Quine's worry about the apparent need to set up an elaborate system of definitions in order to capture the notion of analyticity or L-truth. Carnap points out that, on his view of language, what is needed to capture the notion of an analytic truth is just a semantic system, that is, a Carnapian interpreted language (Creath 1990, 305). The semantic rules (assuming they adequately model standard English) would suffice to guarantee the synonymy of 'spinster' and 'unmarried woman,' even if both were primitive predicates in the language, so definitions are unnecessary. But Carnap still assumes the existence of a semantic system, which Quine would likely consider just as artificial and/ or unreal as a list of definitions or a constitution system.

5.3.2 Quine rejects modal languages

Quine famously holds that if a concept is to be scientifically respectable, then it must be extensional. But analyticity (and necessity) are clearly non-extensional: though 'World War II ended in 1945' and 'World War II ended in 1945 or it did not end in 1945' have the same truth-value, ' "World War II ended in 1945" is analytic' is false, while ' "World War II ended in 1945 or it did not end in 1945" is analytic' is true. In the Harvard conversation notes, Quine approves of a particular proposal for a definition of L-truth, by saying: "Thus we avoid 'state of affairs,' intensional language, and the unclear concept 'logically-possible' " (090-16-10). Carnap's preferred explication of analytic truth at the time was 'true in all states of affairs,' i.e. 'true in all logically-possible cases.' Though this is the only record in the 1940-41 notes of Quine's disapproval of these three interrelated concepts, he was hostile towards intensional languages in general, and modal language in particular, his entire adult life (Quine 2001).

There is abundant evidence of this well-known fact; I will briefly rehearse some of the evidence. First, Quine claims to have been an extensionalist from his college days at Oberlin, and was disappointed that his teachers at Harvard did not share this viewpoint, especially the logically-inclined ones such as Lewis, Sheffer, or his thesis advisor Whitehead (Quine 1991), (Quine 2001). For example, In "Three Grades of Modal Involvement," Quine writes: "In mathematical logic... a policy of extensionality is widely espoused: a policy of admitting statements within statements truth-functionally only" (Quine 1976, 162). Second, Quine reports that the aim of his dissertation was to "reworked the foundations of *Principia Mathematica* in purely extensional terms" (Quine 1991, 266). Third, in one of his first publications, 1934's "Ontological Remarks on the Propositional Calculus" (written when Quine was still Carnap's 'disciple'), Quine argues that the intensional concept of proposition is obscure and unscientific. Finally, Quine argued vehemently against quantified modal logic from the 1940s onwards in print, declaring it unclear, unintelligible, and/or nonsense.[15] Quine's suspicions concerning modality and intensional languages are manifest in the 1940-41 discussions as well, as we saw in the previous paragraph.

---

15. Current commentators on the analyticity debates often side against Quine's antipathy to modal locutions, and not merely because possible-worlds talk is more fashionable amongst philosophers today. Sober (2000) and Stein (1992) both point out that, in our current best natural sciences, modal language is apparently indispensible—and Quine of course holds that there is no higher court of epistemological appeal than our current best scientific theories.

The connection to Quine's increasing skepticism toward the notion of analyticity is clear. For example, for a portion of ordinary English formalized using Carnap's suggestion, the extensions of 'bachelor' and of 'unmarried man' are identical in every L-possible world or state of affairs. And Carnap forwards precisely this characterization of synonymy in the Harvard notes: e.g. two predicates are synonymous in a language (i.e., they designate one and the same property) if and only if, in every possible world, the two predicates are coextensive (102-63-07). Incidentally, this shows that Quine's 'No entity without identity' complaint against properties (and intensional items more generally) relies essentially upon Quine's prior rejection of the modal notion of a logically possible situation or state of affairs. For Carnap has provided, by 1941, an identity-condition for two properties: a property is an extension for each L-possible world, so two properties are identical if, in each L-possible world, they are coextensive. Once Carnap attempts to spell out 'analytic' in modal terms–as he does after taking his semantic turn–Quine's hackles are raised, and the notion that seemed somewhat suspicious to Quine in "Truth by Convention" becomes, in this new intensional form, fundamentally unacceptable. It is interesting that in "Two Dogmas," Quine does not seriously consider Carnap's newer characterization of analyticity in terms of states of affairs, but focuses primarily on Frege-analyticity, which Carnap did not endorse then. One plausible explanation for Quine's passing over Carnap's then-current characterization of analyticity in terms of L-possible worlds/states of affairs is that Quine considered using such notions as the starting point of analysis irredeemably faulty: an attempt to explain the somewhat obscure by the very obscure. Quine says the latter in print: "The notion of analyticity... is clearer to many of us, and obscurer surely to none, than the notions of modal logic" (Quine 1943b, 45). This would explain why, in "Two Dogmas," Quine does not spill much ink attacking the characterization of analyticity Carnap prefers in the 1940s: after Carnap switches to an intensional analysis of analyticity, Quine regards all Carnap's further forays as non-starters. This suggests that the radicalization of Quine's critique of Carnap is prompted, at least in part, by Carnap's shift to intensional approaches to the study of language.

5.3.3 Quine prefers syntactic analyses to semantic ones

Furthermore, speaking generally, Quine is not as impressed as Carnap by semantic approaches to logico-linguistic issues, and prefers syntactic analyses of language. However, Quine's attitude towards semantics (at least, towards what Quine calls the 'Theory of Reference' as opposed to the irredeemably intensional 'Theory of Meaning') is *far* less antagonistic than his attitude toward intensional idioms. For example, Quine accepts Tarski's notion of satisfaction and the resultant definition of truth. However, Quine is not the unequivocal booster of even extensional semantic methods (typified today in classical model theory) that Carnap is. First, very generally, as Decock has noted, "it is quite remarkable that Quine has spent unaccountably little attention to model theory... One can even trace a slight contempt for the methods of model theory" (Decock 2002,

162) (see references there for evidence). This stands in direct contrast to Carnap in the 1940s, who explicitly states that the proof-theoretic view of language is derivative upon or secondary to the semantic one in many respects (Carnap 1942, §39). Furthermore, a few months after the 1940-41 conversations ended, Quine delivered a lecture to Boston University's Philosophy Club, in which he suggested that the semantic program that Tarski brought to prominence had not lived up to its hype:

> I feel that many of the most prominent claims that have been made for semantics are as yet unwarranted. I can't see that any really objective, scientific progress along semantic lines has been made in connection with such supposedly semantic topics as: meaningfulness, protocol sentences, analytic vs. synthetic sentences, indicative vs. expressive use of language. Perhaps progress will be made on some of these topics; but I can think of nothing that I would point to as a definitive semantical accomplishment. (Quine papers, Folder 3058)

Clearly, Quine has not given up on Tarskian semantics in 1941, and he never rejects it, as he does modal language. However, he is far less impressed with the program than Carnap is; apparently not even Tarski's seminal "On the Concept of Truth in Formal Languages" counts as a 'definitive semantical accomplishment' in Quine's eyes.

This general Quinean outlook shows up clearly in remarks Quine makes about logical truth. For example, in a December 1940 lecture, Quine says: " 'Logically true' can be defined syntactically... This is *more elementary* than the semantic characterization with the help of 'true' " (RCC 102-63-04; my emphasis). What is this syntactic characterization? Quine still holds it thirty years later, in *Philosophy of Logic*: "we can simply define a logical truth as any sentence produced by these rules of proof" (Quine 1970, 57), where 'these rules' refers to any set of complete rules for first-order logic, of the sort found in a logic textbook. This is somewhat surprising to contemporary sensibilities: today, most people think that the 'more elementary characterization' of logical truth is semantic— for how could logical truth be a type of *truth*, if it is not semantic? Similarly, in his textbook *Mathematical Logic*, Quine writes: "standards of logical truth can be formulated in terms merely of more or less complex notational features of statements; and so for mathematics more generally" (Quine 1940/1958, 4). So the meanings conferred upon notational features need not be considered when attempting to discern whether a given sentence is a logical (or mathematical) truth.

Although the above texts show that Quine strongly prefers proof-theoretic approaches to semantic ones, someone might reasonably object that elsewhere, Quine does use other formulations of logical truth besides the completely syntactic one just described. In "Truth by Convention" and "Two Dogmas," Quine uses 'truth' in the *definiens* when defining 'logical truth.' There, Quine gives the following definition of logical truth: "If we suppose a prior inventory of logical particles, comprising 'no', 'un-', 'not', 'if', 'then', 'and', etc., then in general a logical truth is a statement which is true and remains true under all reinterpretations of its components other than the logical particles" (Quine 1951, 23). (This is known as the *substitutional* characterization of logical truth; it is usually contrasted with the model-theoretic one, which states that a formula is logically true if and only if that formula is true in all models.) Now, when Quine compares all three various notions of logical truth in *Philosophy of Logic*, he favors the substitutional definition over the model-theoretic one.[16] However, he *also* favors the purely proof-theoretic view, in which a logical truth is just a theorem, over the substitutional characterization, again calling the former "more elementary" (Quine 1970, 57). This is clear evidence that Quine prefers syntactic analyses to semantic ones, at least in the case of analyzing 'logical truth.' So although Quine uses the substitutional characterization in various places, the all-things-considered view of logical truth that he prefers is "independent of the notions of truth and satisfaction" (Quine 1970, 57). To repeat, Quine certainly does not completely reject the notion of truth (or even model theory), as he unreservedly rejects modal and other intensional idioms. However, unlike Carnap, he does not embrace it, and he does without it when possible.

5.3.4 The development of Quine's critique, II: Carnap's changes

These facts suggest another historical conjecture about the development of Quine's critique of analyticity. Quine's view in 1940 about how language should be analyzed is quite close to Carnap's in *Logical Syntax*, six years previous: in that book, Carnap's analysis of every logical characteristic (analyticity included) is declared to be extensional, and avoids talk of meaning. In *Syntax*, Carnap declares he subscribes to the "thesis of extensionality," which states: "a universal language of science may be extensional" (Carnap 1934/1937, 245).[17] Furthermore, Carnap considered intensional language suspect, on the grounds that many sentences couched within it are quasi-syntactic, misleadingly stated in the 'material mode' (Carnap 1934/1937, 246). Finally, Carnap's extensionalism predates the *Syntax*: in the *Aufbau*, he declares that the logical value of a sentence is its truth-value alone (Carnap 1928/1963, 84). Contrast this claim with what Carnap says to Nelson Goodman in 1940, in a conversation about Goodman's dissertation: "My objection against my *Aufbau*:... the extensional conception: definition of qualities etc. by enumeration" (102-44-11), which is of course Quine's preferred approach. Quine's public and private view of how language should be analyzed around 1940 (as well as before and after) is very similar to Carnap's view in *Logical Syntax*; but it is rather different from the explicitly intensional and semantic viewpoint Carnap advocates from 1939's *Foundations* onward. Thus, Quine's break

---

16. Why? "The evident philosophical advantage of resting with this substitutional definition, and not broaching model theory, is that we save on ontology" (Quine 1970, 55).
17. Actually, the type of extensionalism found in *Syntax* is non-standard, since Carnap disallows the notion of truth there, and extensionality is usually characterized in terms of truth: two linguistic expressions have the same extension iff they are intersubstitutable *salva veritate*. A language (or language fragment) L is extensional iff substitution of co-extensive expressions in L never changes any expression's extension.

with Carnap over analyticity can be seen as due to Carnap changing his position as much as Quine changing his: Carnap moves towards an intensional, semantic approach to language analysis, while Quine retains the more extensional approach exhibited in *Logical Syntax*. For example, in the 1934 "Lectures on Carnap," in expounding Carnap's notion of quasi-syntactic utterances, Quine writes: "It is in sentences dealing with reference, mention, meaning, denotation that we must be on our guard; also in modal sentences, both logical and empirical" (Creath 1990, 101). In *Logical Syntax*, Carnap specifically attacks "sentences about meaning" in §75, and explains how to translate suspicious, "quasi-syntactic" intensional language (including the language of modalities) into scientifically hygienic extensional language in §§68-70. In subsequent decades, Quine's guard stays up against intensional language, while Carnap relaxes his.

Interestingly, Quine hints at just such a development of the situation in his "Homage to Carnap," quoted earlier:

> Carnap was my greatest teacher. I got to him in Prague 38 years ago [from 1970, so 1932], just a few months after I had finished my formal studies and received my Ph.D. I was very much his disciple for six years. In later years *his views went on evolving* and so did mine, in divergent ways. (Creath 1990, 464; my emphasis)

Note first that Quine says Carnap's 'views went on evolving.' Part of that evolution, as we have seen, is Carnap's willingness to pursue research on intensional languages. Thus it could be that in Quine's estimation the Harvard discussions played an important role in ending Quine's discipleship under Carnap. More generally, it is possible that Quine sees Carnap's move away from the *Syntax* program as a turning point: Quine read the manuscript of Carnap's *Introduction to Semantics* for the University of Chicago Press in 1940 (Creath 1990, 291), in which Carnap freely uses intensional idioms. In short, the radical critique of analyticity that Quine advocates by 1950 is perhaps as much a product of Carnap changing his views (towards fundamentally intensional, specifically modal approaches, away from exclusively extensional ones) as Quine changing his.

Once Quine's hero commits to spelling out 'analytic' in a modal idiom, he considers Carnap's current characterization of analyticity unacceptable. Quine rejects Carnapian analyticity from 1940 onwards, so his 'discipleship' is presumably over at this point. More speculatively, this move on Carnap's part may have led Quine to be more skeptical of *any* characterization of analytic truth that purports to do heavy epistemological lifting. Why? Seeing the best and brightest (in Quine's eyes) defender of analyticity say that analyticity is intensional and semantic could have further inclined Quine to think no scientifically acceptable characterization could be found. Note that this is a rather indirect influence: the fact that Carnap embraces an intensional account of analyticity from 1940 onward of course does not demonstrate that no account of analyticity could satisfy Quine's various philosophical scruples. But if you are somewhat skeptical about some claim p, and the person you consider world's leading expert on that issue comes forward and states that p really means that pigs can fly, your skepticism about p will likely increase. Of course, you could still believe that there is an alternative understanding of p that does not require flying pigs, and work to find such an interpretation; but in light of the expert's testimony, you might be less optimistic about finding such an interpretation. Analogously, the notion that Quine considered somewhat suspicious in "Truth by Convention" becomes even less appealing, after the great Carnap comes to view analytic truth in much the same way as C. I. Lewis did, a way Quine found unacceptable from his student days onward.[18] However, to repeat, this point is somewhat speculative. (The distinction between Quine's attitudes towards Carnapian analyticity vs. analyticity *tout court* loom large below, in 5.3.5.) [19]

In "Truth by Convention," Quine does not connect worries about analyticity to his distaste for intensional (and especially modal) languages; this is likely because in 1936 he believes that Carnap's preferred explanation of analyticity will be syntactic and extensional. In the discussion notes, Carnap clearly characterizes synonymy as modal: as quoted earlier, two predicates are synonymous if and only if they have the same extension in all possible worlds (102-63-07). This would rankle Quine, who believes 'necessary' is a more "obscure" term than 'analytic' (Quine 1943b, 45), and accordingly the notion of analyticity should be used to explain the notion of necessity, not conversely (Quine 1943a, 121). In the 1941 notes, Quine clearly rejects intensional language in general, and modal language in particular, but he does not yet appear to believe that synonymy of the sort Carnap needs in order to do heavy epistemological lifting has to be cashed out in intensional language.

This brings us to a final question about the historical development of Quine's critique of analyticity. We have seen above that, in a December 1946 lecture, Quine still believed that the task of explicating the notion of analyticity was a 'real' and 'meaningful problem' that was 'worth working on.' What further steps did Quine need to take before he adopted the opposite view? I lack the evidence needed to answer this question conclusively, but I do have two suggestions. First, neither the 1941 discussions, nor Quine's 1946 lecture, nor any earlier text, discusses the argument about synonymy that appears in §3 of "Two Dogmas." There, Quine suggests that a language must contain modal idioms in order to use an interchangeability-*salva-veritate* standard to distinguish between expressions that are truly synonymous and expressions that are merely have the same extension. Perhaps Quine did not think the type of synonymy needed to underwrite an epistemologically useful notion of analyticity was unavoidably modal (as Carnap had in the Harvard discussions) until the late 1940s, and this later realization pushed Quine away from considering the characterization of synonymy to be a project that could yield rewards for the epistemology of mathematics and logic.

---

18. Daniel Isaacson appears to suggest that this is part of Quine's distancing himself from Carnapian analyticity as well (Isaacson 2004, 233-35), though Isaacson holds that this is an "accidental reason" for their later divergence (Isaacson 2004, 238).
19. An anonymous referee greatly improved the line of thought in this paragraph.

Second, one of the most important reasons for appealing to the notion of analyticity is to make sense of the *prima facie* special epistemological status of logic (and mathematics, for logical empiricists and their intellectual allies) within an empiricist framework. Carnap saw this as a, if not the, leading insight of logical empiricism: all substantive knowledge had its source in experience (thereby preserving empiricism), but the claims of math and logic are, in an important sense, empty or non-substantive. That is, they are unavoidable by-products of the language scientists choose to use. Quine always viewed himself as a good empiricist, and perhaps he clung to hope for an eventual clarification of analyticity well into the 1940s in part because he saw no other way for an empiricist to account for the apparently special status of logic and mathematics. (Recall that in "Truth by Convention," Quine says that logic and mathematics are a priori, although he understands 'a priori' behavioristically there.)

In "Two Dogmas," however, Quine finally presents an alternative explanation for the felt difference between the truths 'If grass is white, then grass is white' and 'Over 2 million people live in New York City on January 1, 2010.' This explanation is absent from Quine's criticisms of analyticity in the 1930s and 40s, including the December 1946 lecture mentioned above, which covers many of the same critiques found in "Two Dogmas." In the final section of "Two Dogmas," Quine appeals to the principles of conservatism and simplicity in theory choice to explain why logic and mathematics are felt to be so different from physics and history. Rejecting *modus ponens*, unlike rejecting our estimate of the number of inhabitants of New York City, would likely require a massive overhaul of our sciences, and would most likely complicate our theories of the world horribly. Thus, we are very reluctant to make such a change. By invoking these principles of conservatism and simplicity, we no longer need the notion of analyticity to account for the *prima facie* specialness of logic and mathematics;[20] the type of analyticity Carnap considers essential for understanding the relationship between logico-mathematical inquiry and the natural sciences becomes superfluous to our account of scientific activity, and thus such analyticity should be eliminated. (Of course, on Quine's "Two Dogmas" view, mathematics and logic are not genuinely epistemologically different in kind from natural science; Quine's principles of simplicity and conservatism only explain why they *appear* or *feel* different.) Before his appeal to conservatism and simplicity, no matter how unhappy Quine might have been with extant accounts of analyticity, perhaps he could not see how scientific philosophy could account for the apparently distinctive features of logic and mathematics without some notion of analytic truth. But once Quine found an explanation of this appearance that satisfied him, he gave up trying to find an

---

20. Hylton stresses this point as well. He writes: "Quine appeals to...a 'Maxim of Minimum Mutilation'...to explain why logic and mathematics are often...taken to be a priori and necessary." Hylton then quotes Quine: "We prefer to seek an adequate revision of some more secluded corner of science, where the change would not reverberate so widely through the system. This is how I explain...the inaccessibility of mathematical truth to experiment, and it is how I explain its aura of a priori necessity" (Hylton 2007, 78).

epistemically weighty explication of analytic truth, and thereby opened the way for the view expressed in "Two Dogmas."

5.3.5 *When* did Quine finally break? Creath vs. Mancosu

Suppose the account of the development of Quine's critique of analyticity that has been presented above in 4.2 and 5.3.4 are correct; that is, suppose "Truth by Convention" does not contain the thoroughgoing departure from Carnapian ideas found in "Two Dogmas," and that the 1940-41 conversations did play an important role in radicalizing Quine's critique of analytic truth. A further question to ask is: when exactly did Quine make the fundamental break(s)?

Richard Creath claims that Quine's final rejection of analyticity does not come until 1947, in the context of his three-way correspondence with Goodman and Morton White (Creath 1990, 31). Further, this break occurs only after a slow, gradual disillusionment with the notion of analytic truth that had been building for years: "Quine arrived at that break [viz., his "reject[ion of] Carnap's doctrine that there are analytic truths"]...*only by stages*" (Creath 1990, 31; my emphasis).

Paolo Mancosu has challenged Creath's view of the trajectory of the Quinean attack on analyticity. After presenting historical evidence demonstrating Tarski had been challenging the analytic/synthetic boundary and the unrevisability of logic from 1930 onwards, Mancosu says: "[t]his, however, raises the question of when exactly Quine arrived at the criticism of the analytic-synthetic distinction" (Mancosu 2005, 331). To phrase the question in terms of 'arriving at the criticism' of analyticity may be somewhat prejudicial against Creath's view, since he wishes to portray Quine's criticism as slowly developing and changing over time; on his view, there is no particular moment at which Quine 'arrives' at his critique, since it is a slow evolution. (Additionally, since Quine offers a number of arguments against analyticity, we should perhaps not speak of '*the* criticism' of analyticity.)

But we can set these concerns aside by re-phrasing Mancosu's question as 'When did Quine arrive at the radical rejection of analyticity found in "Two Dogmas"?' Creath, as mentioned above, claims that it was in the summer of 1947, in the three-way correspondence with Goodman and Morton White. Mancosu argues that it was earlier. He offers as evidence a letter from Quine to Woodger, dated May 2, 1942, in which Quine discusses the 1940-41 academic year.

> Carnap, Tarski and I had many vigorous sessions together, joined also, in the first semester, by Russell. Mostly it was a matter of Tarski and me against Carnap, to this effect. (a) C's professedly fundamental cleavage between the analytic and the synthetic is an empty phrase (cf. my 'Truth by Convention'), and (b) consequently the concepts of logic and mathematics are as deserving of an empiricist or positivist critique as are those of physics. In particular, one cannot admit predicate variables (or class variables) primitively without insofar committing oneself to 'the reality of universals.' (Mancosu 2005, 331)

Mancosu believes this letter shows that "already in 1940-1941 Quine had explicitly rejected the notion of analyticity, and in 1942, he considered that rejection to be already in his 1936 paper 'Truth by Convention'" (Mancosu 2005, 331). In short, Mancosu, unlike Creath, believes that Quine's rejection of analyticity was complete long before 1947–rather, by 1942 at the latest. Mancosu does not commit to a position concerning whether this completion comes in 1936, 1940-1941, or some other particular time.

Which picture of Quine's path to the rejection of analyticity is correct, Creath's or Mancosu's? The historical evidence, as we have seen, appears to pull in opposite directions. One could accept Creath's picture and try to explain away all the apparently disconfirming evidence, such as Quine's 1942 letter to Woodger. Or one could adopt Mancosu's position, and attempt to explain away why Quine continues to use the concept of analyticity (albeit reluctantly) throughout the 1940s, such as the December 1946 lecture quoted above in which Quine states, concerning the problems of adequately explicating 'analytic': "my attitude is not one of defeatism, nor one of dismissing the problem as illusory. We have real problems here, meaningful problems worth working on." Alternatively, one could attempt to steer a middle course, and that is the route I will attempt here.

I propose that we make sense of the apparently conflicting pieces of evidence as follows. Quine's letter to Woodger indicates that by 1942 Quine had rejected Carnap's preferred contemporaneous explication of analyticity. However, Quine still thought the notion might eventually be acceptably clarified along non-Carnapian lines: specifically, along empirical, extensional, and hopefully syntactic lines, as opposed to Carnap's a priori, modal, and semantic characterization. This would explain the otherwise puzzling fact that Quine spends relatively little time in "Two Dogmas" dealing directly with Carnap's 1950 view: Quine had abandoned Carnap's preferred characterization of analytic truth several years earlier, around the time of the Harvard discussions, and thus Quine focused in "Two Dogmas" on what he considered more promising or plausible alternatives, such as Frege-analyticity.

This hypothesis provides a *tertium quid* between Creath and Mancosu's views: Quine had completely rejected Carnap's contemporary attempts to explicate analytic truth by 1942 (at the latest), but he was not yet willing to commit himself to the radical view of "Two Dogmas" until shortly before writing that piece, because he held out hope that an acceptable explication could be found. However, certain important parts of Quine's eventual "Two Dogmas" position are already present in "Truth by Convention." Specifically, that (i) on the 'linguistic fiat' explication of analyticity, the class of analytic truths can be indefinitely expanded, and (ii) analyticity must ultimately be cashed out in empirical terms. For this reason, it makes sense that Quine points to "Truth by Convention" in retrospect as providing reasons for his dissent. So Creath may well be right that Quine's mature critique of analyticity, which claims that no coherent characterization of analyticity can do heavy epistemological lifting, does not surface until 1947, while Mancosu is correct that Quine had rejected Carnap's then-current account of analytic truth by 1942 at the latest, in the immediate aftermath of the 1940-41 discussions at Harvard.

Chapter 6
Overcoming Metaphysics through the Unity of Science

A desire to unify human knowledge is both ancient and abiding. Plato, in the seventh book of the *Republic*, suggests that all knowledge is somehow derived from or based upon the Form of the Good. Two millenia later, Descartes' *Rules for the Direction of Mind* stresses the value and importance of developing a universal system of *scientia*. Related discussions continue today: reductionist and anti-reductionist philosophers working in various fields disagree about whether particular domains of knowledge can be unified in their claims, methods, or concepts. The logical empiricists also made the unity of science a central plank of their party platform. A second essential plank of their platform is their antipathy toward metaphysics;[1] this, too, is neither unique to nor original with the logical empiricists. Hume, for example, famously recommended committing metaphysical writings to the flames, and the logical empiricists themselves explicitly acknowledge their historical predecessors in the struggle against metaphysics.[2] And the anti-metaphysical drive is not yet departed: in van Fraassen's *The Empirical Stance*, it is alive and well (van Fraassen 2002).

To most current philosophers, these two topics–the unity of science and the aversion to metaphysics–likely appear *prima facie* rather different. However, the central contention of this chapter is that these two ideas are intimately intertwined in the writings of many logical empiricists. Close attention to the writings of central logical empiricists on the unity of science and the elimination of metaphysics reveals that, metaphorically speaking, these goals are two sides of the same coin. More prosaically, in different logical empiricists, from the 1920s through 1950, we find the following criterion (or an approximation thereof) for detecting metaphysics: an apparently meaningful utterance is metaphysical if and only if it cannot be incorporated into 'unified science' [*Einheitswissenschaft*]. I will focus on Carnap and Neurath, for they wrote most extensively on both the unity of science and the avoidance of metaphysics, and their work is prominent

---

1. Michael Friedman has argued that 'overcoming' is the best term for the logical empiricists' aim with respect to metaphysics (Friedman 2000).
2. Schlick writes: "the denial of metaphysics is an old attitude... for which we can in no way claim priority" (Schlick 1978, 492). Carnap echoes this sentiment: "Anti-metaphysical views have often been put forward in the past, especially by Hume and the Positivists" of the nineteenth century (Carnap 1934/1937, 280).

among both their peers and modern scholars re-evaluating logical empiricism. To conclude, I present an objection to this criterion for identifying metaphysics.

How is this related to previous chapters? Well, one may ask, what is the *point* of undertaking Tarski's project of reconstructing arithmetic within a language of strictly nominalist science, i.e., a language of science that does not countenance the existence of abstracta? As suggested in 2.2, part of the motivation for pursuing this finitist-nominalist project is to purge any noxious metaphysical elements from the language used by scientists, including mathematical language. But why would revising mathematical language (and mathematics itself) achieve that anti-metaphysical end? Because for Carnap and his intellectual allies, the distinguishing mark of a metaphysical claim is (to a first approximation) that it cannot be incorporated into unified scientific language. The burden of the present chapter is to argue for this last assertion.

6.1. Unity of Language, Not Laws

The 'Unity of Science' movement was spearheaded by Otto Neurath and embraced by other logical empiricists.[3] The philosophers associated with the official movement founded the *International Encyclopedia of Unified Science* and organized a series of international conferences, beginning in Paris in 1935. These philosophers were also directly responsible for the journal *Erkenntnis*, whose original English title was *The Journal of Unified Science*. The ideas driving the official movement played role, albeit less direct, in the early activities of *Synthese*: the first sentence of its first issue is "Ours is a time of synthesis," i.e., of unification. During the forties, *Synthese* regularly included articles under the series title 'Unity of Science Forum.'

What did the logical empiricists mean by the phrase 'unity of science'? The unity that the logical empiricists speak of is *not* unity of laws or theories, but rather unity of *language*. This point is increasingly recognized in recent scholarship (Creath 1996), so I will not attempt a complete justification of this claim. Nonetheless, I devote this section to an abbreviated elaboration and defense of this contention. First, to be explicit, Carnap, Neurath, and others stress repeatedly that their thesis is not that the results of biology, psychology, sociology etc. can (or will) be ultimately derived from a single fundamental theory (presumably physics).[4] Thus the logical empiricists of the 1930s unequivocally do not endorse

---

3. To avoid misunderstanding, it should be noted that the Unity of Science movement was not merely a group of advocates for the unity of science thesis. The movement's complex social and political aims are discussed in Reisch (2005).
4. However, commentators nonetheless saddle logical empiricists in general, and Carnap in particular, with this view. Even Thomas Uebel, who usually provides helpful correctives to the stereotypical caricatures of the *Wienerkreis*, appears to succumb to this view of Carnap: "The second large-scale difference between Carnap and Neurath concerned the unity of science. Against the *hierarchy of reductively related theories*, Neurath put a much looser conception of unity...Neurath may well have felt that the supposition of a *reductive hierarchy of special sciences with physics at the base* was just a bit too counterfactual" (Uebel

the kind of 'unity of science' found in (e.g.) "The Unity of Science as a Working Hypothesis" (Oppenheim and Putnam 1958). Rather, the logical empiricists aim to construct a language that can simultaneously express biological, psychological, social, and physical claims. Carnap emphasizes that the reduction of (e.g.) biological laws to chemical or physical laws is an open question: "there is at present no unity of laws... On the other hand, there is a unity of language in science, viz., a common reduction basis for the terms of all branches of science" (Carnap 1938, 61). Neurath's views are similar. He does not demand a unity of laws; as a social scientist, he stresses the autonomy of sociological laws: "Comprehensive sociological laws can be found without the need to be able... to build up these sociological laws from physical ones" (Neurath 1983, 75).

Neurath is more antagonistic than Carnap to this unification of theories or laws. Neurath claims that a desire to fit all knowledge into a single Procrustean bed constitutes a fundamental error of Cartesian and Leibnizean rationalism, and he stresses that the model for unified science is not an axiomatic system, but an encyclopedia: the claims of an encyclopedia, unlike the claims of a system, are not all derivable from a few precise axioms. For example, in the first article in the *International Encyclopedia of Unified Science*, Neurath (the Encyclopedia's editor-in-chief) writes: "the great French Encyclopedia," whose work his new Encyclopedia continues, "was not a '*faute de mieux* encyclopedia' in place of a comprehensive system, but an alternative to systems" (Neurath 1938, 7; cf. 2, 16, 20). This rejection of the single axiomatized system of knowledge in favor of a loosely connected encyclopedia is a *leitmotif* running throughout Neurath's corpus; it is expounded at length in his 1936 piece "Encyclopedia as 'Model'."

What the logical empiricists' unified science requires is not a unity of laws, but something weaker: unity of language. We saw Carnap explicitly state this immediately above; he also emphasizes this distinction in "Psychology in Physical Language": "This question of the deducibility of the laws [of psychology from the laws of inorganic physics] is completely independent of the question of the definability of concepts" (Carnap 1932/1959, 167). For Neurath as well, the crucial kind of unity is linguistic: "We can use the everyday language which we use when we talk about cows and calves throughout our empiricist discussions. This was for me the main element of 'unity' " (Neurath 1983, 233). Philipp Frank provides perhaps the simplest formulation of the unity of science thesis: "there is one and the same language in all fields" of science (Frank 1947, 165). Maria Kokoszynska, who visited the Vienna Circle from Lvov, offers a very similar characterization: "Every scientific sentence can be expressed in one and the same language" (Kokoszynska 1937-38, 326).[5] In *Logical Syntax*, Carnap offers

2001, 214-15; my emphasis). Carnap does not commit to theories' being 'reductively related,' though he does commit to languages being so related. He consistently maintains that law reduction is possible, but that it remains an "open question" (Carnap 1932/1959, 167).

5. Kokoszynska's central contention in this article is an interesting challenge to the unity of science thesis in this standard formulation. Tarski showed in 1933 that, for a given language L (and given a number of relatively natural assumptions) 'true-in-L' is not de-

the following more precise characterization of the thesis: every sub-language of science can be translated without loss of content into one language (Carnap 1934/1937, 320).

The next question is: which languages fit this description? Many logical empiricists agree that the physicalist language does. In *Logical Syntax*, Carnap states that the thesis of physicalism is precisely that the physicalist language can successfully serve as an overarching language for all of science.[6] Carnap defends this thesis most extensively in "*Die Physikalische Sprache als Universalsprache der Wissenschaft*" [The Physicalist Language as the Universal Language of Science], translated into English two years after its initial publication under the non-literal title *Unity of Science* (Carnap 1932/1934). Neurath provides a detailed description of his version of the physicalist language, which he often calls 'Universal Jargon.' It is not restricted to the vocabulary of physics. Neurath describes his Universal Jargon as "an everyday language that avoids certain phrases and is enriched by certain other phrases" (Neurath 1983, 208); specifically, it 'avoids' metaphysical terms, and 'is enriched' by technical terms of the special sciences (Neurath 1983, 91-92). Carnap characterizes the physicalist language as one whose sentences "in the last analysis... express properties (or relations) of space-time domains" (Carnap 1934/1937, 151). Neurath makes similar claims: for someone who uses the physicalist language, "in his predictions he must always speak of entities in space and time" (Neurath 1983, 75). But the 'properties' and 'entities' of biology, chemistry, geology, and (at least) much of psychology and sociology are spatiotemporal, so the language of physicalism is much richer than the language of physics alone. Note that the languages meeting Tarski's (FN 1-4) can be thought of as one kind of physicalist language, in that they completely disallow words referring to abstracta, which are usually conceived of as entities existing outside the spatiotemporal realm.

Although Carnap and Neurath hold that the physicalist language can serve as the language for unified science, they do not maintain that no other language could. For example, in the *Aufbau*, Carnap holds that both the phenomenal,

---

finable in L, on pain of contradiction. However, 'true-in-L' is definable in the metalanguage of L. Kokoszynska's contention is that the sentences of Tarski's metamathematics should count as scientific, so she sees his work as potentially disproving the unity of science thesis: not all scientific sentences can be incorporated into a single language. Neurath demurred (Neurath 1983, 206-8). Much more historical detail and analysis concerning Kokoszynska's interactions with Neurath (and Carnap) concerning Tarski's theory of truth can be found in Mancosu (2008a). Neurath and Carnap's disagreements over the legitimacy of semantics are discussed in Reisch (2005, ch. 10).
6. Carnap writes:
> The thesis of *physicalism* maintains that the physical language is a universal language of science—that is to say, that every language of any sub-domain of science can be equipollently translated into the physical language. From this it follows that science is a unitary system within which there are no fundamentally diverse object-domains, and consequently no gulf, for example, between natural and social sciences. This is the thesis of the *unity of science*. (Carnap 1934/1937, 320)

'autopsychological' language and the physical[7] language could function as languages for unified science. And Neurath writes: "We expect that it will be possible to replace each word of the physicalist ordinary language by terms of the scientific language—just as it is also possible to formulate the terms of the scientific language with the help of the terms of ordinary language" (Neurath 1983, 91). This shows that the 'physicalist ordinary language' is not the only language that Neurath thinks can unify science, since he 'expects' that the technical 'scientific language' will be able to do so as well. However, it should be noted that Neurath sometimes appears to privilege the physicalist language over others: "Unified science contains only physicalist formulations" (Neurath 1983, 54); "[p]hysicalism is the form work on unified science takes in our time" (Neurath 1983, 56). Perhaps Neurath considers the physicalist language best for his purposes, even if not unique. And in 1932, the year after Neurath publishes these remarks, Carnap claims that the physicalist language is the only one currently known to suffice for this purpose of unifying scientific languages.

Additionally, the logical empiricists' unity of science thesis is not refuted by Suppes' observation that the actual terminology used in various sub-disciplines of the sciences is increasingly divergent, with each subfield developing its own jargon (Suppes 1978, 5). Other scholars have already noted that Neurath's and Carnap's unity of science theses do not claim to provide a descriptive account of extant scientific language and practice (Creath 1996). In fact, in §41 of the *Aufbau*, Carnap appears to accept Suppes' position: "as far as the logical meaning of its statements is concerned, science is concerned with only one domain... On the other hand, in its practical procedures, science does not always make use of this transformability [of statements into one domain] by actually transforming all its statements" (Carnap 1928/1963, 70). Carnap, in his most extended defense of the unity of science thesis (Carnap 1932/1934), argues only that the various languages of science *could* be connected in principle, not that they are so connected in everyday scientific practice (if they were, there would be no work left for the *Wissenschaftslogiker* working in the service of the unity of science). In sum, the logical positivists' unity of science thesis, especially as articulated and advocated by Carnap and Neurath, asserts that there exists a language in which all (scientific) knowledge can be couched, but not that this language is actually used, on a day-to-day basis, by scientists.

Finally, one more vision of the unity of science from a logical empiricist sympathizer will be briefly mentioned. One of the most interesting expressions of a unity of science thesis can be found in J. H. Woodger's programmatic "Unity through Formalization":

---

7. Carnap speaks of the 'physical language' in the *Aufbau*, not of the physical*ist* language. This terminological difference is of little consequence; for the 'physical language' in the *Aufbau* is either nearly identical to the (later) physicalist language, or a proper subset of the physicalist language. See Uebel (2007, 134–37) for details about the origins of the term 'physicalism' and its shifting meanings over time and between thinkers.

> some day all the major branches of empirical science may be formalized... the several sciences would differ from one another only in the empirical constants which occur in them... This, then, would be one way, and perhaps the only way, in which a real unity of science could be achieved; and an encyclopedia of the sciences would then consist of lists (with elucidations) of the fundamental constants with cross-references to the axioms in which they occur. (Woodger 1937, 164-65)

Woodger's basic idea is to reformulate all the results of science within the language of *Principia Mathematica* (or another equally rich formal language), and then provide interpretations for the language's non-logical constants. This is precisely what Woodger himself attempts to do for portions of biology and neurology in his *Axiomatic Method in Biology* (Woodger 1937) and *Biology and Language* (Woodger 1952). Note that on Woodger's picture, we again have a unity of language, but not a unity of laws: new empirical constants could be introduced at the level of biology, psychology, or sociology. However, Woodger's vision of a unified science differs from that of Carnap and Neurath outlined above in that Woodger does not explicitly place special stock in the physicalist langauge. He criticizes the physical (not physicalist) language, but does not consider his criticisms absolutely decisive (Woodger 1952, 278, 310).

6.2. Overcoming Metaphysics

The logical empiricists are (in)famous for adopting an anti-metaphysical stance. All the major figures in the group, as well as many of their patron saints, railed against metaphysics. But how exactly did the logical empiricists purport to identify and excise perniciously metaphysical concepts and claims? This question becomes especially pressing if one agrees with Michael Friedman's assertion that "metaphysical neutrality rather than radical empiricism...is...the essence of Carnap's position" (Friedman 1999, 110). Alan Richardson also puts this point strongly: "if there is one defining feature of Carnap's philosophy, it is the claim that both science and philosophy can be done in a way that is neutral with respect to the traditional issues of metaphysics" (Richardson 1992, 45). Such claims need not be restricted to Carnap; metaphysical neutrality was a major, if not fundamental, goal for virtually all leading logical positivists.

How do the logical empiricists purport to expunge metaphysics from science? The stereotypical view, promulgated in Ayer (1959), is that the logical empiricists eliminate metaphysics via a comprehensive application of the verificationist criterion of meaning. This view has already been discounted in Richardson (1992, 59) and, less directly, in Creath (1982). I shall argue that the verificationist criterion of meaning does play a role in some logical empiricist rejections of metaphysics, but its role is a partial one. Thus, focusing exclusively upon it leads to a fundamentally incomplete and therefore distorted image of the logical empiricists' attack on metaphysics. A more complete picture of the logical empiricists' anti-metaphysical project requires keeping their unity of science thesis fully in view. Roughly put, one criterion separating meaningless metaphysics from cognitively significant discourse that holds over several decades for many logical empiricists is the following:

(M) An apparently declarative sentence or apparently descriptive term is *metaphysical* if and only if that (apparent) sentence or term *cannot be incorporated into a total language of science*.

For the logical empiricists, failures of incorporation into unified science usually come in two varieties: a metaphysical claim is either (i) ungrammatical, or (ii) grammatical but inferentially isolated from the rest of scientific language (in a sense to be elaborated presently).

I must stress that (M) is an idealization. No formulation so brief can fully and accurately characterize the logical empiricists' views on metaphysics and unity of science, for the historical situation is fairly complex. Different logical empiricists hold somewhat different views, and a single thinker's ideas about metaphysics often shift over time. Furthermore, the *bi*conditional (M) usually does not appear in the texts as such. Rather, a given logical empiricist virtually always uses only one direction of implication at a time, even though that thinker is committed to both directions, and might use the other direction elsewhere in the same work. So, (M) should be understood as a slogan, from which actual, fuller formulations deviate to a greater or lesser degree, and not as a complete account of logical empiricists' views on the relation between metaphysics and unified science.

The next task, then, is to present a more complete and detailed account of the logical empiricists' rejection of metaphysics across several texts. By examining several variants of (M), we can determine to what extent (M) captures a basic element of logical empiricist thought, and also see what historical nuances and complexities (M) elides. In what follows, I focus on Carnap. More than any other logical empiricist, Carnap works out detailed positions on both the unity of science and the rejection of metaphysics.[8] I then show that Neurath's texts support attributing (M) to him as well, though his expression of the rejection of metaphysics lacks the fine-grained particulars of Carnap's.

6.2.1 *Aufbau*

Let us begin with Carnap's treatment of metaphysics in the *Aufbau*. How does Carnap identify metaphysics there? Carnap discusses the concepts of essence, reality, and the mind-body connection (among others), and concludes that each, if taken in their customary sense, is metaphysical. Each of these purported concepts is deemed metaphysical on the grounds that it cannot be incorporated into any 'constructional system' [*Konstitutionsystem*] of the sorts Carnap describes in

---

8. Schlick writes a good deal about the rejection of metaphysics, but does not discuss the unity of science in much detail; Neurath writes a great deal on the unity of science, but his explanations or justifications for rejecting metaphysics are not as sustained as Carnap's.

the *Aufbau*. We can phrase Carnap's criterion for metaphysics in the *Aufbau* as follows:

(M_{Aufbau}) An apparent sentence is metaphysical if and only if it contains concepts that cannot be constructed in a constructional system.

This connection between non-constructability and metaphysics is clear in Carnap's treatment of the metaphysical 'problem of reality' (i.e., is there an observer-independent reality?):

> The concept of reality (in the sense of independence from cognizing consciousness) does not belong within (rational) science, but within metaphysics. This is now to be demonstrated. For this purpose, we investigate whether this concept can be constructed, i.e., whether it can be expressed through objects of the most important types which we have already considered, namely, the autopsychological, the physical, the heteropsychological, and the cultural. (Carnap 1928/1963, 282)

To show that a concept is metaphysical, it must be shown that that concept cannot be constructed from *any* basic objects–not just from phenomenal, 'autopsychological' ones, but also from physical, heteropsychological, and cultural basic objects. The mind-body problem (in Carnap's terms, the 'parallelism' between mental states and brain states) is similarly unconstructable:

> The question for an *explanation of these findings* [viz., that mental state tokens and brain state tokens can be placed in a one-to-one correspondence–G.F.-A.] *lies outside the range of science*; this already shows itself in the fact that this question cannot be expressed in concepts that can be constructed;... (This holds for any such constructional system and not only for a constructional system of our specific kind.) Rather, the quest for an explanation of that parallelism belongs within metaphysics. (Carnap 1928/1963, 270-71)

The above parenthetical remark indicates that, for Carnap, constructability is a more fundamental criterion than verifiability in determining whether a concept or claim is metaphysical, for presumably the 'specific kind' to which Carnap refers is the constructional system with autopsychological basis. That is, what makes a (pseudo-)concept metaphysical is not whether it can be cashed out in terms of certain first-person conscious experiences, but rather whether it can be incorporated within any constitution system–even one which takes physical or cultural objects as basic.[9] Other metaphysical concepts are shown to have the same property; none can be incorporated into a constructional system.

---

9. If one accepts Carnap's claims in the *Aufbau* that (1) everything that can be said in any construction system can be said in an autopsychological one, and that (2) all concepts can be defined in terms of the autopsychological basis, then 'Concept C cannot be cashed out (defined) in terms of sense experience' will be equivalent to 'C cannot be incorporated into a constructional system.'

Finally, two significant differences between (M_{Aufbau}) and Carnap's later characterizations of metaphysics should be noted: first, in the *Aufbau*, Carnap thinks primarily in terms of concepts; sentences are secondary. Second, the *Aufbau* lacks the claim that many metaphysical sentences are ungrammatical. This idea, drawn from Wittgenstein's *Tractatus*, does not come to prominence in Carnap's writings until after the *Wienerkreis* reads the *Tractatus* intensively together in 1930.

6.2.2 "Overcoming Metaphysics through the Logical Analysis of Language"

Carnap's most focused attack on metaphysics is "Overcoming Metaphysics through the Logical Analysis of Language" Carnap (1932/1959). Here Carnap clearly draws the distinction, described above, between the two kinds of pseudo-sentences that cannot be incorporated into the language of science: (i) ungrammatical strings of symbols, and (ii) grammatical 'sentences' whose terms cannot be connected to the meaningful terms and sentences of the language. I shall deal with each in turn. Carnap begins "Overcoming Metaphysics" by noting that there have been several attempts throughout the centuries to abolish metaphysics from the intellectual landscape. However, he claims that "only" with the "development of modern logic" can "the decisive step be taken" in this pursuit (Carnap 1932/1959, 61). Why? Carnap's justification is that an apparent sentence (even if it contains only meaningful words) is meaningless, i.e. metaphysical, if it cannot be expressed in a logical language of the form found in *Principia Mathematica*. This is why Carnap claims the 'development of modern logic' is essential to overcoming metaphysics: we pick out metaphysical sentences by finding those strings of symbols which appear meaningful, but whose content cannot be expressed in the logical language of the *Principia*.[10] This conception of metaphysics is fundamentally Tractarian: whatever cannot be expressed grammatically in the ideal symbolic language of the *Tractatus* is meaningless metaphysics. Carnap and Neurath explicitly state that their view on the elimination of metaphysics in the early 1930s "was in essentials that of Wittgenstein" (Carnap 1934/1937, 322); see also (Neurath 1983, 54).

This anti-metaphysical strategy is exemplified by one of Carnap's criticisms of Descartes' 'I think, therefore I am.' Carnap claims that the statement 'I am' (or 'Greg Frost-Arnold is,' assuming 'Greg Frost-Arnold' is treated as an individual constant in this sentence's language) cannot be put into the language of classical predicate logic: the concept of existence in the modern logic of Russell and Whitehead's *Principia* is not a predicate, but an operator that acts upon formulae. Thus Carnap claims it is impossible, in such a language, to express that an individual in the domain of discourse exists *simpliciter*: one can only say either '$\exists x P x$' or 'Pa' (in the usual notation), but the string of symbols '$\exists a$' is not an admissible

---

10. Alan Richardson has stressed this idea: "The universal applicability and expressive power of the new logic does all the serious work in the rejection of metaphysics" (Richardson 1998, 26–27).

sentence (Carnap 1932/1959, 74). Carnap concludes that Descartes' assertion is meaningless, since it cannot be expressed in the language of *Principia*.[11] Any other sentence that cannot be expressed in Russell and Whitehead's logical symbolism is also declared meaningless, such as Heidegger's '*Das Nichts nichtet*': Carnap points out that in formal logic, 'nothing' is represented as a concatenation of the negation-sign and an existential quantifier, but Heidegger's sentence treats it as a substantive, which would be represented as an individual constant in the language. And, of course, one cannot (grammatically) place the string '$\neg \exists x$' into an object-variable position of a sentence.

So much for Carnap's account of metaphysical sentences; when is an apparently meaningful term metaphysical, i.e., meaningless? Carnap takes us on a brief detour through sentences, for a term is shown to be meaningless by showing that atomic sentences containing that term are meaningless. He asserts that the question "What is the meaning of [an atomic sentence] S?" is equivalent to each of the following two questions:

(1.) What sentences is S deducible from, and what sentences are deducible from S?

(2.) Under what conditions is S supposed to be true, and under what conditions false?

(Carnap 1932/1959, 62)

Here again we find a version of (M). In this instance, a sentence (and thereby each of its constituents) is shown to be meaningful by placing it within a larger inferential network: (1.) characterizes the network syntactically or proof-theoretically, (2.) characterizes it semantically. The unified language of science provides this inferential network. Grammatical strings that cannot be placed within such a network of scientific claims (e.g. 'God is benevolent'), Carnap maintains, contain metaphysical terms. Which particular term(s) in such a sentence are the metaphysical ones? For a given term t (either a name or a predicate), t is metaphysical if and only if no atomic sentence containing t can be incorporated into the unified language of science. For example, in 'God is male,' 'God' is metaphysical though 'male' is not, for no sentence of the form 'God is F' can be incorporated into the unified language of science, though sentences of the form 'x is male' can be. And the restriction to *atomic* sentences is necessary, because 'God is benevolent' entails 'God is benevolent or water boils at 100 degrees Centigrade,' and is entailed by 'God is benevolent and mammals have hair'; but Carnap wants 'God is benevolent' to count as metaphysical. This view is highly reminiscent of the unconstructable concepts of the *Aufbau*. But, one may wonder, what guarantees that *any* sentences in the larger inferential network are meaningful? Couldn't we construct a network of meaningless words?

---

11. I do not know why Carnap would not allow '$\exists x(x = \text{Greg})$' to express the colloquial 'Greg is' or 'Greg exists'; this is the usual way of expressing the existence of individuals in first-order logic today.

To solve this problem, Carnap appeals to the verificationist criterion of meaning. Carnap states that 'What is the meaning of S?', and hence questions (1.) and (2.) above, are also equivalent to "(3.) How is S to be *verified*?" (Carnap 1932/1959, 62). For Carnap in 1932, this question is answered by specifying the inferential relations between S and the " 'observation sentences' or 'protocol sentences.' It is through this reduction that the word acquires its meaning" (Carnap 1932/1959, 63). However, Carnap explains, the specific nature of the protocol sentences is irrelevant to the elimination of metaphysics: "For our purposes we may ignore entirely the question concerning the content and form of the primary sentences (protocol sentences)": they could deal with "the simplest qualities of sense" (as in Mach), "total experience and similarities between them" (as in the *Aufbau*), or simply "things" (Carnap 1932/1959, 63). Furthermore, in "On Protocol Sentences," Carnap states that which sentences are protocol sentences is a matter of decision (Carnap 1932/1987).[12]

Carnap's claim that a word 'acquires its meaning' through its entailment relationships to observation sentences indicates that Carnap is making the following two assumptions. First, there exists some set of privileged sentences whose meaningfulness is uncontroversial, assumed, or somehow otherwise guaranteed; this set is the protocol sentences. Second, an arbitrary atomic sentence S is meaningful only if S is non-trivially inferentially related to this other set of sentences. Metaphorically, the meaningfulness of the semantically privileged sentences 'filters up,' via inferential relations, to S. These two assumptions about meaning might be called 'semantic foundationalism': just as an epistemic foundationalist holds that there are 'unjustified justifiers' that function as the ultimate source for all claims' justification, a semantic foundationalist holds that there are sentences and/or terms that function as the ultimate source of meaning for all sentences.[13] We can only arrive at the full-fledged verification criterion of meaning (as well as the liberalized empiricist meaning criteria which appear later[14]) by adding to these two assumptions of semantic foundationalism a third: observation sentences (and/or terms) are members of the set of semantically privileged sentences (and/or terms).

We can now see more clearly the respective roles empiricist meaning criteria and a unified language of science play in eliminating metaphysics. Verificationist meaning criteria sanction treating the observational sentences and terms as uncontroversially meaningful. Once we have that assumption, then to determine

---

12. The evolution of Carnap's views on the role and nature of protocol sentences, and their interaction with contemporaneous ideas, is well-catalogued in Uebel (2007).
13. Uebel also sees the protocol language, viz. the language of observation reports, playing a such a role: "Since these primitive protocols remained the termini of the testing of all other statements, this primitive protocol language *provides the basis for all linguistic understanding*" (Uebel 2007, 246; my emphasis).
14. The difference between the earlier, verificationist criterion of meaning and the later, liberalized ones (e.g. in "Testability and Meaning") is that the verification criterion requires that every meaningful atomic sentence is entailed by some set of (possible) observation sentences, whereas later criteria allow weaker logical relations to hold between the observation sentences and other meaningful sentences.

whether a given sentence is meaningful, we must determine whether it is properly inferentially related to the semantic foundation. But from whence are these inferential relations drawn? They are supplied by the unified language of science. If we have a total language of science in which the observational terms and sentences are properly inferentially related to the rest of the scientific language, then all scientific claims are guaranteed to be meaningful. Furthermore, the assumption that certain sentences are uncontroversially meaningful offers a solution to the problem, mentioned above, of constructing an inferential network of meaningless strings. In short, Carnap needs both an empiricist criterion of meaning and a total language of science in order to eliminate all metaphysical claims while preserving all cognitively significant ones: the meaning criterion guarantees that the entire inferential network will not be a meaningless fairy tale, and the unified language of science, shows the sentences of physics, biology, and psychology to be meaningful, by connecting the terms of the individual sciences to the semantically privileged sentences.[15]

6.2.3 *Logical Syntax of Language*

As Carnap's philosophical views change over his career, so too does his characterization of what is metaphysical. In 1934, *Logical Syntax* appears, and with it a slightly modified program for eliminating metaphysics. We find the same basic ideas as in "Overcoming Metaphysics," but with an added wrinkle: the principle of tolerance. In *Logical Syntax*, what counts as metaphysical becomes (to a degree) language relative, as follows:

> (M_{LSL}) An apparently declarative sentence or apparently descriptive term is metaphysical with respect to a language of science L if and only if that (purported) sentence or term cannot be incorporated into L

where 'incorporation' is understood in terms of logical relations, as before.

Carnap describes how the strategy of the anti-metaphysical program must be altered somewhat in order to accommodate the principle of tolerance:

> The view here presented [in accordance with the principle of tolerance] allows great freedom in the introduction of new primitive concepts and new primitive sentences in the language of physics or the language of science in general; yet at the same time it retains the *possibility of differentiating pseudo-concepts and pseudo-sentences* from real scientific concepts and sentences, *and thus of eliminating the former*. This elimination, however, is not so simple as it appeared to be on the basis of the earlier position of the Vienna Circle... On that view it was a question of "the language" in an absolute sense; it was thought possible to reject both concepts and sentences if they did not fit into the language. A newly stated P[hysical]-primitive sentence is shown to be a pseudo-sentence if either no sufficient rules of formation are given... or no sufficient

---

15. Conversations with Jon Tsou greatly improved the preceding two paragraphs.

rules of transformation by means of which it can...be submitted to an empirical test. (Carnap 1934/1937, 322)

Carnap holds that we can still avoid metaphysical pseudo-concepts and pseudo-sentences, even if we adopt the principle of tolerance and thereby reject the notion that there is a single 'correct' language. As in "Overcoming Metaphysics," the 'sentences' that are ungrammatical as well as those apparently descriptive sentences that cannot be tested (i.e. inferentially connected with observation reports) are deemed metaphysical pseudo-sentences. So while there might be more than one acceptable language of science, traditional metaphysical concepts will nonetheless still be excluded, for they will not occur in any language of science, even though they might appear in some other, non-scientific language.

But one might press the efficacy of this anti-metaphysical method as follows: 'You, Carnap, have said that there is an element of convention even at the level of the protocol sentences (Carnap 1932/1987): we can use one or another, and neither is correct or incorrect. But if protocol sentences are semantically foundational, and if the protocol language is conventionally chosen, then it appears that theology *could* re-appear: one simply needs to choose a set of semantically foundational sentences that use (e.g.) the vocabulary of spiritual revelation.' This objection is related to contemporaneous criticisms leveled at Carnap by Neurath and Zilsel, who ask: what remains of empiricism, once even the protocol-sentence language becomes a matter of freely chosen convention (Uebel 2007, 273-75)?

Carnap could resist this objection, and I believe working through this Carnapian response reveals something interesting about the principle of tolerance along the way.[16] The degree of tolerance Carnap allows in the choice of protocol language is *much* more limited than the 'boundless ocean of possible languages' that the principle of tolerance entitles the pure logician to explore. Why? Because protocol sentences must be *observation reports*. The element of convention, according to Carnap, extends to the *form* such reports take: Machian sense-impressions, the *Gestalt* experiences of the *Aufbau*, or the everyday language of physical things, championed by Neurath. Carnap never says that an arbitrary sentence can be turned into a protocol sentence merely by choosing it to be one; a protocol sentence must be a report resulting from observations. Carnap gives an (admittedly rough) account of what makes a linguistic expression observational in "Testablility and Meaning" (Carnap 1936-37, 454). Statements prompted by revealed spiritual experience would not count as observational reports.

Is it reasonable to hold, with Carnap, that what counts as metaphysics is language relative? If we think of metaphysics as nonsense, as the Vienna Circle and Wittgenstein do, then which sentences are labeled 'metaphysical' *should* be

16. Thomas Uebel has a thorough discussion of this interchange (Uebel 2007). The following response is based on "Testability and Meaning," published four years after Neurath and Zilsel's concerns were raised. Carnap's response in 1932 is very interesting: "those statements or written documents (as physical-historical structures) will be designated as 'real protocol statements' that issue from the people of our cultural circle, especially scientists...There is no other distinguishing criterion for 'our' science than the historical one that it is the science of our cultural circle" (Uebel 2007, 273).

indexed to a particular language—for what is meaningful in one language often will not be in another. Let us examine a Carnapian example to illustrate and make plausible the claim that metaphysics could be considered language relative. Consider Languages I and II of *Logical Syntax*: Language I, intended to capture the mathematical intuitionist's point of view, is weaker than Language II, which is expressively rich enough to capture all of classical analysis. Thus, there are sentences that are grammatical in II, but ungrammatical in I, and hence metaphysical from the point of view of someone using Language I. For example, a sentence about so-called unconstructable real numbers would qualify on Carnap's proposal as a metaphysical pseudo-sentence in I, but not in II. Now, intuitionists *do* find something suspect about the unconstructable numbers of classical mathematics, and some would be inclined to call claims about such entities 'metaphysics.' Heyting, expressing the intuitionist viewpoint, writes: "If 'to exist' does not mean 'to be constructed,' it must have some metaphysical meaning" (Heyting 1971/1983, 67). As a second example of the language-relativity of metaphysics, consider the relation between first-order and higher-order logics, much discussed in the 1940-41 conversations: any sentences of second-order logic containing higher-order predicates would, in first-order logic, be metaphysical on Carnap's criterion. And as we have seen above in 2.2, philosophers who find second-order logic suspicious call its quantification over properties 'Platonism', choosing a notorious metaphysician as its namesake. Thus Carnap's suggestion that what one counts as metaphysics depends on the language one uses is borne out in these actual examples. In sum, in *Logical Syntax*, the general means of identifying metaphysics is the same as in Carnap's earlier works, but it is modified to accommodate the principle of tolerance.

6.2.4 "Empiricism, Semantics, and Ontology"

In 1950's "Empiricism, Semantics, and Ontology," Carnap's basic idea for distinguishing metaphysics from acceptable forms of discourse is essentially the same as in earlier decades. However, the terminology has shifted: instead of speaking of constructional systems or languages, Carnap now speaks of linguistic frameworks. But here again, a claim is shown to be non-metaphysical by incorporating it into a (pragmatically) acceptable linguistic framework.

> [T]he concept of reality...in internal questions is...[a] scientific, *non-metaphysical* concept. To recognize something as a real thing or event means to succeed in *incorporating it into the system of things... according to the rules of the framework*. (Carnap 1956a, 207; my emphasis)

The importance of a shared scientific language for identifying metaphysics also recurs here. It is on precisely these grounds that Carnap criticizes philosophers who ask the 'external' question "Are there numbers?":

> Unfortunately, these philosophers have not given a formulation of their question in the common scientific language. Therefore...they have not

succeeded in giving the external question cognitive content. (Carnap 1956a, 209)

And questions without 'cognitive content' are metaphysical. Thus, Carnap's attitude towards metaphysics in 1950 is very closely related to his view in the twenties; linguistic frameworks replace *Konstitutionsysteme*, but the basic strategy for identifying and eliminating metaphysics remains the same.

6.2.5 Neurath

So much for Carnap's views on metaphysics; what of Neurath's? He eschews Carnap's formal, precise languages in favor of his 'universal jargon' or 'universal slang,' which is based on everyday language instead of the language of the exact sciences,[17] and is modeled on the structure of an encyclopedia instead of an axiom system (Neurath 1938, 2, 7, 16, 20), (Uebel 2007, 223*ff.*): in 1936's "Encyclopedia as Model," he writes that "we 'fix up' the empirically given protocol statements a little, without however going so far as 'formalizing' the common language" (Uebel 2007, 152). However, Neurath shares the fundamental idea we have seen in Carnap: an apparently meaningful sentence or term is metaphysical if and only if it cannot be incorporated into unified science.[18] First, let us consider the 'only if' direction: "If it [a proposed scientific sentence] is... meaningless–i.e., metaphysical–then of course it falls outside the sphere of unified science" (Neurath 1983, 58).[19] For Neurath, perhaps even more than for Carnap, unified science is identified with physicalism: "physicalism is the form work in unified science takes in our time" (Neurath 1983, 56). Thus we find assertions such as the following: "If we systematically formulate everything we find in non-metaphysical formulations, we get nothing but physicalist formulations" (Neurath 1983, 73). This differs from Carnap, at least through 1932, since Carnap thinks a non-physicalist language could play the role of a language of science (Uebel 2007, 442).

Neurath explicitly articulates the 'if' direction of the biconditional (M) as well:

> statements that through their structure or special grammar could not be placed within the language of the encyclopedia–in general 'isolated' statements... are statements 'without meaning in a certain language'. For these statements the Vienna Circle has often used the term 'metaphysical statements'. (Neurath 1983, 161)

Note that Neurath mentions the strictures against both ungrammatical and otherwise isolated apparent sentences. As an example of an ungrammatical (and hence

---

17. Carnap, exhibiting his usual tolerance, allows Neurath's proposed physicalist language as a possibility (Uebel 2007, 357).
18. See Uebel (2007, chs. 6–7) for similarities and differences between Neurath and Carnap's physicalisms, as well as for how Carnap's views migrated towards Neurath's during the late 1920s and early 1930s.
19. See also Neurath (1983, 54, 57, 61, 73, 173).

metaphysical) assertion, Neurath offers Kant's categorical imperative. Neurath characterizes it as "a command without a commander," and thus as "a defect of language"; furthermore, such linguistic defects have no place in a language of unified science: "[a]n unblemished syntax is the foundation of an unblemished unified science" (Neurath 1983, 54). Unfortunately, Neurath does not spell out criteria for what counts as a 'blemish' in a language's syntax; he apparently defers to his more logically-inclined colleagues in this matter. In general, where Carnap employs a constitution system or a linguistic framework, Neurath uses an encyclopedic language based on everyday communication instead; but otherwise, their views are very close.

Recall the notion of 'semantic foundationalism' mentioned above (6.2.2): a sentence's meaningfulness is demonstrated by showing that it is connected via inferential relations to sentences whose meaningfulness is given. Carnap identifies these semantically privileged sentences as the protocol or observational ones (though, as we saw, he was willing in 1932 and after to leave open the particular form such sentences take). Neurath, it appears, takes a slightly different set of sentences as antecedently meaningful. Neurath repeatedly states that a language of unified science should take as its starting point everyday language, with minor corrections. Why? One possible reason is that everyday language is (by and large) meaningful if any language is; everyday language would be the most indisputable case of a meaningful language. We are more committed to the meaningfulness of everyday language than any other, since other, more technical vocabulary is 'built on top' of everyday language. Thus, if we have to pick a 'semantic foundation,' everyday language seems most likely the best we can do.[20] (There are other reasons Neurath starts with everyday language: he values the democratization and popularization of scientific knowledge,[21] and he is suspicious of any framework that aims to break free of our present historically given situation–which includes our language–and view the world *sub specie aeternitatis*.)

Neurath's writings make it clear that, for him, a central aim of unifying science is the demolition of barriers between the scientific study of nature [*Naturwissenschaften*] and of the mind [*Geisteswissenschaften*]. Thus, one might allege that my focus on the anti-metaphysical drive misses this aspect of his thought entirely. I certainly concede that Neurath repeatedly and unequivocally urged the value of breaking down these disciplinary barriers. But, interestingly, Neurath claims that the motivation underlying the separation of the sciences is *metaphysical*. As his program is realized,

> each basic decomposition of unified science is eliminated... for example, that into 'natural sciences' and 'mental sciences'... The tenets with

---

20. George Reisch discusses similar matters (Reisch 2005, 114, 177).
21. "A Universal Jargon... would be an advantage from the point of view of popularizing human knowledge, internationally and democratically... [It] seems to me something fundamentally anti-totalitarian" (Neurath 1983, 237).

which we want to justify the division are... always of a metaphysical kind, that is, meaningless. (Neurath 1983, 68)[22]

So, according to Neurath, the assertions used to justify the existence of insuperable boundaries between *Geisteswissenschaft* and *Naturwissenschaft* are metaphysical. If the various sciences were unified, then any such assertion would be ruled out. Thus, unified science, which shows disciplinary barriers are not insuperable, eliminates a certain kind of metaphysics. Specifically, Neurath says, it eliminates any theory that purports to deal with "a special sphere of the 'soul' " (Neurath 1983, 73), distinct from the remainder of the spatiotemporal world. Carnap makes a similar point in "The Task of the Logic of Science," though he characterizes the mental/material division as motivated by "mythological" and "divine" motives, and does not explicitly use the word 'metaphysical' (Carnap 1934/1987, 58-59), though theology is often considered a branch of metaphysics. Unification of the sciences may be valuable for its own sake, but it also serves to eliminate metaphysics.

6.3. A Difficulty: What *Cannot* Be Incorporated into a Language of Science?

As I have argued, a concept or sentence is metaphysical if it cannot be integrated into any unified language (or constitution system, or linguistic framework, etc.) adequate for science. The central and pressing problem for such an account of metaphysics is: how do we know which concepts and claims can be incorporated, and which cannot? The answer to that question will determine what is metaphysical and thus in need of excision from our scientifically respectable language. Let us focus first on the *Aufbau*. When Carnap gets down to the details of showing how essences and theses about the mind-body problem cannot be formulated in any constitutional system, he offers more assertions than arguments.[23] For example, Carnap simply asserts that "essence," taken in its "metaphysical" sense, cannot be constructed in the autopsychological constitution system of the *Aufbau* or in any other constitution system (Carnap 1928/1963, §161).

Carnap's treatment of the mind-body problem is similar, but it better illustrates the potential shortcomings of equating the metaphysical with the uncon-

---

22. See also Neurath (1983, 44, 50, 69).
23. Alberto Coffa expresses surprise at how scanty Carnap's argumentation is here (Coffa 1991, 225). Richardson has suggested that this "lax" argumentation on Carnap's part is due to the fact that "Carnap takes it as a point of agreement between himself and the metaphysicians that metaphysical debates are not scientific debates," i.e., that metaphysical concepts are outside the ken of science (Richardson 1992, 60). However, if that were true, why would Carnap bother writing Part V ("Clarification of Some Philosophical Problems on the Basis of Construction Theory"), which reviews particular metaphysical concepts one by one, and argues that each is not constructable within the system? This indicates Carnap genuinely does intend to show (instead of simply assume) that certain concepts cannot be incorporated into a constitution system, thereby showing more specifically how metaphysical claims are not scientific claims.

structable. In a phenomenal or 'autopsychological' constitution system, Carnap says, we can discern a "parallelism" between two "sequences," one of which corresponds to "the construction of physical objects" and a second which corresponds to phenomenal entities instead. The mind-body problem asks: "how can the occurrence of a parallelism of sequences of constituents be explained?" Carnap responds that this "question cannot be expressed in concepts that can be constructed; for the concept... 'explanation'... [does] not in this sense have any place in a constructional system of objects of cognition," and this holds for "any such constructional system". Therefore, an "explanation of these findings lies outside the range of science" (Carnap 1928/1963, 270). In short, Carnap's position is that 'explanation' is an unconstructable concept, so the mind-body problem is unscientific metaphysics on the grounds that it requests an explanation of a certain parallelism between physical and phenomenal sequences.

But, one may wonder, what if Hempel and Oppenheim's groundbreaking "Studies in the Logic of Explanation" had been published not in 1947 but in 1922? The conception of explanation offered in that article might be sufficiently precise, clear, and scientifically respectable for the Carnap of the *Aufbau* to think that a notion of explanation could be formulated within a constitution system. Regardless of what Carnap's reaction would have been under this particular counterfactual circumstance,[24] this points to a serious and fundamental difficulty. In any case where Carnap (or any other logical empiricist) asserts that a given term or sentence cannot be incorporated into any unified language of science, it is (epistemically) possible that another person could later show how that concept can, in fact, be so integrated. For example, Tarski showed how to define 'truth (in a language)' rigorously, a term that many logical empiricists previously considered the province of speculative metaphysicians (Mancosu 2008a). Claude Shannon gave the concept of information a mathematically tractable characterization, and spawned a fruitful sub-discipline of mathematics. In general, the regimentation of a sentence or term from pre-analyzed usage into a form acceptable for use in a unified language of science can be a difficult process, often requiring substantial intellectual creativity. In short, (M) and its variations are problematic because there is no general procedure for adjudicating claims of the form 'Concept C cannot be incorporated into the unified language of science L' (much less 'into *any* unified language of science L'), because in many cases of interest, such an incorporation, however unexpected, could conceivably be achieved tomorrow, given sufficient ingenuity.[25] Our limited technical creativity is not a demonstration of impossibility. I am not claiming that (M) fails to provide necessary and

24. For example, the Carnap of the *Aufbau* might not have allowed that certain constructable sentences are somehow privileged by being 'laws of nature,' and the Hempel and Oppenheim analysis of explanation requires that we be able to identify such laws. However, in Carnap (1966), Carnap happily accepts and deploys the concept of a law of nature in his account of scientific explanation.
25. Of course, there are results in model theory concerning the definability or indefinability of certain notions in a particular language; e.g., 'finite' cannot be defined within standard first-order logic with identity. My remarks are obviously not intended to apply to cases in which indefinability can be demonstrated.

sufficient conditions for identifying metaphysical terms and claims; it may well be extensionally adequate. Rather, the problem is that, in many cases of interest, we cannot know whether those conditions have been met; thus the criterion cannot be used to determine effectively whether a particular claim is objectionable metaphysics or not.

One might reply to this objection as follows. For example, before Tarski's work, 'true' *was* a metaphysical term, and it only became part of cognitively significant discourse after the publication of his *Wahrheitsbegriff*, and similarly for any other terms and sentences that are not now incorporated into a unified language of science. In effect, this reply suggests a friendly emendation of (M), by modifying the boundary marking off the metaphysical. Specifically, this reply endorses replacing (M) with

(M*) An apparently declarative sentence or apparently descriptive term is metaphysical if and only if that (apparent) sentence or term *is* not incorporated into a total language of science.

The only difference between (M) and (M*) is that the latter lacks the former's modal force: 'cannot' is replaced by 'is not.' Adopting (M*) would constitute a departure from the logical empiricists' original conception of the link between metaphysical neutrality and unified science,[26] but it would also defuse the objection raised in the previous paragraph.

However, (M*) creates a problem at least as severe as the one it solves: (M*) makes the line dividing metaphysics from cognitively significant discourse overly sensitive to the intellectual abilities and interests of the *Wissenschaftslogiker*. Suppose a new theory, employing a set of new terms, is introduced into the developmental psychology literature this year. If the people constructing a unified language of science are either underinformed or simply too dense to see how to connect these new terms with older, antecedently meaningful ones, then these novel terms will qualify as metaphysical under (M*). Even worse, under (M*) what qualifies as metaphysics will depend on the particular interests of the *Wissenshaftslogiker*. Suppose that no one in the group formulating a unified language has an interest in ecology; their efforts are focused instead upon incorporating (e.g.) chemical and psychological language into the unified language. Because time and resources are finite, the terms unique to ecology may not be incorporated into the unified language now (or ever), and thus large chunks of ecology would be classified as metaphysics by (M*), simply because no one managed to fit that project into the schedule. The obvious remedy for this unacceptable delineation of the metaphysical is to hold that these new terms from developmental psychology and the terms unique to ecology may not be incorporated into a unified language of science yet, they nonetheless *could* be, and for that reason are not metaphysical. But that position is just the original (M).

---

26. As Jon Tsou pointed out to me, (M*) also appears to run counter to Carnapian tolerance, since new language forms 'under construction' would apparently count as metaphysical.

A more sustained criticism or defense could be made for (M) and/or its conceptual kin. However, I will not dwell on this matter further, in part because there is relatively little contemporary interest in separating out scientific elements in our discourse from metaphysical ones.

6.4. Conclusion: The Origin of the Term 'Unified Science'

Thus far I have argued that, in the writings of central logical empiricists, there is a close conceptual connection between the unity of science thesis and the elimination of metaphysics, and that this connection is approximately captured by (M). In closing, I present one piece of evidence that this connection is not merely conceptual, but also genealogical. That is, the term 'unified science' [*Einheitswissenschaft*], suggested by Neurath, sprung directly out of the Vienna Circle's program to overcome metaphysics. Neurath, recalling the Circle's discussion of the *Tractatus*, explains how he came to introduce the term.

> Eliminating 'meaningless' sentences became a kind of game... But I very soon felt uneasy, when members of our Vienna Circle suggested that we should drop the term 'philosophy' as a name for a set of sentences... but use it as a name for the activity engaged in improving given sentences by 'demetaphysicalizing' them[27]... Thus I came to suggest as our object, the collection of material, which we could accept within the framework of scientific language; for this I thought the not-much-used term 'Unified Science' (*Einheitswissenschaft* ...) a suitable one. (Neurath 1983, 231)

Thus, the very term 'unified science' arose directly from a desire to re-name the anti-metaphysical goal of the *Wienerkreis*. The two goals are, metaphorically, two sides of the same coin: the elimination of metaphysics is the negative or destructive part, while the production of a unified scientific language constitutes its positive or constructive aspect.

What does the unity of science movement have to do with the finitist-nominalist project pursued in 1940-41? The primary point of contact is the anti-metaphysical animus, which animates the unity of science as well as nominalism, both in 1941 and later. The initial suspicion towards classical mathematical language, for its *prima facie* commitment to strange abstract entities, is overcome by showing that a substantial portion of such suspicious language can be captured in a language that is thoroughly empirical: the domain of its existential quantifiers are empirical, concrete things only. Mathematical discourse is shown to be meaningful, instead of metaphysical, by embedding it within paradigmatically

---

27. This is similar to *Tractatus* 6.53: "The correct method in philosophy would really be the following: to say nothing except what can be said, i.e. propositions of natural science...and then, whenever someone wanted to say something metaphysical, to demonstrate to him that he had failed to give a meaning to certain signs in his propositions."

meaningful discourse. And as this chapter endeavored to show, for Carnap and his intellectual allies, any concept or claim that can be incorporated into a unified language of empirical science is not metaphysical.

What, in the end, should we make of Carnap's 1940-41 Harvard notes as a whole? I must confess that when I began studying these documents, I was initially somewhat disappointed by the participants' primary foci of conversation. Although it was certainly surprising that Carnap, Tarski and Quine were discussing a seemingly strange set of questions about what arithmetic should look like if the number of things in the world should turn out to be finite, I did wonder whether these notes might simply be a historical curiosity, along the lines of 'Isn't it odd that these great minds spent the year discussing such a strange question, tangential to their primary interests and achievements?' That is, I wished that Carnap, Tarski, and Quine had concentrated their efforts on issues that we consider to lie at the heart of their various logico-philosophical enterprises; for example, I hoped for 75 pages of a *tête-à-tête-à-tête* over analytic truth, or new information that would decisively settle outstanding historical disputes among historians of analytic philosophy.

As my initial disappointment faded, and I began to think about the notes in greater detail, it became clearer to me that these philosophers actually were working on a set of issues not so far removed from those considered central to them—and to us today. For example, the relationship between mathematical theories and theories about the natural world is absolutely central for almost all of those caught up in the intellectual currents of logical empiricism, and for Carnap in particular. He saw Tarski's finitist-nominalist project, and Quine's support for it, as a retrogressive slide back into Mill's empiricist view of mathematics. Carnap took a public stand against saddling empiricism with nominalism in "Empiricism, Semantics, and Ontology" a decade later. Furthermore, Carnap viewed Tarski's program as closely related to his own long-standing project of investigating the relationship between what Carnap usually called the 'observational' and 'theoretical' parts of scientific language; this again shows that the 1940-41 conversations should not be considered an 'outlier' irrelevant to Carnap's wider goals. The demand for intelligibility, as I argued in 2.1.3, is very closely tied to the issue of linguistic meaning, a central concern of both the logical empiricists and many philosophers who came after them. And despite my initial disappointment that the notes are not simply a sustained, direct confrontation over the analytic/synthetic distinction, the issue nonetheless makes prominent appearances. For example, in a FN language certain parts of arithmetic become synthetic, and some light was shed on the historical trajectory that led Quine to "Two Dogmas."

I firmly believe that much more of historical and conceptual worth can be mined from these dictation notes. I hope more of value will be. As interest continues to grow in the history of analytic philosophy, and in the history of philosophy of science in particular, there is—thankfully—good reason to believe this hope will be fulfilled.

Appendix A
Translation

These notes were originally written in German, in Stolze-Schrey stenographic shorthand. They were first transcribed into German longhand by (in all likelihood) Richard Nollan, and his transcription was corrected and improved by Brigitta Arden.

The typographic conventions are as follows:
Carnap used underlining for emphasis in his handwritten notes; in what follows, I have replaced underlined text with italicized text. All single square brackets '[...]' and parentheses are Carnap's own. My additions are placed within double square brackets '[[...]]'.

090–16–09 *Conversation with Tarski, Chicago, March 6 1940*
1. 'L-true'. 'logical-descriptive'.
I: My intuition about the distinction between L-true–F-true is clearer than between logical–descriptive. But I can nevertheless explain the latter by indicating the simplest logical constants in the customary systems and declare that everything definable from them should also be logical.
He: He has no such intuition; one could equally well reckon 'temperature' as logical as well.
I: One determines the truth of a closed sentence of the temperature functor via measurement.
He: But one can decide upon a fixed theory of truth [[unreadable]][1] in the face of all observations.
I: Then it is a mathematical function, and a logical sign, and not the physical concept of temperature. In the case of a closed sentence containing the physical temperature-functor, we cannot find the truth-value through mere calculation.
He: That proves nothing, since often that is not possible for mathematical functions either, because there are undecidable sentences; no fundamental difference between mathematical but undecidable sentences, and factual sentences.
I: It appears to me that there is.
  I explain that the difficulty lies only in general semantics; in the special semantics of a fixed language, it is easy to define the above-mentioned concepts

---

1. Probably 'unrevisable.'

so that they agree with our intuitions. If we do this for the metalanguage, then one can also give general definitions for the object language as well. 2 options: 1.) Intensional metalanguage, with modality; 2.) metalanguage divided into M_1 and M_2 (see MS "Part I", §16).[2]

He: That will probably work, even though the division appears arbitrary to him. Is it possible to formalize L-semantics, i.e. to set up a calculus in the metalanguage, which represents the previously set out means of deduction in the metalanguage, and is still a calculus with finite rules? Then and only then will the whole thing be understandable and acceptable to him (even though arbitrary in the division).

I: One can certainly formalize L-semantics; whether with only finite rules, I cannot foresee at the moment. Can one do the corresponding thing for simple semantics (concept of truth)? He: Certainly. (It appears to me that the following problem must be generally investigated: if we have a calculus with transfinite rules, under which conditions can we then formalize its syntax, and have a calculus with only finite rules?)

[[p. 2]]

2. He: For him, a calculus is an ordered pair, consisting of a class (of sentences) and a relation (consequence). *What, according to me, is a semantic system?* I: When we set aside L-concepts (a class (of sentences); but this is unnecessary, since field of [relations])[3] a relation ('designation' for sentences, or if without sentences, the property 'true'). *But*: this relation or the property 'true' must be taken as intensional—as a property, not as a class. I.e., if two systems agree on the extension of this property, then they still are not necessarily identical. It certainly does not suffice (as he thought, and what his conception ('semantic system') apparently is) to take the class of true sentences, because the interpretation is not thereby fixed. How this class is defined is essential. This is evident in the case of the L-concepts. For a semantic system there is only one adequate concept 'L-true'; but if only the extension and not the definition of 'true' is given, then several very different concepts of 'L-true' are possible. He: He does not understand that, since his whole idea proceeds in an extensional language. I: But then important distinctions fall away, which we make in everyday life. For example, a certain class of people can be defined in different ways. Then if I only know the extension, not the defining property, under certain conditions I cannot make a certain prediction without certain additional factual knowledge

---

2. This refers to (the manuscript version of) *Introduction to Semantics*, section 16, entitled "L-Concepts in General Semantics." There Carnap outlines four possibilities for "defining an adequate concept of L-truth in general semantics" (Carnap 1942, 83); he refers here to the second of the four ways. In *Introduction to Semantics*, he describes this method as follows: "M consists of two parts M_1 and M_2, where M_1 contains the radical terms of general semantics ('designation,' 'true,' etc.) and M_2 contains the means of logical deduction in M_1 either in a syntactical or in an L-semantical form" (Carnap 1942, 85–86).
3. Text very uncertain.

Translation |41|

(namely, about the extensional equivalence of the related concepts).

[[p. 3]]

3. *Logic without types*. The best form is that which was originally created by Zermelo; now on the basis of this, improved systems of *Bernays* (distinction between classes and sets) and *Mostowski* (without this distinction). Quine, in his system, makes too many exceptional truths (e.g., so that Cantor's theorem does not hold), which deters the mathematician, and which indicate that the system is not useful. I: Should we make the language of science with or without types?

He: Perhaps something completely different will develop. It would be a wish and a guess that the entirety of *general set theory*, as beautiful as it is, will *disappear in the future*.[4] *With the higher types, Platonism begins*. The tendencies of Chwistek and others ("Nominalism") to talk only about designatable things are healthy. The only problem is finding a good implementation. Perhaps roughly of this kind: in the first language numbers as individuals, as in language I, but perhaps with unrestricted operators; in the second language individuals that are identical with or correspond to the sentential functions in the first language, so properties of natural numbers expressible in the first language; in the third language, as individuals those properties expressible in the second language, and so forth. Then one has in each language only individual variables, albeit dealing with entities of different types.

I: This restriction to the expressible real numbers, functions of them, and so on, corresponds to finitism and intuitionism; the tendency (since Poincaré) of this restriction is healthy and sympathetic; but didn't it turn out that mathematics is thereby complicated intolerably, and that the restriction is arbitrary? He: The intuitionists did not carry out such a construction on a good basis, especially since e.g. they throw out the law of the excluded middle etc., which produces unnecessary complications. It could indeed turn out that theorems in the restricted domain analogous to theorems of classical mathematics are valid, if choices are made appropriately (e.g. doing much more with addition, multiplication, and recursive functions).

102–63–09   *For discussion with Russell*. In the *logic group*
October 18, 1940
I. "*Underlying metaphysics*"
Example: Tarski and Russell: "platonic logic"
Russell says: A *Platonism* underlies talk of 'letter x' (and so the use of any predicate?) *see 1b
Tarski: A *Platonism* underlies the higher functional calculus (and so the use of predicate variables, especially higher types).
Russell: The metaphysical words "*In the beginning was the word*" underlies the

---

4. Mancosu identifies general set theory with Tarski's theory of classes presented in §5 of his *Wahrheitsbegriff* monograph (Mancosu 2005, 334).

philosophies of Plato and Carnap (and most of the philosophers in between).
I:

1. An unspoken opinion is frequently implied, whether the author is aware of it or not.

    a. We can show him: you make these tacit assumptions; or else you cannot draw this conclusion. Or
    b. We can show him: you make these tacit assumptions; this is revealed in your practical behavior.
    In this way, all kinds of opinions can be uncovered: rational, absurd, magical, even contradictory.

   (Interesting related question: Can we infer (and how?) that someone believes a determinate logic that deviates from ours from pure behavior or from their use of factual sentences?)

2. A *metaphysical theory* can never be implied in this way, i.e. to be necessary (or merely useful) for a conclusion or for an explication of an action. For metaphysical theory has *no cognitive content*. (Here 'metaphysical' is not meant in the empirical sense = general propositions about the world, e.g. "each thing consists of particles, which neither come into existence nor pass out of existence, but rather only their situation (and condition) change.")

3. That someone accepts a determinate metaphysical theory *cannot be uncovered* from his *practical behavior* (without language); it cannot be uncovered from his cognitive utterances, but rather only *from metaphysical utterances*, i.e., from non-cognitive utterances, which he treats as cognitive. ('*pseudo-cognitive*') (But it is possible to infer, from the utterance of a determinate metaphysical theory, that the person also accepts another metaphysical claim. For a kind of quasi-logical connection also exists between pseudo-cognitive utterances. E.g. "There exists an omnipotent being" follows logically from "God is omnipotent.")

   Fundamental *difference between metaphysics and magic*: Magic is cognitive, even though false; a magical belief can therefore be inferred from the conclusions that a man makes, or from his practical behavior. *There are no metaphysical opinions, rather only metaphysical utterances*! An *animal* can have magic, but no metaphysics! (*Perhaps it can be conceded*, that we sometimes *can make psychological inferences* that someone accepts a certain metaphysics, since he shows the symptoms that are known often to accompany the corresponding metaphysics. (E.g. if a certain theology is not magical, but rather metaphysical, and we observe that a man belongs to its sect, and he makes the other utterances of the corresponding religion, then we can surmise that he could be brought to utter the same metaphysics. But this is different from the inference of a factual belief; while this is logically connected to the belief that he expresses or on the basis of which he acts, it is *merely a psychological connection*.)

[[p. 2]]

R.: Example ([Fane] 18 to proposition 4): "*Logic... is thus incurably (!) Platonic*";[5]
If I say "this is black" and "that is black," then I wish to say the same thing about both, but I do not succeed; I can only do this when I say "this and that are black," but I am saying something different than what I said earlier about this and about that. The *generality* via repeated use of the word 'black' is an *illusion*; in reality there is only similarity.
[? No. I can decide to make sounds of a certain kind (thus similar to one another) under particular conditions, and thereby to express generally the existence of those conditions.]
R.: Logic takes for granted that the same word can occur on different occassions. But this is misleading.

102-63-11 *For discussion in logic group.*
October 27, 1940.
The concept proposition. Many friends raise objections.
(Here, we put to one side: general objections to semantics; so we assume: semantics with relation *Des* for names and predicates.)
Analogy:

---

5. This is a quotation from Russell (1940, 70).

"Number"	"*proposition*"
Assume a language with numerals, but without the word 'number'	Language with sentences, but without the word '*proposition*'.
1. *without numerical variables.* We introduce 'number' as follows: if '...' is a numeral, then (but perhaps not only then) '...is a number' is true.	1. *without propositional variables.* We introduce 'proposition' as follows: if '...' is a sentence, then (but perhaps not only then) '...is a *proposition*' is true.
2. *with numerical variables 'n', 'm'.* Definition: $Nu(n) =_{df} n = n$ (any analytic sentential function in 'n')	2. *with propositional variables 'p', 'q'.* Definition: $Prop(p) =_{df} \neg p \vee p$ (any analytic sentential function in 'p') With 'F' and 'x' alone (assuming that all sentences have the form $\mathfrak{pr}(in)$): $Prop(F(x)) =_{df} ..F..x..$ analytic (e.g. '$F(x) \vee \neg F(x)$'). Here 'Des_p' can be defined: $Des_p(u, F(x)) =_{df} (\exists v, w)(u = v^\frown w . Des(v, F) . Des(w, x))$. Or with p (in an intensional language with 'N'): $Des_p(u, p) =_{df} (\exists v, w, F, x)(u^\frown w . Des(v, F) . p=F(x))$; where $p = q =_{df} N(p \equiv q)$.

102–63–10 On '*proposition*'.
November 3, 1940
singular connectives:

	Characteristic		
c_1	T T	This is the *concept proposition*; '$c_1 A$' = in English 'A is prop.'	$A \vee \neg A$
c_2	T F	The *absolute concept of truth*; '$c_2 A$' is L-equiv. with 'A.' Thus *unneccessary*.	A
c_3	F T	The *absolute concept of falsity*; = negation sign; '$c_3 A$' is L-equiv. with '$\neg A$'	$\neg A$
c_4	F F	*Contradictory*	$A . \neg A$

English translation for '$c_r A$'
$c_1 A$: A or not A; A is a *prop*.
$c_2 A$: A is *true*; it is true that A.
$c_3 A$: *not-A*; A is *false*; it is false that A.
$c_4 A$: A & not-A.

No hypostasis; we are not substantializing, we are not treating anything as a thing which is not a thing.

102-63-05 Quine, on *general semantics (and syntax)*. Conversation, November 23, 1940.

Quine: It would be more useful *to have names not for single signs, but rather for the operations* used to construct sentences: "the disjunction of $\mathfrak{S}_i$ and $\mathfrak{S}_j$", "the universal sentence from ... (with respect to the variable ..)" and so forth.

Advantage: the inessential[6] features (whether disjunction is expressed with or without brackets, before the signs or between them, etc.) are not taken into consideration; the signs that sometimes occur several times, which together only serve for *one* operation, need not be treated separately (e.g. '(...) ∨ (–)'). He thus prefers to speak of *statement composition*, instead of *connectives*.

Tarski: He has already used this method earlier.

090-16-02 Tarski, *On general semantics*, and systems without types (short conversation)
Nov. 23, 1940

1. The system-variable 'S' in the metalanguage M is not allowed to refer unrestrictedly to all systems; otherwise the antinomies will appear.

   In general I will take as the values of 'S' poorer systems than M, so that 'true in S' is definable in M. But in general semantics such a restriction is in fact not necessary. I also assume that it is possible to compute the values of 'S' in M; to let 'for all S...' sentences include M in their scope (e.g., "if $\mathfrak{S}_i$ is L-true$_S$, then it is true$_S$" and the like); but since 'true$_M$' is not definable in M, we cannot formulate the instance of M in M, so we also cannot derive [[the instance]] from the universal sentence in M, although it is intended as well. Analogy: a universal sentence "all real numbers..." refers to all, although the instances for the undefinable real numbers in the corresponding language cannot be formulated and so cannot be derived, but they are nonetheless intended along with the others in the universal sentence.

2. It appears unneccessary in *general semantics* in M to attempt (as I do) to treat all possible systems. For all practical occurrences and all important problems, it *indeed suffices to restrict oneself* to systems with a certain *relatively simple structure*, namely those *with individual variables* and predicate constants. Then all of set theory can be expressed in Zermelo's way, with the help of the predicate '∈' for individuals. This simplifies general semantics and syntax extraordinarily, and indeed also will be more fruitful, since more results will be obtained.

   For general syntax this is probable (for the purpose of treating systems similar to the theory of sets). But how does he believe it is in semantics? (He says: see the appendix to "*Wahrheitsbegriff*"!) In the interpretation

---

6. The transcript actually reads 'essential,' but 'inessential' makes more sense in the context.

we must say that '$a \in b$' means that a is an element of b. Then should M likewise have this structure, or one with types?

This must be thought over!

[[p. 2]]

3. Process for *predicates with arguments of different types*.

   a. *Reservations about transfinite types*: the rules will surely become complicated. (I: We take variables that run through all finite types.) He: We also need variables that run through all types; e.g., when we want to define 'true.'

   b. *Without types*: *Two sub-kinds*:
      1. *Zermelo*-Fraenkel (- von Neumann?)
      2. *Quine*. Through which the absolute total-class can occur (and "other *peculiarities*")

   He appears to prefer (1). There, 'true' can be easily defined according to his method (see appendix to "*Wahrheitsbegriff*"). Difficulties proper to (2): we must have a stronger system for the definition of 'true'; presumably it will be strengthened (as Quine assumes) neither through new fundamental concepts (which Quine would then call 'non-logical'!), nor through new kinds of variables (here Quine agrees), but rather through added postulates. (Whereas with other systems (I believe he means (1)), certain postulates are given up and will be replaced by new ones, new ones will be added here.) These new postulates must make it the case that a sentence signifying the existence of a model for the old postulates becomes provable; namely the existence of a class of sufficiently higher cardinal number, so that its elements are understood as identical with (or corresponding to) the entities (elements and non-elements) of the old system. Quine: is it certain that such a thing is possible? Tarski: if not, then he would have doubts whether the old system is free of contradiction.

090–16–03   Dec. 9, 1940
Tarski and Quine, on general semantics
On the definition of 'entity u is *covered* by system S' ((I) D17-1)
Tarski: One should also include: Elements of designated classes, elements of elements of classes, and so forth.
Quine: The definition must be flexible, so that it also holds for languages in which universality is not expressed via variables, e.g. *Schönfinkel*'s system.

Tarski and Quine: General remarks on general semantics:
It is hardly worthwhile to refer the definitions and theorems in a system of general

semantics to the class K of all languages, which can be handled in M, rather better only to a partial class K' such that:

1.) Each language of K (or each that we want to consider) is translatable into a language of K',

2.) All languages of K' have certain usual structures.

In the simplest case, and for all further practical purposes: we only refer to languages that have individual variables and constants, predicate constants, and identity; also the connectives and operators. So the lower functional calculus (but without predicate variables (so how I took them in (II)) is thereby justified: with the help of the special relation '$\in$' (but which here is not presupposed as occurring in each language), we can translate set theory and mathematics into the lower functional calculus. This is *the difference between logic and mathematics: Mathematics = logic + '$\in$'*. Through '$\in$' the system becomes non-finitistic, and incomplete.

102-63-13 For logic group.
December 12 1940
The Kolmogorov-Doob interpretation of probability (as Mises explained it in the sc. of sc. group,[7] and which I showed to be more satisfactory than the limit of the frequency interpretation)
It uses the same concepts as I do, with *'state of affairs' and 'range'*.
A certain series of trials are made; a certain series of results will occur.

We consider all possible sequences of results	= the *states of aff.* (*Leibniz's* possible worlds).
We consider classes of such possible sequences, for which something determinate occurs	= *range*
We ascribe *measures* to these classes.	

102-63-04 Quine, MS, (without title; something like) "*Lng., Math., Sci.*"
Read in the *Logic group, December 20, 1940*.

General semantics must be restricted, otherwise it will be trivial.
Proposal: we want to investigate languages which contain only:
Constants, Predicates, joint denial, universal quantification. With only one type of variable; only closed sentences.
Is this too strict? We can translate into such languages:
All of mathematics ('$\in$' the sole predicate)
Syntax:

---

7. This presumably refers to the 'Science of Science' group that met at Harvard during the same academic year Carnap, Tarski, and Quine were there. See section 1.1 above and Hardcastle (2003).

Protosyntax: 'M'[8]; definable: concatenation, identity, names of particular signs. Further syntax: for that purpose '∈'.

Individual constants and functors can be introduced via contextual definition. (Advantage, see ML[9] 27: 1. technical: the theory of quantification can be simplified; 2. philosophical: questions of meaningfulness are separated from questions of existence.)

Can all languages be translated into such a language? This is the problem of the *thesis of extensionality*.

Conversely: Are there interesting, weaker languages (i.e., which would not be derived from the described space), that would be worth investigating? It appears doubtful. If they occur, they could be set aside and investigated.

Proposal: '*Logic*' = *Theory of joint denial and quantification*.
'*Mathematics*' = (Logic +) Theory of ∈.
'*Physics*' = (Logic +) (Mathematics +) Theory of other predicates.
(Or: elementary logic, logic, and physics. But: the stricter sense of 'logic' is perhaps in greater agreement with the spirit of the long historical tradition.) The boundary between logic and the the rest of science (including mathematics) is important!

Important differences between logic and mathematics:

1. *There are no logical sentences*, because there are no logical predicates. Investigations of logical processes are metatheoretical.
'p', 'q',... 'F', 'G'... do not occur (or only as translatable expedients). Instead of these, uttered syntactic signs.
But: there are pure *mathematical sentences*, with '∈' (e.g. '$(x)(x \in x)$'). We obtain content with these; mathematical *subject matter* (while logic deals only with the form).

[[p. 2]]

2. Logic demands no special objects, its scope never [[has]] a determinate size; if a normal sentence [[is]] logically true from the standpoint of an infinite domain of discourse, then [[it is logically true in]] all finite domains as well, and conversely. The logical truths are valid for almost all philosophies, including nominalism and realism; exception: intuitionism, but perhaps to be satisfied by extralogical restrictions (no non-constructive predicates).
Predicates bring *first* ontological claims (not because they signify, they hold here syncategorematically, since variables never occur for them; rather: a predicate demands certain objects as values for the argument variable; so *e.g.* '∈' *demands classes*, universals; thus *mathematics is Platonic, logic is not.*

'*Logically true*' can be defined syntactically, and even *protosyntactically* (following Gödel's completeness proof):

---

8. For an explanation of this ternary predicate and its intended interpretation, see Quine (1940/1958, 288).
9. Throughout, 'ML' abbreviates Quine's *Mathematical Logic*.

Infinite sets of axioms of quantification (axiom schemata, as in M.L.) and modus ponens.

This is more elementary than the semantic characterization with the help of 'true.' Here, *no epistemological theory of logical truth* is proposed, as e.g. in conventionalism, intuitionism, or empiricism; I no longer understand these apparently mutually contradictory theories. 'Logical consequence' is easily definable (e.g. the conditional is logically true; or: derivable).

Extra-logical notations (e.g. mathematical, biological, etc.): introduction of suitable predicates; and *axioms. Theorems* = logical consequence of the axioms. *Logic is thus the common part of all (non-trivial) theories.*
E.g.: elementary arithmetic, e.g. using 'P':
Px, y, z means: $x = y^z$.
Then identity will be defined; and definite description, via contextual definition.
For $y^z =_{df} (\iota x) Px, y, z$
$x \cdot y =_{df} (\iota z)(w)(w^z = (w^x)^y)$
$x + y =_{df} (\iota z)(w)(w^z = w^x \cdot w^y)$.

The entirety of mathematics through '$\in$'. Axiomatization (e.g.: finite set of axioms, as in Bernays (who follows von Neumann), or infinite set of axoims, as in M.L.).

The theorems are the logical consequences of the mathematical axioms. But they do not exhaust mathematical truth (Gödel).

[[p. 3]]

Universal *language of science*. Large set of predicates.
Ontology, i.e. values of the variables: very different objectivity, among electrons, atoms, bacteria, tables, sense-qualities; (objects which are not things:) also centimeters, distances, temperatures, electric charges, energy, lines, points, classes (or properties).

Some people see certain universals as more problematic than others, and they therefore reduce these problematic ones (e.g. Whitehead: points to volumes; Carnap and Jeffreys: distances and temperatures to pure numbers.)

I maintain: in the end, all universals have the same nature as points, centimeters, and so forth. Classes are probably no exception. I do not demand that classes or other objects which are not things should be eliminated; perhaps they are necessary for science. In each case, if we do reduce, it is in order to reduce the obscure to the clearer; but then there is no reason to maintain the existence of the things; one would like to reduce electrons to larger things, and perhaps all things to phenomena. But the way is not clear: greater clarity, or epistemological plurality. I believe that we must *follow Carnap*: the non-positivistic or non-phenomenological language form of science as an *ineliminable assumption*. I conjecture that C. is right: there is only piecewise clarification, not a complete, definitional elimination. This clarification appeared through investigation of the relations of confirmation between sentences at some remove and those of a more immediate kind.

Science is full of myth and hypostasis; goal: to situate the chaotic behavior of everyday things in a more understandable wider-world; ultimate task: predictions covering the everyday things; this is psychologically possible only in consequence of the greater "clarity of arrangement" (sic) of the wider-world, which is construed by science as an *intermediary device*. The trichotomy: phenomena–*common sense* world–wider-world of science holds only roughly; it is a question of degree. Tables are hypostases just as electrons, but to a lesser degree. We can infer the common sense world from the wider-world. Not conversely (underdetermined); just as the common sense world is underdetermined from *experience*.

I conceive of mathematics in the same way. The theory of the real numbers is confirmed by the points of contact with the theory of the rational numbers. The general theory of classes gives familiar *common sense* results for finite classes, parallel to *common sense* laws about heaps (!). But the general theory of classes is not thereby univocally determined. Therefore, one must consciously search for a myth; I did so, after I read about the paradoxes: Russell's myth, Zermelo's, my own.

By the way: to me, such considerations make Gödel's (incompleteness) theorem appear less *anomalous* than before.

090-16-29 Dec. 20, 1940.
Quine is discussed.

Can we perhaps conceive of the higher, non-finitistic parts of logic (mathematics) thus: their relation to the finitistic parts is analogous to the relation of the higher parts of physics to the observation sentences? Non-finitistic logic (mathematics) would thus become non-metaphysical (like physics). Perhaps light is thereby also thrown on the question whether a fundamental difference exists between logic-mathematics and physics.

102-63-06 *Remarks on Quine's lecture* in the logic group, Dec. 20 1940. January 10, 1941

1. Yes, certain *analogy between mathematics and physics*, between '$\in$' and 'temperature.' But *problem*: *What is the difference?*

2. "*myth & hypostasis*"
   Myth is at most psychologically necessary, not logically necessary. But certainly helpful. *Distinguish*: theoretical, cognitive content and *accompanying* [[unreadable]] (pictorial content).

102-44-11 *For conversation with Goodman, on Dr. Thesis.* Jan 2, 1941

To my surprise, he assumes *that I did not see certain defects of Quasi-analysis*: p. 113 ff:

Thing	Colors
1	bg
2	rg
3	br

(1, 2, 3) yields a color class, though not the same color.

p. 115 "C. is here the victim of a dangerous... fallacy. It consists in inferg." that if 2 of three classes overlap, all three overlap. Actually, I knew about this defect of quasianalysis. The general description of a problem case in "Aufbau" p. 100 appears to be exactly Goodman's example! (G. himself says 116) In my MS "Quasianalysis" (1922-23) I dealt with similar cases. There, a precisification of the method is given, through which my case is eliminated; nevertheless, Goodman's case is still not eliminated.

For me: class h = i, m, o, p
i = d, f, a
m = f, a
o = c, e, a
p = c, f

The last four are completely similar to Goodman's.

Similarly, he says in the article with Leonard (JSL 5, 1940) p. 53 and below (see SD): "...mistakenly supposg. that a class of things, each member of which is similar to each other, is a class of things which are all similar."

p. 139. Literal quotation of my warning that we must distinguish between similarity in a certain relation and similarity in any relation. Only the first is trivial. "...how is it poss. for him to point out this fallacy so clearly and even to refer to Section 70, without realizg. that he has there committed essentially the same error?"

[[p. 2]]

My objection against my "Aufbau": (it is not so much the particular mistakes of quasianalysis, which I already knew about.)

The extensional conception: definition of qualities etc. by enumeration.

(Of course this is only with the explanations with "pair-lists" etc. The actually given definitions, on the other hand, are not extensional, but rather "per intensionem," if also in extensional language. But the justification of the method of quasianalysis often makes reference to these pair lists etc.)

Result: I would take more fundamental concepts today; notwithstanding the fact that one can take "nominalistic basic elements."
(I do not see in the least the disadvantage or the advantage of Goodman's method.)

102-63-12 Further discussion of Quine's remarks, logic group January 10, 1941.

I: Shouldn't 'logical consequence' be taken more widely, so that a universal sentence follows from the infinite class of its instances? For example:
..0..
..0'..
⋮
⇓
$(x)..x..$

Quine and Tarski: better: $(x)(Nx \supset ..x..)$, ['N' = natural number]

But: We need the axioms in order to know that $0, 0',\ldots$ are *all* N.

I: In the conception without 'N', the universal sentence follows on the basis of the meaning of '(x)'.

Tarski: We only want to apply 'logically true' and 'logical consequence' when it holds for *every* meaning of the non-logical constants.

(So perhaps I should go back again to the definition in *Foundations of Logic and Mathematics*, where the meaning of the descriptive[10] signs were excluded. But then a difficulty with '$P \supset Q$', if there is a logical connection between both properties. For the truth is then a priori also!)

Quine: '0' can not occur as a primitive in a [[unreadable]] language. Important: only primitive predicates, in order that the formal rules settle nothing about existence. In arithmetic '0' is easily replaceable through a definite description. But then we again need the axioms, for univocality.

Tarski : The universal sentence is not even a logical consequence from its instances and the Peano axioms taken together;

I: Yes, since for the 5 axioms, or many more axiom schemata here, other interpretations are possible, so that the whole is not necessarily a progression. So the universal sentence follows only mathematically, but not even with the mathematical axioms, but rather with a particular interpretation. (not certain).

Quine: The "specification" [[rule]] $(x)(..x..) \rightarrow ..0..$ is also not a logical consequence here; instead of '0' we must use a description, and then the axioms are necessary in order to secure the existence of 0.

[[p. 2]]

I: If the specification [[rule]] is not logical, then I also no longer have the intuition against it, or against excluding the above-mentioned transfinite deduction from logic.

Wundheiler: Following Tarski-Lindenbaum (On the Restriction of Means of Expression...[11]), the logically-true sentences are in a domain of individuals, each of which remain the same throughout any one-one transformation.[12]

---

10. The transcript reads 'diskreten.'
11. This is a reference to Tarski and Lindenbaum (1936), translated into English in Tarski (1983, 384–92).
12. As Mancosu (2005, 340) notes, this is the characterization of logical truth that Tarski eventually endorses in Tarski (1986).

Quine: Yes, and the *mathematical truths* are those that remain the same through any ∈ transformation.

I: Naturally; that says no more than that mathematics (in a certain formulation) is characterized through ∈.

Wundheiler: Can we perhaps characterize the difference between logic, mathematics, and physics through transformation groups, just as we characterize projective, affine, and metrical geometry through transformation groups?

Tarski: It is doubtful whether the concept of *group* helps much in this context.

Open question that we want to discuss next time: how is the *difference between mathematics and physics* to be understood?

Quine: It is a difference in the kind of evidence; in mathematics we do not need experiments as we do in physics, so it is a priori in a behavioristic sense.

I: I prefer to characterize the a priori non-behavioristically; behaviorism is only a difference of degree (Bridgman's *pen and paper* operation).

090-16-28 Jan. 10, 1941.
Tarski, Finitism. Remark in discussion in the logic group.

Tarski: I only fundamentally understand a language that fulfills the following conditions:

1. *Finite* number of individuals.
2. *Reistic* (Kotarbiński): The individuals are physical things.
3. *Non-Platonic*: Only variables for individuals (things) occur, not for universals (classes etc.)

I only "understand" any other language in the way I "understand" classical mathematics, namely as a calculus; I know what I can derive from what (rather, what I have derived; "derivability" in general is already problematic).

With any *higher* "platonic" statements in a discussion, I interpret them to myself as statements that a fixed sentence is derivable (or derived) from certain other sentences. (He really believes the following: the assertion of a certain sentence is interpreted as signifying: this sentence holds in the fixed, presupposed system; and this means: it is derivable from certain basic assumptions.)

Why is even elementary arithmetic, with countable domain, excluded? Because, following Skolem, all of classical mathematics can be represented through a countable model, so it can be expressed in elementary arithmetic, e.g. when one takes ∈ as a certain relation between natural numbers.

102-63-07 *Logical, Mathematical, and Factual truth.*
January 11, 1941
Logical truth is truth that depends only on the meaning of the logical signs, so it also remains in existence when the non-logical constants are replaced by others, or in other words: when the non-logical constants have a different meaning.

Perhaps then: a priori truth is truth which depends only on the meaning of signs, so it remains when different facts are assumed, but the same meaning is assumed.
Mathematical truth = a priori, non-logical truth.
Problem: What exactly is "depends on," "is determined by"?

1. *Subjective formulation*: B depends upon A (is determined by A, is a function of A): If one knows A, then one knows B. *But*: this subjective conception is not good, since it introduces inessential factors, namely psychological ones. E.g.: the three angles of a triangle are determined by its three sides (and one can easily make this clear to a beginner). But a more complicated method is necessary in order to actually calculate the angles, given the sides; it is not right to say that anyone who knows the three sides also knows the angles.

2. *Objective formulation*: B depends upon A, is a function of A: if A remains the same after a given transformation, then B does also. *Difficulty*: How is meaning to be represented? What is a "transformation after which the meaning remains the same"?

[[p. 2]]

'P' and 'P'' have the same meaning when P and P' have the same extension not only in the actual world, but rather in every possible world, thus in every total-state ('state' in Semantics (I)[13]).
Assume that we have *two meanings* for a given series of (non-logical?) constants (e.g. '$\in$', 'temp.',...), i.e., two definitions of '$true_S$' that apply to the same set of sentences S.

1. $\mathfrak{S}_i$ is $true_S =_{df} ..P_1 ... P_n ...$
2. $\mathfrak{S}_i$ is $true'_S =_{df} ..P'_1 ... P'_n ...$

the definition of (2) results from that of (1) in the following manner: certain non-logical constants of the metalanguage [M] (like 'P_1',..., 'P_n' ...) are replaced by others (like 'P'_1',..., 'P'_n'...).

102-63-15 January 11, 1941
In *Physics* universal sentences (laws) do not suffice to determine everything. In *mathematics* perhaps they do??
In Peano's AS we could hardly manage with only universal sentences; "There is at most one beginning element" cannot be formulated as a general sentence. But how is it, when we introduce the numbers as cardinal numbers, i.e., as classes of classes?
But also in the *general theory of classes* we have others as universal sentences, e.g.: principle of comprehension, i.e. for each condition, there is a corresponding principle. Axiom of choice.

---

13. *Introduction to Semantics* (Carnap 1942).

102-63-08 *Non-standard models of the Peano axiom-system.*
January 11, 1941.
AS: R is one-one, exactly one beginning-element, no final element;
 Induction: Axiom schema: $((..0..) \cdot (x)(y)(..x.. \cdot R(x,y) \supset ..y..) \supset (z)(..z..))$ This says: a property expressible by R, which is hereditary with respect to R and holds for 0, holds for every number.
 The AS is expressed in a Quinean language, so without predicate variables, and without individual constants ('0' is an abbreviation of a description).
 Models: The individuals are ordered pairs of natural numbers:
$(0,0) \xrightarrow{R} (0,1) \xrightarrow{R} (0,2) \to (0,3) \to (0,4) \to (0,5) \dashrightarrow (0,n)$
$(1,0) \to (1,1) \to (1,2) \to (1,3) \to (1,4) \dashrightarrow (1,n)$
$R(x,y) =_{df} x = (r,s) \wedge y = (t,u) \wedge (r = 0 \vee r = 1) \wedge t = r \wedge s + 1 = u$. The axiom "at most one beginning-element" states exactly: "if x and y are beginning-elements, then $x = y$". And "$x = y$" says: "x and y have all *properties expressible by R* in common." But this is also satisfied by both the beginning-elements in the above model, namely the pairs $(0,0)$ and $(1,0)$.
 Simpler non-normal models: [[Pictures]]

102-63-03 *Logic group, January 20, 1941*
 Quine: A sentence is *logically true* (in the strict sense, not mathematically true), if its truth remains constant throughout arbitrary transformations of all its entities (not only the individuals); (this is because the '∈'-relation must not be included; thereby an individual is allowed to be a class!). With his language-form such a transformation is thereby accomplished (because there are no individual constants in the primitive vocabulary: each atomic formula is replaced by an arbitrary form (not necessarily an atomic formula). (The following is intended: an atomic formula 'Pxy' is replaced by an arbitrary sentential function with exact 'x' and 'y', such as '$..x..y..$'; but then different occurrences of the same predicate must be replaced by the corresponding sentential function (e.g. 'Puv' by '$..u..v..$').
 I: Wundheiler has offered as a criterion for logical truth: truth is invariant under *arbitrary transformations of individuals*. Isn't this perhaps characteristic of mathematical truth? A class is thereby transformed into the class of the correlates of its elements. But the discussion of the example '$(x)(P(x) \supset Q(x))$' shows, *that this factual sentence also satisfies the criterion!*
 I: I am inclined to take the following sentence as L-true as well (it would be logically or mathematically true): '$(x)(P(x) \supset Q(x))$', where 'P' is interpreted as 'black table,' and 'Q' is 'black.'
 Quine: Yes, you can arrive at that, when you state an interpretation via the definition of 'synonym,' as a relation between expressions of the object language and either the metalanguage or perhaps a richer object language. ('Synonym' is intended so that it holds only for L-equivalent predicates, not for F-equivalent ones.) The above sentence then corresponds to a sentence '$(x)(P_1(x) \wedge P_2(x) \supset$

$P_1(x))$', which is logically true. So a criterion for logical truth: either logically provable or transformable through synonyms into a logically-provable sentence.

I: (1) In the encyclopedia brochure[14], I took a sentence to be L-true, when it is true on the basis of the meaning of logical signs alone. In the new MS[15]: (2) on the basis of all signs. I prefer the latter, because of cases like the above one.

Someone (Quine?): Perhaps (1) can be taken for 'logically true,' (2) for 'logically or mathematically true'? This appears to agree with Quine's concept 'logically true', if we take as logical signs the connectives and the *quantifiers* only, so '$\in$' is not logical.

[[Pictures]]

090-16-25 Jan. 31, 1941.
Conversation with Tarski and Quine on Finitism, I
Result: p. 4

I: Three points of *unclarity between Tarski and me*:
1. Finitism. I.e., talking about *what kind of variables do we understand*?
2. Modalities. 'N'; *intensional* language.
3. L-Concepts.

(3) is the easiest. Let's take Quine's language form (or another, similar one). We give the *logical constants* through *enumeration*. Then 'L-true' is easy to define. (We can leave aside here certain modifications, perhaps necessary on account of the example that I brought up in the previous meeting.)

(2). If 'L-true' is defined, then *'N' can be easily explicated*; in essentials:
1. 'N(...)' is translated as '...,' in case the latter is L-true, otherwise as '¬(...).' (We here assume: only closed sentences, as with Quine.)
2. '(x)N(...)' is translated into 'N(x)(...).'[16]

(1) is the most difficult. In what sense do we "understand" e.g. arithmetic with bound number variables (for natural numbers).

On (2) and (3) see my pages "Conversation...; *Modalities*"

[[p. 2]]

Finitism.
Tarski: I truly understand only a *finite language* S_1: only individual variables, whose values are things; whose number is not claimed to be infinite (but perhaps also not the opposite). Finitely many descriptive primitive predicates. *Numbers*: they can be used in a finite realm, in that we think of the ordered things, and we interpret the numerals as the corresponding things. We can then use arithmetical

---

14. *Foundations of Logic and Mathematics* (Carnap 1939).
15. *Introduction to Semantics* (Carnap 1942).
16. This is now known as the *Barcan formula* (Marcus 1946).

concepts; but many arithmetical sentences cannot be proved here, since we do not know how many numbers there are.

One can also ascribe a cardinal number to a class.

Quine: E.g. by the introduction of '$(\exists 3x)\ldots$' as an abbreviation for '$(\exists x)(\exists y)(\exists z)(\neg.. = .. \wedge \ldots)$'."[17] (where '=' is either assumed as a logical fundamental sign, or as quasi-identity, defined on the basis of finitely many predicates.)

I: Or also 'NC(3, P)', in case we allow predicates of higher types, but only as abbreviations.

Tarski: The psychological puzzle is the following: The mathematician also appears to understand infinite arithmetic in a definite sense. In the case of an undecidable sentence (e.g., that of Gödel), they are able, without looking back to the axioms, to say that they recognize this sentence as true. And I (Tarski) share this feeling to a certain degree.

I: It seems to me that, in a certain sense, I really understand *infinite arithmetic*. Let us call it *language S_2*: only variables for natural numbers, with operators (so also negative universal sentences) for the purpose of recursive definitions. To Tarski and Quine's question, as I take it, if the number of things is perhaps in fact finite: I don't know exactly, but perhaps by [[using]] pure locations instead of things (Tarski: This conception in *Syntax* [[*The Logical Syntax of Language*]] made a great impact upon him at the time, but he thinks there are still difficulties with it.) A position is an arrangement-possibility for a thing. I do not feel as averse toward the concept of possibility as Tarski and Quine do. It seems to me that the possibility always exists of taking another step in forming the number series. Thus a potential, not an actual infinity (Tarski and Quine say: they do not understand this distinction.)

[[p. 3]]

I: Perhaps there is also an in-between stage, similar to language I, without negative universal sentences. (Tarski: This does not appear to be an essential difference to him, since he conceives of a sentence with free variables as an abbreviation for a sentence with a [[universal]] operator.)

We can conceive of a universal sentence for natural numbers as the joint assertion of all its instances, since for each natural number, an expression is on hand (Tarski: but not a real expression as a thing, in case the number of things is finite.)

Tarski: For the *metalanguage M* we naturally use a richer language than S_1, if we want to have 'true' relate to a non-impoverished language. But *this semantics in M cannot be considered as providing true understanding, rather only as a calculus* with finite rules, which are *formulated in S_1 as a part of M*. When we say '... is true$_0$' we mean by that: " '... is true$_0$' is proven in M" and this is a sentence in the part S_1 of M. 'Provable' naturally cannot be defined in S_1.

---

17. Presumably, Quine intends the following:
$\exists 3x(\phi x) \equiv \exists x \exists y \exists z (x \neq y \wedge y \neq z \wedge z \neq x \wedge \phi x \wedge \phi y \wedge \phi z)$.

Quine: We must replace this with the definite concept 'x is a proof of y.'

I: Or a term 'proven,' which is not defined, rather for which we have the rule that 'y is proven' follows from 'x is a proof of y,' while 'not-proven' does not occur.

[[p. 4]]

We together: So now *a problem*: What sort of part S of M can we take as a kind of *nucleus*, such that

1.) S is *understood* in a definite sense by us, and

2.) S suffices for the formulation of the syntax of all of M, as far as is necessary for science, in order to treat the syntax and semantics of the complete language of science.

1. It must be investigated, if and how far the *poor nucleus* (i.e. the finite language S_1) suffices here. If it does, then that would certainly be the happiest solution. If not, then two paths must be investigated:

2a. How can we justify the *rich nucleus* (i.e., infinite arithmetic S_2)? I.e., in what sense can we perhaps say that we really understand it? If we can, then we can certainly set up the rules of the calculus M with it.

2b. If S_1 does not suffice to reach classical mathematics, couldn't one perhaps nevertheless take S_1 and *perhaps* show that *classical mathematics is not really necessary for the application of science in life*. Perhaps we can set up, on the basis of S_1, a calculus for a *fragment of mathematics*, which suffices for all practical purposes (i.e. not something just for everyday purposes, but also for the most complicated technological tasks).

[[p. 5]]

Quine on 2a: The following are considerations against allowing S_2 as the nucleus: if we understand S_2, we understand all of set theory, not only as a calculus that we can construct, but rather we can formulate it in S_2. Because of Löwenheim-Skolem, there is a countable model for the theory of sets, thus a relation R between natural numbers with the meaning of '$\in$' in Quine's system, which satisfies all the axioms there. We then take 'R' as a logical predicate in S_2.

I: This appears to be a very essential addition to me. Then it becomes doubtful whether we can still say that we understand S_2.

Quine: Yes. This probably shows that 'R' is not definable in S_2, as stated earlier.

I: On this route, the difference still remains between the understanding of elementary arithmetic (S_2) and the understanding of general set theory. For me, subjectively: I believe I understand S_2 (not completely clearly like S_1, but still real understanding, not merely the operation of a calculus). On the other hand, with general set theory: if I would venture to say that I understand it, then I would at least wish to stress a large though gradual difference.

[[p. 6]]

A special question:
I: If 'T' is introduced as a *predicate for truth in M* only through syntactical rules, but we only understand a part of S, not all of M, how do we gather that 'T' signifies truth?

Tarski: The syntactical rules will be made so that the condition of adequacy is fulfilled, i.e., that for each $\mathfrak{S}_i$, '$\mathfrak{S}_i$ is true ≡ ...' is provable.

[But: This still holds only for an object language which is a part of M. Tarski appears to assume this situation for the most part. Otherwise, not $\mathfrak{S}_i$, but the translation of $\mathfrak{S}_i$ must be taken for '...'; but again, then it is not known that 'T' signifies truth!]

I: If two predicates fulfill the conditions of adequacy, then are they equivalent with certainty? If so, then the meaning of 'T' really is determined through the specified rules.

Tarski: That does not appear to be the case.

[But: If 'T$_1$' and 'T$_2$' fulfill the condition, then it holds for each $\mathfrak{S}_i$, that $\mathfrak{S}_i$ is T$_1$ ≡ ... ≡ $\mathfrak{S}_i$ is T$_2$; thus $\mathfrak{S}_i$ is T$_1$ ≡ $\mathfrak{S}_i$ is T$_2$.

Then the last sentence is provable. Then aren't T$_1$ and T$_2$ necessarily extensionally equivalent?]

090-16-26   Feb. 13, 1941
Conversation with Tarski.
On Systems without Types.

Tarski says: *1. Systems with types*. One can indeed extend PM [[*Principia Mathematica*]] to transfinite types, but not in a simple way. One needs not only variables that run through all finite types, but rather should also run through all present types. But then it is actually superfluous to still have bound variables at each type as well. Then, finally, the types fall out completely.

I: Doesn't one still need the types for the constants, especially the non-logical ones?

T: Perhaps one may still need them; but perhaps also the ontological types suffice.

2. Systems without types. T. intuitively prefers these. 2 cases here:
 a. Those with "*principles of production*" (e.g., axioms of sums, of powersets, of set separation, of set replacement, etc.). These have the great advantage that [[a]] future, unforeseen strengthening can be introduced by new principles of this kind, without thereby losing the older ones. Here, one has everything present which one needs in practice; and if it becomes apparent that the practice will be exhausted, then one can introduce new principles.

Here belongs: *Zermelo, von Neumann, Bernays*. Bernays's general system is the latest and perhaps the best at present.

Further considerable advantage (in *comparison to Quine's* system): for the lower functional calculus (with schemata, without predicate variables), only *finitely many axioms* are introduced (so no ∈-schemata, as in Quine's case).

[[p. 2]]

b. Quine's System: Disadvantage: It appears as though everything were finished, since one cannot see any simple steps to strengthen the system. (If Quine's ML were the only logic book found after 1000 years, while all the others were destroyed and forgotten, it would be another 300 years before the people would discover that one can make an entirely different system.) There is no simple, clear, visible path to strengthening: one can see no natural alternative possibility for the stratification condition; one cannot introduce (ontological) types, since the universal-class is already present; no principles of production.

(I believe *Quine* would say: strengthening is achieved through new axioms, on the basis of which further entities are explained as elements.)

T: He told Quine, even before publication [[of *Mathematical Logic*]], that it certainly would not be advisable to ground a logic textbook on such a system that was not yet fully investigated, that perhaps had problematic disadvantages, and that will perhaps even be found contradictory.[18] It is also a disadvantage that *Cantor's theorem* cannot be proved.

T: *The Warsaw Logicians*, especially *Leśniewski and Kotarbiński*, considered a *system like PM* [[*Principia Mathematica*]] (but with a simple theory of types) completely self-evident as a formal system. This limitation worked strongly and suggestively on all the students, and on T. himself until "*Wahrheitsbegriff*" (where neither transfinite types nor a system without types is considered, and finitude of types is implicitly presupposed; they were first articulated in the appendix, added later). But then Tarski saw that an entirely different system-form is used in *set theory* with great success. So he finally came to consider this system-form without types as more natural and simpler.

[[p. 3]]

I: The types appear to me completely natural and understandable; to a certain extent, stratification too. But how should one understand Quine's "*non-elements*" or the corresponding "classes" of Bernays? *T*: That is not so bad. There are also systems without non-elements. It simply depends on the *order of the language*. We are speaking now not of syntactic types but rather of *ontological types*. When the non-elements are simply the elements of the highest type, then in that case such [[non-elements]] exist. But when the order of the system (i.e.,

---

18. This final suspicion of Tarski's proved to be justified. Rosser found an inconsistency in Quine's axioms for classes in the first edition of *Mathematical Logic* (published in 1940). Quine rectified the situation in the second edition. (See the second preface to the second edition, p. *ix*.)

the smallest ordinal number greater than the number of all previous types) is a *limit number*, in the simplest case ω, then there is no highest type and thus no non-elements. (He thinks this is not really known at present; he wants to publish something to draw attention to it.)

For many purposes, allowing a *system of type ω would be the most useful*. In this case we are of course not allowed to erect the axiom of infinity in Zermelo's form (then $\{\Lambda; \{\Lambda\}; \ldots\}$[19] is itself of type ω, so it requires a language of order $< \omega$). But, instead of this, one can simply assume an axiom of infinity which says that the *number of individuals is infinite*. (Of course, here again Russell's scruples would be violated; while Zermelo's form has the disadvantage that an infinite set of *logical* entities is constructed.) (The principle of extensionality must naturally then be restricted to proper sets, i.e. non-individuals.)

090-16-27 Feb. 16, 1941
On finitistic syntax.
(Stimulated by conversation with Tarski on finitism, Jan. 31, 1941)

Tarski thinks we ought to take as expressions, sentences, and proofs only items that are *actually written-down*. But this is much too narrow. Then PM [[*Principia Mathematica*]] does not contain a single proof of a theorem.

But we can make it *finitistic nonetheless*: we take as symbols only actual things, but as expressions and proofs not only certain actual spatial arrangements of these things, but rather (non-spatial) sequences of these things, designated either by the series of names of these things, separated by commas (elementary sequence expression), or designated by descriptions, e.g. as the union of two previously-described sequences, for which we have introduced abbreviations. (So sequences of things, not of kinds of things; the symbols are thus only tokens, i.e., we do not assume things in different places are the same; nevertheless, we can express what we usually formulate thus: "different occurrences of the same sign," namely: different places in different sequences for the same thing.)

Example:

Object language symbols	x	y	z	P	(	)	¬	∨	∃
Their metalinguistic names	a_1	a_2	a_3	a_4	a_5	a_6	a_7	a_8	a_9

The sequential expression 'a_4, a_5, a_1, a_6' then designates the sentence '$P(x)$', even if this sentence never actually occurs (as a spatial series of four things of this type).

Problem: Is this talk of sequences whose length is greater than the number of things in the world compatible with the principle of finitism? I.e., is such a sentence understandable for the finitist?

We can then define the following properties of sequences:
'Sentence' (The rules of formation of the object language)

---

19. Here 'Λ' denotes the empty set.

'Axiom' (The rules of deduction for the object language)
'Directly derivable'
'Proof'
'Derivation'

There are still only *finitely many symbols* of the object language. But we can speak of expressions whose length is greater than the number of things. E.g.
$\| a_7, a_1, a_{100}, \ldots | 5 \|$
Here [[*viz.* '...']] I write in a sequential expression, which designates a certain very long expression of the object language. This [[*viz.* the whole expression]] should be the designation of the expression in the object language that *5 identical partial expressions* of the written form stand next to each other.

090–16–24   Feb 16, 1941
Empirical vs. Logical Finitism. Tarski's finitism is a logical one. He claims: perhaps the number of things in the world is finite; in this case, one can only speak of finitely many natural numbers as well.

I counter: We are empiricists. Thus we say: our *knowledge* is restricted to the finite; i.e., each confirmation is based on a finite amount of evidence, i.e., a finite set of observation sentences.

But: We can nonetheless speak about finite classes of arbitrary higher cardinal numbers, also about the single natural numbers (e.g. $1000 \neq 1001$), without bringing the number of things in the world under consideration. So *logic and arithmetic will be independent of the contingent number of things in the world*. Nevertheless, logic and arithmetic also remain in another sense finitistic, if they should really be understood.

Arithmetic (of the natural numbers) was in fact discovered without our knowing with certainty (up to the present) if the number of things in the world is finite or not. And no one doubts the proven sentences; the concrete sentences (i.e., without variables) appear especially indubitable. Thus arithmetic can indeed be independent[20] of a factual hypothesis about the world.

Also, if the number of things (e.g., electrons etc.) is finite, then nonetheless the *number of events* can be assumed to be *infinite* (not only the number of temporal-points within an interval, as a consequence of the density, but rather also the number of temporal-points a unit distance away from one another, in other words: infinite length of time). Is this a factual hypothesis? Or is it not again connected to *logical possibility*?

---

20. Carnap has written 'dependent,' but that makes no sense given the context.

090-16-23 Feb 19 1941[21]
Conversation with Tarski and Quine, on finitism, II: 17.2.41

I: If we have only finitely many things, and thus finitely many names 'a,' 'b,'... 'Q,' then we can build *arbitrarily long sequences*:
$R(a,a)$
$S(a,a,a)$
$T(a,a,a,a)$
$\vdots$

Naturally, in the same world, we cannot write down arbitrarily long sequences; but with the help of abbreviations, we can indeed talk about them. With these, we can build an unrestricted arithmetic.

Quine: The decisive question here is whether we introduce variables for these sequences. We must do so in order to make an unrestricted arithmetic. But then we are making an ontological assumption, namely about the existence of sequences. But if we do this, then we can in the same way also assume *classes, classes of classes etc.*; with that we also obtain an unrestricted arithmetic. But with that we would give up reistic finitism.

Tarski: We want the (perhaps finitely many) things of the world ordered in some arbitrary way (see the earlier conversation): $0, 0', 0'', \ldots$. The thing-names also serve as numerals. Then axioms analogous to those of Peano hold good for them, but without the assumption of infinity (so we must construct the Peano AS such that this becomes an axiom, and then is omitted). ~~For example, we can explain thus: for each (too long) accented-expression, which no longer denotes a thing in the series, should denote 0 again. (But then 0 has a predecessor! And if these expressions denote another thing, then these 2 have different predecessors!)~~ On the basis of this we should attempt

[[p. 8]]

to construct a *recursive arithmetic*.
Free variables as well (only as an abbreviation for a sentence with universal operator, but without universal negated sentences).

I: Then *similar to Language I*.[22] Accented expressions for sufficiently large numbers cannot be written out, because there are not enough symbols in the world. We assumed the *Peano axioms*,
Quine: including the axiom of complete induction, but without the axiom of infinity. (For example, we can formulate the Peano AS such that the assumption of infinity becomes an axiom, and then *cross it out*.)

---

21. The page numbers of this section begin with page 7. This presumably continues RCC 090-16-25, since it has six pages and is titled "Conversation with Tarski and Quine on Finitism, I".
22. The notes have 'II' here, but that cannot be correct.

I: But one can indirectly build up numerals for the large numbers, with the help of recursively defined functions, e.g. 'power(10, 30)' ($= 10^{30}$).

Quine: Perhaps one could fix it such that all numerals that are so-and-so high do not denote some further thing, but rather they denote some fixed, chosen thing (e.g. 0; but then 0 has a predecessor; or another thing, but then this has 2 different predecessors), instead of needing a certain change in the Peano Axioms. Or rather: we do not understand 'prod(a, b) = prod(c, d)' as a relation between two things (which are not there), but rather as a relation between 4 things a, b, c, d; and analogously for more complicated sentences. Or perhaps even better: only predicates are introduced via recursive definitions, not functions; then no unmeaningful numerals appear.

[[p. 9]]

On the formulation of syntax in finitistic language.

I: Should we here understand as expressions only those actually written down in ink, or arbitrary conceivable sequences composed of actually existing things? (So that the alphabet will only need to be written down once, somewhere.)

Quine: Neither. We also conceive of parts of things as things; so all wholes, of parts of electrons and so forth, exist, even if not spatially interconnected. A 'P' is then a thing of a certain form; for such things there is a minimal quantity, since they should be composed of electrons. But every location of space where similarly sufficient material is, e.g. here in the wall, then a 'P' is present. (I believe this agrees with an earlier idea of mine, which I explained years ago.)

I: Even if space is finite, isn't *time infinite*?

Tarski: Not with certainty. 1. Perhaps quantum theory will give up continuity and density, so that each interval of time has only finitely many parts (so there are no arbitrarily small parts of time.) 2. Time in the large is possibly finite, in that only finitely many points of space and finitely many things return to the same state of affairs, so time runs back upon itself; circular structure. In any case, we want to build the structure of the language so that this is not excluded from the beginning.

Quine: In order to compare space with time, we should take *quanta of energy* instead of electrons as the smallest parts; so all wholes composed out of such parts as things (individuals).–A linguistic expression is a spatially interconnected thing (i.e. a sign's parts must be sufficiently close to one another).

[[p. 10]]

I: If, for syntax, we consider only the actual arrangements, not the possible ones, then paradoxical consequences follow. For there is e.g. a sentence S_1, which more-or-less fills up a star, and another sentence S_2, which does the same; but there is no conjunction nor disjunction of both these sentences, since there are no sufficiently large interconnected things. Another example: S_1 is proved through a proof which more-or-less fills up the largest star; further, a derivation of S_2 from S_1 more-or-less fills up the same star. But the concatenation of both chains of sentences is nowhere. Consequently, according to the proposed finitistic concepts, we cannot say that we have proved S_2. But every logician will surely want to say that if S_1 is proven and S_2 is derived from S_1, then S_2 is also proved (not merely "provable," which is inexpressible in this language).

It appears to me that the entire proposal suffers from a mistaken conception of arithmetic: the numbers are reified; arithmetic is made dependent on contingent facts, while in reality it deals with conceptual connections; if one likes: with possible, not with actual facts.

[[p. 11]]

Tarski: Perhaps the paradoxes in the syntax can be avoided by referring to the Gödel numbers of sentences. "a is a proof of b" is a relation between two numbers.

I: But the Gödel numbers for proofs are so stunningly high that they very quickly exceed the limits of the numbers (which are things here) present here.

Quine: Perhaps we should indeed conceive of expressions as spatially interconnected things, but not demand the same of proofs and derivations as well. It suffices that the sentences of a proof are present somewhere.

I: But the order of sentences in a proof is essential!

Inserted on Feb. 19, 1941
Perhaps the difficulties which I recorded can be at least technically avoided in the following way. The sentences which I would like to utter, but cannot assert as true because of the paradoxes, we cannot assert or prove in S_1, but in calculus M; so [[these sentences can be asserted]] in the more comprehensive language, which is only a calculus, but is not actually understood, whose rules are formulated in S_1.

This would indeed technically overcome the difficulties. But my reservations concerning the factual conception of arithmetic are not thereby removed.

090–16–06 Feb. 21 1941
Finitistic Language, through modification of Language I.
(In connection with the conversations with Tarski and Quine on finitism.)

We order all things in the world
0 is the beginning-thing; x' is the successor of x.

Problem: How should we interpret the accented expressions that are too large, for which no further thing exists? These accented expressions themselves naturally cannot be written down (assuming that the speech is only of one world, i.e., that the world in which we write is the same as the one about which we write). But abbreviations of such accented expressions can in fact be constructed. Let 'k'

be the abbreviation-name for the *final thing*. What should 'k''', 'k'''', etc. signify? Different possibilities:

a. $k' = k'' = \ldots = k$. The final thing is its own successor.

b. 'k''', 'k'''', etc. should all signify 0: $k' = k'' = \ldots = 0$. (Quine proposed this.) But that *runs into problems*; for from $k' = 0$ follows $k'' = 0'$, at least if we have '$(x = y) \supset (x' = y')$,' which is surely natural.

c. $k' = 0; k'' = 0'$; etc.

[[Picture of a circle of arrows (c.); followed by a picture of (a.), namely, a one-dimensional chain ending in a loop from the last element to itself.]]

[[p. 2]]

We want to try to use recursive definitions and restricted operators. Perhaps it will thereby become apparent, which of the above interpretations (a), (b), or (c), is the most appropriate.

In language I we have 2 axiom-schemes, which in a certain way *recursively* introduce the *restricted universal operator*:

PSI4. $(x)0(..x..) \equiv ..0..$

PSI5. $(x)y'(..x..) \equiv (x)y(..x..) \wedge (..y'..)$

In (b) and (c) we would have: $k' = 0$; Let S_1 be: '$(x)k'(P(x))$'. S_1 can be transformed: since $k' = 0$: $(x)0(P(x))$; by (4): $P(0)$. S_1 can be transformed via (5): $\underbrace{(x)k(P(x))}_{\text{This says } everything\text{'s P!}} \wedge \underbrace{(P(k'))}_{P(0)}$;

So *we must accept interpretation (a)!*
$(\exists x) \ldots (..x..)$ and $(Kx) \ldots (..x..)$ can be interpreted correspondingly.

Axioms of Arithmetic.
PSI9: $\neg(0 = x')$; remains valid on interpretation (a). (Not on (b) and (c)!)
On the other hand *PSI10*: $(x' = y') \supset (x = y)$ will be *invalid on (a)*! (Also for (b); on the other hand, it would be valid on (c).)
So *accents*! (In case we want to take (a).)
(On the basis of (a) and PSI9, PSI10 signifies *invalidity in the domain of things*.)

'$\underbrace{(x)k(P(x))}$' is equivalent to '$(x)k'(P(x))$', to '$(x)k''(P(x))$', etc.; this is true≡Everything is P

K-Operator: PSI 11:

$Q[(Kx)y(P(x))] \equiv [\neg(\exists x)y(P(x)) \wedge Q(0)$
$\vee (\exists x)k'[P(x) \wedge (z)x(\neg(z = x) \supset \neg P(z)) \wedge Q(x)]$

Thus:

$Q[(Kx)k'(P(x))] \equiv [\underbrace{\neg(\exists x)k'(P(x))}_{\text{nothing is P}} \wedge Q(0)]$
$\vee (\exists x)k'[P(x) \wedge (z)x(\neg(z = x) \supset \neg P(z)) \wedge Q(x)]$

is excluded, only let $k(= k' = k'' = \ldots)$ be P; when this $[['(z)x\neg(z = x) \supset \neg P(z)']]$ is true, then each thing (until k') that is $\neq k'$ (so $\neq k$) is not P.
So axioms other than PSI10 remain valid!

Can we prove $(x = y) \supset (x' = y')$?
Premise: $a = b$ (1)
PSI8: $(x = y) \supset ((x' = z') \supset (y' = z'))$ (2)
(1), (2) $(a' = z') \supset (b' = z')$ (3)
(3) $(a' = a') \supset (b' = a')$ (4)
(4), PSI7: $b' = a'$ (5)

From this it follows: if $a = a'$, then $a' = a''$, $a'' = a'''$, etc.
We *define*: $\text{Ult}(x) = x = x'$;
From this it follows: $\text{Ult}(x) \supset (x' = x'') \wedge (x'' = x''') \ldots$
$\ldots x = x' = x'' = \ldots$
We can define a *function* l such that for each *normal* number a: $l(a) = 0$, and for $k(= k'$ etc.$)$: $l(k) = k$;
Def: $l(x) = (Ky)x(y = y')$.

We assume *all the rules RI 1-4, including complete induction!* The rule of induction means: each thing is reachable in finitely many steps from 0; i.e., there are no things besides those we denote by accented-expressions (or their abbreviations).

$\neg\text{Ult}(a)$ means: a is not the final thing; thus $a \neq a'$, $a \neq a''$, etc. thus: a is a *normal number*.

From $\text{Ult}(a)$ follows $a = a'''^{\cdots}$, thus $\text{Ult}(a'''^{\cdots})$.
Thus there is *at most one final thing*. (And none, if the number of things is infinite.)

From $\neg\text{Ult}(a)$ follows: $(x)a(\neg\text{Ult}(x))$; i.e. if a is normal, then so are all earlier things (numbers).

We can now set up *recursive definitions*. Not only for predicates, but *also for functors*. Then closed expressions, even if "too high," are interpreted on the basis of (a).

Thus all the syntactic concepts can be defined, as in [*Syntax*] Ch. II; instead of the syntax of I, the syntax of a stronger language, which contains *general set theory*, can be formulated in the same way, *e.g. II*, or *Quine's system, or Bernays' system, etc.*

090–16–12 Feb. 23, 1941
The Language of Science, on a finitistic basis.
(In connection with the conversations with *Tarski and Quine* on finitism; see pages.)
(Cf. here also: "Finitistic language, through modification of Language I" from Feb. 21, 1941)

We begin with a basic system BS.

This language is *understood, finitisitic*.

Individuals: certain *observable things* and their observable parts; we name them in some successive series as we need them, by 'α', 'α'', 'α''', etc. Let 'k' be the abbreviation of the name of the *last thing* (i.e.: of the last thing for which we have constructed a name, not of the last thing in the world).

universe of discourse: a certain *finite class of things of the world*!

Variables :   'u', 'v', ...
Restricted operators : $(u)..(..u..)$
                           $(\exists u)..(..u..)$ These will be introduced later by
                           $(Kx)..(..u..)$ *definitions*!
                           ↑
                           limit expn.

Free variables (as in I)? *Perhaps we do not need them!!* We want to try to manage *without them*!

[[p. 2]]

S_n	^{n-1}g and ^{n-1}f, also bound.	*Semantics*. 'true$_{S_{n-1}}$' etc.
	⋮	⋮
S_3	^2g and ^2f, also bound. *Theory of functions* for real and complex numbers; infinitesimal calculus	*Semantics*: 'true$_{S_2}$'.
S_2	^1g and ^1f: $F_1 \ldots;\, f_1 \ldots;\, (F);\, (\exists F)$ *Arithmetic of the real numbers*. *Physics*: *coordinate system*. Physical laws as axioms.	*Semantics*: 'true$_{S_0}$', 'true$_{S_1}$'.
S_1	Unrestricted: $(x), (\exists x), (\mathrm{K}x)$. $0, 0', 0'' \ldots$ *Number-variables* $x, y, \ldots$. *Arithmetic of the natural numbers*.	*Syntax* (on the basis of definite rules) for S_0; $\ldots S_n; \ldots$ '*provable*', '*derivable*'
BS (=I without PSI 10)	$\alpha, \alpha', \alpha'', \ldots$ (These are *observable things* and their observable parts!)	*Syntax* (axioms and rules of inference) are formulated here for: S_0; $S_1, S_2, \ldots$
	Restricted operators: $(u)..(..u..);$ $(\exists u)..(..u..);\, (\mathrm{K}u)..(..u..)$ *Primitive Description*: observable thing-predicates: $P_1, P_2, \ldots$	*only definable*: '*directly derivable*', '*proof sentence*' etc.

[[p. 3]]

Axioms in BS
The axiom-schemata are as in language I, but:
1. *Not* PSI 10 $((x' = y') \supset (x = y))$, since, in conjunction with the others, it entails *infinity*.
((1.3.:)[23] For a language without defined signs, the 𝔖t are the only 𝟛, so the physical 𝔣u would be taken as primitive.)
  2. *Instead of the free variables*, closed number-expressions:

---

23. I believe this indicates an insertion added on March 1.

So:
in PSI 5   '3_2' replaced by   '3_2'
       6   ,,   ,,
       7   '$\check{3}_1$'   '$\check{3}_1$'
       8   '$\check{3}_1$' and '$\check{3}_2$'   '$\check{3}_1$' resp. '$\check{3}_2$'
     and   '$\begin{pmatrix} \check{3}_1 \\ \check{3}_2 \end{pmatrix}$' by   '$\begin{bmatrix} \check{3}_1 \\ \check{3}_2 \end{bmatrix}$',
       9   '$\check{3}$' by 3
      11   '$\check{3}_2$'   '3_2'

Rules in BS: as in Language I, but:
R1 is *eliminated* (Substitution)
R4 is *eliminated* (*complete induction*)!
There *remains* only R2 (*connectives*) and R4 (Implication).
Perhaps *complete induction*, but in *restricted form*:

$$\frac{\ldots\alpha\ldots \quad (u)--[(\ldots u\ldots) \supset (\ldots u'\ldots)]}{(u)--'(\ldots u\ldots)}$$

Or perhaps thus (if k is the final designated thing):

$$\frac{\ldots\alpha\ldots \quad (u)k[(\ldots u\ldots) \supset (\ldots u'\ldots)]}{(u)k(\ldots u\ldots)}$$

This *indeed holds*, but it does *not need* to be postulated as a special rule, but rather it can be formulated as a 'derived rule.'

Explicit and recursive definitions.

They will be formulated as *rules of definition*, not as definition-sentences as in I; but completely analogous to those in I.
D1. '$nf(u)$' for 'u''. (This is unnecessary).
D2. 1. '$sum(0, v)$' for 'v',
     2. '$sum(u', v)$' for '$(sum(u, v))'$'

Or, in the form of *schemata*:
D1. $\mathfrak{fu}_1(\mathfrak{Z}_1)$ *for* $\mathfrak{Z}'_1$
D2. 1. $\mathfrak{fu}_2(\mathfrak{nu}, \mathfrak{Z}_2)$ for $\mathfrak{Z}_2$,
     2. $\mathfrak{fu}_2(\mathfrak{Z}_1, \mathfrak{Z}_2)$ for $\mathfrak{fu}_1(\mathfrak{fu}_2(\mathfrak{Z}_1, \mathfrak{Z}_2))$.

Problem: In the formulation of the axioms, the rules and definitions of BS are in BS.
'$\mathfrak{S}_1$', '$\mathfrak{Z}_1$' and the like occur. These are *free metavariables*! Can we get *rid* of them? We must *replace them via restricted bound variables!*

As a *restriction* we take the *number* k; we have denoted $k + 1$ things with accented-expressions. This does not mean that there are only $k + 1$ things in the world, but rather only that we have only gotten that far with the task of naming the things.

E.g. *Axiom 1* (D 103):[24] Instead of '$GrS1(u) \equiv \ldots u \ldots$',
(This [[$\ldots u \ldots$]] means: u has the form $\mathfrak{S}_1 \supset (\neg \mathfrak{S}_1 \supset \mathfrak{S}_2)$)
or $\mathfrak{pr}_{103}(\mathfrak{Z}_i)$ for $\ldots \mathfrak{Z}_i \ldots$,
we write: $(u)k[GrS1(u) = \ldots u \ldots]$.

Or: We can just as well still *use free variables*, but they do *not signify unrestricted universality*, but rather only run through the $k + 1$ designated things:
thus '$\ldots u \ldots$' is not an abbreviation for '$(u)(\ldots u \ldots)$',
but rather for '$(u)k(\ldots u \ldots)$'.
In other words: as an abbreviation for a conjunction with $k + 1$ components:
$(\ldots \alpha \ldots) \wedge (\ldots \alpha' \ldots) \wedge \ldots \wedge (\ldots \alpha^{(k)} \ldots)$;
(that is: we can just as well introduce unrestricted operators in place of free variables! See page 6 below) So *fundamentally only a molecular*[25] *language; everything else is an abbreviation!*

[[p. 6]]

Construction of BS_k (i.e., the basis system for k things)
Fundamental symbols: ( ) , $\alpha' = |$; *physical* $\mathfrak{pr}$ *and* $\mathfrak{fu}$ *as well*.
The *definitions serve only as abbreviations, including* where they have recursive form; then *elimination is possible*!
We *define*:
1. from '|': the *connectives*: $\neg \vee \wedge \supset \equiv$
(in Language I, instead of $\equiv$, we had '=').
2. *Restricted universal operators*:
    1. '$(u)\alpha(..u..)$' for '$..\alpha..$';
    2. '$(u) - -'(..u..)$' for '$(u) - -(..u..) \wedge (.. - -'..)$'. This must be expressed more exactly through *schemata*. (1.3.) Better to add: '"$(.. - -'..)$" is omitted, if it is not a sentence.' This makes a restricted universal sentence always meaningful, if $\mathfrak{S}_i \begin{bmatrix} `\alpha' \\ u \end{bmatrix}$ is meaningful (where $\mathfrak{S}_i$ is the operand). This addition (or something similar) is necessary e.g. for the formulation of the principle of complete induction, see page 8 below.
3. *Restricted existential operator*: '$(\exists u) - -(..u..)$' for '$\neg(u) - -(\neg(..u..))$'.
4. *Restricted K-operator*: '$\cdot - \cdot(Ku) - -(..u..) \cdot -\cdot$' for
'$[\neg(\exists u) - -(..u..) \wedge \cdot - \cdot \alpha \cdot -\cdot] \vee (\exists u) - -[(v)u(..v.. \equiv v = u) \wedge \cdot - \cdot u \cdot -\cdot]$'
5. 'k' for '$\alpha^{'''''\ldots}$' (Here we write in the final accented-expression used, namely that with k accents). (For technical simplification, we can naturally introduce for 'k' decimal-expressions for natural numbers.)

---

24. See Carnap (1934/1937, §23): "**D 103**. $GrS1(x) \equiv (\exists y)x(\exists z)x[Satz(x) \wedge (x = imp(y, imp[neg(y), z]))]$," In words, **D 103** says that x is a primitive sentence of the form of PSI I: $\mathfrak{S}_1 \supset (\neg \mathfrak{S}_1 \supset \mathfrak{S}_2)$.
25. In Carnap's terminology, "a molecular sentence is one not containing variables but consisting of atomic sentences... and connectives...; a general sentence is one containing a variable" (Carnap 1942, 17).

6. *Free variables*: '...u...' for '$(u)k(...u...)$'.
(1.3.:) Or instead of free variables: *unrestricted operators*:
6. '$(u)(...u...)$' for '$(u)k(...u...)$'.
7. '$(\exists u)(...u...)$' for '$(\exists u)k(...u...)$'.

The unrestricted universal- and existential-operators are translatable into conjunctions [[resp. disjunctions]] with $k+1$ components.
The *rules of formation* (for $\mathfrak{z}\mathfrak{z}$, $\mathfrak{St}$, $\mathfrak{z}$, $\mathfrak{Arg}^n$, and $\mathfrak{S}$) are the same as in I, (1.3.:)
But: addition: '$A\,\mathfrak{St}$ *has at most k accents*'!
(or, if we allow longer $\mathfrak{St}$: 'a *proper* $\mathfrak{St}$ has *at most k accents*').

[[p. 7]]

Axiom schema for BS_k. We formulate them such that they *do not assume* the presence of *variables*.
1. Those of the *propositional calculus*.
2. For *identity*:
   a. $\mathfrak{z}_i = \mathfrak{z}_i$.
   b. $(\mathfrak{z}_i = \mathfrak{z}_j) \supset (\mathfrak{S}_\mathfrak{l} \supset \mathfrak{S}_\mathfrak{l}\begin{bmatrix}\mathfrak{z}_i\\\mathfrak{z}_j\end{bmatrix})$
3. For α (i.e., the *first thing*): $\neg(\alpha = \mathfrak{z}_i')$.
4. For k (the *last thing*): ($k = k\underbrace{'''\cdots}_{\text{one or more accents}}$.) $\mathfrak{St}_k = \mathfrak{St}_k''^{\cdots}$.

(1.3.:) *But this axiom* is *unnecessary if* we allow only proper $\mathfrak{St}$ in the rules of formation!

Here, in place of 'k', its definiens '$\underbrace{\alpha'''^{\cdots}}_{\mathfrak{St}_k}$' can be written; this is better, if we do not take 'k' as primitive, but rather as defined (see page 6 (5)). In cases where we take 'k' *as a primitive*, (4) can be written in the simple form with 'k'; but then we must replace the definition of k with the following *axiom*:
5. $k = \underbrace{\alpha'''^{\cdots}}_{\mathfrak{St}_k}$. (1.3.: *This is a better definition!* For 'k' *is not a fundamental sign!*

(1.3.:) Since we have eliminated PSI 10, we must indicate via other fundamental axioms that two differing expressions between $\mathfrak{St}$ *and* $\mathfrak{St}_k$ are not the same:
6. $\neg(\mathfrak{St}_i = \mathfrak{St}_j)$, where $\mathfrak{St}_i$ and $\mathfrak{St}_j$ are two different *proper* $\mathfrak{St}$ (i.e., ones with at most k accents).
Simpler, completely *analogous to PSI 10!*:
6. $(u)(v)[(u' = v') \supset (u = v)]$. (Because of the addition in the *middle of p. 6*, this cannot be applied to '$k''^{\cdots}$'.)
Better without variables: 6. $\mathfrak{z}_i' = \mathfrak{z}_j' \supset \mathfrak{z}_i = \mathfrak{z}_j$.
Thus: axiom-schemata for BS_k correspond to the group (a), (c), (d) for I; but without variables!
Rules for BS_k: only the *rule for implication*.

[[p. 8]]

Complete induction, even in the general form as in I (which here is not really general, but rather restricted to the finite), can now be proved in BS_k; a special rule is not necessary.

	Premises	
	$P(\alpha)$	(1)
	$P(u) \supset P(u')$	(2)
(1) (2)	$P(\alpha')$	(3)
(3) (2)	$P(\alpha'')$	(4)
	$\vdots$	
	$P(\underbrace{\alpha''^{\cdots}})$	(k + 2)
	k accents	
(1) (3) (4) ... (k + 2)	$P(\alpha) \wedge P(\alpha') \wedge P(\alpha'') \wedge \ldots P(\alpha^{(k)})$	(k + 3)
(k + 3), def. univ. oper.	$(u)\alpha^{(k)} P(u)$	(k + 4)
(k + 4), def. of k	$(u)k(P(u))$	(k + 5)
(k + 5), def. free var's	$P(u)$	(k + 6)

(1.3.:) After the introduction of *unrestricted operators*, the *principle of complete induction* becomes *provable!*:

$$P(0) \wedge (u)[P(u) \supset P(u')] \supset (v)P(v)$$

For the value k for 'u', '$P(u')$' is not a sentence (since 'k'' is not a numeral); nonetheless the bigger '$(u)[P(u) \supset P(u')]$' is a sentence, if a suitable addition is made in the definition of the unrestricted universal operator (as given earlier, see the middle of p. 6).

[[p. 9]]

Are the operators truly eliminable? Even if the *restriction is descriptive*? Yes. *Example*: $(w) \underbrace{(Ku)5(P(u))}_{\text{restricted}}(Q(w))$.

This becomes:

$$\neg(\exists u)5[(P(u)) \wedge (w)\alpha(Q(w))] \vee (\exists u)5[(v)u(P(v) \equiv v = u) \wedge (w)u(Q(w))]$$

Each of the two $(\exists u)5$ operators are eliminated, and give a 6-component disjunction.
The $(w)\alpha$ operator is eliminated, disappears
For $(v)u$ and $(w)u$: Through the elimination of 'u' these universal operators (which appear in all six disjunction components) each become a accented-expression (between α and α''''') through the restriction; then they will be eliminated; it yields a conjunction with at most six components.

[[p. 10]]

BS_k as syntax-language, for BS itself and for other calculi.
What do we want to express in BS_k?

Perhaps at best we restrict ourselves to those calculi that have only finitely many kinds of symbols; but each symbol type is allowed to contain infinitely many symbols; we do not need names for all these symbols in the syntax language, but only a $\mathfrak{pr}^2$ for identity '*eq*'. Thereby *language II, e.g., is excluded*, since an infinite number of types. To represent the syntax of a richer language, we use a full arithmetical language, whose syntax is stated in BS_k.
(Or should we *restrict ourselves even further, to calculi with finitely many symbols? And deal with all other calculi as we do in II*?)
1.3.: *Yes*; then in BS_k we can only speak of finitely many objects!

Naturally, we cannot define '*provable*' in BS_k, rather only the definite concepts 'axiom' and '*directly derivable*'; 'sentence' is indeed definite ; but perhaps we can restrict ourselves here to the fundamental concepts 'Atomic formula' and 'directly constructible.'
Perhaps it is not necessary here to define '*proof*' and '*proof sentence*' as well; similarly 'construction sequence' (for formulae). The practical determination to accept each sentence, as soon as it is proven, is implicitly held, if we decide:

1. We want to accept each axiom;

2. If we have accepted $\mathfrak{S}_1$ and $\mathfrak{S}_2$, and $\mathfrak{S}_3$ is directly derivable from them, then we also want to accept $\mathfrak{S}_3$.

This then leads to acceptance of the proven sentence, and of each sentence which can be derived from the already accepted sentences.

[[p. 11]]

Problem: what should we take as *expressions*?
Different possibilities:
An *expression in K* is
    1. a thing with spatial, linearly ordered parts (-sign).
    or 2. a sequence of things (-sign)
    or 3. a number n (expressed by a accented-expression, so = thing number n).
    or 4. a numerical pair m, l, namely of the mth expression of length l, in a lexigraphical ordering (something like: we fix an alphabetical order for the (finitely many) symbols of K. Then we order the expressions of length l alphabetically,

e.g. for $l = 3$:

			No.
a_1	a_1	a_1	1
·	·	a_2	2
·	·	a_3	3
a_1	a_2	a_1	4 (This would be 4, 3).

090-16-21   Feb. 23 1941
Another interpretation of the higher numerals

Setting $k = k' = k''$ etc. is probably dubious. (In the original Tarskian outline, at least, it remains unknown that each proven equation is also an arithmetical truth in the customary interpretation.) Then sentences that agree with customary arithmetic are valid, and this can lead to great disadvantages in syntax. On the other hand, we need names for expressions in syntax, and thus for finite sequences of things. We now wish to signify *the higher numerals by abbreviated names*:

Sequences of length 2:	Name:
α, α	k'
$\alpha, 1$	k''
$\alpha, 2$	k'''
$\vdots$	
α, k	
$1, \alpha$	$\vdots$
$1, 1$	
$1, 2$	
$\vdots$	
$1, k$	
$\vdots$	
k, α	
$k, 1$	
$\vdots$	
k, k	$k + (k+1)^2$
Length 3: α, α, α	$k + (k+1)^2 + 1$
$\alpha, \alpha, 1$	$k + (k+1)^2 + 2$
$\vdots$	$\vdots$
k, k, k	

and so on.

We can easily reach *this result via the following rules*:
1. Accented-expressions: $\alpha, \alpha', \ldots$; let the longest proper accented-expression be $\mathfrak{St}$. ('k' is an abbreviation for $\mathfrak{St}_k$, but is not itself a $\mathfrak{St}$.)
2. *Sequence expression* $\mathfrak{Sq}$ is composed of a finite number of accented-expressions, separated by commas: $\mathfrak{St}_1, \mathfrak{St}_2, \ldots \mathfrak{St}_n$
3. $(\mathfrak{Sq}_i)' = \mathfrak{Sq}_j$, where $\mathfrak{Sq}_j$ is built out of $\mathfrak{Sq}_i$ as follows:
   Let $\mathfrak{Sq}_i$ be $\mathfrak{St}_1, \mathfrak{St}_2, \ldots \mathfrak{St}_n$.
1. Let $\mathfrak{St}_m$ be the last (i.e., furthest to the right) $\mathfrak{St}$ that is not $\mathfrak{St}_k$; $\mathfrak{St}_m$ will be replaced by $\mathfrak{St}'_m$.

2. Each of the n $\mathfrak{St}$ in $\mathfrak{Sq}_i$ that are $\mathfrak{St}_k$:
$(\mathfrak{Sq}_i)' = \underbrace{\alpha, \alpha, \ldots \alpha}_{n+1}.$

(So: we replace each $\mathfrak{St}$ with 'α,' and add one more new 'α'.)

090–16–04 March 1, 1941.
On Finitism. Conversation with Tarski; also Quine, Goodman, III.

I explain my language-system (see pages from Feb 23): it refers to a finite number of designated things, with a largest $\mathfrak{St}$ ($\mathfrak{St}_k$); $k+1$ things.

Tarski: I would like to have a system of arithmetic that makes no assumptions about the quantity of numbers at hand, or assumes at most one number (0).

Let A_n be the system of those sentences of customary arithmetic which are valid, if there are only numbers $< n$; so A_0 has no numbers; A_1 only has 0; and so forth. Let A_ω be the entirety of customary infinite arithmetic. For the purposes of simplification we want to exclude A_0, so we assume the existence of at least *one* number. My (i.e. Tarski's) system should contain all and only the sentences that are valid in each of the systems A_n ($n = 1, 2, \ldots \omega$). Here belong, e.g., all sentences of the following form: no functors occur, all universal operators at the beginning of a formula are not negated, no existential operators.

Perhap we should first have only predicates, not functors, since these introduce existence assumptions. We can let '0' be the fundamental symbol, but in place of the successor-functor ''' the successor-predicate '*Succ*' is better.

We could use *recursive* definition to a much greater degree; not only the primitive recursions, and the so-called general recursions, but also, e.g., those that appear in the definition of the semantic concept "satisfaction" (especially not the place where the corresponding sentential function itself contains a universal operator). Then we do understand such recursion. The definition of "satisfaction" is the definition of a predicate, not a function, for we need a universal operator in the definition. Here there is almost the whole Peano system, except for the claim that each number has a successor. But as a kind of replacement, we have here the claim '$x \neq x'$', namely in the form '$(x)(y)(\mathrm{Succ}(y,x) \supset x \neq y)$'.

[[p. 2]]

(Tarski:) Perhaps this system is similar to that of C. (see my pages of Feb 23); but it does not include the sentences that contain 'k'. If we took 'k' as a parameter, both systems would perhaps become completely similar. *In reality we never want to assume a completely fixed number k.*

We have variables in the language from the beginning; these run through all the things in the world; but it remains open how many things there are. Instead of '$prod(2,3) = 6$', we say: 'if x is a successor of a successor of 0, and $y\ldots$, and $z\ldots$, then '$prod(x,y) = z$' (or instead of this, $prod(x,y,z)$). In a similar way one must perhaps translate universal sentences with functors into implicit sentences;

Question: can we introduce functors generally, so that we obtain definite translation rules of this kind? Quine: this agrees very well with the old pre-Russellian, [[unreadable]] conception of mathematics (which is also represented by Bennett), that mathematics only makes conditional assertions.

Common conversation:
If a certain basis system BS that we completely understand is constructed, then there are *2 options* for the construction of the complete language W of science:

1. We introduce ever more items into BS *through definitions*, e.g. infinite arithmetic of the natural numbers, theory of real numbers, of functions, and so on; all of physics. If this could be completed, it would be the ideal solution. But it appears quite doubtful whether it is possible. Perhaps one will be able to obtain a fragment of mathematics and physics W' (in agreement with classical mathematics and physics); perhaps even as much as is needed for all practical goals of science. Then that would still be a very good solution.

2. If this cannot be carried out far enough, then we must use BS as a syntax language, in order to construct W as a calculus, without laying claim to interpretation. (W receives a piecewise interpretation by means of W').

[[p. 3]]

Quine: Then W is really only a myth.
I: No, not a myth, simply a machine. It would be merely a myth, if we were to add a pseudo-interpretation to part of the machine (symbolic calculus), via references to entities that do not actually exist.
Tarski: But option (2) would have this unsatisfactory consequence: it would remain truly *mysterious* how the machine worked correctly, i.e., how do we explain that when we feed true sentences into the machine (as premises), then true sentences also come out (as conclusions).
We: Perhaps that is not an unsolvable riddle. We build the machine for this goal, and we reject it if we notice that it does not accomplish this goal. Perhaps even in BS one can show: if a machine is constructed in such and such a manner, then it delivers true conclusions from true premises.
Tarski: The rules for recursive definition of predicates are still not developed.
[I: It appears to me that the restricted operators are important here; we will allow $n + 1$ such operators in the definiens for the argument, with the restriction that only n can be used.
Think this over!]

090–16–19 March 2, 1941
"$\mathfrak{k}$-*numerical identical Formulae*, after Hilbert-Bernays, *Grundlagen der Mathematik*.
Volume I, p.119 ff. [in German edition] (without identity!):

A formula of the lower functional calculus is $\mathfrak{k}$-numerical identical ($\mathfrak{k}$ is finite, $\neq 0$) $=_{df}$ it turns into an identical formula of the propositional calculus (i.e., a tautology) via interpretation in a $\mathfrak{k}$-numerical individual domain. The intended interpretation is as follows:

$(x)\mathfrak{A}(x)$ is replaced by $\mathfrak{A}(1) \wedge \mathfrak{A}(2) \wedge \ldots \mathfrak{A}(k)$,

$(\exists x)\mathfrak{A}(x)$ is replaced by $\mathfrak{A}(1) \vee \mathfrak{A}(2) \vee \ldots \mathfrak{A}(k)$.

Theorem (p. 121). *If a formula is $(\mathfrak{k} + 1)$-numerically identical, then it is also $\mathfrak{k}$-numerically identical.* (Then we can replace the argument '$\mathfrak{k} + 1$' with '$\mathfrak{k}$' everywhere, for the formula remains identical in the propositional calculus.) (This *only holds for calculi without '='!*)

So: if a formula is $\mathfrak{k}$-numerical identical, then it is also identical for all numbers smaller than $\mathfrak{k}$, but not necessarily for the larger numbers as well. For each number there are formulae that are identical (and for all smaller numbers), but are not identical for the larger. As $\mathfrak{k}$ changes, the classes of identical formulae become ever smaller:

[[Picture: Concentric circles, with the largest labeled '1-numerically identical,' then '2', next largest '3', then ellipsis, and a final smallest circle. An arrow connects the smallest circle to the words: 'Identical in the finite (i.e., for each finite k)']]

p. 121. *Theorems*.

1. *Every* formula *provable* in the lower functional calculus (Hilbert's "Predicate Calculus") is identical in the finite.

2. (Wajsberg). If we add an arbitrary formula to the calculus as an axiom that is $\mathfrak{k}$-numerically identical but not $\mathfrak{k} + 1$-numerically identical, then $\mathfrak{k}$-numerically identical formulae will be provable.

p. 123. 3. For the *monadic* predicate calculus, the *converse of (1)* also holds: every formula identical in the finite is provable.

But: with the help of $\mathfrak{pr}_2$, formulae can be built that are identical in the finite, but are not provable; namely, those that are valid only in the finite (which can be taken as *conditions of finitude*); they are the negations of those formulae that are satisfiable only in the infinite.

Example: 1. "R is irreflexive and transitive; each individual is a first element (so: without a final element)."

2. "S has a first element, is *one-many* (expressed without identity), has no final element."

[[p. 2]]

p. 129. *Gödel's completeness theorem.* Each formula of the predicate calculus is either contradictory or satisfiable (in a countable domain).

Thus: *every generally valid formula is provable*.

But this theorem *cannot* be taken over into *finitistic* proof theory.

But there is a corresponding finitistic completeness claim.

Predicate calculus with identity.

Here there are formulae that are only $\mathfrak{k}$-numerical identical, but neither for larger nor smaller numbers; namely those that signify that there are exactly ℓ individuals. Also *(1) holds* here. And *Gödel's completeness theorem too.*

090–16–18 March 18, 1941.
Finitistic Language.
  Only recursively defined *predicates*, not functors, since these require existence assumptions. Also, no successor functor, but rather the predicate ('*Succ*') or, even better, '*Pred*'.
  Axioms: [Ignore this, if the other system with '*Pred*' meets with approval.]
I. Propositional Calculus.
II. Arithmetic:
  1. $\neg Succ(0, x)$ 0 is first element
  2. $Succ(x, y) \wedge Succ(x, z) \supset y = z$
  3. $Succ(x, z) \wedge Succ(y, z) \supset x = y$ is one-one
  No axiom that no final element exists; so it remains open whether the domain is finite or infinite.
III. Identity.
  1. $x = x$
  2. $(x = y) \supset (\ldots x \ldots \supset \ldots y \ldots)$.   Schema like PSI8
IV. Restricted universal, existential and K-operators.
(like PSI4, 5, 6, 11.)
(for PSI5:) $Succ(z, y) \supset [(x)z(\ldots x \ldots) \equiv (x)y(\ldots x \ldots) \wedge (\ldots z \ldots)]$;
  Rules:

$$\left.\begin{array}{rl} 1. & \textit{Substitution} \\ 2. & \textit{Implication rule} \\ 3. & \textit{Complete induction} \end{array}\right\} \text{(as in I).}$$

$$\frac{\ldots 0 \ldots \quad \ldots x \ldots \wedge Succ(y, x) \supset \ldots y \ldots}{\ldots x \ldots}$$

[[p. 2]]

Recursive definitions: General schema:
1. $R(-, -, -, 0) \equiv -------$
2. $Succ(z, y) \supset [R(-, -, -, z) \equiv --------- R(-, -, -, y) ---]$
The three argument places '$-, -, -$' on the right must not be the same as those on the left, but rather arbitrary! They ought to be bound as well! *Why is the usual identity of the arguments demanded??* And demanded that they not be bound?

$(x = y + z)$ $Sum(x, y, z)$:
1. $Sum(x, y, 0) \equiv x = y$,
2. $Succ(v, z) \supset [Sum(x, y, v) \equiv (\exists u)x(Succ(x, u) \wedge Sum(\underbrace{u}_{\text{new bound variable}}, y, z))]$

$(x = y \cdot z)$ $Prod(x, y, z)$:
1. $Prod(x, y, 0) \equiv x = 0$.

2. $Succ(v, z) \supset [Prod(x, y, v) \equiv (\exists u)x(Prod(u, y, z) \wedge Sum(x, u, y))]$.

[[p. 3]]

Perhaps it is simpler with the predecessor-functor δ? (As in Bernays: 1.)$\delta(0) = 0$; 2.)$\delta(n') = n$.) (Or it can be written "'x', since this is a special sign, analogous to the usual successor sign "'", and because no functors should appear besides.
Axioms for 'δ':
$(\delta(y) = x) \equiv [(y = 0) \wedge (x = 0)] \vee [\neg(y = 0) \wedge Succ(y, x)]$.

090–16–16 March 19, 1941
Finitistic Arithmetic
(Outline on the basis of conversations with Tarski, III, of March 1 1941.)

Only predicates, not functors, since these imply existence assumptions.
Recursive definition for predicates, of a new kind, since no successor-sign is at hand.
Predecessor predicate: '*Pred*'. (is more convenient than '*Succ*', since the series of the arguments is the same as succession in the series.)

[[p. 2]]

The whole thing goes very well with '*Pred*' for predecessor; this is easier, because the succession of arguments is the succession in the series.
Axioms.
I. *propositional calculus.* II. *Operators.*
(for PSI5:) $Pred(y, z) \supset [(x)z(\ldots x \ldots) \equiv (x)y(\ldots x \ldots) \wedge (\ldots z \ldots)]$
PSI 4, 6 (Existence), 11 (K) as in I.
III. *Identity.* As in I.
IV. *Arithmetic.*
    1. $\neg Pred(x, 0)$ 0 is a first element
    2. $Pred(x, y) \wedge Pred(x, z) \supset y = z$
    3. $Pred(x, z) \wedge Pred(y, z) \supset x = y$
No axiom that there is no final element; so *whether the domain is finite or infinite remains open.*
Rules:

                1. Substitution
                2. Implication rule   } (as in I).
                3. *Complete induction*

$$\frac{\ldots 0 \ldots \quad \ldots x \ldots \wedge Pred(y, x) \supset \ldots y \ldots}{\ldots x \ldots}$$

Translation

[[p. 3]]

Question: Must we still maintain that *0 is the only beginning element*?
$$\neg Pred(x, \ldots) \downarrow \ldots = 0.$$
Perhaps a new rule is necessary?

Can we perhaps express it with a universal operator?
Perhaps a new axiom: $(x)y(\neg Pred(x, y)) \equiv y = 0$.   (a)
Or is this *provable* with the help of the earlier axioms? *Yes*, through complete induction on y:

1. It is trivial for $y = 0$.
2. We must prove:
$[(x)y(\neg Pred(x, y)) \supset y = 0] \wedge Pred(y, z) \supset [(x)z(\neg Pred(x, z)) \supset z = 0]$

from a modified PSI5:

$Pred(y, z)$	$\supset$	$[(x)z(\neg Pred(x, z))$	$\equiv$	$(x)y(\neg Pred(x, z) \wedge (\neg Pred(z, z)))]$
			$\supset$	$(x)y(\neg Pred(x, z))$
	(use:	$(x)y(\ldots x..) \supset ..y..$	$\vdots$	
			$\supset$	$\neg Pred(y, z)$
$Pred(y, z)$	$\supset$	$[Pred(y, z)$	$\supset$	$\neg(x)z(\neg Pred(x, z))]$
$Pred(y, z)$			$\supset$	"
			$\supset$	$[(x)z(\neg Pred(x, z)) \supset \underbrace{\ldots}_{\text{arbitrary}}]$
			$\supset$	$[$ " $\supset z = 0]$

From (1) and (2), after complete induction: *(a)*.
So a new axiom is not necessary, and neither is a rule. The derivation according to the above rule follows thus:
$\neg Pred(x, \ldots)$

Th.13.6b (based on complete induction): $(x) \ldots (\neg Pred(x, \ldots))$
               (a) $\ldots = 0.$

[[p. 4]]

Recursive definitions:
General schema:
1. $R(-, -, -, 0) \equiv -----$
2. $Pred(u, v) \supset [R(-, -, -, v) \equiv -----R(\cdot, \cdot, \cdot, u) -----]$
The three argument places '$\cdot$, $\cdot$, $\cdot$' must not be the same as those on the left. They ought to be bound as well (see example above)!
A different way is better! See p.5!

Why is the usual identity of the arguments demanded?? And that they are not bound? Like Hilbert-Bernays, perhaps Gödel too?

$(x = y + z)$ $Sum(x, y, z)$:
1. $Sum(x, y, 0) \equiv x = y$,
2. $Pred(u, v) \supset [Sum(x, y, v) \equiv (\exists z)x(Pred(z, x) \wedge Sum(z, y, u))]$
   $u' = v$ $x = y + v$ $z' = x$ $z = y + u$
                    $x = y + u'$ v, z, u bound!

$(x = y \cdot z)$ $Prod(x, y, z)$:
1. $Prod(x, y, 0) \equiv x = 0$.
2. $Pred(u, v) \supset [Prod(x, y, v) \equiv (\exists u)x(Prod(u, y, z) \wedge Sum(x, u, y))]$.

[[p. 5]]

Perhaps *Recursion schema as follows*:
1. $R(x, \cdot, \cdot, 0) \equiv \underbrace{------}_{x}$
2. $Pred(u, v) \wedge R(w, \cdot, \cdot, u) \supset [R(x, \cdot, \cdot, v) \equiv \underbrace{------}_{u,v,w,x}]$.

Example:

1. $Sum(x, y, 0) \equiv x = y$,
2. $Pred(u, v) \wedge Sum(w, y, u) \supset [Sum(x, y, v) \equiv Pred(w, x)]$
   $u' = v$ $w = y + u$ $x = y + v$ $w' = x$
                                                        $= y + u'$

1. $Prod(x, y, 0) \equiv x = 0$.
2. $Pred(u, v) \wedge Prod(w, y, u) \supset [Prod(x, y, v) \equiv Sum(x, w, y)]$
   $u' = v$ $w = y \cdot u$ $x = y \cdot v$
                                                        $= y \cdot u'$

090–16–17 April 16, 1941
Perhaps we can introduce '$0''''$' through contextual definition:
$P(0''') =_{df} (x)(Pred^3(0, x) \supset P(x))$; we must get rid of the operator; but are we allowed to use free variables in the definiens??
But that's surely what's meant: if the right-hand side is provable then it's L-true.

090–16–15 May 21, 1941
Tarski, on the functional calculus.
(In conversation with Quine and me, May 7 1941)

For the lower functional calculus without predicate variables and with only closed sentences, the following holds:

Translation   183

1. If $\mathfrak{S}_n$ is provable in FC (or analytic, which, following Gödel, is the same thing), then there is a finite series (out of infinitely many) axioms of FC such that $\mathfrak{S}_1 \wedge \mathfrak{S}_2 \wedge \cdots \wedge \mathfrak{S}_m \supset \mathfrak{S}_n$ is a tautology (on the basis of truth-tables).

2. If $\mathfrak{S}_n$ is derivable from other sentences in FC, then there is a finite sequence $\mathfrak{S}_1 \ldots \mathfrak{S}_m$ composed of the axioms of FC and those premises such that $\mathfrak{S}_1 \wedge \cdots \wedge \mathfrak{S}_m \supset \mathfrak{S}_n$ is a tautology.

Tarski: This is especially advantageous for use in *Quine's system* (ML); there the propositional calculus is replaced by truth-tables; then there are axioms of quantification and for $\in$,[26] and modus ponens as a single rule; if the above presentation is used, then *we no longer need a consequence-rule*.

090–16–13   May 26, 1941
Tarski, formal system with quotes.
(Conversation with Tarski, Quine, Goodman, *May 26 '41*)

Tarski: One can easily build an exact formal system that uses quotes to speak about particular expressions, or several together. (*I*: or also about other languages, which perhaps contain other sentences but not other signs).

For *primitive* signs: Variables $x, \ldots$; $\neg, \rightarrow, \Pi$.

Δ: "Δ '$\ldots$' " means: '$\ldots$' is provable; or it can mean 'true' or whatever else as well; no axiom for 'Δ' is put forth, so the meaning remains entirely open.

S: "Sxy" is the expression that results from x, when y is substituted for all its free variables. Schema-axiom for S:
"S '$\ldots$' '$- - -$' " = '$- \cdot -$' if '$- \cdot -$' results from '$\ldots$,' through $- - -$.

I: Doesn't the use of quotes force complications in the rules? E.g., the substitution rule.

Tarski: No.

I: But then "free variables" must be defined so that the variables are not free inside the quotes.

Tarski: Yes.

Tarski: Here the *antinomies* can now be analyzed in a simpler way. Furthermore, a *theorem analogous to Gödel's* can be proven; *without arithmetization*.
(Quine: the proof of incompleteness of protosyntax already exists without arithmetic as well.)
Namely, 'α' can be defined such that $\alpha = $ '$\neg \Delta \alpha$'; this can be done for each predicate, using 'Δ'. Thus we obtain in a very easy way an undecidable sentence. But this does not replace Gödel's result, for here the incompleteness of *arithmetic* does not follow.

090–16–14   May 26, 1941
Quine's "frames".
(Conversation with Tarski, Quine, Goodman, *May 26, 1941*)

---

26. not certain

Quine uses '*frames*', i.e. expressions like '$x = y$', '$p \supset q$', perhaps even '$F(x)$' etc.; these contain signs that do not occur in the object language; but they do not belong to the metalanguage, but rather they are always in quotes; they are used to speak about certain forms of the object language. Thus they are replacements, so to speak, for schemata in the metalanguage.

Tarski: Thay are especially useful if, for didactic reasons, the elaborate schemata of the metalanguage should not be used, as e.g. in the article on definability in *Erkenntnis*.[27]

Quine: 'p' etc. will be used in the new introductory logic book.

090-16-08 May 26, 1941
Conversation with Tarski and Quine (and Goodman), *May 26, 1941*

Tarski: It will be very practical in the future to develop a syntax and semantics of a particular *standard language-form*. And then it will be very useful for each theory (construed thus) to have this form, for all general theorems can be applied to these theories without further ado. This *standard language-form*:

1. No free variables (these often lead students to make mistakes); see also e.g. Uschenko's confusion; for didactic purposes it is best to avoid them);

2. Modus Ponens as the single rule; since there are no free variables, every other rule can be replaced by a corresponding implication sentence as an axiom.

3. For the propositional calculus, no axioms, rather a direct (definite) definition of '*tautology*' (like Quine).

4. Perhaps thus (see other page): in place of proofs and derivations as sequences of sentences, simply: the corresponding impl. sentence is a tautology. In place of the complicated statement of a proof, the statement of the related axioms (i.e. instances of the axiom schemata) (these must be declared, otherwise the assertion of provability is not definitely checkable; or, on the practical grounds of easier 'checkability,' a statement of the related instances of certain previously-proven theorems.

5. '$\in$' *as the single* primitive predicate, even for physics etc. Here '$\in$' is one of the *logical* constants (as I would like) (Quine says: it is taken as a *mathematical* expression).

6. *Individual constants as the single descriptive primitive constants.* But these constants are "individuals" only in the syntactic sense: they are constants for the single occurring variable-type. But considered semantically: they designate classes, classes of classes,

[[p. 2]]

reals etc., namely entities of the $\in$-system, as in Quine.

---

27. This refers to "Einige methodologische Untersuchungen über die Definierbarkeit der Begriffe" (Tarski 1935), translated into English as "Some Methodological Investigations on the Definability of Concepts," in Tarski (1983).

Quine: This appears to be the reverse process from that in ML: there, certain atomic predicates are introduced as the single descriptive, primitive constants (but they cannot be replaced by variables and thus have no designata); while all constants for the values of variables are introduced through definitions, namely as abbreviations for descriptions. Tarski believes his process appears natural. Quine is not certain of the two is preferable.

Tarski: With this language form (individual constants as the single primitive descriptive signs), one can define '*Models* of the corresponding theory' in a simple way: namely, the sequence of corresponding entities that are designated by the constants. Each theory will be conceived of as dealing with certain individuals or things (neither understood in their usual sense), with certain entities, namely classes, relations, and the like.

[*I*: Perhaps we could also incorporate Quine's idea (to not take as primitive any proper individual constants, i.e., a name a for non-class) into Tarski's plan: only take signs for classes as primitive descriptive constants, while signs for proper individuals (i.e. non-classes) will be defined by description, as in Quine. So for each such constant 'a' we assume an axiom: for each corresponding entity, there is an element not identical to the class.

$(\exists x)(x \in a \wedge x \neq a)$.]

7. It is questionable whether the standard language form should also contain *functions*. *Quine* wants n-place functions to be replaced by $n + 1$-ary relations. But *Tarski* thinks that perhaps sometimes it would be technically simpler to allow functors in arithmetic, e.g. '+' etc., so as not to deviate so considerably from the common language form. The question will not be unequivocally decidable.

Quine: The elimination of primitive individual constants in ML also occurred on a philosophical basis: nothing about the existence of objects should be claimed in advance, simply on the grounds that all the expressions of the language are meaningful. But this can in fact be reached using Tarski's form; we can therefore somehow worry that an individual constant, which turns out to signify nothing, signifies Λ.

090-16-30 June 2, 1941
Is there "probabilistic consequence"?, (For discussion with Tarski and Quine)

Consequences in deductive logic (*semantic* sentences):

S_1 is true S_1 is true S_1 is L-true
$\underline{S_1 \rightarrow S_2}$ $\underline{S_1 \rightarrow_L S_2}$ $\underline{S_1 \rightarrow_L S_2}$
S_2 is true S_2 is true S_2 is L-true

(The case in which S_2 follows from S_1 physically is a special case of '$\rightarrow$').
Problem: Is there something analogous, if in place of $\rightarrow$ or $\rightarrow_L$ *a probabilistic- or confirmational-consequence* or something similar appears? Something designated by '--→'. Naturally, the consequence cannot yield "S_2 is true (or L-true)," but rather at most "S_2 is highly probable (or highly confirmed)," or something similar.
(But what does 'probable' mean?)

Since probability, confirmation etc. only make sense as relative concepts, their absolute use must be understood as elliptical for a reference to a standard reference, e.g. the entirety of my knowledge now, or a fixed class K of observation sentences or the like.

The consequence would then be of the form:

$K \dashrightarrow S_1$
$S_1 \dashrightarrow S_2$
$\overline{K \dashrightarrow S_2}$

So, in other words: *Problem: is* '$\dashrightarrow$' *transitive?*: If $\dashrightarrow$ | $\dashrightarrow$, then $\dashrightarrow$.
What happens if one of the two relations in the premisses is $\rightarrow_L$?

$S_1 \dashrightarrow S_2$
1. $\underline{S_2 \rightarrow_L S_3}$ this is *correct*.
$S_1 \dashrightarrow S_3$

But
$S_1 \rightarrow_L S_2$
2. $\underline{S_2 \dashrightarrow S_3}$?
$S_1 \dashrightarrow S_3$

This does not hold generally. It can be the case that S_1, S_3 is only very poorly confirmed (e.g., of 300 observed things, only 100 are P) while S_2, a part of the observations of S_1, S_3 is very well confirmed (namely the 100 P things).

[[p. 2]]

The creation of a "probabilistic consequence" appears *plausible*.

Tomorrow it will probably rain.
E.g.: $\underline{\text{If it rains, then the street will probably (usually, most times) get wet.}}$
Tomorrow the street will probably get wet.

But this consequence is *not valid*! The second premise leaves open the possibility that the street will sometimes not become wet with rain, e.g., if it is covered. Now if the first premise and the conclusion contain a tacitly assumed reference, e.g. to my present knowledge that the street will be covered tomorrow, then the conclusion is false, even if both premises are true.

090–16–11 June 10, 1941
States of Affairs and models.

[[Picture]]
state = assignment of primitive descriptive predicates of the corresponding language to the individuals (of the universe of discourse of the language). Then each $\mathfrak{pr}^1$ is coordinated with a class of individuals, each $\mathfrak{pr}^2$ is coordinated with a class of ordered pairs of individuals.

So must we *only* take into consideration *the extension* of the $P_{..}$??
Let the actual state of affairs of the world be thus:

Translation 187

[[Picture: P_1 is a proper subset of P_2]]

So that: $(x)(P_1(x) \supset P_2(x))[= \mathfrak{S}_1]$ is *true*.
Now here it happens that, for the *meaning* of P_1 and P_2, there are *2 different* cases: 1. The sentence $\mathfrak{S}_1$ already follows from the meanings of both predicates (i.e., from the semantic rules); $\mathfrak{S}_1$ is L-true. Here, it must hold that in each other state $P_1 \subset P_2$.
2. $\mathfrak{S}_1$ *is F-true*. Then this is also allowed as a *state*:

[[Picture: P1 and P2 partially overlap each other, but neither is a subset of the other.]]

Models. Tarski apparently refers to a partially-interpreted calculus, namely, all logical symbols are interpreted; for the usual signs, it is only determined that they are descriptive; but their interpretation is left open.
A *model* for this system = a sequence of n entities, which are coordinated (as designata) to n descriptive signs (for which a fixed ordering, the "alphabetical" one, is presupposed).
The following would be given:
1. A *calculus C*, with an interpretation of the logical signs and with uninterpreted[28] descriptive signs 'P_1', 'P_2', $\cdots$ 'P_n'.
2. A *semantic system S* with the same sentences and signs, but everything is interpreted, and so 'P_1' designates the property E_1, etc.
We construct a *correlation K* between the *model* (M) for C and the state of *affairs* (Z) for S:
$K(M, Z) =_{Df}$ for each r (for $r = 1$ to n): the "classes" of individuals coordinated with $\mathfrak{pr}_r$ (i.e. 'P_r') in M = classes of individuals that have the property E_r in Z.
But: if logical relations obtain between the 'P_r' in S (and so the E_r) (e.g., the earlier example), then certain assignments will thereby be eliminated as impossible, i.e., certain models in C then correspond to no states of affairs in S. In order to avoid this, we could only consider those S where *no logical relations hold between the 'P_r'*. It appears that *then the correlation K is unique*.
Here we have paid attention only to the *type-relations*, e.g., in a model for 'P_r' only classes of individuals are allowed. One could also use *'model' in a further sense*: arbitrary entities are correlated with the descriptive signs.

range of $\mathfrak{S}_i =_{Df}$ $\begin{cases} 1. & \text{\textit{Classes of states of affairs of S}, in which } \mathfrak{S}_i \text{ is true.} \\ 2. & \text{\textit{Classes of models of C}, in which } \mathfrak{S}_i \text{ is true.} \end{cases}$

$\mathfrak{S}_i$ is L-*true* $=_{Df}$ $\begin{cases} 1. & \mathfrak{S}_i \text{ is \textit{true in every state} of affairs of } S. \\ 2. & \mathfrak{S}_i \text{ is \textit{true in each model} of } C. \end{cases}$

---

28. The document actually reads 'interpreted.'

090–16–10 June 18, 1941
Tarski on "state of affairs",
Conversation (with Quine, Goodman, Hempel), June 18, 1941.

Let a language S be given. If more descriptive primitive signs occur, even infinitely many, we can replace them by one thing, namely by the sequence of the corresponding entities. Then we have 4 primitive signs: 3 for logic (including '∈'), and the descriptive names (name = something that denotes an entity, i.e., a value of a variable).

2 entities are equivalent $=_{df}$ for every sentential function in the language, both satisfy it or both do not. Then: they are either identical or their differentiating properties cannot be expressed in the language. The class of entities equivalent to a given entity corresponds to a state; another choice: the class of those sentential functions in S that are satisfied directly by any one (and thus by each) element of this class.

I: Isn't it the case that this no longer corresponds to a *state description*? For example, for a language with 'T' for temperature as the only descriptive constant, I understand as states every function of 4 real numbers, so each entity of T's type.

Tarski: It is better to take each entity in general. We should abolish the types completely. A state corresponds to an entity, of a class of states that we cannot distinguish in S, a class of equivalent entities.

I: But a physicist who introduced 'T' will not refuse '2, 3 ∈ T' as F-false, but rather as L-false, since he doesn't need an experiment to show that it is false. Could one perhaps proceed as follows?:

$\mathfrak{S}_i$ is L-true$_1$ in 0 $=_{Df}$ ... (taking 'T' as a descriptive sign);

$\mathfrak{S}_i$ is L-true$_1$ in M $=_{Df}$ ... (analogously, taking the descriptive signs in M that we use for the semantic rules for 'T'.)

$\mathfrak{S}_i$ is L-true$_2$ in 0 $=_{Df}$ the sentence '$\mathfrak{S}_i$ is true in 0' is L-true$_1$ in M.

But a problem: reduction sentences for 'T' cannot be taken as properly semantic rules; and if we simply use 'temperature' in M, then L-true$_1$ and $_2$ collapse. (But perhaps not, if other words are used in a properly semantic rule, not only a reduction sentence; e.g. 'P_1' designates horse, 'P_2' white horse; then '$P_1 \supset P_2$' is L-true$_2$, but it is not L-true$_1$.)

Tarski: Better as follows: just as we define 'descriptive' through an ultimately arbitrary enumeration, in the same way we also define the further concepts ('L-true$_2$' or whatever) through an enumeration of sentences in S about T, so that the logical consequences ('L-implies$_1$') are taken as L-true$_2$. These sentences signify, for example: T is only quintuples, and furthermore quintuples of real numbers such that no 2 quintuples differ only in their first element, and that for every quadruple, there is a quintuple with a unique first element; but furthermore also: the function should be continuous, should have a first derivative, perhaps also a second etc., (he strongly thinks

[[p.2]]

perhaps rational values for rational arguments, or (Quine) limited to algebraic numbers; but I think a physicist would not want that).

Quine: Thus we avoid "*state of affairs*," intensional language, and the unclear concept 'logically possible.'

Tarski: The physicist chooses these sentences as conditions that a proposed claim about T must satisfy, in order to be assumed as (logically) correct, before experiments about the truth are made.

Quine: It is then the task of a behavioristic investigation to determine what conditions of this kind physicists set up.

I: No, that would give only the corresponding pragmatic concept. As with all other semantic (and syntactic) concepts, here also the pragmatic concept gives only a suggestion, and is not determined univocally.

My considerations on the above.
Corresponds to:

a state	an entity
	or: an entity, which satisfies the additional conditions (not simply: types, rather what Tarski hinted at above; these conditions are set forth by a physicist) = a model of S
- L-range of $\mathfrak{S}_i$	The class of those models of S which satisfy the logical sentential function corresponding to $\mathfrak{S}_i$.
- Actual *state*	the entity denoted via 'T' (here, 'denotes' as an extensional concept)

090–16–05 June 18, 1941
Final conversation about the nucleus-language, with Tarski, Quine, Goodman, and Hempel; *June 6 1941*.

Summary of earlier conversations. The *nucleus language* should serve as the syntax-language for the construction of the complete language of science (including classical mathematics, physics, etc.). The language of science thereby receives a piecewise interpretation, since the *n.l.* is assumed to be understandable, and the *n.l.* is either a part of the entire language, or is coordinated to a part; and the syntactic symbols ($\to_C$) between this part and the rest are conceived such that they represent logical symbols ($\to_L$) (or something similar).

1. The *logico-arithmetic* part of the *n.l.*: unrestricted operators, also [[unreadable]]. (The restriction to recursive arithmetic with only free variables is apparently unnecessary.) Here there are no considerations of finitistic [[unreadable]], since the values of variables are only physical things. Thus it remains undetermined whether their quantity is finite or infinite. The things themselves will be taken as numbers, for which an order is established, on the basis of the successor-relation. (Functions only indirectly used, as an abbreviation of more complicated sentences with the successor-relation.)

2. The *descriptive* part. We have not agreed among ourselves whether it is better to begin with thing-predicates or sense-data-predicates. For the first: I and

Tarski; Hempel follows Popper. For the second: Goodman and Quine. Finally: the language should be as intelligible as possible. But perhaps it is not clear, what we properly mean by that. Should we perhaps ask children psychological questions about what the child learns first, or most easily? I stress the difference between the mere having of experiences, e.g. perceptions, and knowledge. Knowledge, cognition = ability for expression (more generally: for some sort of a discriminatory response).

090–16–20 [[no date]]

For the discussion on finitism.
Tarski proposes looking to Heyting and Weyl, as they reflect upon the construction of mathematics and physics upon intuitionistic principles.
I believe that Gödel's interpretation of classical mathematics via translation into intuitionistic mathematics is also important for us.

090–16–22 [[no date]]
Number and thing.
Following *Eddington*, there are 2^{256} particles $= 2^{(10 \times 25.6)} = (2^{10})^{25.6} = (10^3)^{25.6} = 10^{3 \times 25.6} = 10^{77}$.

Quine takes the things to be classes of particles: $2^{(2^{256})} = 2^{(10^{77})} = 2^{(10 \times 10^{76})} = (2^{10})^{10^{76}} = (10^3)^{(10^{76})} = 10^{(3 \times 10^{76})}$.

Appendix B
German Transcription

090-16-09 *Gespräch mit Tarski, Chic., 6.3.40*
1. '*L-wahr*'. '*logisch-deskriptiv*'. Ich: meine Intuition ist klarer in der Unterscheidung L-wahr–F-wahr, als in logisch-descriptiv. Die Letztere kann ich aber immerhin erklären durch Aufweisung der einfachsten logischen Konstanten in den üblichen Systemen und angabe, dass Alles daraus Definierbaren auch logisch sein soll.
Er: Er hat keine solche Intuition; man könnte ebenso gut 'Temperatur' auch als logisch rechnen.
Ich: Die Wahrheit eines Vollsatzes des Temperaturfunktoren bestimmt man durch Messung.
Er: Man kann aber beschliessen, an einem festgesetzten Wahrheitslehre [unleserlich][1] trotz aller Beobachtungen.
Ich: Dann ist es eine mathematische Funktion, und ein logisches Zeichen, und nicht der physikalische Temperaturbegriff. Bei einem Vollsatz des physikalischen Temperaturfunktores können wir nicht durch blosses rechnen den Wahrheitswert finden.
Er: Das beweist nichts, denn auch für eine mathematische Funktion ist das oft nicht möglich, weil es unentscheidbare Sätze gibt; kein fundamentaler Unterschied zwischen den mathematischen, aber unentscheidbaren Sätzen und den faktischen Sätzen.
Ich: Das scheint mir doch.
   Ich erkläre, dass die Schwerigkeit nur in der allgemeinen Semantik liegt; in der speziellen Semantik einer bestimmten Sprache ist es leicht, die gennanten Begriffe so zu definieren, dass sie mit der Intuition übereinstimmen. Wenn wir das für die Metasprache tun, das kann man indirect für die Objektsprache auch zu allgemeinen Definition können. 2 Wege: 1.) Intensionale Metasprache, mit modalität; 2.) Metasprache geteilt in M_1 und M_2 (siehe MS "Part I", §16).
   Er: Das wird wohl gehen, wenn auch für ihn die Zweiteilung einer willkürlich erscheinen. Ist es möglich, die L-Semantik zu formalisieren, d.h. in der MMSprache ein Kalkül aufzustellen, der die in der MSprache vorgesetzte Deduktion Mittel darstellt, und zwar einen Kalkül mit finiten Regeln? Dann und nur dann wird das ganze für ihn verständlich und annehmbar sein (wenn auch immer

---

1. wahrscheinlich 'unredivierlich'

noch willkürlich in der Abgrenzung). Ich: Man kann die L-Semantiksicher formalisieren; ob mit nur finiten Regeln, übersehe ich im Augenblick nicht. Kann man das Entsprechende für die einfache Semantik (Wahrheitsbegriffe) tun? Er: Sicherlich. (Mir scheint, folgendes Problem muss mal allgemein untersucht werden: wenn wir einen Kalkül mit transfiniten Regeln haben, unter welchen Bedingungen können wir dann seine Syntax wiederum formalisieren, haben[2] wir einen Kalkül mit nur finiten Regeln?)

[[s. 2]]

2. Er: Für ihn ist ein Kalkül ein geordnetes Paar aus einer Klasse (der Sätze) und einer Relation (Folgerung). *Was ist bei mir ein semantisches System?* Ich: Wenn wir L-Begriffe beiseite lassen: (eine Klasse (der Sätze); das ist aber unnötig, weil Feld der [Relation])[3] eine Relation ('designation' auch für Sätze; oder, wenn ohne Sätze, noch die Eigenschaft 'wahr'). *Aber*: diese Relation oder die Eigenschaft 'wahr' muss intensional genommen werden, als Eigenschaft, nicht als Klasse. D.h. wenn zwei Systeme im Umfang dieser Eigenschaft übereinstimmen, so sind sie trotzdem nicht notwendig identisch. Inbesondere genügt es sicherlich nicht (wie er dacht, und was anscheinend seine Auffassung ('semantisches System') ist), die Klasse der wahren Sätze zu nehmen, weil dadurch die Interpretation nicht bestimmt ist. Es ist wesentlich, wie diese Klasse definiert ist. Das zeigt sich dann bei den L-Begriffen. Für ein semantisches System gibt es nur einen adäquaten Begriff 'L-Wahr'; wenn aber nur der Umfang, nicht die Definition, von 'wahr' gegeben word, so sind sehr viele sehr verschiedene Begriffe 'L-wahr' möglich. Er: Das versteht er nicht, weil sine ganzes Denken in einer extensionaler Sprache vor sich geht. Ich: Damit fallen aber wichtige Unterscheidungen fort, die wir auch im täglichen Leben machen. Zum Beispiel eine gewisse Klasse von Personen kann in verschiedenen Weisen definiert werden. Wenn ich dann nur dem Umfang, nicht die definierende Eigenschaft kenne, kann ich unter Umständen eine gewisse Voraussage nicht machen ohne eine bestimmte hinzukommende faktische Kenntnis (nämlich über die Umfangsgleichheit der betreffenden Begriffe).

[[s. 3]]

3. *Logik ohne Typen.* Die beste Form ist die, die ursprünglich von Zermelo gemacht worden ist; auf Grund davon jetzt verbesserte Systeme von *Bernays* (Unterscheidung von Klassen und Mengen) und *Mostowski* (ohne diese Unterscheidung). *Quine* macht in seinen Systemen zu viele Sonderwahrheiten (z.B. so, dass Cantors Theorem nicht stimmt), die die Mathematiker abschrecken, und die anzeigen, dass die Systemform nicht zweckmässig ist.

2. Text unsicher
3. Text sehr unsicher

Ich: Sollen wir die Sprache der Wissenschaft mit oder ohne Typen machen? Er: Vielleicht wird sich etwas ganz anderes enwickeln. Es wäre zu wünschen und vielleicht zu vermuten, dass die ganze *allgemeine Mengenlehre*, so schöne sie auch ist, *in der Zukunft verschwinden* wird. *Mit den höheren Stufen fängt der Platonismus an.* Die Tendenzen von Chwistek und anderen ("Nominalismus"), nur über Bezeichenbarem zu sprechen, sind gesund. Problem nur, wie gute Durchführung zu finden. Vielleicht in ungefähr dieser Art: in der ersten Sprache natürliche Zahlen als Individuen, wie in Sprache I, aber vielleicht mit unbeschränkten Operatoren; in der zweiten Sprache Individuen, die identisch sind oder entsprechen den Satzfunktionen in der ersten Sprache, also den in der ersten Sprache *ausdrücken* Eigenschaften natürlicher Zahlen; in der dritten Sprache als Individuen die in der zweiten Sprache ausdrückbaren Eigenschaften usw. So hat man in jeder Sprache nur Individuumvariable, behandelt aber trotzdem Entitäten verschiedener Stufen. Ich: Diese Beschränkung auf die ausdrückbaren reellen Zahlen, Funktionen von solchen, usw. entspricht dem Finitismus und Intuitionismus; die Tendenz (seit Poincaré) dieser Beschränkung ist gesund und sympathetisch; hat sich aber nicht herausgestellt, dass dadurch die Mathematik unerträglich kompliziert wird und dass die Beschränkung immer eine Willkürliche ist? Er: Die Intuitionisten haben einen solchen Aufbau nie durchgeführt auf einer guten Basis, sondern z.B. den Satz vom ausgeschlossen Dritten verworfen usw. Damit unnötige Komplikationen erzeugt. Es könnte sich doch herausstellen, dass zu den Theoremen der klassischen Mathematik analoge Theoreme in dem beschränkten Gebiete gelten, wenn dieses in geeigneter Weise ausgewält wird (z.B. mit Addition, Multiplikation, und recursive Funktionen lässt sich doch schon sehr viel machen).

102-63-09 Für Diskussion mit Russell. In *Logikgruppe* 18.10.40
    I. "Underlying metaphysics"
Beispiel: Tarski und Russell: "*platonic logic*"
Russell sagt: Ein *Platonismus* unterliegt dem Sprechen von 'Buchstabe x' (also den Gebrauch irgendeines Prädikates?) *)siehe 1b
    Tarski: Ein *Platonismus* unterliegt dem höheren Funktionskalkul (also den Gebrauch einer Prädikatenvariable, besonders höherer Stufe).
    Russell: Die metaphysischen Wörter „*Im Anfang war das Wort*" unterliegt den Philosophien von *Plato und Carnap* (und den meisten dazwischenliegenden Philosophen).
    Ich:

1. Eine nicht-ausgesprochene Ansicht ist häufig impliziert, ob dem Autor bewusst oder nicht.

    a. Wir können ihm zeigen: Du machst diese stillschweigenden Annahmen; denn sonst könntest du diesen Schluss nicht ziehen. oder

b. Wir können ihm zeigen: Du machst diese stillschweigenden Annahmen; daraus erklärt sich dein praktisches Verhalten.
   In dieser Weise können alle Arten von Meinungen erschlossen werden, vernünftige, absurde, magische, sogar contradiktorische.

(Interessante Nebenfrage: Können wir (und wie?) aus blossem Verhalt oder aus dem Gebrauch von Faktischen Sätze schliessen, dass jemand eine bestimmte Logik glaubt die von unserer abweicht?)

2. Eine *metaphysische Lehre* kann niemals in dieser Weise impliziert sein, d.h. notwendig (oder auch nur brauchbar) sein für einen Schluss oder für Erklärung einer Handlung. Denn metaphysische Lehre hat *keinen cognitive Gehalt*. (Hier 'metaphysisch' nicht im empirischen Sinne = allgemeinste Sätze über die Welt, z. B. "jedes Ding besteht aus Partikeln, die weder entstehen noch vergehen, sondern nur ihre Lage (und Zustand) ändern."

3. Dass jemand eine bestimmte *metaphysische Lehre* akzeptiert, *kann nicht erschlossen werden* aus seinem *praktischen Verhalten* (ohne Sprache); kann nicht erschlossen werden aus seinem kognitiven Äusserungen; sondern nur aus metaphysischen Äusserungen, d.h. aus nicht-kognitiven Äusserungenm die er als kognitiv behandelt. ('pseudo-cognitive') (Es ist aber möglich, aus der Äusserung einer bestimmten metaphysischer Lehre zu schliessen, dass der Mann auch eine andere metaphysischer Lehre vertritt. Denn auch zwischen pseudo-kognitiven Äusserungen kann eine Art quasilogische Beziehung bestehen. Z.B. aus "Gott ist allmächtig" folgt logisch "Es gibt ein allmächtiges Wesen.")

Fundamentaler *Unterschied zwischen Metaphysik und Magik*: Magik ist kognitiv, wenn auch falsch; ein magischer Glaube kann daher aus Schlüsse, die der Mann macht, oder aus praktischem Verhalten erschlossen werden. *Es gibt keine metaphysische opinions, sondern nur metaphysische Äusserungen*! Ein Tier kann Magie haben, aber keine Metaphysik! (*Vielliecht ist zuzugeben*, dass wir zuweilen *psychologisch erschliessen können*, dass jemand eine gewisse Metaphysik akzeptiert, weil er einige symptome zeigt, die oft zusammen mit dem bekennen der betreffenden Metaphysik auftreten. (Z.B. wenn eine gewisse Theologie nicht magisch, sondern metaphysisch ist, und wir beobachten, dass ein Mann zu deren Sekte gehört und die übrigen Äusserungen der betreffenden Religion mitmacht, so können wir vermuten, dass er dahin gebracht werden könnte, auch dieselbe Metaphysik zu äussern. Dies ist aber dann verschieden von dem Erschliessen eines faktischen Glaubens; während dieser logisch verknüpft ist mit dem Glauben, den er ausdrückt oder auf Grund dessen er handelt, ist dort *nur psychologischer Zusammenhang*.)

[[s. 2]]

R. Beispiel ([Fane] 18 zu Absatz 4): "*Logic...is thus incurably [!] Platonic*"; wenn ich sage "Dies ist schwarz" und "das ist schwarz", so möchte ich dasselbe über beides sagen, aber das gelingt mir nicht; das kann ich nur wenn ich sage "Dies und das sind schwarz", dann aber sage ich etwas verschieden von dem was ich früher über dies und über das gesagt habe.

Die *Generalität* durch wiederholten Gebrauch des Wortes 'schwarz' ist eine Illusion; in Wirklichkeit ist da nur Ähnlichkeit.
[? Nein. Ich kann beschliessen, unter gewissen Bedingungen Laute einer gewissen Art zu machen (also ähnlich mit einander), und dadurch das Vorliegen jener Bedingungen generell auszudrücken.]

R: *Logik* takes for granted dass dasselbe Wort bei verschiedenen Gelegenheiten vorkommen kann. Aber das ist irreführend.

102-63-11 *Für Diskussion in Logikgruppe.*
27.10.40
Begriff proposition. Vielle Freunde einwenden.
(Wir lägen hier beiseite: allgemeine Einwände gegen Semantik; wir nehmen also an: Semantik, mit Relation Des für Namen und Prädikaten.)
Analogie:

„Zahl"	„Proposition"
Angennomen, Sprache mit Zahlausdruck, aber ohne das Wort 'Zahl'	Sprache mit Sätzen, aber ohne das Wort 'proposition.'
1. *Ohne nummerische Variabel.*	1. *ohne Propositionsvariable.*
Wir führen 'Zahl' ein derart, dass '...ist eine Zahl' dann (aber vielleicht nicht nur dann) wahr ist wenn '...' ein Zahlausdruck ist.	Wir führen 'proposition' ein derart, dass '...ist eine proposition' wahr ist dann (aber vielleicht nicht nur dann) wenn '...' ein Satz ist.
2. *mit nummerischer Variable 'n', 'm'.* Definition: $Nu(n) =_{df} n = n$ [irgendeine analytische Satzfunktion in 'n'.]	2. *mit Propositionsvariable 'p', 'q'.* Definition: $Prop(p) =_{df} \neg p \vee p$ [irgendeine analytische Satzfunktion in 'p'] Mit 'F' und 'x' allein (angenemmen, dass alle Sätze die Form $\mathfrak{pr}(\mathfrak{in})$): $Prop(F(x)) =_{Df} ..F..x..$ analytisch (z.B. '$F(x) \vee \neg F(x)$'). Hier kann 'Des_p' *definiert* werden: $Des_p(u, F(x)) =_{Df} (\exists v, w)(u = v\frown w \wedge Des(v, F) \wedge Des(w, x))$. Oder mit p (in intensionaler Sprache mit 'N'): $Des_p(u, p) =_{df} (\exists v, w, F, x)(u\frown w \wedge Des(v, F) \wedge p = F(x))$; $p = q =_{Df} N(p \equiv q)$.

102-63-10 3.11.40
Über 'proposition'. Singulary connv's:

	Charac-teristik		
c_1	T T	Dies ist *Begriff proposition*; '$c_1 A$' = in englisch 'A is prop.'	$A \vee \neg A$
c_2	T F	Der *absolute Wahrheitsbegriff*; '$c_2 A$' ist L-equiv. mit 'A.' Also *überflussig*.	A
c_3	F T	Der *absolute Falscheitsbegriff*; = *negation sign*; '$c_3 A$' ist L-equ. mit '$\neg A$'	$\neg A$
c_4	F F	Kontradiktorisch	$A \wedge \neg A$

englische Übersetzung
für '$c_r A$'
$c_1 A$: A or not A; A is a *prop*.
$c_2 A$: A is *true*; it is true that A.
$c_3 A$: *not-A*; A is *false*; it is false that A.
$c_4 A$: A & not-A.

Kein hypostasis; wir substanzialisieren nicht, wir betrachten nicht als Ding, was kein Ding ist.

102-63-05 Quine, über *allgemeine Semantik (und Syntax).*
Gespräch, 23.11.40.
Quine: Es wäre zweckmässiger, *nicht Namen für die einzelnen Zeichen zu haben, sondern für die Operationen*, mit denen Sätze gebildet werden: „die Disjunction aus $\mathfrak{S}_i$ und $\mathfrak{S}_j$", „der Universalsatz aus .. (in bezug auf die Variable ..)" usw. Vorteil: die wesentlichen[4] Züge (ob die Disjunktion mit oder ohne Klammern, durch Voranstellung oder Zwischenstellung des Zeichens, usw. ausgedrückt wird) bleiben unberücksichtigt; die manchmal auftretenden vielen Zeichen, die zusammen nur für eine Operation dienen, brauchen nicht einzeln behandelt zu werden (z.B. '(...)(–)'). Er spricht daher lieber von statement composition, anstatt von den connectives.
Tarski: Er hat diese Methode schon früher angewendet.

090-16-02 Tarski, *Über allgemeine Semantik, und Systeme ohne Stufen*
(kürzes Gespräch)
23.11.40
1. Die *Systemvariable* 'S' in der Metasprache M darf *sich nicht* unbeschränkt *auf alle* Systeme beziehen; sonst treten Antinomien auf.
Im Allgemeinen will ich als Werte von 'S' ärmere Systeme als M nehmen, damit in M 'wahr in S' definierbar ist. Aber in der allgemeinen Semantik ist solche Beschränkung wohl nicht nötig. Ich vermute, dass es möglich ist, auch M zu den Werten von 'S' zu rechnen; also universelle Sätze mit 'S' auch für M gelten zu lassen (z.B. „wenn $\mathfrak{S}_i$ L-wahr$_S$, so wahr$_S$" und dergleichen); da aber 'wahr$_M$' nicht definierbar in M, so können wir die Instanz für M nicht in M formulieren,

---

4. Die Text sagt „unwesentlich."

also auch nicht aus dem universellen Satz in M ableiten, obwohl sie mitgemeint ist. Analogie: ein universeller Satz „Alle reellen Zahlen..." bezeiht sich auf alle; dagegen können die Instanzen für die in der betreffenden Sprache nicht definierbaren reellen Zahlen dort nicht formuliert und daher nicht abgeleitet werden, sind aber trotzdem in dem universellen Satz mitgemeint.

2. Es scheint unnötig, sich zu bemühen (wie ich es tue), in der *allgemeinen Semantik* in M alle möglichen Systeme zu behandeln. Für alle praktisch vorkommenden und alle wichtigen Probleme *genügt es wohl*, sich auf Systeme einer gewissen, *relativ einfachen Struktur zu beschränken*, nämlich etwa solche mit Individualvariable und Prädikatenkonstanten. In der Zermeloschen Weise kann dann die ganze Mengenlehre hier ausgedrückt werden, mit Hilfe des Prädikat '$\in$' für Individuen. Das vereinfacht die allgemeine Semantik (und Syntax) ausserordentlich, und wird wohl auch fruchtbarer, weil mehr Ergebnisse zu erzielen.

Für allgemeine Syntax geht das wohl (für den Zweck der Behandlung von Systemen ähnlich der Mengenlehre). Aber wie meint er es in der Semantik? (Er sagt: siehe Anhang zu "Wahrheitsbegriff"!) In der Interpretation müssen wir doch sagen, dass '$a \in b$' heisst dass a ein Element von b ist. Soll dann M ebenfalls diese Struktur haben, oder die mit Stufen?

Dies muss überlegt werden!

[[s. 2]]

3. Verfahren für *Prädikate mit Argumenten verschiedener Stufen*.
   a. *Bedenken gegen transfinite Stufen*: die Regeln werden doch recht kompliziert. (Ich: wir nehmen Variable, die durch alle endlichen Stufen laufen.) Er: wir brauchen wohl auch *Variable die durch alle Stufen laufen*; z.B. wenn wir 'wahr' definieren wollen.
   b. *Ohne Stufen: zwei Unterarten*:
   1. *Zermelo*-Fraenkel (- von Neumann?)
   2. *Quine*. Dadurch charakterisiert, dass absolute Allklassen vorkommen (und durch „andere peculiarities")

Er scheint (1) vorzuziehen. Dort kann 'wahr' leicht nach seiner Methode definiert werden (siehe Anhang zu „Wahrheitsbegriff"). Bei (2) dagegen eigentümliche Schwerigkeiten: wir müssen für Definition von 'wahr' stärkeres System haben; es wird vermutlich nicht dadurch starker sein (wie Quine vermutete), dass neue Grundbegriffe hinzukommen (die Quine dann "nicht-logisch" nennen würde!), auch nicht durch neue Variablenart (hierin stimmt Quine zu), sondern durch hinzugefügte Postulate. (Während bei anderen Systeme (Ich glaube, er meint (1)) gewisse Postulate aufgegeben und durch neue ersetzt werden, werden hier neue hinzugefügt.) Diese neuen Postulate müssen bewirken, dass ein Satz beweisbar wird, der die Existenz eines Modelles für die alten Postulate besagt; nämlich die Existenz einer Klasse von hinreichend höher Kardinalzahl, sodass ihre Elemente aufgefasst werden als identisch mit (oder korrespondierend zu) den Entitäten (Elementen und nicht-Elementen) des alten Systems. Quine: ist es sicher, dass so etwas möglich ist? Tarski: wenn nicht, so würde er Zweifel haben, ob das alte System widerspruchsfrei ist.

090–16–03 *Tarski und Quine, über allgemeine Semantik.*
9.12.40

Zur Definition von 'entity u is *covered* by sm. S' ([I] D17-1) *Tarski*: Man sollte auch noch einbegreifen: Elemente von bezeichneten Klassen, Elemente von Elementen von Klassen usw.

Quine: Die Definition müsste so elastisch sein, dass sie auch für Sprachen gilt, die Universalität anders als durch Variable ausdrückt, z.B. *Schönfinkels* System.

Tarski und Quine: Allgemeine Bemerkung zur allgemeinen Semantik:
Es ist wohl kaum lohnend, die Definitionen und Theoreme eines Systems der allgemeinen Semantik auf die Klasse K aller Sprachen zu beziehen, die in M behandelt werden können, sondern lieber nur auf eine Teilklasse K' die so ist, dass:

1.) Jede Sprache von K (oder jede solche, die wir mit in Erwägung ziehen wollen) ist übersetztbar in eine Sprache von K',

2.) Alle Sprachen von K' haben gewisse üblichen Strukturen.

Am Einfachsten, und für alle praktischen Zwecke hinreichend weit: wir beziehen uns nur in Sprachen, die Individualvariable und Konstanten, Prädikatenkonstanten, und Identität haben; doch Verknüpfungen und Operatoren. Also niederer Funktionskalkül (aber ohne Prädikatenvariable [also so, wie ich ihnen in [II] genommen habe]). Rechtfertigung hierfür: mit hilfen der besondern Relation '$\in$' (die aber hierbei nicht als in jeder Sprache vorkommend vorausgesetzt wird) können wir die Mengenlehre und Mathematik in den niederen Funktionskalkülen übersetzen.

Dies ist *die Unterscheidung zwischen Logik und Mathematik*: *Mathematik = Logik + '$\in$'*. Durch das '$\in$' wird das System non-finitistisch, und vollständig.

102–63–13 *Für Logikgruppe.*
12.12.40

Die *Kolmogorov-Doob Deutung der Wahrscheinlichkeit* (wie Mieses sie in der Sc. Of Sc. Gruppe erklärt hat, und auf die ich hingewiesen hat als befriedigender als die Limit der Gehäufigkeit Deutung)

Verwendet dieselben Begriffe wie ich bei *'state of aff.'* und *'range'*. Eine bestimmte Versuchsreihe wird gemacht; eine destimmte Reihe von Resultaten wird erfolgen.

Wir betrachten alle möglichen Sequenzen von Resultaten	= die *states* of aff. (*Leibniz* mögliche Welten).
Wir betrachten Klassen von solchen möglichen Sequenzen, für die etwas bestimmtes zutrifft	= *range*
Wir schreiben diesen Klassen *measures* zu.	

102-63-04 Quine, MS, (ohne Titel; etwa) „*Lg., Math., Sc.*" gelesen in *Logikgruppe, 20.12.1940.*

Allgemeine Semantik muss beschränkt werden, sonst wird sie trivial. Vorschlag: wir wollen die Sprache untersuchen, die nur folgendes enthält: *Konstante, Prädikate, joint denial, univ. quantification. Mit nur einer Art von Variable; nur geschlossene Sätze.*
Ist dies zu eng? In solche Sprachen können wir übersetzen:
Die ganze mathematik (einziges Prädikat '∈')
Syntax; Protosyntax: 'M'; damit definierbar: concatenn., Identität, Namen von einzelnen Zeichen.
Weitere syntax: dazu '∈'.
Individs Konstante und Funktoren können durch contextual Definition eingeführt werden. (Vorteil, siehe ML 27: 1. technisch: Theorie der Quantifikation kann vereinfacht werden; 2. philosophisch: Fragen der Sinnvollität werden getrennt von Fragen der Existenz.)
Können alle Sprachen in solche übersetzt werden? Das ist das Problem der *Extensionalitätsthese.*
Umgekehrt: gibt es interesante schwächere Sprachen (d.h. solche, die den beschriebenen Raum nicht ausschöpfen würden), die eine Untersuchung Wert sind? Scheint zweifelhaft. Wenn sie vorkommen, können sie getrennt untersucht werden.
Vorschlag: '*Logik*' = *Theorie von joint denial und quantifn.* (Oder auch: Elementarlogik, Logik. *Aber*: der engere Sinn von 'Logik' ist vielleicht besser in Übereinstimmung mit dem Geist der langen Tradition.)
'*Mathematik*' = (Logik +) Theorie von ∈.
'*Physik*' = (Logik +) (Mathematik +) Theorie anderer Prädikate.
Die Grenze zwischen Logik und der übrigen Wissenschaft (einschliesslich Mathematik) ist wichtig!
Wichtige Unterschiede zwischen Logik und Mathematik:
1. *Es gibt keine logische Sätze*, weil es keine logische Prädikate gibt. Untersuchungen der Logikverfahren *metatheoretisch.*
'p', 'q',... 'F', 'G'... kommen nicht vor (oder nur als übersetzbare Hilfsmittel). Stattdessen aussprechende syntaktische Zeichen.
Aber: Es gibt reine *mathematische Sätze*, mit '∈' (z.B. '$(x)x \in x$'). Damit becomment wir *content*; *mathematische subj.-matter* (während Logik nur die Form betrifft).

[[s. 2]]

2. Logik verlangt keine besonderen Objekte, nicht einmal eine bestimmte Grösse des Bereiches; wenn ein normaler Satz logisch wahr vom Gesichtspunkt eines Unendlichkeitsbereichs, so auch aller endlichen Bereiche, und umgekehrt. Die logischen Wahrheiten gelten für beinahe alle Philosophien, einschliesslich Nominalismus und Realismus; Ausnahme: Intuitionismus, aber

vielleicht zu befriedigen durch ausserlogischen Beschränkungen (keine nicht-konstructionalistische Prädikate). *Erst Prädikate* bringen *ontologische* Anfordungen (nicht weil sie bezeichnen; sie gelten hier als synkategorematisch, da niemals Variable für sie vorkommen; sondern: ein Predikät verlangt gewisse Objekte als Werte für die Argumentenvariable; so *verlangt z.B.* '∈' *Klassen*, Universalen; daher ist *Mathematik platonisch, Logik nicht*.

'*Logisch Wahr*' kann syntaktisch definiert werden, und sogar *protosyntaktisch* (wegen Gödels Vollständigkeitsbeweis):
Unendliche Menge von Axiomen der Quantifikation (Axiomen Schemata, wie in M.L.) und modus ponens.
Dies ist mehr elementar als die semantische Charakterisierung mit Hilfe von 'wahr.'
Hiermit wird *keine epistemologische Theorie der logischen Wahrheit* aufgestellt, wie z.B. in Konventionalismus oder Intuitionismus oder Empirismus; ich verstehe diese anscheinend einander entgegengesetzte Theorien immer noch nicht.
'Logische Folge' ist leicht definierbar (z.B. conditional ist logisch wahr; oder: ableitbar).

Extra-log'l. Notations (z.B. mathematisch, biologisch, usw.): Einführung geeigneter Prädikate; und *Axiome. Theoreme* = logischen Folgen der Axiome. Die *Logik ist so das gemeinsame Stück aller (nicht-trivialer) Theorien*.
Z.B.: Elementararithmetik, z.B. durch 'P'
Px, y, z bedeutet: $x = y^z$.
Dann wird Identität definiert; und descrn., durch Kontextdefinition.
Dann $y^z =_{Df} (\iota x) Px, y, z$
$x \cdot y =_{Df} (\iota z)(w)(w^z = (w^x)^y)$
$x + y =_{Df} (\iota z)(w)(w^z = w^x \cdot w^y)$.

Die ganze Mathematik durch '∈'. Axiomatisierung (z.B.: endliche Menge von Axiome, wie bei Bernays (der von Neumann folgt), oder unendliche Menge von Axiome, wie M.L. Die Theoreme sind die logischen Folgen der mathematischen Axiome. Aber sie erschöpfen die mathematische Wahrheit nicht (Gödel).

[[s. 3]]

Universelle *Sprache der Wissenschaft*. Grosse Menge von Prädikaten.
Ontologie, d.h. Werte der Variablen: sehr verschiedene Objektivität, darunter Elektronen, Atomen, Bakterien, Tische, Sinnesqualitäten;
(undingliche Objekte:) auch Zentimeters, Distanzen, Temperaturen, elektrische Ladungen, Energie, Geraden, Punkte, Klassen (oder Eigenschaften).

Einige Leute sehen gewisse Universellen als mehr problamatisch an als andere und reduzieren sie deshalb auf diese (z.B. Whitehead: die Punkte auf Volumina; Carnap und Jefferys: Distanzen und Temperaturen auf reine Zahlen.)

Ich betone: alle Universellen haben schliesslich dieselbe Natur wie punkte, Zentimeter, usw. Klassen sind wahrscheinlich keine Ausnahmen. Ich verlange nicht, dass Klassen oder andere undingliche Objekte eliminiert werden sollen;

vielleicht sind sie nötig für die Wissenschaft. Jedenfalls, wenn wir es tun, so, um Obskures auf Klareren zu reduzieren; dann aber ist kein Grund, bei den Dingen stehen zu bleiben; man möchte Elektronen auf grössere Dinge reduzieren, und vielleicht alle Dinge auf Phänomene. Aber die Richtung grösserer Klarheit oder epistemologische Pluralität ist nicht klar.

Ich glaube eher, wir müssen *Carnap folgen*: die nicht-positivistische oder nicht phänomenalistische Sprechweise der Wissenschaft ist *uneliminierbar annehmen*. Ich vermute, C. hat recht: es gibt nur teilweise Klärung, nicht vollständige definitionale Eliminierung. Diese Klärung geschieht durch Untersuchung der Relationen der Konfirmation zwischen Sätze der entfernteren und solchen der mehr unmittelbaren Art.

Wissenschaft ist voll von myth und hypostasis; Zweck: das chaotische Verhalten der gewöhnlichen Dingen einzubetten in eine mehr verständliche Überwelt; Endaufgabe: prediction inbezug auf die gewöhnlichen Dinge; das ist psychologisch möglisch nur infolge der grösseren "übersichtlichkeit" (sic) der Überwelt, die von der Wissenschaft als intermediary device construiert wird. Die Trichotomie: Phänomene, common sense Welt, Überwelt der Wissenschaft, gilt nur grob; es handelt sich um Grade. Tische sind Hypostasen ebenso wie Elektronen, aber in geringerem Grade. Von der Überwelt können wir auf die gewöhnliche Welt schliessen. Nicht umgekehrt (unterdeterminiert); ebenso ist die gewöhnliche Welt unterdetermineirt durch experience.

Ebenso fasse ich Mathematik auf. Die Theorie der reellen Zahlen prüft sich an den den Berührungspunkten mit der Theorie der rationalen Zahlen. Die allgemeinen Theorie der Klassen gibt gewöhnliche common sense Resultate für endliche Klassen, parallel zu comm. S. Gesetze über heaps [!]. Aber dadurch ist die allgemeine Theorie der Klassen nicht eindeutig determiniert. Daher muss man bewusst nach einem myth suchen; ich tat so, nachdem ich von den Paradoxien las: Russells Mythe, Zermelos, meine eigene.

Nebenbei: solche Überlegungen lassen mir Gödels Theorem (Unvollständigkeit) weniger anomalous erscheinen als früher.

090-16-29 *20.12.40 Quine wird diskutiert*:
Können wir vielleicht die höheren, nicht-finitistischen Teile der Logik (Mathematik) so auffassen, dass ihre Beziehung zu den finitistischen Teilen analog ist mit der beziehung der höheren Teile der Physik zu den Beobachtungssätzen? Dadurch würde die nicht-finitistische Logik (Mathematik) nicht-metaphysisch (wie die Physik). Vielleicht wird dadurch auch leicht geworfen auf die Frage, ob fundamentaler Unterschied zwischen Logik-Mathematik und Physik besteht.

102-63-06 *Bemerkungen zu Quines Vortrag* in Logikgruppe, 10.12.40. 10.1.41
1. Ja, gewisse *Analogie zwischen Mathematik und Physik*, zwischen '$\in$' und 'temp'.
aber *Problem: Was ist der Unterschied?*

2. *"myth & hypostasis"*.

Mythe ist höchstens psychologisch nötig, nicht logisch nötig. Aber sicher hilfreich. *Unterschieden*: theoretischer cogn. Gehalt und *Begleit[[unleserlich]]* (pictorial content)

102-44-11   *Für Gespräch mit Goodman, über Dr.-These.*
2.1.41
Zu meiner Überraschung nimmt er an, *dass ich gewisse Defekte der Quasianalyse nicht gesehen habe*:
p. 113 ff:

Thing	Colors
1	bg
2	rg
3	br

(1, 2, 3) ergibt sich als eine Farbklasses, obwohl keine gemeinsame Farbe.

p. 115 "C. is here the victim of a dangerous... fallacy. It consists in inferg." dass wenn je 2 von drei Klassen überlappen, alle drei überlappen. In Wirklichkeit habe ich diesen Defekt der Quasizerlegung gekannt. Die allgemeine Beschreibung eines Fehlfalles "Aufbau" p.100 unten trifft genau auf Goodmans Beispiel zu! (G. selbst sagt 116) In meiner MS "Quasizerlegung" (1922-23) habe ich ähnliche Fälle behandelt. Dort ist eine Verschärfung der Methode gegeben, durch die mein Fall ausgeschaltet wird; Goodmans Fall wird allerdings doch noch nicht ausgeschaltet.

For me: class h = i, m, o, p
i = d, f, a
m = f, a
o = c, e, a
p = c, f

Dies [[letztes vier]] ist ganz ähnlich wie bei Goodman.

Ähnlich sagt er im Aufsatz mit Leonard (JSL 5, 1940) p. 53 unten (siehe SD): "...mistakenly supposg. that a class of things each member of which is similar to each other is a class of things which are all similar."

p.139. Wörtliches Zitat meiner Warnung, dass wir unterscheiden müssen zwischen Ähnlichkeit in einer bestimmten Beziehung und Ähnlichkeit in irgendeiner Beziehung. Nur die erste ist trivial. "...how is it poss. for him to point out this fallacy so clearly and even refer to section 70 without realizg. that he has there committed essentially the same error?"

[[s. 2]]

Mein Einwand gegen meinen "Aufbau": (ist nicht so sehr die bestimmten Fehler der Quasianalyse, die ich ja schon wusste.)
Die *extensionalistische Auffassung*: Definition von Qualitäten usw. durch Aufzählung.

(Allerdings ist das nur mit Erläuterungen mit "Paarliste" usw. Die wirklich gegeben Definitionen dagegen nicht extensionalistisch, sondern "per intensionem," wenn auch in extensionaler Sprache. Aber die Rechtfertigung der quasianalytische Methode nimmt doch häufig auf diese Paarliste usw. Bezug.)

Folge: Ich würde heute mehr Grundbegriffe nehmen; trotzdem kann man "nominalistische Grundelemente" nehmen.

(Ich sehe nicht in Geringsten den Nachteil davon oder den Vorteil von Goodmans Methode.)

102-63-12   Weitere Diskussion über Quines Bemerkungen, Logikgruppe, 10.1.41.

Ich: Sollte 'logische Folge' nicht weiter genommen werden, sodass ein universeller Satz aus der unendlichen Klasse seiner Instanzen folgt? z.B.:

..0..
..0'..
⋮
⇓
$(x)..x..$

Quine und Tarski: besser: $(x)(Nx \supset ..x..)$, ['N' = natürliche Zahl]

Aber: Wir brauchen die Axiome, um zu wissen, dass $0, 0', \ldots$ *alle* N sind.

Ich: In der Fassung ohne 'N' folgt der Universalsatz auf Grund der Deutung von '(x)'.

Tarski: Wir wollen 'logisch wahr' und 'logische Folge' nur anwenden, wenn es gilt für jede Deutung der nicht-logischen Konstanten.
(Also sollte ich vielleicht doch wieder zu der Definition in [Found.] zurückgehen, wo die Deutung der descriptiven Zeichen ausgeschlossen wurden?? Aber dann Schwierigkeit mit '$P \supset Q$', wenn logisch zusammen zwischen den beiden Eigenschaften. Die Wahrheit ist dann doch auch a priori!)

Quine: '0' kann in einer [[unleserlich]] Sprache nicht als primitiv vorkommen. Wichtig: nur primitive Prädikate, um durch die Formregeln nichts über Existenzauszumachen. In Arithmetik leicht ist ersetzbar durch description. Aber dann brauchen wir wieder die Axiome zur Eindeutigkeit.

Tarski: Der Allsatz ist nicht einmal eine logische Folge aus den Instanzsäten und den Peano Axiomen zusammen;

Ich: Ja, weil für das 5. Axiome, oder vielmehr hier Axiomenschema, andere Deutungen möglich, sodass das Ganze nicht notwendig eine Progression ist. So folgt also der Allsatz nur mathematisch, aber nicht einmal mit den mathematischen Axiomen, sondern derart bei bestimmer Deutung. (nicht sicher.)

Quine: Die „Spezifikation" $(x)(..x..) \rightarrow ..0..$ ist auch keine logische Folge hier; statt '0' müssen wir deskriptione nehmen, und dann sind die Axiome nötig zur Sicherung der Existenz von 0.

[[s. 2]]

Ich: Wenn Spezifikation nicht logisch, so habe ich auch kein Gefühl mehr dagegen, auch die genannte transfinite Deduktion aus der Logik ausgeschlossen zu sehen.

Wundheiler: Nach Tarski-Lindenbaum (Über die Beschränkung der Ausdrucksmittel...) sind die logisch-wahren Sätze in einem Bereich von Individuen diejenigen, die bei jeder eineindeutigen Transformation erhalten bleiben.

Quine: Ja, und die mathematisch-wahren sind die, bei denen erhalten bleibt. Ich: Naturlich; das sagt nicht mehr, als dass die Mathematik (in gewisser Formulierung) durch charakterisiert ist.

Wundheiler: Können wir vielleicht den Unterschied zwischen Logik, Mathematik, und Physik durch die Transformationsgruppe charakterisiert, so wie wir projective, 'affine,' und metrische geometrie charakterisieren durch Transformationsgruppe?

Tarski: Es ist zweifelhaft, ob in diesen Zusammenhang der Gruppenbegriff viel hilft.

Offene Frage, die wir nächstes Mal Diskutieren wollen: Wie ist der *Unterschied zwischen Mathematik und Physik* zu erfassen?

Quine: Es ist ein Unterschied in der Art der Evidenz, bei Mathematik brauchen wir nicht ebenso Experimente wie bei Physik, also Apriori in behavioristischem Sinne.

Ich: Ich glaube, lieber das "A priori" nicht behavioristisch charakterisieren; Behaviorismus ist nur Gradunterschied (Bridgmans pen and paper Operation).

090-16-28 *Tarski, Finitismus*. Bemerkung in Diskussion in der Logikgruppe, *10.1.41*.

Tarski: Ich verstehe im Grunde nur eine Sprache die folgende Bedingungen erfüllt:

1. *Finite* Anzahl der Individuen.
2. *Reistisch* (Kotarbiński): Die Individuen sind physikalische Dinge;
3. *Nicht-Platonisch*: Es kommen nur Variable für Individuen (Dinge) vor, nicht für Universalien (Klassen usw.)

Eine andere Sprache „verstehe" ich nur so, wie ich die Klassische Mathematik „verstehe", nämlich als Kalkül; ich weiss, was ich aus anderen Ableiten kann (oder abgeleitet habe; „Ableitbarkeit" im Allgemeinen schon problematisch).

Bei irgendwelchen *höheren*, „Platonischen" Aussagen in einer Diskussion deute ich sie mir als Aussagen, dass ein bestimmter Satz aus gewissen anderen Sätzen ableitbar (bzw. abgeleitet) ist. (Er meint wohl so: Die Behauptung eines gewissen Satzes wird gedeutet als besagend: dieser Satz gilt in dem bestimmten, vorausgesetzten System; und das heisst: er ist ableitbar aus gewissen Grundannahmen.)

Warum wird auch schon die elementare Arithmetik, mit anzahlbarem Bereich, ausgeschlossen? Weil, nach Skolem, die ganze klassische Mathematik sich durch ein anzählbares Modell darstellen lässt, also in der elementare Arithmetik ausdrücken lässt, z.B. indem man ∈ als eine gewisse Beziehung zwischen natürlichen Zahlen nimmt.

102-63-07 *Logische, mathematische, und faktische Wahrheit.* 11.1.41
Logische Wahrheit ist Wahrheit, die nur von der Deutung der logischen Zeichen abhängt, also auch bestehen bleibt, wenn die nicht-logischen Konstaten durch andere ersetzt werden, oder mit andern Worten: wenn die nicht-logischen Konstanten anders gedeutet werden.

Vielleicht so: *a priori Wahrheit* ist Wahrheit, die nur von der Deutung der Zeichen abhängt, also bestehen bleibt, wenn andere Fakten angenommen werden, aber dieselbe Deutung genommen wird.

Mathematische Wahrheit = a priori, nicht logische Wahrheit.

Problem: Was heisst genau „hängt ab von", „ist bestimmt durch"?

1. *Subjektivistische Formulierung*: B hängt von A ab (ist determiniert durch A, ist eine Funktion von A): Wenn man A weiss, so kann man B finden.

Aber: diese subjektivistische Fassung ist nicht gut, weil sie unwesentliche, nämliche psychologische Faktoren hineinbringt. Z.B.: durch die drei Seiten eines Dreiecks sind die Winkel destimmt (und das kann man leicht einem Anfänger klarmachen). Aber es ist eine komplizierte Methode nötig, um die Winkel wirklich aus den Seiten zu berechnen; es stimmt nicht, dass jeder der die Seiten weiss, auch die Winkel weiss.

2. *Objektivistische Formulierung*: B hängt von A ab, ist function von A: wenn bei einer Transformation A erhalten bleibt, so auch B. *Schwerigkeit*: Wie ist Deutung darzustellen? Was heisst „Transformation, bei der die Deutung erhalten bleibt"?

[[s. 2]]

'P' und 'P'' haben *dieselbe Deutung*, wenn P und P' nicht nur in der wirklichen Welt denselben Umfang haben, sondern in jeder möglichen Welt, also in jedem Gesamtzustand ('state' in Semantik [I]).

Angenommen, wir haben *Zweideutungen* für eine gegebene Reihe von (nicht-logischen?) Konstanten (z.B. '∈', 'temp',...), d.h. zwei Definitionen für 'wahr$_S$' inbezug auf dieselbe Satzmenge S.

(1.) $\mathfrak{S}_i$ ist wahr$_S =_{Df} ..P_1...P_n...$

(2.) $\mathfrak{S}_i$ ist wahr$'_S =_{Df} ..P'_1...P'_n...$

Derart, dass das Definiens von (2) aus dem von (1) dadurch entsteht, dass gewisse nicht-logische Konstanten der Metasprache M (etwa 'P_1',.. 'P_n'..) durch andere ersetzt werden (etwa 'P'_1',.. 'P'_n'..).

102-63-15 11.1.
In der *Physik* genügen Allsätze (Gesetze) nicht, um alles zu bestimmen.
In der *Mathematik* vielleicht ja??

In Peanos AS können wir wohl kaum mit nur Allsätze auskommen;
„Es gibt mindestens ein Anfangsglied" kann nicht als Allsatz formuliert werden.

Wie aber, wenn wir die Zahlen als Kardinalzahlen einführen, d.h. als Klassen von Klassen?

Aber auch in der *allgemeinen Klassentheorie* haben wir andere als Allsätze, z.B.: Prinzip der Komprehension, d.h. für jede Bedingung gibt es eine entsprechende Klasse. Auswahlprinzip.

102-63-08 *Nicht-Normale Modelle des Peano AS.* 11.1.41

AS: R ist eineindeutig, genau 1 Anfangsglied, kein Endglied; Induktion: Axiomschema: $((..0..) \cdot (x)(y)(..x.. \cdot R(x,y) \supset ..y..) \supset (z)(..z..))$

Dies besagt: eine *durch R ausdrückbare Eigenschaft*, die [erblich] inbezug auf R ist und der 0 zurkommt, kommt jeder Zahl zu.

Das AS ist ausgedrückt in einer *Quineschen Sprache*, also ohne pred. Variablen, und ohne indiv. Konstanten ('0' ist Abkürzung für Deskription).

Modelle: Die Individuen sind geordnete Paare natürlicher Zahlen:

$(0,0) \xrightarrow{R} (0,1) \xrightarrow{R} (0,2) \to (0,3) \to (0,4) \to (0,5) \dashrightarrow (0,n)$
$(1,0) \to (1,1) \to (1,2) \to (1,3) \to (1,4) \dashrightarrow (1,n)$
$R(x,y) =_{Df} x = (r,s) \land y = (t,u) \land (r = 0 \lor r = 1) \land t = r \land s+1 = u$.

Das Axiom „höchstens ein Anfangsglied" heisst genau: "wenn x und y Anfangsglieder sind, so $x = y$".

Und "$x = y$" heisst: "x und y haben alle *durch R ausdrückbaren Eigenschaften* gemein". Dies ist aber auch erfüllt für die beide Anfangsglieder in dem obigen Modelle, nämlich die Paare $(0,0)$ und $(1,0)$.

Einfachere nicht-normale Modelle:

[[Bilder]]

102-63-03 *Logikgruppe, 20.1.41*

Quine: Ein Satz ist *logisch-wahr* (im engeren Sinne, nicht mathematisch-wahr), wenn seine Wahrheit erhalten bleibt bei beliebiger Transformation aller Entitäten (nicht nur der Individuen); (dies ist so gemeint, dass ∈-Relation nicht erhalten werden muss; dabei darf ein Individuum auch in eine Klasse überführt werden!). Bei seiner Sprachform wird eine solche Transformation so durchgeführt (weil es in primitiver Schreibweise keine individuellen Konstanten gibt): jede Atomformel wird durch eine beliebige Form (nicht notwendig Atomformel) ersetzen. (Das ist wohl so gemeint: eine Atomformel 'Pxy' wird durch eine beliebige Satzfunktion mit genau 'x' und 'y' ersetzt, etwa '$..x..y..$'; dann muss aber ein anderes vorkommen desselben Prädikates durch die korrespondierende Satzfunktion ersetzt werden (z.B. 'Puv' durch '$..u..v..$').

Ich: Wundheiler hat als Kriterium für logisch-wahr angegeben: Wahrheit ist invariant inbezug auf *beliebige Transformation der Individuen*. Ist dies nicht vielleicht charakteristisch für mathematisch-wahr? Dabei wird eine Klasse transformiert in die Klasse der Korrelata der Elemente.

Die Diskussion eines Beispieles '$(x)(P(x)\ supset Q(x))$' zeigt aber, *dass dieser faktische Satz auch das Kriterium erfüllt*!

Ich: Ich bin geneigt, den folgenden Satz auch L-wahr zu nennen (sei es logisch oder mathematisch wahr): '$(x)(P(x) \supset Q(x))$'. 'P' interpretiert als: black table, 'Q': black

Quine: Ja, das kann man erreichen, indem man Interpretation durch Definition von 'Synonym' angibt, als Relation zwischen Ausdrücken der Objectsprache und entweder der Metasprache oder vielleicht einer reicheren Objektsprache. Dies Definition von 'synonym' ist so gemeint, dass es nur für L-äquivalente Prädikate gilt, nicht für F-äquivalente). Der genannte Satz entspricht dann einen Satz '$(x)[P_1(x) \wedge P_2(x) \supset P_1(x)]$', der logisch wahr ist. Also Kriterium für logisch-wahr: entweder logisch-beweisbar oder durch synonyme Transformation umformbar in logisch-beweisbaren Satz.

Ich: (1) In Enzyklopädiebroschüre nannte L-wahr, wenn wahr auf Grund der Deutung der logischen Zeichen allein. Im neuen MS (2) auf Grund aller Zeichen. Das Letztere ziehe ich vor wegen solcher Fälle wie oben.

Jemand (Quine?): Vielleicht kann (1) für logisch wahr, (2) für logisch oder mathematisch-wahr genommen werden? Das scheint mit Quines Begriff 'logisch-wahr' übereinzustimmen, wenn wir als logische Zeichen nur die konnektive und 'quantifiers'] nehmen, also '$\in$' als nicht-logisch.

[[Bilder]]

090–16–25 *Gespräch mit Tarski und Quine über Finitismus, I*
31.1.41
Ergebnis: p. 4.

Ich: *Schwierigkeiten der Verständigung zwischen Tarski und mir*, hauptsächlich in drei Punkten:

1. *Finitismus*. D.h.: Sprachen mit *was für Variablen verstehen* wir? (Das ist der schwerigste Punkt; für mich Frage des Grades. Aber nicht ganz klar.)

2. *Modalitäten*. „N'; *intensionale* Sprache.

3. *L-Begriffe*.

(3) ist am leichtesten. Nehmen wir Quines Sprachform (oder andere, ähnliche). Wir geben die *logischen Konstanten* durch *Aufzählung* an. Dann ist 'L-wahr' leicht definierbar. (Gewisse Modifikationen, die vielleicht nötig sind wegen des Beispiels, dass ich in der vorigen Sitzung gebracht habe, mögen wir hier beiseite lassen.)

(2). Wenn 'L-wahr' definiert, so *kann 'N' leicht erklärt* werden; im wesentlichen:

1. 'N(...)' wird übersetzt in '...', falls dies L-wahr, anderenfalls in '$\neg$(...)'. (Wir nehmen hierbei an: nur geschlossene Sätze, wie bei Quine.)

2. '$(x)\mathrm{N}(\ldots)$' wird übersetzt in '$\mathrm{N}(x)(\ldots)$'.
(1) ist am schwerigsten. In welchem Sinn „verstehen" wir z.B. Arithmetik mit gebundenen Zahlvariablen (für natürlichen Zahlen).
Über (2) und (3) siehe meine Blätter „Gespräch...; *Modalitäten*".

[[s. 2]]

Finitismus.
Tarski: Ich verstehe richtig nur eine *endliche Sprache* S_1: nur Individuumsvariable, ihre Werte sind Dinge; für deren Anzahl wird nicht Unendlichkeit behauptet (aber vielleicht auch nicht das Gegenteil). Endlich viele deskr[[iptive]] primitive Prädikate. *Zahlen*: sie können verwendet werden, in endlichem Bereich, indem wir die Dinge geordnet denken, und unter den Zahlzeichen die betreffenden Dinge verstehen. Wir können dann arithmetische Begriffe verwenden; aber viele arithmetische Sätze können hier nicht beweisen werden, weil wir nicht wissen, wie viele Zahlen vorhanden sind.
Man kann auch einer Klasse eine Kardinalzahl zuschreiben.
Quine: Z.B. durch Einführung von '$(\exists 3 x) \ldots$' als Abkürzung für '$(\exists x)(\exists y)(\exists z)[\neg .. = .. \wedge \ldots]$' (wobei '$=$' entweder als logisches Grundzeichen angenommen wird, oder als Quasi-Identität auf Grund der endlich vielen Prädikate definiert.)
Ich: Oder auch '$\mathrm{NC}(3, P)$', falls wir Prädikate höherer Stufe zulassen, aber nur als Abkürzungen.
Tarski: Das psychologische Rätsel ist folgendes: Die Mathematiker scheinen in einem gewissen Sinn auch die unendliche Arithmetik zu verstehen. Nämlich bei einem unentscheidbaren Satz (z.B. dem von Gödel) sind sie imstande, ohne Rücksicht auf die Axiome, zu sagen, dass sie den Satz als wahr anerkennen. Und ich (Tarski) teile dieses Gefühl in einem gewissen Grade.
Ich: Mir scheint, in einem gewissen Sinn verstehe ich wirklich die *unendliche Arithmetik*, sagen wir etwa *Sprache* S_2: nur Variable für natürliche Zahlen, mit Operatoren (sodass auch negierten Allsätzen), dazu recursive Definitionen. Auf Tarskis und Quines Frage, wie ich das deute, wenn die Anzahl der Dinge doch vielleicht endlich ist: ich weiss nicht genau, aber vielleicht durch blosse Stellen anstatt Dinge (Tarski: Diese Auffassung in [Syntax] hat ihm damals grossen Eindruck gemnacht, er findet aber doch Schwerigkeiten dabei). Eine Stelle ist eine Anordnungsmöglichkeit für ein Ding. Ich habe nicht die gefühlsmässige Ablehnung gegen den Möglichkeitsbegriff wie Tarski und Quine. Mir scheint die Möglichkeit des immer Weiterschreitens die Grundlage der Zahlenreihe. Also potentials, nicht aktuales unendlich (Tarski und Quine sagen: sie verstehen diesen Unterschied nicht).

[[s. 3]]

Ich: Vielleicht gibt es auch noch Zwischenstufe, ähnlich Sprache I, ohne negierte Allsätze. (Tarski: Dies scheint ihm kein wesentlicher Unterschied, da er

Satz mit freier Variable als Abkürzung für Satz mit Operator auffasst.)
Ein Allsatz für natürliche Zahlen können wir auffassen als gemeinsame Behauptung aller Instanzen, da ja für jede natürliche Zahl ein Ausdruck vorhanden ist (Tarski: aber nicht ein wirklicher Ausdruck als Ding, falls die Anzahl der Dinge endlich ist.)

Tarski: Als *Metasprache M* brauchen wir natürlich reichere Sprache als S_1, wenn wir 'wahr' inbezug auf eine nicht zu arme Sprache haben wollen. Aber *diese Semantik in M darf nicht als wirklich verstanden aufgefasst werden, sondern nur als Kalkül* mit finiten Regeln, die *in S_1 als einem Teil von M formuliert* werden. Wenn wir sagen '... ist wahr$_0$' so meinen wir damit: " '... ist wahr$_0$' ist beweisen$_M$ " und dies ist ein Satz im Teil S_1 von M. 'Beweisbar' kann natürlich in S_1 nicht definiert werden.

Quine: Statt dessen müssen wir den definiten Begriff 'x ist Beweis für y' nehmen.

Ich: Oder einen Term 'beweisen', der nicht definiert wird, sondern für den wir nur die Regel haben, dass aus 'x ist Beweis für y' folgt 'y ist bewiesen', während 'nicht-beweisen' nicht vorkommt.

[[s. 4]]

Wir zusammen: also *jetzt Problem*: Was für einen Teil S von M können wir *nucleus* nehmen derart,
dass 1.) S in einem gewissen Sinn von uns *verstanden* wird,
und 2.) S hinreicht zu Formulierung der Syntax von ganz M, soweit sie nötig ist für die Wissenschaft, um in M die Syntax und Semantik der Gesamtwissenschaftssprache zu behandeln.

1. Es muss untersucht werden, ob und wie weit der *poor nucleus* (d.h. endliche Sprache S_1) hierfür ausreicht.
Wenn ja, so wäre das sicherlich die befriedigendste Lösung.
Wenn nein, so müssen 2 Wege untersucht werden:
2a. Wie können wir den *rich nucleus* (d.h. unendliche Arithmetik S_2) rechtfertigen? D.h. in welchem Sinn können wir vielleicht doch sagen, dass wir ihn wirklich verstehen? Wenn ja, so können wir damit sicherlich die Regeln des Kalküls M aufstellen.
2b. Wenn S_1 nicht ausreicht, um die klassische Mathematik zu erreichen, könnte man dann nicht vielleicht trotzdem S_1 nehmen und *vielleicht* zeigen, dass die *klassische Mathematik nicht wirklich nötig ist für die Anwendung der Wissenschaft im Leben*. Können wir vielleicht auf Grund von S_1 einen Kalkül für eine fragmentare Mathematik aufstellen, die für alle praktischen Zwecke genügt (d.h. nicht etwa nur für Alltagszwecke, sondern auch für die kompliziertesten Aufgaben der Technik.)

[[s. 5]]

Quine zu 2a: Bedenken gegen S_2 als Kern ergeben sich daraus, dass wenn wir S_2 verstehen, wir die ganze Mengenlehre verstehen, nicht nur als Kalkül aufbauen können, sondern in S_2 formulieren können. Nach Löwenheim-Skolem gibt es ein abzählbares Modell für Mengenlehre, also eine Relation R zwischen natürlichen Zahlen als Deutung für '∈' etwa in Quines System, die alle Axiome dort erfüllt. Wir nehmen dann 'R' als logisches Prädikat in S_2.

Ich: Dies scheint mir aber doch eine sehr wesentliche Hinzufügung. Es wird dann zweifelhaft, ob wir noch sagen können, dass wir S_2 verstehen.

Quine: Ja. Es wird sich vermutlich herausstellen, dass 'R' nicht in S_2, wie früher angegeben, definierbar ist.

Ich: Auf diese Weise bleibt also doch der Unterschied zwischen dem Verstehen der elementaren Arithmetik (S_2) und dem Verstehen der allgemeinen Mengenlehre bestehen. Für mich subjektiv: Ich glaube S_2 zu verstehen (nicht ganz so klar wie S_1, aber doch wirkliches Verstehen, nicht nur Kalkülen operieren). Dagegen mit allgemeinen Mengenlehre: wenn ich mich getrauen würde zu sagen, dass ich sie verstehen, so würde ich doch zumindest einen sehr grossen graduellen Unterschied betonen.

[[s. 6]]

Eine besondere Frage:

Ich: Wenn 'T' als *Prädikat für Wahrheit* in M nur durch syntaktischen Regeln eingeführt wird, wobei wir aber nur den Teil S, nicht ganz M verstehen, woraus ist dann zu ersehen, dass 'T' Wahrheit bedeutet?

Tarski: Die syntaktischen Regeln werden so gemacht, dass die Bedingungen der Adequätheit erfüllt ist, d.h. dass für jede nach $\mathfrak{S}_i$ '$\mathfrak{S}_i$ ist wahr ≡ ...' beweisbar ist. [Aber: Dies gilt doch nur für eine Objektsprache, die Teil von M ist. Diese scheint Tarski meist anzunehmen. Anderenfalls muss für '...' nicht $\mathfrak{S}_i$, sondern die Übersetzung von $\mathfrak{S}_i$ genommen werden; aber dann ist wieder nicht erkennbar, dass 'T' Wahrheit bedeutet!]

Ich: Wenn 2 Prädikate die Adequätheitsbedingungen erfüllen, sind sie dann sicher äquivalent? Wenn das der Fall ist, ist durch die genannten Regeln wirklich die Bedeutung von 'T' bestimmt.

Tarski: Das scheint lieber nicht der Fall zu sein.
[Aber: wenn 'T_1' und 'T_2' die Bedingungen erfüllen, so gilt für jedes $\mathfrak{S}_i$, $\mathfrak{S}_i$ ist $T_1 \equiv ... \equiv \mathfrak{S}_i$ ist T_2; also $\mathfrak{S}_i$ ist $T_1 \equiv \mathfrak{S}_i$ ist T_2.
Der letztere Satz ist dann also beweisbar. Sind dann nicht T_1 und T_2 doch notwendigerweise umfangsgleich?]

090-16-26 *Gespräch mit Tarski, 13.2.41.*
Über Systeme ohne Typen.
Tarski sagt: *1. Systeme mit Typen*. Man kann zwar PM erweitern durch transfinite Stufen, aber nicht in *einfacher* Weise. Man braucht dann nicht nur Variable, die alle endliche Stufen durchlaufen, sondern auch soll, die *alle* vorhanden Stufen

durchlaufen. Dann aber ist es eigentlich überflüssig, Stufen gebundene Variable daneben auch noch zu haben. So fallen dann schliesslich die Stufen überhaupt fort.

Ich: Braucht man nicht die Stufen doch immer noch für die Konstanten, besonders die nicht-logischen?

T: Vielleicht kann man sie noch brauchen; vielleicht genügen aber doch auch die ontologischen Stufen.

2. *Systeme ohne Typen*. T. zieht diese intuitive vor. Hier 2 arten:

a. Solche mit „*Erzeugungsprinzipien*" (z.B. Axiomen der Summe, der Potenzmenge, der Aussonderungsmenge, der Ersetzungsmenge, usw.). Diese haben den grossen Vorteil, dass bei zukünftiger, unvorhergesehener Verstärkung einfach neue Prinzipien dieser Art hinzugefügt werden können, ohne dass die alten dabei verletzt werden. Hier ist worklich alles vorhanden, was man in der Praxis braucht; und wenn sich mal zeigt, dass die Praxis darüber hinausgehen will, so fügt man neue Prinzipien hinzu.

Hierher gehören: *Zermelo*, *von Neumann*, *Bernays*. Bernays Hauptsystem ist das letzte ist [*sic*] vielleicht gegenwärtig das beste.

Ferner erheblicher Vorzug (im *Vergleich zu Quines* System): zum niederen Funktionskalkül (mit Schemata, ohne Prädikatsvariable) werden nur *endlich viele Axiome* hinzugefügt (also keine ∈-Schemata wie bei Quine).

[[s. 2]]

b. Quines System. Nachteil: es gibt den Anschein, als ob alles fertig wäre; weil man keine einfachen Schritte sehen kann, um das System zu verstärken. (Wenn Quines ML als einziges Logikbuch nach 1000 Jahren aufgefunden wurde, während alles übrige zerstört und vergessen wäre, so würde es 300 Jahre dauern, bis die Leute entdecken würden, dass man ganz andere Systeme machen kann.) Es gibt keinen *einfachen*, deutlich sichtbaren Weg zur Verstärkung: für die Stratifikationsbedingungen sieht man keine natürliche Änderungsmöglichkeit; (ontologische) Stufen kann man nicht hinzufügen, weil die Allklasse schon vorhanden ist; keine Erzeugungsprinzipien.

[Ich glaube, *Quine* würde sagen: Verstarküng wird erreicht durch neue Axiome, auf Grund von denen weitere Entitäten als Elemente erklärt werden.]

T: Er hat Quine gesagt, schon vor Veröffentlichung, dass es sicherlich nicht ratsam wäre, ein Lehrbuch der Logik auf einen solches, noch nicht hinreichend untersuchtes System zu gründen, dass vielleicht schwere Nachteile hat, vielleicht sogar als widerspruchsvoll befunden werden wird. Ein Nachteil ist auch, dass *Cantors Theorem* nicht beweisen werden kann.

T: *Die Warschauer Logiker*, besonders *Leśniewski und Kotarbiński*, sahen ein *System wie PM* (aber mit einfacher Typentheorie) ganz selbstverständlich als die Systemform an. Diese Beschränkung wirkte stark suggestive auf alle Schüler; auf T. selbst noch bis zu „Wahrheitsbegriff" (wo weder transfinite Stufen noch stufenlose System betrachtet wird, und Endlichkeit der Stufen stillschweigend vorausgesetzt wird, erst im später hinzugefügten Anhang werden sie besprochen).

Dann aber sah T., dass in der *Mengenlehre* mit grossem Erfolg eine ganz andere Systemform verwendet wird. So kam er schliesslich dazu, diese stufenlose Systemform als natürlicher und einfacher anzusehen.

[[s. 3]]

Ich: Die Stufen erscheinen mir ganz natürlich und verständlich; daher einigermassen auch die Stratifikation. Aber was soll man sich unter Quines "*Nicht-Elementen*" oder den entsprechenden „Klassen" bei Bernays vorstellen?

T: Das ist nicht so schlimm. Es gibt auch Systeme ohne Nicht-Elemente. Das hängt einfach ab von der *Ordnung der Sprache*. Wir sprechen jetzt nicht von syntaktischen Stufen, sondern von *ontologischen Stufen*. Da sind die Nicht-Elemente ja einfach die Entitäten der höchsten Stufe, falls es eine solche gibt. Falls aber die Ordung des Systems (d.h. die kleinste Ordinalzahl grosser als alle vorkommenden Stufen Zahlen) eine *Limitzahl* ist, im einfachsten Falle also ω, so gibt es keine höchste Stufe und daher keine Nicht-Elemente. (Er meint, das wird gegenwärtig nicht deutlich erkannt; er möchte etwas veröffentlichen, um die Aufmerksamkeit darauf zu lenken.)

Für viele Zwecke dürfte daher wohl ein *System der Stufe ω am zweckmässigsten* sein. In diesem Fall dürfen wir allerdings nicht ein Unendlichkeitsaxiom in Zermelos Form aufstellen (denn $\{\Lambda; \{\Lambda\}; \ldots\}$ ist ja selbst von der Stufe ω, benötigt also eine Sprache von einer Ordnung $> \omega$). Aber statt dessen kann man einfach ein Unendlichkeitsaxiom nehmen, dass besagt, dass die *Anzahl der Individuen unendlich* ist. [Hier würde allerdings Russells Bedenken wieder auftreten; während Zermelos Form gerade den Vorteil hatte, dass eine unendliche Menge von *logischen* Entitäten konstruiert wird.] (Das Extensionalitätsprinzip muss dann natürlich auf eigentlichen Mengen, d.h. Nicht-Individuen, eingeschränkt werden.)

090-16-27 *Über finitistischen Syntax.* 16.2.41
(Angeregt durch Gespräch mit Tarski über Finitismus, 31.1.41)

Tarski meinte, wir sollten als Ausdrücke und Sätze und Beweise nur die *wirklich Hingeschriebenen* nehmen. Aber das ist viel zu eng. Dann enthält PM nicht einen einzigen Beweis für ein Theorem.

Aber wir können es *doch finitistisch* machen: wir nehmen als Zeichen nur wirkliche Dinge, aber als Ausdrücke und Beweise nicht nur gewisse wirkliche räumliche Anordnungen von diesen Dingen, sondern (nicht-räumliche) *Sequenzen dieser Dinge*, entweder bezeichnet durch die Reihe der Namen dieser Dinge, getrennt durch Kommata (elementarer Sequenzausdruck), oder durch Deskriptionen, z.B. als Verbindung zweier früher angegebener Sequenzen, für die wir Abkürzungen eingeführt haben. (Also Sequenzen von Dingen, nicht von Dingarten; die Zeichen sind also nur Tokens, d.h. wir setzen keine gleichen Dinge an verschiedenen Orten voraus; trotzdem können wir ausdrücken, was wir gewöhn-

lich so formulieren: "verschiedene Vorkommnisse desselben Zeichens", nämlich: verschiedene Stellen in verscheidene Sequenzen für dasselbe Ding.)
Beispiel:
Zeichen der Objektsprache $\quad x \quad y \quad z \quad P \quad (\quad) \quad \neg \quad \vee \quad \exists$
Ihre Namen in der Metasprache $\quad a_1 \quad a_2 \quad a_3 \quad a_4 \quad a_5 \quad a_6 \quad a_7 \quad a_8 \quad a_9$

Der Sequenzausdruck 'a_4, a_5, a_1, a_6' bezeichnet dann den Satz '$P(x)$' auch wenn dieser Satz niergends wirklich vorkommt (als räumliche Reihe von 4 Dinge dieser Arten).
Problem: Ist das Sprechen von Sequenzen, deren Länge grosser ist als die Anzahl der Dinge in der Welt, verträglich mit dem Prinzip des Finitismus? D.h. ist ein solcher Satz verständlich für den Finitisten?

[[s. 2]]

Wir können dann folgende Eigenschaften von Sequenzen definieren:
'Satz' (Die Formregeln der Objektsprache)
'Grundsatz' (die Deduktionsregeln der Objektsprache)
'direkt ableitbar'
'Beweis'
'Ableitung'
Es gibt zwar nur *endlich viele Zeichen* der Objektsprache. Aber wir können über Ausdrücke sprechen, deren Länge grosser ist als die Anzahl der Dinge. Z.B.
$\| \ a_7, a_1, a_{100}, \ldots \ldots | 5 \|$

Hier [[*viz.* '......']] schreibe ich einen Sequenzenausdruck hin, der einen gewissen sehr langen Ausdruck der Objektsprache bezeichnet.
Dies [[*viz.* die ganze Ausdruck '| | ... | | ']] soll Bezeichnung desjenigen Ausdrucks der Objektsprache sein, der aus *5 gleichen Teilausdrücke* der beschriebenen Form besteht.

090-16-24 *Empiristischer vs. logischer Finitismus* 16.2.41
Tarskis Finitismus ist ein logischer. Er meint: vielleicht ist die Anzahl der Dinge in der Welt endlich; in diesem Fall kann man auch nur von endlich vielen natürlichen Zahlen sprechen.
Ich dagegen: Wir sind Empiristen. Daher sagen wir: unser *Wissen* ist auf Endliches beschränkt; d.h. auf eine endliche Menge von Evidenz, d.h. endliche Menge von Beobachtungsaussagen.
Aber: Wir können trotzdem über endliche Klassen von beliebig hoher Kardinalzahl sprechen, also auch über die einzelnen natürlichen Zahlen (z.B. 1000 ≠ 1001), ohne die Anzahl der Dinge in der Welt inbetracht zu ziehen. So werden *Logik und Arithmetik unabhängig von der zufälligen Anzahl der Dinge in der Welt.*
Trotzdem bleiben auch Logik und Arithmetik in einem gewissen anderen Sinn finitistisch, wenn sie wirklich verstanden werden sollen.

Die Arithmetik (der natürlichen Zahlen) ist ja tatsächlich entwickelt geworden, ohne dass wir bis heute mit Sicherheit wissen, ob die Anzahl der Dinge in der Welt endlich ist oder nicht. Und die bewiesene Sätze werden von niemandem bezweifelt; besonders die konkreten Sätze (d.h. ohne Variable) scheinen doch unzweifelhaft. Also kann die Arithmetik doch wohl abhängig sein von einer faktischen Hypothese über die Welt.

Auch wenn die Anzahl der Dinge (z.B. Elektronen usw.) endlich ist so kann trotzdem die *Anzahl der Ereignisse als unendlich* angenommen werden (nicht nur die Anzahl der Zeitpunkte innerhalb eines Intervalls infolge der Dichte, sondern auch die Anzahl der Zeitpunkte im Einheitsabstand von einander, mit anderen Worten: unendliche Länge der Zeit). Ist dies eine faktische Hypothese? Oder hängt es nicht auch wieder mit *logischer Möglichkeit* zusammen?

090-16-23 19.2.41 [[s. 7]]
Gespräch mit Tarski und Quine, über Finitismus, II: 17.2.41
Ich: Auch wenn wir nur endlich viele Dinge und daher endlich viele Namen 'a', 'b',... 'Q' haben, so können wir doch *beliebig lange Sequenzen* bilden:
$R(a,a)$
$S(a,a,a)$
$T(a,a,a,a,)$
$\vdots$

Natürlich können wir sie in derselben Welt nicht beliebig lang hinschreiben; aber mit Hilfe von Abkürzungen können wir doch über sie sprechen. Damit können wir dann doch unbeschränkte Arithmetik bilden.

Quine: Die entscheidende Frage ist hier, ob wir Variable für diese Sequenzen einführen. Das müssen wir doch wohl, um unbeschränkte Arithmetik zu machen. Dann aber machen wir damit eine ontologische Annahme, nämlich über die Existenz von Sequenzen. Wenn wir aber das machen, so können wir *ebenso gut auch Klassen, Klassen von Klassen* usw. Annehmen; damit bekömen wir auch eine unbeschränkte Arithmetik. Aber damit würden wir den reistischen Finitismus aufgeben.

Tarski: Wir wollen die (vielleicht endlich vielen) Dinge der Welt in irgendeiner beliebigen Weise ordnen (siehe früheres Gespräch): $0, 0', 0'', \ldots$. Die Dingnamen dienen zugleich auch als Zahlzeichen. Für sie gelten dann Axiome analog denen von Peano, aber ohne Annahme der Unendlichkeit (also müssen wir das Peano AS so umformen, dass dies ein Axiom wird, und dies dann weglassen). ~~Z. B. können wir so deuten: jeder (zu lange) Strichausdruck, der nicht mehr ein Ding der Reihe bezeichnet, sollen wieder 0 bezeichnen. (Dann aber hat 0 einen Vorgänger! Und diese Ausdrücke ein anderes Ding bezeichnen, so hat dieses 2 verschiedene Vorgänger!)~~ Auf Grund hiervon sollten wir versuchen,

[[s. 8]]

eine *rekursive Arithmetik* aufzubauen. Dabei freie Variable (nur als Abkürzung für Satz mit Alloperator, aber ohne negierte Allsätze). Ich: also *ähnlich Sprache I*.[5] Strichausdrücke für zu grosse Zahlen können gar nicht hingeschrieben werden, weil nicht so viele Zeichen in der Welt vorhanden sind. Wir nahmen die *Peano Axiome*.

Quine: einschliesslich der vollständigen Induktion, aber ohne Unendlichkeitsaxiom. (Wir können z.B. das Peano AS so umformulieren, dass die Undendlichkeitsannahme ein Axiom wird, und dieses dann *wegstreichen*.)

Ich: Man kann aber indirect, mit hilfe von recursiv definierten Funktoren, Zahlausdrücke für zu grosse Zahlen bilden, z.B. 'power(10, 30)' ($= 10^{30}$).

Quine: Man könnte vielleicht bestimmen, dass alle Zahlausdrücke, die so hoch sind, dass sie kein Ding mehr bezeichnen, als Bezeichnungen für ein bestimmtes gewähltes Ding gedeutet werden. (Z.B. für 0; dann aber hat 0 einen Vorgänger; oder für anderes Ding, dann aber hat dieses 2 verschiedene Vorgänger; also) dafür bestimmte Änderung der Peanoschen Axiome nötig. Oder aber: wir verstehen 'prod(a, b) = prod(c, d)' nicht als Beziehung zwischen den 4 Dingen a, b, c, d; und analog für kompliziertere Sätze. Oder vielleicht noch besser: *nur Prädikate, nicht Funktoren* durch recursive Definitionen einführen; dann treten keine ungedeutete Zahlausdrücke auf.

[[s. 9]]

Über die Formulierung der Syntax in der finitistischen Sprache.

Ich: Sollen hier als Ausdrücke nur die wirklich mit Tinte hingeschrieben verstanden werden, oder beliebige denkbare Sequenzen aus wirklich vorhandenen Dingen? (Sodass das Alphabet nur einmal irgendwo nur einmal irgendwo hingeschrieben zu werden brauchte.)

Quine: Beides nicht. Wir fassen auch Teile von Dinge als Dinge auf; also alle Ganzen, der Teile etwa Elektronen usw. sind, auch wenn nicht räumlich zusammenhängend. Ein 'P' ist dann ein Ding gewisser Form; für solche Dinge gibt es eine minimale Grösse, weil sie aus Elektronen bestehen sollen. Aber das jeder Stelle des Raumes, wo ähnlich hinreichend Materie ist, z.B. hier in der Mauer, ist dann ein 'P' vorhanden. (Ich glaube, dies stammt von einer früheren Idee von mir, die ich mal vor Jahren erklärt habe.)

Ich: Auch wenn der Raum endlich ist, ist nicht die *Zeit unendlich?*

Tarski: Nicht mit Sicherheit. 1. Die Quantentheorie wird vielleicht die Kontinuität und Dichtheit aufgeben, sodass jedes Zeitintervall nur endlich viele Teile hat (es gibt dann keine beliebig kleinen Zeitteile). 2. Die Zeit im Grossen ist möglicherweise endlich, indem bei nur endlich vielen Raumpunkten und endlich vielen Dingen derselbe Zustand wiederkehrt, also die Zeit in sich zurückläuft; zirkuläre Struktur. Jedenfalls wollen wir die Sprache so aufbauen, dass dies nicht van vornherein ausgeschlossen ist.

5. MS: 'Sprache II'

Quine: Um neben dem Raum auch die Zeit gleich mit einzubeziehen, sollten wir anstatt der Elektronen die Energiequanten als kleinste Teile nehmen; also als Dinge (Individuen) alle Ganzen aus solchen Teilen. –Ein Ausdruck der Sprache ist ein räumlich zusammenhängendes Ding (d.h. Zeichen als Teile müssen als Teile hinreichend nahe zu einander sein.)

[[s. 10]]

Ich: Wenn wir für die *Syntax* nur die wirklichen, nicht die möglichen Anordnungen in Betracht ziehen, so ergeben sich *paradoxe Folgen*. Es gibt dann z.B. einen Satz S_1, der den Fixstern ziemlich ausfüllt, und ein anderen Satz S_2, der dasselbe tut; es gibt aber keine Konjunktion oder Disjunktion dieser beiden Sätzen da es keine hinreichende grossen zusammenhängenden Dinge gibt. Anderes Beispiel: S_1 sei bewiesen durch einen Beweis, der den grössten Stern ziemlich aüsfullt; ferner fülleeine Ableitung von S_2 aus S_1 denselben Stern ziemlich aus. Für die Aneinanderreihung der beiden Satzketten ist nirgends [Platz]. Folglich können wir nach den vorgeschlagenen finitistischen Begriffen nicht sagen, dass wir S_2 beweisen haben. Aber jeder Logiker wird doch sagen wollen, dass, wenn wir S_1 beweisen und S_2 aus S_1 abgeleitet ist, S_2 auch bewiesen ist (nicht nur "beweisbar", was in dieser Sprache nicht ausdrückbar ist).

Mir scheint der ganze Vorschlag an einer *Fehlauffassung der Arithmetik* zu kranken: Die Zahlen werden reifiziert; die Arithmetik wird von kontingenten Fakten abhängig gemacht, während sie in Wirklichkeit von begrifflichen Zusammenhängen handelt; wenn man so will: von möglichen, nicht von wirklichen Fakten.

[[p. 11]]

Tarski: Vielleicht können die Paradoxe dadurch vermeiden werden, dass wir die Syntax auf die gödelschen Zahlen der Sätze beziehen. "a ist beweis für b" ist ein Relation zwischen 2 Zahlen.

Ich: Aber die gödelschen Zahlen für Beweise sind so ungeheuer hoch, dass sie sehr schnell die Grenzen der hier vorhandenen Zahlen (die ja hier Dinge sind) überschreiten.

Quine: Vielleicht sollten wir zwar Ausdrücke als räumlich zusammenhängende Dinge auffassen, aber dasselbe nicht auch für Beweise und Ableitungen verlangen. Es genügt, dass die Sätze des Beweises irgendwo vorhanden sind.

Ich: Aber die Ordnung der Sätze im Beweis ist wesentlich!

[[Später Einfügung:]] 19.2.41 Veilleicht lassen sich die Schwerigkeiten, die ich aufgezeigt habe, wenigstens technisch in folgender Weise vermeiden. Die Sätze, die ich aussprechen möchte, aber paradoxermassen hier nicht als wahre Sätze behaupten kann, können wir zwar nicht in S_1, wohl aber in Kalkül M behaupten und beweisen; also in der umfassenderen Sprache, die nur ein Kalkül ist, aber nicht wirklich verstanden wird; deren Regeln in S_1 formuliert werden.

Dies würde wohl die Schwerigkeiten technisch überwinden. Aber meine Bedenken gegen die faktische Auffassung der Arithmetik werden dadurch nicht beseitigt.

090-16-06 21.2.41

Finitistische Sprache, durch Modifikation von Sprache I.
(Im Anschluss an die Gespräche mit *Tarski und Quine über Finitismus*.)
Wir ordnen alle Dinge in der Welt 0 ist das Anfangsding; x' ist der Nachfolger von x.

Problem: Wie sollen wir die zu grossen Strichausdrücken deuten, für die kein Ding mehr ist? Diese Strichausdrücke selbst können natürlich nicht hingeschrieben werden (vorausgesetzt, dass nur von einer Welt die Rede ist, d.h. dass die Welt, in wir schreiben, dieselbe ist, über die wir schreiben). Aber Abkürzungen solcher Strichausdrücke können doch gebildet werden. 'k' sei abkürzender Name für das *letzte Ding*. Was soll 'k'', 'k''', usw. bedeuten? Verschiedene Möglichkeiten:

a. $k' = k'' = \ldots = k$. Das letzte Ding ist sein eigener Nachfolger.

b. 'k'', 'k''', usw. soll alle wieder 0 bedeuten: $k' = k'' = 0$. (so schlug Quine vor). Das *geht aber nicht leicht*; denn aus $k' = 0$ folgt doch wohl $k'' = 0'$, wenigstens wir '$(x = y) \supset (x' = y')$' haben, was doch wohl natürlich ist.

c. $k' = 0; k'' = 0';$ usw.

[[Bildern von c. und a.]]

[[s. 2]]

Wir wollen versuchen, *rekursive Definitionen* und *beschränkte Operatoren* zu verwenden. Vielleicht ziegt sich dabei, welche der obigen Deutungen (a), (b), (c) die geeignetste ist.

In Sprache I haben wir 2 Grundsatzschemata, die den *beschränkten Alloperator* gewissermassen *rekursiv* einführen:

PSI4. $(x)0(..x..) \equiv ..0..$

PSI5. $(x)y'(..x..) \equiv (x)y(..x..) \wedge (..y'..)$

In (b) und (c) hatten wir: $k' = 0$; S_1 sei: '$(x)k'(P(x))$'.
S_1 kann umgeformt werden: wegen $k' = 0$: $(x)0(P(x))$; nach (4): $P(0)$.
S_1 kann umgeformt werden nach (5): $\underbrace{(x)k(P(x))} \wedge \underbrace{(P(k'))}$;
  Dies heisst, dass *alle* Dinge P sind! $P(0)$
Also *müssen wir Deutung (a) nehmen*!

Entsprechend können auch $(\exists x)\ldots(..x..)$ und $(Kx)\ldots(..x..)$ gedeutet werden.

[[s. 3]]

Grundsätze der Arithmetik.
PSI9: $\neg(0 = x')$; bleibt gültig für Deutung *(a)*. (Nicht für (b) und (c)!)
  Dagegen *PSI10*: $(x' = y') \supset (x = y)$ wird *ungültig für (a)*! (Auch für (b); dagegen wäre es gültig für (c)).
  Also *Streichen!* (Falls wir (a) nehmen wollen).
(Auf Grund von (a) und PSI9, besagt PSI10 die *Ungültigkeit des Dingbereiches*.)
  Wir nehmen (a) an.
  $\underbrace{(x)k(P(x))}$' ist äquivalent mit '$(x)k'(P(x))$', mit '$(x)k''(P(x))$', usw.;
Dies ist wahr $\equiv$ alle Dinge sind P

K-Operator: PSI 11:
$Q[(Kx)y(P(x))] \equiv [\neg(\exists x)y(P(x)) \wedge Q(0)$
$\vee (\exists x)k'[P(x) \wedge (z)x(\neg(z = x) \supset \neg P(z)) \wedge Q(x)]$

Also:

$Q[(Kx)k'(P(x))] \equiv [\ \underbrace{\neg(\exists x)k'(P(x))}\ \wedge Q(0)]$
$\qquad\qquad\qquad\qquad\quad\text{es gibt kein Ding, dass P ist}$
$\vee (\exists x)k'[P(x) \wedge (z)x(\neg(z = x) \supset \neg P(z)) \wedge Q(x)]$

angenommen, nur $k(= k' = k'' = \ldots)$ sei *P*; dies [[*viz.* '$(z)x\neg(z = x) \supset \neg P(z)$']] stimmt dann, denn jedes Ding (bis k') dass $\neq k'$ (also $\neq k$)it, ist nicht *P*.
Also Grundsätze ausser PSI10 bleiben also gültig!

[[s. 4]]

  Können wir beweisen $(x = y) \supset (x' = y')$?
Prämisse: $\quad a = b$ \hfill (1)
PSI8: $\qquad (x = y) \supset ((x' = z') \supset (y' = z'))$ \hfill (2)
(1), (2) $\qquad (a' = z') \supset (b' = z')$ \hfill (3)
(3) $\qquad\quad (a' = a') \supset (b' = a')$ \hfill (4)
(4), PSI7: $\quad b' = a'$ \hfill (5)
  Hieraus folgt: wenn $a = a'$, so $a' = a'', a'' = a'''$, usw.
Wir *definieren*: $Ult(x) = x = x'$;
  Hieraus folgt: $\text{Ult}(x) \supset (x' = x'') \wedge (x'' = x''')\ldots$
$\ldots x = x' = x'' = \ldots$
  Wir können eine *Funktion* l definieren derart, dass für jede *normale* Zahl a: $l(a) = 0$,
und für $k(= k' \text{ usw.})$: $l(k) = k$;

Def: $l(x) = (Ky)x(y = y')$.

[[s. 5]]

 Wir nehmen die *Regeln RI1-4 alle* an, *einschliesslich der vollständigen Induktion!*
Die Regel der Induktion besagt: jades Ding ist in endlich viellen Schritten von 0 aus erreichbar; d.h. es gibt keine andere Dinge als die wir Strichausdrücke (beziehungsweise deren Abkurzungen) bezeichen[baren].
$\neg Ult(a)$ heisst: a ist nicht das letzte Ding; daher $a \neq a'$; $a \neq a''$; usw.
also: a ist eine *normale Zahl*.
Aus $Ult(a)$ folgt $a = a'''\cdots$, also $Ult(a''''\cdots)$.
Also gibt es *höchstens ein letztes Ding*. (Und keins, falls die Anzahl der Dinge unendlich ist).
Aus $\neg Ult(a)$ folgt: $(x)a(\neg Ult(x))$;
d.h., wenn a normal, so auch alle frühere Dinge (Zahlen).

[[s. 6]]

Recursive Definitionen können wir jetzt aufstellen.
Nicht nur für Prädikate, sondern *auch für Funktoren*. Denn deren vollständigen Ausdrücke, auch wenn "zu hoch", sind ja auf Grund von (a) gedeutet.
So können alle die syntaktischen Begriffe definiert werden, wie in [Syntax] Ch.II;
Anstatt der Syntax von I, können ebenso die Syntax einer mächtigeren Sprache, die die *allgemeine Mengenlehre* umfasst, formuliert werden, *z.B. von II, oder Quines System, oder Bernays System, usw*.

090-16-12 23.2.41
Die Sprache der Wissenschaft, auf finitistischer Basis.
(Im Anschluss an die Gespräche mit *Tarski und Quine* über Finitismus; siehe Blätter)
(Vgl. Hierzu auch: "Finitistische Sprache, durch Modifikation von Sprache I" vom 21.2.41)
Wir beginnen mit einem *Basic System BS*.
Diese ist eine *verstandene Sprache, finitistische*.
Individuen: gewisse *beobachtbare* Dinge und ihre Beobachtbare teile; wir benennen sie in irgendeiner Reihenfolge, etwa so wie wir sie brauchen, mit 'α', 'α'', 'α''', usw. 'k' sei Abkürzung für die Bezeichnung gebildet haben, nicht des letzten Dinges in der Welt)
univ. of disc.: eine gewisse, *endliche Klasse von Dingen der Welt*!

Variable : 　　　　　'u', 'v', ...
Beschränkte Operatoren : 　$(u)..(..u..)$
　　　　　　　　　　　　　$(\exists u)..(..u..)$　　Dies wird später durch
　　　　　　　　　　　　　$(Kx)..(..u..)$　　　　*Definitionen* eingeführt!
　　　　　　　　　　　　　　　↑
　　　　　　　　　　　　　limit expn.

Freie Variable (wie in I)? *Vielleicht brauchen wir nicht!!* Wir wollen versuchen, *ohne sie* auszukommen!

[[s. 2]]

S_n	^{n-1}g und ^{n-1}f, auch gebunden.	*Semantik*. usw.	'true$_{S_{n-1}}$'
	⋮	⋮	
S_3	^2g und ^2f, auch gebunden. *Theorie der Funktion* reeller und komplexer Zahlen; Infinitesimal-Kalkül	*Semantik*: 'true$_{S_2}$'.	
S_2	^1g und ^1f: F_1...; f_1...; (F); $(\exists F)$ *Arithmetik der reellen Zahlen.* *Physik*: *Koordinates System*. Physikalische Gesetze als Grundsätze.	*Semantik*: 'true$_{S_0}$', 'true$_{S_1}$'.	
S_1	Unbeschränkt: $\quad (x), (\exists x), (Kx)$. $0, 0', 0''$ ... *Zahlvariable* $x, y, ...$ *Arithmetik der natürlichen Zahlen.*	*Syntax* (auf Grund definiter Regeln) für S_0; ...S_n; ... '*provb.*', '*derb.*'	
BS (=I ohne PSI 10)	$\alpha, \alpha', \alpha'', ...$ (Dies sind *beobachtbare Dinge* und ihre beobachtbare Teile!) Beschränkte Operatoren: $(u)..(..u..)$; $(\exists u)..(..u..)$; $(Ku)..(..u..)$ *Primitive Descri*: *Observ. thing-preds*: $P_1, P_2, ...$	*Syntax* (*Grundsätze* und *Schlussregeln*) wird hier formuliert für: S_0; $S_1, S_2, ...$ *Nur definit*: '*dir. derb.*', '*proof sent.*' und dergl.	

[[s. 3]]

Grundsätze in BS:
Die Grundsatzschema wie in Sprache I, aber: 1. *Nicht* PSI10 $((x' = y') \supset (x = y))$, weil es zusammen mit den Anderen *Unendlichkeit* besagt. (d.h.:) Für

die Sprache ohne definierten Zeichen sind die $\mathfrak{St}$ die einzigen $\mathfrak{Z}$, es sei denn, dass physikalische $\mathfrak{fu}$ sind primitiv genommen werden.

2. *Anstatt der freien Variablen* geschlossene Zahlausdrücke;
also:

in PSI 5   wird '$\mathfrak{z}_2$' durch   '$\mathfrak{Z}_2$' ersetzt,
6   "   "
7   '$\mathfrak{z}_1$'   '$\mathfrak{Z}_1$'
8   '$\mathfrak{z}_1$' und '$\mathfrak{z}_2$'   '$\mathfrak{Z}_1$' bzw.. '$\mathfrak{Z}_2$'
   und '$\begin{pmatrix} \mathfrak{z}_1 \\ \mathfrak{z}_2 \end{pmatrix}$,'   durch '$\begin{bmatrix} \mathfrak{Z}_1 \\ \mathfrak{Z}_2 \end{bmatrix}$'.
9   '$\mathfrak{z}$' durch $\mathfrak{Z}$
11   '$\mathfrak{z}_2$'   '$\mathfrak{Z}_2$'

Regeln in BS: wie in Sprache I, aber:
R1 wird *gestrichen* (substi.)
R4 wird *gestrichen* (*vollständige Induktion*)!

Es *bleiben* nur: R2 (connvs.), und R3 (Impli).
Vielleicht *doch vollständige Induktion*, aber in beschränker Form:

$$\frac{\ldots\alpha\ldots \quad (u)--[(\ldots u\ldots) \supset (\ldots u'\ldots)]}{(u)--'(\ldots u\ldots)}$$

oder vielleicht so (wenn k das letzte bezeichnete Ding ist):

$$\frac{\ldots\alpha\ldots \quad (u)k[(\ldots u\ldots) \supset (\ldots u'\ldots)]}{(u)k(\ldots u\ldots)}$$

Dies [[Regel]] *gilt zwar*, aber *braucht nicht* aufgestellt zu werden als besondere Regel, sondern kann als "abgeleitete Regel" gefunden werden.

[[s. 4]]

Explizite und recursive Definitionen.
indexdefinition!recursive

Sie werden als *Definitionsregeln* formuliert, nicht als Definitionssätze wie in I; aber ganz analog zu denen in I.

D1. '$nf(u)$' for 'u''. (Dies ist überflüssig).
D2.   1.   '$sum(0, v)$' for 'v',
     2.   '$sum(u', v)$' for '$(sum(u, v))$'

Oder auch in Form von *Schemata*:
D1. $\mathfrak{fu}_1(\mathfrak{Z}_1)$ *for* $\mathfrak{Z}_1'$
D2.   1. $\mathfrak{fu}_2(\mathfrak{nu}, \mathfrak{Z}_2)$ for $\mathfrak{Z}_2$,
     2. $\mathfrak{fu}_2(\mathfrak{Z}_1, \mathfrak{Z}_2)$ for $\mathfrak{fu}_1(\mathfrak{fu}_2(\mathfrak{Z}_1, \mathfrak{Z}_2))$.

[[s. 5]]

Schwierigkeit: In der Formulierung der Grundsätzen, der Regeln und der Definitionen von BS in BS

Kommen vor: '$\mathfrak{S}_1$', '$\mathfrak{Z}_1$', und dergleichen. Dies sind *freie Metavariable*! Können wir sie vermeiden? Wir müssen sie *durch beschränkte gebundene Variable ersetzen*!

Als *Schränke* nehmen wir die Zahl k derart, dass wir $k + 1$ Dinge mit Strichausdrücke bezeichnet haben. Dies bedeutet nicht, dass nur $k + 1$ Dinge in der Welt sind, sondern nur, dass wir mit der Namengebung so weit fortgeschritten sind.

Z.B. *Grundsatz 1* (D 103):[6] Anstatt '$GrS1(u) \equiv \ldots u \ldots$,'
('$\ldots u \ldots$' heisst: u hat die Form $\mathfrak{S}_1 \supset (\neg \mathfrak{S}_1 \supset \mathfrak{S}_2)$)
oder $\mathfrak{pr}_{103}(Z_i)$ für $\ldots \mathfrak{Z}_i \ldots$,
schreiben wir: $(u)k[GrS1(u) = \ldots u \ldots]$.

Oder: Ebenso gut *können wir aber doch freie variable* verwenden, aber sie *nicht als unbeschränkte Allgemeinheit* deuten, sondern als nur durch die $k + 1$ bezeichnete Dinge laufen:

also '$\ldots u \ldots$' *als Abkürzung* nicht für '$(u)(\ldots u \ldots)$', sondern für '*(u)k*$(\ldots u \ldots)$'.

Mit anderen Worten: *als Abkürzung für eine Konjunction* mit $k + 1$ Gliedern: $(\ldots \alpha \ldots) \wedge (\ldots \alpha' \ldots) \wedge \ldots \wedge (\ldots \alpha^{(k)} \ldots)$;

(d.h.: ebenso gut können wir statt freier Variable gleich unbeschränkte Operatoren einführen! Siehe 6 unten)

Also *im Grunde nur molekulare Sprache*; *alles übrige ist Abkürzung!*

[[s. 6]]

Konstruktion von BS_k (d.h. das Basissystem für $k + 1$ Dinge).
Grundzeichen: ( ) , $\alpha' = |$; dazu *physicalische* $\mathfrak{pr}$ *und* $\mathfrak{fu}$.

Die *Definitionen dienen nur zur Abkürzung, auch* wo sie recursive Form haben; denn es ist *stets Elimination möglich*!

Wir *definieren*:
1. aus '$|$': die *connv.s*: $\neg \vee \wedge \supset \equiv$
(Anstatt '$\equiv$' hatten wir in Sprache I einfach auch '$=$').

2. *Beschränkte Alloperatoren*: 1. '$(u)\alpha(..u..)$' für '$..\alpha..$';
2. '$(u) - -'(..u..)$' für '$(u) - -(..u..) \wedge (.. - -'..)$'

Muss genauer durch *Schemata* ausgedrückt werden.

(1.3.:)[7] Wohl besser hinzufügen: "Das zweite Konjunktionsglied wird fortgelassen, falls es kein Satz ist." Dies macht einen beschränkten Allsatz immer sinnvoll, wenn $\mathfrak{S}_i \begin{bmatrix} \text{`}\alpha\text{'} \\ u \end{bmatrix}$ sinnvoll ist (wo $\mathfrak{S}_i$ der Operand ist). Dieser

---

6. *LSL* §23: "**D 103.** $GrS1(x) \equiv (\exists y)x(\exists z)x[Satz(x) \wedge (x = imp(y, imp[neg(y), z]))]$."
7. d.h. hinzufügt März 1

Zusatz (oder etwas ähnlich) ist z.B. nötig für Formulierung des Prinzips der vollständigen Induktion, siehe 8 unten.

3. *Beschränkte Existenzoperator*: '$(\exists u) - -(..u..)$' for '$\neg(u) - -(\neg(..u..))$'.

4. *Beschränkter K-operator*: '$\cdot - \cdot (Ku) - -(..u..) \cdot -\cdot$' for
'$[\neg(\exists u) - -(..u..) \wedge \cdot - \cdot \alpha \cdot -\cdot] \vee (\exists u) - -[(v)u(..v.. \equiv v = u) \wedge \cdot - \cdot u \cdot -\cdot]$'

5. 'k' for '$\alpha^{'''''\cdots}$' (Hier schreiben wir den zuletzt benutzten Strichausdruck hin, nämlich den mit k Akzenten). (Zur technischen Vereinfachung können wir natürlich vor 'k' zunächst Dezemalausdrücke für natürlichen Zahlen einführen.)

6. *Freie Variable*: '$\ldots u \ldots$' for '$(u)k(\ldots u \ldots)$'.

(1.3.:) Oder anstatt freier Variable: *unbeschränkte Operatoren*:

6. '$(u)(\ldots u \ldots)$' for '$(u)k(\ldots u \ldots)$'.

7. '$(\exists u)(\ldots u \ldots)$' for '$(\exists u)k(\ldots u \ldots)$'.

Die unbeschränkten All- und Existenzsätze sind *rückübersetzbar* in Konjunktion[8] mit $k + 1$ Gliedern.

Die *Formregeln* (für $_{33}$, $\mathfrak{St}$, $\mathfrak{Z}$, $\mathfrak{Arg}^n$, und $\mathfrak{S}$) sind dieselben *wie in I*,

(1.3.:) *Aber*: Zusatz: '*Ein $\mathfrak{St}$ hat höchstens k Striche*'!
(oder, wenn wir längere $\mathfrak{St}$ zulassen: „ein *eigentliche* $\mathfrak{St}$ hat *höchstens k Striche*").

[[s. 7]]

Grundsatzschemata für BS_k. Wir formulieren sie so, dass sie *nicht* das Vorhandensein von *Variablen voraussetzen*.

1. die des propl. calc.

2. Für *Identität*:
 a. $\mathfrak{Z}_i = \mathfrak{Z}_i$.
 b. $(\mathfrak{Z}_i = \mathfrak{Z}_j) \supset (\mathfrak{S}_{\mathfrak{l}} \supset \mathfrak{S}_{\mathfrak{l}} \begin{bmatrix} \mathfrak{Z}_i \\ \mathfrak{Z}_j \end{bmatrix})$

3. Für α (d.h., das *erste Ding*): $\neg(\alpha = \mathfrak{Z}_i{}')$.

4. Für k (das *letzte Ding*): $(k = k\underbrace{'''\cdots}_{\text{ein oder mehrere Akzente}}.) \mathfrak{St}_k = \mathfrak{St}_k''{}^{\cdots}$.

1.3.:) *Dieser Grundsatz ist aber überflüssig, wenn* wir in den Formregeln *nur eigentliche* $\mathfrak{St}$ *zulassen!*

Hier kann anstatt 'k' auch sein Definiens '$\underbrace{\alpha^{'''\cdots}}_{\mathfrak{St}_k}$' geschreiben werden; dies ist besser, wenn wir 'k' nicht als primitiv nehmen, sondern definieren (siehe 6 (5).) (Falls wir 'k' als primitiv nehmen, können (4) in der einfachen Form mit 'k' geschrieben werden; dann müssen wir aber anstatt der Definition von k noch folgenden Grundsatz aufstellen:

5. $k = \underbrace{\alpha^{'''\cdots}}_{\mathfrak{St}_k}$. (1.3.:) *Besser dies als Definition! Also 'k' nicht als Grundzeichen!*)

(1.3.:) Da wir PSI10 gestrichen haben, müssen wir durch anderen Grundsatzaus-

---

8. unsicher

sagen, dass je 2 verschiedenen $\mathfrak{St}$ *bis* $\mathfrak{St}_k$ nicht dasselbe bezeichnen:
6. $\neg(\mathfrak{St}_i = \mathfrak{St}_j)$, wo $\mathfrak{St}_i$ und $\mathfrak{St}_j$ zwei verscheidene *eigentliche* $\mathfrak{St}$ sind (d.h., solche mit höchstens k Strichen).
Einfacher, ganz *analog zu PSI10!*:
6. $(u)(v)[(u' = v') \supset (u = v)]$. (Auf Grund des Zusatzes *6* Mitte kann dies nicht auf '$k''^{...}$' angewendet werden.)
Besser ohne Variable: 6. $3'_i = 3'_j \supset 3_i = 3_j$.
Also: Grundsatzschemata für BS_k entsprechen das Gruppen (a), (c), (d) für I; aber ohne Variable!
Regeln für BS_k: nur *Impli. Regel*.

[[s. 8]]

Die vollständige Induktion, sogar in der allgemein Form wie in I (die aber hier in Wirklichkeit nicht allgemein ist, sondern auf Endliches beschränkt), kann jetzt in BS_k gezeigt werden; eine besondere *Regel ist nicht nötig*.

Prämissen		
	$P(\alpha)$	(1)
	$P(u) \supset P(u')$	(2)
(1) (2)	$P(\alpha')$	(3)
(3) (2)	$P(\alpha'')$	(4)
$\vdots$		
	$P(\alpha\underbrace{''^{...}}_{k\text{ Striche}})$	$(k+2)$
(1) (3) (4)...$(k+2)$	$P(\alpha) \wedge P(\alpha') \wedge P(\alpha'') \wedge \ldots P(\alpha^{(k)})$	$(k+3)$
$(k+3)$, def. Alloper.	$(u)\alpha^{(k)} P(u)$	$(k+4)$
$(k+4)$, def. von 'k'	$(u)k(P(u))$	$(k+5)$
$(k+5)$, def. freie Var	$P(u)$	$(k+6)$

1.3.: Nach Einführung der *unbeschränkten Operatoren* wird dann das *Prinzip der vollständingen Induktion beweisbar*!:

$$P(0) \wedge (u)[P(u) \supset P(u')] \supset (v)P(v)$$

Für den Wert k für 'u', '$P(u')$' kein Satz (weil 'k'' kein Zahlausdruck ist); trotzdem ist das Ganze [['$(u)[P(u) \supset P(u')]$']] ein Satz, wenn in der definition des unbeschränkten Alloperators ein geeigneter Zusatz gemacht wird (wie früher angegeben, siehe *6* Mitte).

[[s. 9]]

Sind die Operatoren wirklich stets eliminierbar? Auch wenn die *Schränke deskriptiv ist? Ja.*
Beispeil: $(w) \underbrace{(Ku)5(P(u))}_{\text{Schränke}}(Q(w))$.

Dies wird:

$$\neg(\exists u)5[(P(u)) \wedge (w)\alpha(Q(w))] \vee (\exists u)5[(v)u(P(v) \equiv v = u) \wedge (w)u(Q(w))]$$

Jede $(\exists u)5$ wird eliminiert, gibt 6-gliedrige Disjunktion.
$(w)\alpha$ wird eliminiert, verschwindet
$(v)u$ und $(w)u$: Durch die Eliminierung von 'u' bekommen diese Alloperatoren (die in allen 6 Disjunktionsgliedern auftreten) überall einen Strichausdruck (zwischen α und α''''') als Schränke; sie werden dann eliminiert; es ergibt sich jeweils Konjunktion von höchstens 6 Gliedern.

[[s. 10]]

BS_k als Syntaxsprache, für BS_k selbst und für andere Kalküle.
Was wollen wir in BS_k ausdrücken?
Vielleicht beschränken wir uns am Besten auf solche Kalküle, die nur endlich viele Zeichenarten haben; jede Zeichenart darf aber unendlich viele Zahlen enthalten; wir brauchen in der Syntaxsprache nicht Namen für diese Zeichen, sondern nur ein $\mathfrak{pr}^2$ für Gleichheit 'Eq'. Hierdurch ist *z.B. II ausgeschlossen*, da unendliche Zahlen von Typen. Zur Darstellung der Syntax solcher reicheren Sprachen verwenden wir dann eine volle arithmetische Sprache, deren Syntax in BS_k angegeben ist.
(Oder sollen wir *uns sogar auf Kalküle mit endlich vielen Zeichen beschränken? Und alle anderen Kalküle behandeln wie II*?)
1.3.: *Ja*, doch wohl; denn in BS_k können wir doch nur über endlich viele Gegenstände sprechen!
In BS_k können wir natürlich nicht 'provb.' Definieren, sondern nur die definiten Begriffe 'Grundsatz' und 'dir. derb.'; 'Satz' ist zwar definit; aber vielleicht können wir auch hier uns auf die Urbegriffe 'Atomformel' und 'direkt construierbar' beschränken. Vielleicht ist es gar nicht nötig, hier auch 'proof' und 'Proof Sent.' zu definieren; ebenso 'Konstruktionsreihe' (für Formeln). Der praktische Beschluss, jeden Satz, sobald er bewiesen ist, anzuerkennen, ist ja implizit enthalten, wenn wir beschliessen:

1. Wir wollen jeden Grundsatz anerkennen;

2. Wenn wir $\mathfrak{S}_1$ und $\mathfrak{S}_2$ anerkennt haben, und $\mathfrak{S}_3$ ist direct ableitbar aus ihnen, so wollen wir auch $\mathfrak{S}_3$ anerkennen.

Dies führt ja dann von selbst zur Anerkennung des bewiesenen Satzes, und jedes Satzes, der aus schon Anerkannten abgeleitet worden ist.

[[s. 11]]

Problem: Was sollen wir als *Ausdrücke* nehmen?
Verschiedene Möglichkeiten:
Ein *Ausdruck in K* ist

1. ein *Ding* mit räumlich linear geordneten Teile (-Zeichen).

Oder 2. ein *Sequenz* von Dingen (-Zeichen)

Oder 3. ein *Zahl* n (ausgedruckt durch ein Strichausdruck, also =Ding No. n).

Oder 4. ein *Zahlpaar* m, l, nämlich der m-te Ausdruck der Länge l, in lexikographische Anordnung (etwa so: wir bestimmen eine alphabetische Anordnung für die (endlich viele) Zeichen von K. Dann ordnen wir die Ausdrücke der Länge l

			No.
a_1	a_1	a_1	1
·	·	a_2	2
·	·	a_3	3
a_1	a_2	a_1	4 (Dies hier wäre z.B. 4, 3).

alphabetisch, z.B. für $l = 3$:

090–16–21 Andere Deutung der hohen Zahlausdrücke

Es hat wohl ergebliche Bedenken, $k = k' = k''$ usw. zu setzen. (Beim ursprünglichen Tarskischen Entwurf blieb dies wenigstens unbekannt, sodass jede bewiesene Gliechung auch arithmetisch wahr war in üblicher Deutung.) Denn dann gelten Sätze, die nicht ohne übereinstimmung sind mit der üblichen Arithmetik, und das kann doch wohl in der Syntax zu grossen Nachteile führen. Anderenseits brauchen wir für die Syntax Bezeichnungen für Ausdrücke, also für endliche Sequenzen von Dingen. Wir wollen nun *die hohen Zahlausdrücke als abkürzende Bezeichnungen solcher Sequenzen* deuten:

Sequenzen der Länge 2:	Bezeichnung:
α, α	k'
$\alpha, 1$	k''
$\alpha, 2$	k'''
$\vdots$	
α, k	
$1, \alpha$	$\vdots$
$1, 1$	
$1, 2$	
$\vdots$	
$1, k$	
$\vdots$	
k, α	
$k, 1$	
$\vdots$	
k, k	$k + (k+1)^2$
Länge 3: α, α, α	$k + (k+1)^2 + 1$
$\alpha, \alpha, 1$	$k + (k+1)^2 + 2$
$\vdots$	$\vdots$
k, k, k	

usw.

Diese Ergebnis können wir einfach *durch folgende Regeln* erreichen:
1. Strichausdrücke: $\alpha, \alpha', \ldots$; der längste eigentliche Strichausdruck sei $\mathfrak{St}$. ('k' ist Abkürzung für $\mathfrak{St}_k$, gilt aber nicht selbst als $\mathfrak{St}$.)
2. *Sequenzausdrücke* $\mathfrak{Sq}$ bestehen aus einer endlichen Anzahl von Strichausdruucke, durch Kommata getrennt: $\mathfrak{St}_1, \mathfrak{St}_2, \ldots \mathfrak{St}_n$
3. $(\mathfrak{Sq}_i)' = \mathfrak{Sq}_j$, wo $\mathfrak{Sq}_j$ aus $\mathfrak{Sq}_i$ gebildet wird:
   $\mathfrak{Sq}_i$ sei $\mathfrak{St}_1, \mathfrak{St}_2, \ldots \mathfrak{St}_n$.
1. $\mathfrak{St}_m$ sei das letzte (d.h. am meisten rechts stehende) $\mathfrak{St}$, dass nicht $\mathfrak{St}_k$ ist; $\mathfrak{St}_m$ wird ersetzt durch $\mathfrak{St}'_m$.
2. Jeder der n $\mathfrak{St}$ in $\mathfrak{Sq}_i$ sei $\mathfrak{St}_k$:
$(\mathfrak{Sq}_i)' = \underbrace{\alpha, \alpha, \ldots \alpha}_{n+1}$.

(Also: wir ersetzen jeder $\mathfrak{St}$ durch '$\alpha,$' und fügen noch ein neues 'α' hinzu.)

090-16-04 *Über Finitismus. Gespräch mit Tarski; auch Quine, Goodman, III 1.3.41.*

Ich erkläre mein Sprachsystem (siehe Blätter vom 23.2): Es bezieht sich auf eine endliche Anzahl von bezeichneten Dingen, mit einem grössten $\mathfrak{St}$ ($\mathfrak{St}_k$); $k + 1$ Dinge.

Tarski: Ich möchte ein Arithmetiksystem haben, dass keine Annahmen über die Anzahl der vorhandenen Zahlen macht, oder höchstens eine Zahl (0) annimmt.

A_n sei das System derjenigen Sätze der gewöhnlichen Arithmetik, die auch gelten, wenn es nur die Zahlen $< n$ gibt; also A_0 ohne Zahlen; A_1 nur mit 0; usw. A_ω sei die ganze unendliche gewöhnliche Arithmetik. Wir wollen zur Vereinfachung A_0 ausschliessen, also wenigstens die Existenz einer Zahl annehmen. Mein (i.e. Tarskis) System soll alle die und nur die Sätze enthalten, die in jedem der Systeme $A_n (n = 1, 2, \ldots \omega)$ gelten. Hierher gehören z.B. alle Sätze von folgender Form: keine Funktoren kommen vor, alle universellen Operatoren stehen unnegiert am Anfang, keine Existenzoperatoren.

Wir sollten vielleicht zunächst nur Pradikaten haben, keine Funktoren, da diese Existenzannahmen hineinbringen. Wir können '0' als Grundzeichen zulassen, aber anstatt Nachfolgerfunktor `''`, lieber nur Nachfolgerprädikat 'Succ'.

Wir könnten *recursive* Definition in sehr weitem Masse zulassen; nicht nur die primitive Rekursionen, und die sogenannte generelle Rekursionen, sondern auch z.B. solche, wie sie in der Definition des semantischen Begriffes "erfüllen" auftreten (besonders nicht der Stelle, wo die betreffende Satzfunktion selbst ein Alloperator enthält). Denn solche Rekursion verstehen wir ja. Die Definitionen von "erfüllen" ist die Definition eines Prädikates, nicht eines Funktores, denn wir brauchen im Definiens ein Alloperator. Es gibt hier wohl so ziemlich das ganze Peanosche System, ausgenommen der Satz, dass jede Zahl einen Nachfolger hat. Aber, als einen gewissen Ersatz, haben wir hier doch den Satz '$x \neq x'$', nämlich in der Form '$(x)(y)(Succ(y,x) \supset x \neq y)$'.

[[s. 2]]

(Tarski:) Vielleicht ist dieses System ähnlich dem von C. (Siehe meine Blätter vom 23.2); es enthält aber nicht die Sätze dort, die 'k' enthalten. Wenn wir 'k' als Parameter auffassen, werden die beiden Systeme vielleicht ganz ähnlich. *In Wirklichkeit wollen wir ja niemals eine ganz bestimmte Zahl k annehmen.*

Wir haben von Anfang an Variable in der Sprache; diese durchlaufen alle Dinge der Welt; es bleibt aber offen, wie viele Dinge es gibt.

Anstatt '$prod(2, 3) = 6$' sagen wir: 'wenn x Nachfolger eines Nachfolgers von 0 ist, und $y \ldots$ und $z \ldots$, so ist '$prod(x, y) = z$' (oder stattdessen: $Prod(x, y, z)$). In ähnlicher Weise muss man vielleicht allgemeine Sätze mit Funktoren übersetzen in implizite Sätze; Frage: können wir Funktoren allgemein so einführen, dass wir definite übersetzungsregeln dieser Art bekommen?

Quine: dies stimmt ganz gut mit der alten vor-Russellschen, [[unleserlich]] Auffassung der Mathematik überein (die auch noch Bennett vertreten wird), dass die Mathematik nur Bedingungsaussagen macht.

Gemeinsames Gespräch:

Wenn ein gewisses Basissystem BS, dass wir ganz verstehen, konstruiert ist, so gibt es für den Aufbau der Gesamtsprache W der Wissenschaft *2 Wege*: 1. Wir führen *durch Definition* immer mehr Sachen in BS ein, z.B. unendliche Arithmetik der Natürlichen Zahlen, Theorie der reellen Zahlen, der Funktionen, usw.; die ganze Physik. Wenn dies vollständig ginge, wäre es die ideale Lösung. Es scheint aber recht zweifelhaft, ob das möglich ist. Vermutlich wird man eine (im Vergleich zur klassischen Mathematik und Physik) fragmentare Mathematik und Physik W' erreichen können; vielleicht sogar soviel, wie überhaupt für die praktischen Zwecke der Wissenschaft nötig ist. Das wäre dann immer noch eine sehr gute Lösung.

2. Wenn sich das nicht hinreichend weit durchführen lässt, so müssen wir BS als Syntaxsprache anwenden, um W als Kalkül aufzubauen, ohne Anspruch der Interpretation. (Eine teilweise Interpretation erhält W durch W').

[[s. 3]]

Quine: W ist dann eigentlich nur ein Mythos.

Ich: Nein, kein Mythos, einfach eine Maschine. Es wäre nur ein Mythos, wenn wir den Maschinenteil (Kalkülzeichen) Pseudointerpretation beilegen würde, durch Hinweise auf Entitäten, die es in Wirklichkeit nicht gibt.

Tarski: Weg (2) hatte aber dies unbefriedigende, dass es eigentlich *Mysteriös* bleibe, wie so die Maschine richtig wirkt, d.h. wie es zu erklären ist, dass wenn wir wahre Sätze von BS in die Maschine stecken (als Prämissen), dann auch wahre Sätze (als Konklusionen) wieder herauskommen.

Wir: Das ist vielleicht kein unlösbares Geheimnis. Wir bauen ja die Maschine zu diesem Zweck, und verwurfen sie, wenn wir merken, dass sie dies nicht leistet. Vielleicht kann man sogar in BS zeigen: wenn eine Maschine so und so konstruiert ist, so liefert sie zu wahren Prämissen stets wahren Konklusionen.

Tarski: Die Regeln für recursive Definition für Prädikaten sind noch nicht entwickelt.

[*Ich*: Mir scheint, dass hier die beschränkte Operatoren wichtig sind; wir werden erlauben, im Definiens für das Argument $n+1$ solche Operatoren mit der Schränke n zu gebrauchen. *Überlegen!*]

090-16-19 2.3.41

"$\mathfrak{k}$-*Zahl identische Formeln*", nach Hilbert-Bernays, Grundlagen der Mathematik.

Band I, p. 119 (ohne Identität!):

Ein Formel des niederen Funktionskalküls ist $\mathfrak{k}$-zahlig identisch ($\mathfrak{k}$ ist endlich, $\neq 0$) $=_{Df}$ sie geht bei Anwendung auf einen $\mathfrak{k}$-zahligen Individuum-bereich in eine identische Formel des Aussagenkalküls (d.h. Tautologie) über. Die Anwendung ist so gemeint:

$(x)\mathfrak{A}(x)$ wird ersetzt durch $\mathfrak{A}(1) \land \mathfrak{A}(2) \land \ldots \mathfrak{A}(k)$,

$(\exists x)\mathfrak{A}(x)$ wird ersetzt durch $\mathfrak{A}(1) \lor \mathfrak{A}(2) \lor \ldots \mathfrak{A}(k)$.

Theorem (p.121). Wenn eine Formel $\mathfrak{k} + 1$ *zahlig identisch, so auch $\mathfrak{k}$-zahlig identisch*. (denn wir können ja für das Argument '$k+1$' überall 'k' setzen; dann bleibt die Formel identisch im Aussagenskalkül.) (Das *gilt nur für Kalküle ohne* '='!)

Also: wenn eine Formel $\mathfrak{k}$-zahlig identisch, so auch für alle Zahlen kleiner als $\mathfrak{k}$, aber nicht notwendig auch für die grösseren. Für jede Zahl gibt es Formeln, die für sie (und alle Kleineren), aber nicht für die grösseren identischen sind. Mit wechselndem $\mathfrak{k}$ werden also die Klassen der identischen Formeln immer kleiner:
[[Bild]]

p.121. *Theoreme*. 1. *Jeder* im niederen Funktionskalkül (Hilbert „Prädikatenkalkül") *beweisbare* Formel ist im Endlichen identisch.

2. (Wajsberg). Fügen wir zu den Kalkülen eine beliebige Formel, die $\mathfrak{k}$-zahlig, aber nicht $\mathfrak{k}+1$ zahlig identisch ist, als Grundsatz hinzu, so werden also $\mathfrak{k}$-zahlig identische Formeln beweisbar.

p.123. 3. Für den *einstelligen* Prädikatenkalkül gilt auch die *Umkehrung von (1)*: jede im Endlichen identische Formel ist beweisbar.
Aber: mit Hilfe von $\mathfrak{pr}^2$ lassen sich Formeln bilden, die im Endlichen identisch, aber nicht beweisbar sind; nämlich solche, die nur im Endlichen gelten (die also als *Endlichkeitsbedingung* genommen werden können); sie sind Negationen von solchen, die nur im Unendlichen erfüllbar sind.

Beispiel: 1. "R ist irreflexiv und transitive; jedes Individuum ist ein Erstglied (also: ohne Endglied)".

2. "S hat einen Anfangsgleid, ist one-many (wird ohne Identität ausgedrückt), hat kein Endglied".

[[s. 2]]

p.129. *Gödels Vollständigkeitstheorem*. Jede Formel des Prädikatenkalkül ist entweder widerlegbar, oder erfüllbar (und zwar im abzählbaren Bereich).

Daher: *jede allgemein gültige Formel ist beweisbar*.
Dieses Theorem kann aber *nicht* in die *finitistische* Beweistheorie übernommen werden. Es gibt aber einen entsprechenden finitistischen Vollständigkeitssatz.

Prädikatenkalkül mit Identität.
Hier gibt es Formeln, die nur $\mathfrak{k}$-zahlig identisch ist, weder für grössere noch für kleinere Zahlen; nämlich solche, die besagem dass es genau $\mathfrak{k}$ Individuen gibt.

Auch hier *gilt (1)*. Und *auch Gödels Vollständigkeitssatz*.

090-16-18 *Finitistische Sprache*.
18.3.41

Nur rekursiv definierte *Prädikate*, nicht Funktoren, weil diese Existenzannahmen voraussetzen. Auch kein Nachfolgerfunktor, sondern stattdessen Prädikat ('*Succ*') lieber mit '*Pred*'.

Grundsätze: [Vernichten, falls die andere System mit '*Pred*' Anklang findet.]
I. Satzkalkül.
II. Arithmetik:
1. $\neg Succ(0, x)$ 0 ist Anfangsglied
2. $Succ(x, y) \wedge Succ(x, z) \supset y = z$
3. $Succ(x, z) \wedge Succ(y, z) \supset x = y$ eineindeutig

Kein Grundsatz, dass kein Endglied; so bleibt offen, ob der Bereich endlich oder unendlich ist.

III. Identity. 1. $x = x$
2. $(x = y) \supset (\ldots x \ldots \supset \ldots y \ldots)$.   *Schema* wie PSI8

IV. Restricted univ, exist. & K-operators.
(wie PSI4, 5, 6, 11.)
(für PSI5:) $Succ(z, y) \supset [(x)z(\ldots x \ldots) \equiv (x)y(\ldots x \ldots) \wedge (\ldots z \ldots)]$;
Regeln:

$$\left.\begin{array}{rl} 1. & \textit{Substi.} \\ 2. & \textit{Impli. Regel} \\ 3. & \textit{Vollständige Induktion} \end{array}\right\} \text{(wie in I)}.$$

$$\frac{\ldots 0 \ldots \qquad \ldots x \ldots \wedge Succ(y, x) \supset \ldots y \ldots}{\ldots x \ldots}$$

[[s. 2]]

Recursive Definitionen: Allgemeine Schema:
1. $R(-, -, -, 0) \equiv -------$
2. $Succ(z, y) \supset [R(-, -, -, z) \equiv ---------- R(-, -, -, y) ---]$

Diese Argumente '$-, -, -$' müssen nicht dieselbe sein wie links, sondern beliebig! Sie dürfen auch gebunden sein! *Warum ist gewöhnlich Gleichheit der Argumente gefordert??* Und gefordert, dass sie nicht gebunden sind?

$(x = y + z)$ $Sum(x, y, z)$:
1. $Sum(x, y, 0) \equiv x = y$,
2. $Succ(v, z) \supset [Sum(x, y, v) \equiv (\exists u)x(Succ(x, u) \wedge Sum(\underbrace{u}, y, z))]$

neue Variable, gebunden!

$(x = y \cdot z)$ $Prod(x, y, z)$:
1. $Prod(x, y, 0) \equiv x = 0$.
2. $Succ(v, z) \supset [Prod(x, y, v) \equiv (\exists u)x(Prod(u, y, z) \wedge Sum(x, u, y))]$.

[[s. 3]]

Vielleicht einfacher mit *Vorgänger-Funktor* δ? (Wie bei Bernays: 1.) $\delta(0) = 0$; 2.) $\delta(n') = n$.)
(Oder auch so geschrieben "'x', weil dies ein Sonderzeichen ist, analog zum üblichen Nachfolgerzeichen''", weil sonst keine Funktoren vorkommen sollen.
Grundsätze für 'δ':
$(\delta(y) = x) \equiv [(y = 0) \wedge (x = 0)] \vee [\neg(y = 0) \wedge Succ(y, x)]$.

090-16-16 *Finitistische Arithmetik.*
19.3.41
(Entwurf auf Grund des Gespräches mit Tarski, III, vom 1.31.41)

Nur Prädikate, nicht Funktoren, weil diese Existenzannahmen emplizieren.
Rekursiv Definition für Prädikat, von neuer Art, weil kein Nachfolgerzeichen vorhanden.

Vorgänger Prädikat: '*Pred*'. (ist bequemer als '*Succ*', weil Reihenfolger der Argumente dieselbe ist wie Reihenfolge in der Reihe.)

[[s. 2]]

Die Ganze geht ebenso gut mit '*Pred*' für *Vorgänger*; dies ist sogar bequemer, weil die Reihenfolge der Argumente die Reihenfolge in der Reihe ist.

Grundsätze.
I. *Satzkalkül*. II. *Operatoren.*
(für PSI5:) $Pred(y, z) \supset [(x)z(\ldots x \ldots) \equiv (x)y(\ldots x \ldots) \land (\ldots z \ldots)]$
PSI 4, 6 (Existenz), 11 (K) wie in I.
III. *Identity*. wie in I.
IV. *Arithmetik.*
 1. $\neg Pred(x, 0)$ 0 ist ein Anfangsglied.
 2. $Pred(x, y) \land Pred(x, z) \supset y = z$
 3. $Pred(x, z) \land Pred(y, z) \supset x = y$

Kein Grundsatz, dass kein Endglied; so *bleibt offen, ob der Bereich endlich oder unendlich ist.*

Regeln:
 1.   Subst
 2.   Impli. Regel   } (wie in I).
 3.   *vollständige Induktion*

$$\frac{\ldots 0 \ldots \qquad \ldots x \ldots \land Pred(y, x) \supset \ldots y \ldots}{\ldots x \ldots}$$

[[s. 3]]

Frage: Müssen wir noch zum Ausdruck bringen, dass 0 *das einzige Anfangsglied ist?*

$$\neg Pred(x, \ldots)$$
Vielleicht neue Regel nötig? $\downarrow$
$$\ldots = 0.$$

Können wir es vielleicht mit Alloperator ausdrücken?
Vielleicht neuen Grundsatz: $(x)y(\neg Pred(x, y)) \equiv y = 0$.   (a)
Oder ist dies *beweisbar* mit Hilfe der bisherigen Grundsätzen? *Ja*, durch vollständige Induktion inbezug auf y:
 1. Für $y = 0$ ist es trivial.

2. Wir müssen beweisen:
$[(x)y(\neg Pred(x,y)) \supset y = 0] \wedge Pred(y,z) \supset [(x)z(\neg Pred(x,z)) \supset z = 0]$

aus geändertem PSI5:
$Pred(y,z) \quad \supset \quad [(x)z(\neg Pred(x,z)) \quad \equiv \quad (x)y(\neg Pred(x,z) \wedge (\neg Pred(z,z))]$
$\supset \quad (x)y(\neg Pred(x,z))$

(verwenden: $\quad (x)y(..x..) \supset ..y..$
Wendung $\quad \supset \quad \neg Pred(y,z)$
$Pred(y,z) \quad \supset \quad [Pred(y,z) \quad \supset \quad \neg(x)z(\neg Pred(x,z))]$
$Pred(y,z) \quad \supset \quad$ "
$\supset \quad [(x)z(\neg Pred(x,z)) \supset \underbrace{\ldots}_{\text{beliebig}}]$
$\supset \quad [\quad " \quad \supset z = 0]$

Aus (1) und (2), nach vollständiger Induktion: *(a)*.
Also kein neuer Grundsatz nötig, und auch keine Regel. Die Ableitung laut obiger Regel ergibt sich so:
$\neg Pred(x, \ldots)$

Th.13.6b (beruht auf vollständige Induktion): $\quad (x)\ldots(\neg Pred(x,\ldots))$
(a) $\quad \ldots = 0.$

[[s. 4]]

Recursive Definitionen:
Allgemeine Schema:
1. $R(-,-,-,0) \equiv -----$
2. $Pred(u,v) \supset [R(-,-,-,v) \equiv ------R(\cdot,\cdot,\cdot,u)-----]$
Diese Argumente '·, ·, ·' müssen nicht dieselben sein wie links. Sie dürfen auch gebunden sein (siehe Beispiel unten!)
Besser anders! Siehe s.5!

Warum wird gewöhnlich Gleichheit der Argumente gefordert?? Und dass sie nicht gebunden sind? So z. B. Hilbert-Bernays, vielleicht auch Gödel?

$(x = y + z) \quad Sum(x,y,z):$
1. $Sum(x,y,0) \equiv x = y,$
2. $Pred(u,v) \quad \supset [Sum(x,y,v) \quad \equiv (\exists z)x(Pred(z,x) \quad \wedge Sum(z,y,u))]$
$\quad u' = v \qquad\qquad x = y + v \qquad\quad z' = x \qquad\qquad z = y + u$
$\qquad\qquad\qquad x = y + u' \qquad\qquad\qquad\qquad\qquad v, z, u$ bound!
$(x = y \cdot z) \quad Prod(x,y,z):$
1. $Prod(x,y,0) \equiv x = 0.$
2. $Pred(u,v) \supset [Prod(x,y,v) \equiv (\exists u)x(Prod(u,y,z) \wedge Sum(x,u,y))].$

[[s. 5]]

Vielleicht *Rekursionschema* so:
1. $R(x,\cdot,\cdot,0) \equiv \underbrace{-----}_{x}$
2. $Pred(u,v) \wedge R(w,\cdot,\cdot,u) \supset [R(x,\cdot,\cdot,v) \equiv \underbrace{------}_{u,v,w,x}]$.

Bespiel:

1. $Sum(x,y,0) \equiv x = y$,
2. $Pred(u,v) \quad \wedge \quad Sum(w,y,u) \quad \supset \quad [Sum(x,y,v) \quad \equiv \quad Pred(w,x)]$
   $u' = v \qquad\qquad w = y+u \qquad\qquad x = y+v \qquad\qquad w' = x$
   $\qquad\qquad\qquad\qquad\qquad\qquad\qquad\qquad = y+u'$

1. $Prod(x,y,0) \equiv x = 0$.
2. $Pred(u,v) \quad \wedge \quad Prod(w,y,u) \quad \supset \quad [Prod(x,y,v) \quad \equiv \quad Sum(x,w,y)]$
   $u' = v \qquad\qquad w = y \cdot u \qquad\qquad x = y \cdot v$
   $\qquad\qquad\qquad\qquad\qquad\qquad\qquad\qquad = y \cdot u'$

090-16-17 16.4.41

Vielleicht können wir dann '$0''''\cdots$' durch Kontext-Definition einführen:
$P(0''') =_{df} (x)[Pred^3(0,x) \supset P(x)]$; den Operator müssen wir weglassen; aber dürfen wir freie Variable im Definiens verwenden??

Aber das trifft doch wohl nur das Gemeinte, wenn dies [[$(x)[Pred^3(0,x) \supset P(x)]$]] beweisbar, also L-wahr ist.

090-16-15 *Tarski, über Funktionskalkül.*
21.5.41
(Im Gespräch mit Quine und mir, 7.5.41)

Für niederen Funktionskalkül ohne Prädikatvariable und mit nur geschlossenen Sätzen gilt: 1. Wenn $\mathfrak{S}_n$ im FC beweisbar ist (oder analytisch, was nach Gödel dasselbe ist), so gibt es eine endliche Reiche (aus den unendlichen vielen) Axiomen von FC derart, dass $\mathfrak{S}_1 \wedge \mathfrak{S}_2 \wedge \cdots \wedge \mathfrak{S}_m \supset \mathfrak{S}_n$ eine Tautologie ist (auf Grund der Wahrheitswerttafeln).
2. Wenn $\mathfrak{S}_n$ aus anderen Sätzen ableitbar in FC ist, so gibt es eine endliche Reihe $\mathfrak{S}_1 \ldots \mathfrak{S}_m$ aus den Axiomen des FC und jenen Prämissen derart dass $\mathfrak{S}_1 \wedge \cdots \wedge \mathfrak{S}_m \supset \mathfrak{S}_n$ eine Tautologie ist.

Tarski: Dies ist besonders vorteilhaft zu verwenden in *Quines System* (ML); dort ist jetzt der Satzkalkül ersetzt durch Wahrheitswerttafeln; dann gibt es Axiome der Quantifikation und für $\in^9$, und modus ponens als einzige Regel; wenn die obige Darstellung angewendet wird, *brauchen wir gar keine Schlussregel mehr!*

9. unsicher

090–16–13 Tarski, formalisiertes System mit Quotes.
(Gespräch mit Tarski, Quine, Goodman, *26.5.41*)

Tarski: Man kann leicht ein exaktes, formalisiertes System aufbauen, dass Quotes verwendet, um über die eigenen Ausdrücke oder einige davon zu sprechen (*Ich*: oder auch über andere Sprachen, die vielleicht andere Sätze, aber nicht andere Zeichen enthalten). Zu den *primitiven* Zeichen: Variable $x, \ldots$; $\neg, \rightarrow, \Pi$.

Δ: "Δ '...' " heisst: '...' ist beweisbar; es kann aber auch "wahr" oder irgendetwas anderes bedeuten; es werden keine Axiome für 'Δ' aufgestellt, so bleibt die Bedeutung ganz offen.

S: "Sxy" ist der Ausdruck, der aus x entsteht, indem für alle freien Variablen y eingesetzt wird.

Schema-Axiom für S:
"S '...' '– – –' " = '– · –' wenn '– · –' aus '...' dadurch entsteht, dass –––.

Ich: Zwingt der Gebrauch von Quotes nicht zu Komplikationen in den Regeln? Z.B. substi. Regel.
Tarski: Nein.
Ich: Dann muss aber "freie Variable" so definiert werden, dass die Variable innerhalb von Quotes nicht frei sind.
Tarski: Ja. *Tarski*: Hier können nun in einfacher Weise die *Antinomien* analysiert werden. Ferner kann ein *Theorem analog zu Gödels* beweisen werden; *ohne Arithmetisierung*.
(Quine: der Beweis der Unvollständigkeit der Protosyntax ist auch schon ohne Arithmetik.)
Es kann nämlich 'α' so definiert werden, dass α = '$\neg \Delta \alpha$'; das kann für jades Prädikat anstelle von 'Δ' gemacht werden. So bekommen wir in höchst einfacher Weise einen unentschiedenen Satz. Dies ersetzt aber nicht etwa Gödels Resultat; denn hier folgt nicht die Unvollstandigkeit der Arithmetik.

090–16–14 Quine's "frames".
(Gespräch mit Tarski, Quine, Goodman, *26.5.41*)

Quine verwendet 'frames', d.h. Ausdrücke wie '$x = y$', '$p \supset q$', vielleicht sogar '$F(x)$' usw.; diese enthalten Zeichen, die in der Objektsprache nicht vorkommen; sie gehören aber nicht zur Metasprache, sondern sind immer in Quotes; dienen dazu, um über gewisse Formen der Objektsprache zu sprechen. Also gewissermassen Ersatz für Schemata in der Metasprache.

Tarski: Sie sind besonders nützlich, wenn aus didaktischen Gründen die elaboraten Schemata der Metasprache nicht verwendet werden sollen, wie z.B. im Aufsatz über Definierbarkeit in "*Erkenntnis.*"

Quine: 'p' usw. werden in dem neuen einführenden Logikbuch verwendet werden.

090–16–08 Gespräch mit Tarski und Quine (und Goodman), *26.5.41*.

Tarski: In Zukunft wird es sich immer mehr als praktisch herausstellen, dass wir eine Syntax und Semantik einer gewissen *Standardsprachform* entwickeln.

Und es wird dann für jede zu konstruierende Theorie sehr nützlich sein, diese Form zu haben, damit alle allgemeinen Theoreme ohne weiteres auf sie angewendet werden können. Diese *Standardsprachform*:

1. Keine freie Variablen (diese richten bei Studenten oft Verwirrung an; siehe auch z.B. Ushenkos Konfusion; für didaktischen Zwecke am besten vermieden);

2. Modus Ponens als einzige Regel; da keine freie Variablen, so kann jede andere Regel durch entsprechende impl. Satz als Grundsatz ersetzt werden,

3. Für Satzkalkül keine Grundsätze, sondern direkte (definite) Definitionen für '*Tautologie*' (wie Quine).

4. Vielleicht so (siehe anderes Blatt): anstatt Beweise und Ableitungen als Reihe von Sätzen, einfach: der entsprechende impl. Satz ist eine Tautologie. An Stelle der umständlichen Angabe des Beweises genügt Angabe der betreffenden Grundsätze (d.h. Instanzen der Grundsatzschemata) (diese müssen angegeben werden, sonst ist die Behauptung der Beweisbarkeit nicht definit nachprüfbar); oder, aus praktischen Gründen der leichteren Nachprüfbarkeit, Angabe der betreffenden Instanzen gewisser vorher bewiesener Theoreme.

5. '$\in$' als einziges primitiven Prädikat, sogar für Physik usw. '$\in$' wird also hier (wie ich möchte) den logischen Konstanten gleichgestellt (*Quine* sagt: es wird als *mathematisches* Zeichen genommen).

6. *Individuum-Konstanten als einzige deskriptive primitive Konstante*. Diese Konstante sind aber "Individuum" nur im syntaktischen Sinn: Konstanten für die einzige vorkommende Variablenart. Semantisch betrachtet aber: sie bezeichnen Klassen, Klassen von Klassen,

[[s. 2]]

reellen usw., nämlich Entitäten des $\in$-Systemes, wie bei Quine.

Quine: Dies scheint das umgekehrte Verfahren von dem in ML: dort als einziger deskriptiver primitiver Konstante gewisse Atomprädikate (die aber nicht einsetzbar sind für Variable und daher keine Designata haben), während alle Konstanten für Werte der Variablen erst durch Definitionen eingeführt werden, nämlich als Abkürzungen für Deskriptionen. Tarski meint, sein Verfahren erscheint natürlich. Quine ist nicht sicher, welches von beiden vorzuziehen ist.

Tarski: Bei dieser Sprachform (Individuum-Konstante als einziges primitive deskriptives Zeichen) kann man in einfacher Weise '*Modelle* der betreffenden Theorie' definieren: nämlich die Reihe der betreffenden Entitäten, die durch die Konstanten bezeichnet sind. Jede Theorie wird somit aufgefasst als handelnd von gewissen Individuen oder Dingen (Beides nicht im üblichen Sinn verstanden), von gewissen Entitäten, nämlich Klassen, Relationen oder dergleichen.

[*Ich*: Vielleicht könnten wir auch Quines Idee, keine eigentlichen Individuum-Konstanten (d.h. Name für Nicht-Klasse) als primitiv zu nehmen, in Tarskis Plan hineinnehmen: als primitive deskriptive Konstanten nur Zeichen für Klassen nehmen, während Zeichen für eigentliche Individuen (d.h. Nicht-Klassen) wie bei Quine durch Deskription definiert werden. Also für jede solche

Konstante 'a' Axiom nehmen: es gibt ihn mit der betreffenden Entität nicht-identischen Elemente von ihr.
$(\exists x)(x \in a \wedge x \neq a)]$

7. Es ist fraglich, ob die Standardsprachform auch *Funktoren* enthalten soll. Bei *Quine* werden Funktion durch einmehrdeutige Relationen ersetzt. Tarski meint aber, es sei vielleicht doch zuweilen technisch einfacher, Funktoren zu zulassen, z.B. '+' usw. in Arithmetik, um nicht zu stark von der üblichen Sprachform abzuweichen. Die Frage wird nicht eindeutig entschieden.

Quine: Die Ausschaltung von primitiven Individuum-Konstanten in ML geschah auch aus dem philosophischen Grund, dass durch die blosse Sinnhaftigkeit aller Ausdrücke der Sprache nicht schon etwas über Existenz von Gegenständen ausgesagt werden; wir können irgendwie dafür sorgen, dass ein Individuum-Konstante, für die sich herausstellt, dass sie sonst nichts bezeichnet, Λ bezeichnet.

090-16-30 *Gibt es einen "Wahrscheinlichkeitsschluss"?* (Für Diskussion mit Tarski und Quine)
2.6.41

Schlüsse in deductiver Logik: (*Semantische* Sätze)

S_1 ist wahr S_1 ist wahr S_1 ist L-wahr
$S_1 \to S_2$ $S_1 \to_L S_2$ $S_1 \to_L S_2$
S_2 ist wahr S_2 ist wahr S_2 ist L-wahr

(Der Fall, dass S_2 *physikalisch* aus S_1 folgt, ist ein Spezialfall von '$\to$').

Problem: Gibt es etwas Analoges, wenn anstatt $\to$ oder $\to_L$ *eine Wahrscheinlichkeits- oder Konfirmations-Beziehung* oder ähnliches genommen wird? Etwa bezeichnet '$--\to$'. Natürlich kann dann der Schluss nicht aus "S_2 ist wahr (oder L-wahr)", sondern höchstens "S_2 ist hoch wahrscheinlich (oder hoch konfirmiert)" oder ähnliches.

Was aber bedeutet 'wahrscheinlich'?

Da Wahrscheinlichkeit, Konfirmation usw. nur als relative Begriffe einen Sinn haben, so muss ihre absolute Verwendung verstanden werden als elliptisch für Bezugnahme auf ein standard Referenz z.B. meine Gesamtkenntnis jetzt, oder eine festgelegte Klasse K von Beobachtungssätzen oder dergleichen.

Der Schluss wäre also dann von der Form:
$K --\to S_1$
$S_1 --\to S_2$
$K --\to S_2$

Also mit anderen Worten: *Problem: ist '$--\to$' transitiv?*: wenn $--\to$ | $--\to$, so $--\to$.

Wie steht es, wenn eine der beiden Relationen in den Prämissen $\to_L$ ist?

1. $\dfrac{S_1 --\to S_2 \quad S_2 \to_L S_3}{S_1 --\to S_3}$ dies ist *richtig*.

Aber 2. $\dfrac{\begin{array}{c}S_1 \to_L S_2\\ S_2 \dashrightarrow S_3\end{array}}{S_1 \dashrightarrow S_3}$?

Dies stimmt nicht allgemein. Es kann sein, dass S_1, S_3 nur sehr schlecht konfirmiert (z.B., von 300 beobachteten Dinge nur 100 P sind) während S_2, ein Teil der Beobachtungen von S_1, S_3 sehr gut konfirmiert (nämlich die 100 P-Dinge).

[[s. 2]]

Es scheint *plausible*, "Wahrkeinlichsschluss" zu machen.
z.B.:
Morgen wird es wahrscheinlich regnen.
Wenn es regnet, wird wahrscheinlich (gewöhnlich, meistens) die Strasse nass.
Morgen wird wahrscheinlich die Strasse nass.

Aber dieser schluss ist *nicht gültig!* Die zweite Prämisse lässt die Möglichkeit offen, dass die Strasse zuweilen bei Regen nicht nass wird, z.B. wenn sie überdacht wird. Wenn nun die für die erste Prämisse und den Schlußsatz stillschweigend angenommene Referenz, z.B. mein gegenwärtiges Wissen, den Satz enthält, dass die Strasse morgen überdacht wird, so ist der Schlusssatz falsch, obwohl beide Prämisse wahr sind.

090-16-11 *States of aff. und Modelle.*
10.6.41

[[Bild]]
state = Verteilung der primitiven Prädikate der betreffenden Sprache auf die Individuen (des universe of disc. der Sprache).
Dabei ist als jeden $\mathfrak{pr}_1$ eine Klasse von individuen zugeordnet, jedem $\mathfrak{pr}_2$ eine Klasse von geordneten Paaren von Individuen.
Müssen wir dabei *nur die Extension* der P.. berücksichtigen??
Die wirkliche Zustand der welt sei so: [[Bild: $P_1 \subset P_2$]]
Sodass also $(x)(P_1(x) \supset P_2(x))[= \mathfrak{S}_1]$ wahr ist.
Hier kommt es nun doch auf die Bedeutung von 'P_1' und 'P_2' an;
2 Fälle unterscheiden: 1. Der Satz $\mathfrak{S}_1$ folgt schon aus der Bedeutung der beiden Prädikaten (d.h. aus den semantischen Regeln); $\mathfrak{S}$ ist L-wahr. Hier muss auch in jedem anderen state $P_1 \subset P_2$ sein.
2. $\mathfrak{S}_1$ ist F-wahr. Dann ist auch z.B. als state zugelassen: [[Bild: $P_1 \cap P_2 \neq \emptyset$, $P_1 \not\subseteq P_2$, und $P_1 \not\supseteq P_2$]]
Modelle. Tarski bezieht sich anscheinend auf einen teilweise interpretieren Kalkül, nämlich alle logischen Zeichen sind interpretiert; für die übrigen Zeichen ist nur bestimmt, dass sie deskriptiv sind; aber ihre Interpretation ist offen gelassen.
Eine Modell für dieses System = eine Sequenz von n Entitäten, die den n deskriptiven Zeichen (für die eine bestimmte Anordnung, die "alphabetisch",

vorausgesetzt) zugeordnet werden (als Designata).

[[s. 2]]

Es sei gegeben:
1. Eine *Kalkül C*, mit Interpretation der logischen Zeichen und mit nicht[10] interpretierten deskriptiven Zeichen 'P_1', 'P_2', $\cdots$ 'P_n'.
2. Ein *Semantisches System S* mit denselben Sätzen und Zeichen, aber alles interpretiert; und zwar bezeichnet 'P_1' die Eigenschaft E_1, usw.
Wir konstruieren eine *Korrelation K* zwischen den *Modellen* (M) für C und den *Zuständen* (Z) für S:
$K(M, Z) =_{Df}$ für jedes r (für $r = 1$ bis n): die dem $\mathfrak{pr}_r$ (d.h. 'P_r') in M zugeordneten Klassen von Individuen = Klasse der Individuen, die in Z die Eigenschaft E_r haben.
Aber: wenn zwischen den 'P_r' in S (also den E_r) logische Beziehungen bestehen (z.B. früheres Beispiel), dann werden dadurch gewisse Verteilungen als unmöglich ausgeschlossen, d.h. gewisse Modelle in C entsprechen dann keine Zustände in S. Um dies zu vermieden, könnten wir so vorgehen, dass wir nur solche S in Betracht ziehen, wo *keine logischen Beziehungen zwischen den 'P_r'* bestehen. Es scheint, dass dann die *Korrelation K eineindeutig* ist.
Hierbei haben wir immer die *Typenverhältnisse beachtet*, z.B. dadurch, dass in einem Modell für 'P_r' nur Klassen von Individuen zugelassen werden. Man könnte auch *'Modell' in weiterem* Sinn verwenden: den deskriptiven Zeichen werden beliebige Entitäten zugeordnet.

range von $\mathfrak{S}_i =_{Df}$ $\begin{cases} 1. & \textit{Klasse der Zuständen inbezug auf S, in denen } \mathfrak{S}_i \\ & \textit{wahr ist.} \\ 2. & \textit{Klasse der Modelle inbezug auf C, für die } \mathfrak{S}_i \textit{ wahr} \\ & \textit{ist.} \end{cases}$

$\mathfrak{S}_i$ ist *L-wahr* $=_{Df}$ $\begin{cases} 1. & \mathfrak{S}_i \text{ ist } \textit{wahr in jedem Zustand} \text{ inbezug auf } S. \\ 2. & \mathfrak{S}_i \text{ ist } \textit{wahr für jedes Modell} \text{ auf } C. \end{cases}$

090-16-10 *Tarski über "state of affairs"*,
Gespräch (dabei Quine, Goodman, Hempel), 18.6.41.
Eine Sprache S sei gegeben. Wenn mehrere, sogar auch unendlich viele, deskriptiven primitiven Zeichen vorkommen, können wir sie durch eines ersetzen, nämlich für die Sequenz der betreffenden Entitäten. Dann haben wir 4 *primitiven Zeichen*: 3 für Logik (einschliesslich '$\in$'), und *die deskriptiven Namen* (Namen = etwas, dass eine Entität bezeichnet, d.h. einen Wert der Variabeln).

---

10. Im Text fehlt „nicht".

2 Entitäten sind äquivalent $=_{Df}$ für jede Satzfunktion in der Sprache, beide erfüllen sie oder beide nicht. Also: sie sind entweder identisch, oder ihre unterscheidenden Eigenschaften können in der Sprache nicht ausgedrückt werden.

Die Klasse der mit einer gegebenen Entität äquivalenten Entitäten entspricht einen state; anders gewählt: die Klasse derjenigen Satzfunktionen in S, die gerade durch irgendein (und daher durch jedes) Element dieser Klasse erfüllt werden.

Ich: Entspricht dies nicht vielmehr einer state description? Unter einem state z.B. für eine Sprache mit 'T' für Temperatur als einziges deskriptives Zeichen verstehe ich jede Funktion von 4 reellen Zahlen, also jede Entität des Typus von T.

Tarski: Es ist besser, jede Entität überhaupt zu nehmen. Die Typen sollten wir ganz abschaffen. Einem state entspricht eine Entität, einer Klasse von states, die wir in S nicht unterscheiden Klasse von states, die wir in S nicht unterscheiden könnten, eine Klasse von äquivalenten Entitäten.

Ich: Ein Physiker, der 'T' eingeführt hat, wird aber '2, 3 $\in$ T' nicht nur als F-falsch ablehnen, sondern schon als L-falsch, denn er braucht kein Experiment, um es als falsch zu zeigen. Könnte man vielleicht so vorgehen?:

$\mathfrak{S}_i$ ist L-wahr$_1$ in 0 $=_{Df}$ ... (mit bezug auf 'T' als deskriptives Zeichen);

$\mathfrak{S}_i$ ist L-wahr$_1$ in M $=_{Df}$ ... (analog inbezug auf die deskriptiven Zeichen in M, die wir für die semantische Regel für 'T brauchen.)

$\mathfrak{S}_i$ ist L-wahr$_2$ in 0 $=_{Df}$ der Satz '$\mathfrak{S}_i$ ist wahr in 0' ist L-wahr$_1$ in M.

Aber Schwerigkeit: Reduktionssätze für 'T' können nicht als eigentlichen semantischen Regeln genommen werden; und wenn wir einfach 'Temperatur' in M verwenden, fallen wohl L-wahr$_1$ und $_2$ zusammen. [Vielleicht aber nicht, wenn andere Wörter verwendet werden, in eigentlicher semantischer Regel, nicht nur Reduktionssatz; z.B. 'P_1' bezeichnet Pferd, 'P_2' weisses Pferd; dann wird '$P_1 \supset P_2$' L-wahr$_2$, obwohl es nicht L-wahr$_1$ ist.]

Tarski: Wohl besser so: wie wir 'deskriptiv' durch eine, schliesslich willkürliche, Aufzählung[11] definieren, so definieren wir auch den weiteren Begriff ('L-wahr$_2$' oder was immer) durch eine Aufzählung von Sätzen in S über T, derart, dass die logische Folgen ('L-impli.$_1$') dieser Sätze als L-wahr$_2$ genommen werden. Diese Sätze besagen z.B.: nur Quintupel in T, und zwar Quintupel von relleen Zahlen, und zwar so, dass keine 2 Quintupeln nur im ersten Glied verschieden sind, und dass es für jedes Quadrupel ein Quintupel mit geeignetem ersten Glied gibt; ferner aber auch: die Funktion soll stetig sein, soll einen ersten dif.quote haben, vielleicht

[[s. 2]]

auch zweiten usw., (er meint halt: vielleicht rationale Werte für rationale Argumente, oder (Quine) beschränkt auf algebraische Zahlen; aber ich meine, das würde ein Physiker nicht wünschen).

---

11. Text: 'Abzählung'

Quine. So vermeiden wir „state of aff.", intensionale Sprache, und den unklaren Begriff 'logisch-möglich'.

Tarski: Der Physiker wählt diese Sätze, als Bedingungen, die eine vorgeschlagene Behauptung über T erfüllen muss, um überhaupt als (logisch) korrekt angenommen zu werden, bevor noch Experimente über die Wahrheit gemacht werden.

Quine: Es ist dann Aufgabe einer behavioristische Untersuchung, festzustellen, welche Bedingungen dieser Art die Physiker aufstellen.

Ich: Nein, das gäbe nur den entsprechenden pragmatischen Begriff. Wie bei allen anderen semantischen (und syntaktischen) Begriffen, gibt auch hier der pragmatische Begriff nur ein Suggestion, bestimmt nicht eindeutig.

Meine überlegung hierzu.
So entspricht also:

einem state	einem Entität
	Oder: eine Entität, die die zusätzlichen Bedingungen erfüllt (nicht einfach: Typen, sondern wie oben von Tarski angedeutet; diese Bedingungen werden vom Physiker aufgestellt) = ein Modell von S
- L-range von $\mathfrak{S}_i$	Die Klasse derjenigen Modelle von S die die dem $\mathfrak{S}_i$ entsprechende logische Satzfunktion erfüllen.
- Wirkungs-state	die durch 'T' bezeichenete Entität. ('bezeichnet' hier als extensionaler Begriff)

090-16-05 *Letztes Gespäch über nucleus-Sprache*, mit Tarski, Quine, Goodman; dabei Hempel;
18.6.41.

Zusammenfassung des Bisherbesprochenen. Nucleus lang., soll dienen als Syntaxsprache für Aufbau der Gesamtwissenschaftssprache (einschliesslich klassische Mathematik, Physik, usw.). Die Wissenschaftssprache bekommt eine teilweise Intereretation dadurch, dass die n.l. als verstanden vorausgesetzt wird und entweder ein Teil der Gesamtsprache ist oder einem Teil zugeordnet ist, und dass die syntaktische Beziehungen ($\to_C$) zwischen diesem Teil und dem Rest so aufgefasst werden, dass sie logische Beziehungen ($\to_L$) darstellen (oder etwas ähnliches).

1. Der *logisch-arithmetische* Teil der n.l.: unbeschränkte Operatoren, auch [[unleserlich]]. (Die Beschränkung auf recursive Arithmetik mit nur freien Variabeln ist anscheinend als unnötig aufgegeben worden). Hiergegen keine Bedenken vom finitistischen [[unleserlich]], weil die Werte der Variabeln nur physikalische Dinge sind. Dabei bleibt es unbestimmt, ob deren Anzahl endlich oder unendlich ist. Als Zahlen werden die Dinge selbst genommen, für die eine Ordnung vorangesetzt wird, auf Grund einer Nachfolgerrelation. (Funktoren nur indirect verwendet, zur abkürzung komplizierter Sätze mit der Nachfolgerrelation.)

2. Der *deskriptive* Teil. Wir haben uns nicht geeinigt, ob man besser mit Dingprädikaten oder sense data Prädikaten anfängt. Für das Erstere: Ich,

wohl auch Tarski; Hempel führt Popper an. Für das Zweite: Goodman und Quine. [[unleserlich]]: die Sprache soll möglichst gut intelligible sein. Es ist aber nicht klar, was wir eigentlich damit meinen. Sollen wir vielleicht die Kinder psychologisch fragen, was das Kind zuerst oder am leichtesten lernt? Ich betone den Unterschied zwischen dem blossen Haben von Erlebnisse, z.B. Wahrnehmungen, und dem Wissen. Wissen, Erkenntnis, = Fähigkeit zum Aussagen (allgemeiner: zu irgender diskriminitiven Response).

– Zwei mehr, aber ohne Daten –

090–16–20 *Zur Diskussion über Finitismus.*
Tarski schlägt vor, Heyting und Weyl nachzusehen, wie sie sich den Aufbau der Mathematik und *Physik* auf intuitionistische Grundlagen denken.
Ich glaube, auch *Gödels* Interpretation der klassischen Mathematik durch Übersetzung in die Intuitionistische ist für uns wichtig.

090–16–22 *Zahl und Ding.*
Nach Eddington gibt es 2^{256} Partikel; $= 2^{(10 \times 25.6)} = (2^{10})^{25.6} = (10^3)^{25.6} = 10^{3 \times 25.6} = 10^{77}$.
Quine nimmt die Dinge als Klassen von Partikeln: $2^{(2^{256})} = 2^{(10^{77})} = 2^{(10 \times 10^{76})} = (2^{10})^{10^{76}} = (10^3)^{(10^{76})} = 10^{(3 \times 10^{76})}$.

References

Awodey, S. and Carus, A. 2007. "Carnap's Dream: Gödel, Wittgenstein, and Logical Syntax." *Synthese* 159(1), pp. 23-45.

Ayer, A. J. 1959. *Logical Positivism*. Glencoe, IL: Free Press.

Baldwin, T. 2007. "C. I. Lewis: Pragmatism and Analysis." In *The Analytic Turn*, M. Beaney, ed., London: Routledge, pp. 178-95.

Bays, T. 2001. "On Tarski on Models." *Journal of Symbolic Logic* 66, pp. 1701-26.

Ben-Menahem, Y. 2006. *Conventionalism: From Poincaré to Quine*. New York: Cambridge University Press.

Benacerraf, P. 1965/1983. "What Numbers Could Not Be." In *Philosophy of Mathematics: Selected Readings*, P. Benacerraf and H. Putnam, eds., New York: Cambridge University Press, 2nd edn., pp. 272-94.

Bernays, P. 1935/1983. "On Platonism in Mathematics." In *Philosophy of Mathematics: Selected Readings*, P. Benacerraf and H. Putnam, eds., New York: Cambridge University Press, 2nd edn., pp. 258-71.

Betti, A. 2008. "Polish Axiomatics and Its Truth." In *New Essays on Tarski and Philosophy*, D. Patterson, ed., New York: Oxford University Press, pp. 44-71.

Bouveresse, J. 2005. "On the Meaning of the Word 'Platonism' in the Phrase 'Mathematical Platonism'." *Proceedings of the Aristotelian Society*, pp. 55-70.

Brandom, R. 1994. *Making It Explicit*. Cambridge, MA: Harvard University Press.

Burgess, J. 1983. "Why I Am Not a Nominalist." *Notre Dame Journal of Formal Logic* 24, pp. 93-105.

Burgess, J. and Rosen, G. 1996. *A Subject with No Object*. New York: Oxford University Press.

Carnap, R. 1928/1963. *The Logical Structure of the World*. Chicago and La Salle, IL: Open Court.

——. 1932/1934. *Unity of Science*. London: Kegan Paul.

——. 1932/1959. "The Elimination of Metaphysics through Logical Analysis of Language." In *Logical Positivism*, A. J. Ayer, ed., Glencoe, IL: Free Press, pp. 60-81.

——. 1932/1987. "On Protocol Sentences." *Nous* 21, pp. 457-70.

——. 1934/1937. *Logical Syntax of Language*. Chicago and La Salle, IL: Open Court.

——. 1934/1987. "The Task of the Logic of Science." In *Unified Science*, B. McGuinness, ed., Dordrecht: Reidel, vol. 19 of *Vienna Circle Collection*, pp. 46-66.

——. 1936-37. "Testability and Meaning." *Philosophy of Science* 3-4, pp. 419-71 and 1-40.

——. 1936/1949. "Truth and Confirmation." In *Readings in Philosophical Analysis*, H. Feigl and W. Sellars, eds., New York: Appleton, Century, Crofts, pp. 119-27.

——. 1938. "Logical Foundations of the Unity of Science." In *The International Encyclopedia of Unified Science*, O. Neurath, ed., Chicago: University of Chicago Press, vol. 1, pp. 42-62.

——. 1939. *Foundations of Logic and Mathematics*, vol. I of *The International Encyclopedia of Unified Science*. Chicago: University of Chicago Press.

——. 1942. *Introduction to Semantics*. Cambridge, MA: Harvard University Press.

——. 1954/1958. *Introduction to Symbolic Logic and Its Applications*. New York: Dover.

——. 1956a. *Meaning and Necessity*. Chicago: University of Chicago Press, 2nd edn.

——. 1956b. "The Methodological Character of Theoretical Concepts." In *Minnesota Studies in the Philosophy of Science*, H. Feigl and M. Scriven, eds., Minneapolis: University of Minnesota Press, vol. I, pp. 38-76.

——. 1963. "Intellectual Autobiography." In *Philosophy of Rudolf Carnap*, P. Schilpp, ed., Chicago and La Salle, IL: Open Court, vol. 11 of *The Library of Living Philosophers*, pp. 3-85.

——. 1966. *Introduction to the Philosophy of Science*. New York: Basic Books.

Carus, A. 2007. *Carnap and Twentieth-Century Thought: Explication as Enlightenment*. New York: Cambridge University Press.

Casullo, A. 1988. "Necessity, Certainty, and the A Priori." *Canadian Journal of Philosophy* 18, pp. 43-66.

Chihara, C. 1990. *Constructibility and Mathematical Existence.* New York: Oxford University Press.

Chwistek, L. 1933. "Die Nominalistische Grundlegung der Mathematik." *Erkenntnis* 3, pp. 367-88.

———. 1935/1949. *The Limits of Science.* London: Routledge and Kegan Paul.

Coffa, A. 1991. *The Semantic Tradition from Kant to Carnap.* New York: Cambridge University Press.

Colyvan, M. 2001. *The Indispensibility of Mathematics.* New York: Oxford University Press.

Creath, R. 1982. "Was Carnap a Complete Verificationist in the *Aufbau*?" *Philosophy of Science Association (Proceedings 1982)*, pp. 384-93.

———. 1987. "The Initial Reception of Carnap's Doctrine of Analyticity." *Nous* 21, pp. 477-99.

———. 1990. *Dear Carnap, Dear Van.* University of California Press.

———. 1996. "The Unity of Science: Carnap, Neurath, and Beyond." In *The Disunity of Science: Boundaries, Contexts, and Power*, P. Galison and D. Stump, eds., Stanford, CA: Stanford University Press, pp. 417-27.

———. 2004. "Quine on the Intelligibility and Relevance of Analyticity." In *The Cambridge Companion to Quine*, J. Roger Gibson, ed., New York: Cambridge University Press, pp. 48-64.

Dalla Chiara, M. L. and di Francia, G. 1995. "Quine on Physical Objects." In *On Quine*, P. Leonardo and M. Santambrogio, eds., New York: Cambridge University Press, pp. 104-12.

Decock, L. 2002. *Trading Ontology for Ideology.* Boston: Kluwer.

Detlefsen, M. 1986. *Hilbert's Program: An Essay on Mathematical Instrumentalism.* Boston: D. Reidel.

Etchemendy, J. 1988. "Tarski on Truth and Logical Consequence." *Journal of Symbolic Logic* 53, pp. 51-79.

Feferman, A. B. and Feferman, S. 2004. *Alfred Tarski: Life and Logic.* New York: Cambridge University Press.

Field, H. 1972. "Tarski's Theory of Truth." *Journal of Philosophy* 69, pp. 347-75.

———. 1980. *Science Without Numbers: A Defense of Nominalism.* Princeton, NJ: Princeton University Press.

———. 2001. *Truth and the Absence of Fact.* New York: Oxford University Press.

Fodor, J. and Lepore, E. 1991. "Why Meaning (Probably) Isn't Conceptual Role." *Mind and Language* 6, pp. 328-43.

Folina, J. 1992. *Poincaré and the Philosophy of Mathematics.* New York: St. Martin's Press.

Frank, P. 1947. "The Institute for the Unity of Science: Its Background and Purpose." *Synthese* 6, pp. 160-67.

Friedman, M. 1999. *Reconsidering Logical Positivism.* New York: Cambridge University Press.

———. 2000. *A Parting of the Ways.* Chicago and La Salle, IL: Open Court.

———. 2001. *The Dynamics of Reason.* Stanford: CSLI Press.

Frost-Arnold, G. 2004. "Was Tarski's Theory of Truth Motivated by Physicalism?" *History and Philosophy of Logic* 25, pp. 265-80.

George, A. 2000. "On Washing the Fur without Wetting it: Quine, Carnap, and Analyticity." *Mind* 109, pp. 1-24.

Gödel, K. 1963/1983. "What is Cantor's Continuum Problem?" In *Philosophy of Mathematics: Selected Readings*, P. Benacerraf and H. Putnam, eds., New York: Cambridge University Press, pp. 470-85.

Gomez-Torrente, M. 1996. "Tarski on Logical Consequence." *Notre Dame Journal of Formal Logic* 37, pp. 125-51.

Goodman, N. 1956. "A World of Individuals." In *The Problem of Universals: A Symposium*, Notre Dame, IN: University of Notre Dame Press, pp. 15-31.

———. 1966. *The Structure of Appearance.* Indianapolis: Bobbs-Merrill, 2nd edn.

Hacking, I. 1979. "What Is Logic?" *Journal of Philosophy* 76, pp. 285-319.

Hailperin, T. 1992. "Herbrand Semantics, the Potential Infinite, and Ontology-Free Logic." *History and Philosophy of Logic* 13, pp. 69-90.

Hardcastle, G. 2003. "Debabelizing Science: The Harvard Science of Science Discussion Group, 1940-41." In *Logical Empiricism in North America*, G. Hardcastle and A. Richardson, eds., Minneapolis: University of Minnesota Press, pp. 170-96.

Hellman, G. 1989. *Mathematics without Numbers: Towards a Modal-Structural Interpretation.* New York: Oxford University Press.

Heyting, A. 1971/1983. "Disputation." In *Philosophy of Mathematics: Selected Readings*, P. Benacerraf and H. Putnam, eds., New York: Cambridge University Press, 2nd edn., pp. 66-76.

Hilbert, D. 1926/1983. "On the Infinite." In *Philosophy of Mathematics: Selected Readings*, New York: Cambridge University Press, 2nd edn., pp. 183-201.

Hudson, R. 2010. "Carnap, the Principle of Tolerance, and Empiricism." *Philosophy of Science* 77, pp. 341-58.

Hylton, P. 2001. "'The Defensible Province of Philosophy': Quine's 1934 Lectures on Carnap." In *Future Pasts: The Analytic Tradition in Twentieth-Century Philosophy*, J. Floyd and S. Shieh, eds., New York: Oxford University Press, pp. 257-76.

———. 2007. *Quine. Arguments of the Philosophers*. New York: Routledge.

Isaacson, D. 2004. "Quine and Logical Positivism." In *The Cambridge Companion to Quine*, J. Roger Gibson, ed., New York: Cambridge University Press, pp. 214-69.

Kokoszynska, M. 1937-38. "Bemerkungen über die Einheitswissenschaft." *Erkenntnis* 7, pp. 325-35.

Kotarbiński, T. 1929/1966. *Gnosiology: The Scientific Approach to the Theory of Knowledge*. Oxford: Pergamon Press.

———. 1935/1955. "The Fundamental Ideas of Pansomatism." *Mind* 64, pp. 488-500.

Krynicki, M. and Zdanowski, K. 2005. "Theories of Arithmetics in Finite Models." *Journal of Symbolic Logic* 70, pp. 1-28.

Lasnik, H. 2000. *Syntactic Structures Revisited: Contemporary Lectures on Classic Transformational Theory*. Cambridge, MA: MIT Press.

Leśniewski, S. 1992. *Collected Works*. Boston: Kluwer.

Lewis, C. I. 1929. *Mind and the World Order: Outline of a Theory of Knowledge*. New York: Charles Scribners.

Maddy, P. 1990. *Realism in Mathematics*. New York: Oxford University Press.

Mancosu, P. 2001. "Mathematical Explanation: Problems and Prospects." *Topoi* 20, pp. 97-117.

———. 2005. "Harvard 1940-1941: Tarski, Carnap and Quine on a Finitistic Language of Mathematics for science." *History and Philosophy of Logic* 26, pp. 327-57.

———. 2006. "Tarski on Models and Logical Consequence." In *The Architecture of Modern Mathematics*, J. Ferreiros and J. Gray, eds., New York: Oxford University Press, pp. 209-38.

———. 2008a. "Tarski, Neurath, and Kokoszynska on the Semantic Conception of Truth." In *New Essays on Tarski and Philosophy*, D. Patterson, ed., New York: Oxford University Press, pp. 192-224.

———. 2008b. "Quine and Tarski on Nominalism." In *Oxford Studies in Metaphysics*, D. Zimmerman, ed., New York: Oxford University Press, vol. 4, pp. 22-55.

Marcus, R. B. 1946. "A Functional Calculus of First Order Based on Strict Implication." *Journal of Symbolic Logic* 11, pp. 1-16.

Mormann, T. 2007. "The Structure of Scientific Theories in Logical Empiricism." In *The Cambridge Companion to Logical Empiricism*, A. Richardson and T. Uebel, eds., Cambridge University Press, pp. 136-64.

Mostowski, M. 2001. "On Representing Concepts in Finite Models." *Mathematical Logic Quarterly* 47, pp. 513-23.

Neurath, O. 1938. "Unified Science as Encyclopedic Integration." In *The International Encyclopedia of Unified Science*, Chicago: University of Chicago Press, vol. I, pp. 1–27.

———. 1946. "After Six Years." *Synthese* 5, pp. 77–82.

———. 1983. *Philosophical Papers*. Boston: Reidel.

Oppenheim, P. and Putnam, H. 1958. "The Unity of Science as a Working Hypothesis." In *Concepts, Theories, and the Mind-Body Problem*, H. Feigel, M. Scriven, and G. Maxwell, eds., Minneapolis: University of Minnesota Press, vol. II of *Minnesota Studies in the Philosophy of Science*, pp. 3–36.

Patterson, D. 2012. *Alfred Tarski: Philosophy of Language and Logic*. History of Analytic Philosophy. New York: Palgrave MacMillan.

Poincaré, H. 1902/1905. *Science and Hypothesis*. New York: Dover.

Priest, G. 1994. "Is Arithmetic Consistent?" *Mind* 103, pp. 337–49.

———. 1997. "Inconsistent Models of Arithmetic I: Finite Models." *Journal of Philosophical Logic* 26, pp. 223–35.

Psillos, S. 2000. "Rudolf Carnap's 'Theoretical Concepts in Science'." *Studies in the History and Philosophy of Science: Part A* 31, pp. 151–72.

Pullum, G. and Scholz, B. 2010. "Recursion and the Infiniteness Claim." In *Recursion in Human Language*, H. van der Hulst, ed., Berlin: De Gruyter Mouton, vol. 108 of *Studies in Generative Grammar*, pp. 113–38.

Quine, W. V. O. 1939. "Designation and Existence." *Journal of Philosophy* 36, pp. 701–9.

———. 1940/1958. *Mathematical Logic*. Cambridge, MA: Harvard University Press, revised edn.

———. 1943a. "Notes on Existence and Necessity." *Journal of Philosophy* 40, pp. 113–27.

———. 1943b. "On the Problem of Interpreting Modal Logic." *Journal of Symbolic Logic* 12, pp. 43–48.

———. 1947. "On Universals." *Journal of Symbolic Logic* 12, pp. 74–84.

———. 1951. "Main Trends in Recent Philosophy: Two Dogmas of Empiricism." *Philosophical Review* 60, pp. 20–43.

———. 1960. *Word and Object*. Cambridge, MA: MIT Press.

———. 1961. *From a Logical Point of View*. Cambridge, MA: Harvard University Press, 2nd edn.

———. 1970. *Philosophy of Logic*. Cambridge, MA: Harvard University Press.

———. 1974. *The Roots of Reference*. Chicago and La Salle, IL: Open Court.

———. 1976. *The Ways of Paradox*. Cambridge, MA: Harvard University Press, 2nd edn.

———. 1985. *The Time of My Life: An Autobiography*. Cambridge, MA: The MIT Press.

———. 1986. *The Philosophy of W. V. Quine*, vol. 18 of *Library of Living Philosophers*. Chicago and La Salle, IL: Open Court.

———. 1991. "Two Dogmas in Retrospect." *Canadian Journal of Philosophy* 21, pp. 265-74.

———. 2001. "Confessions of a Confirmed Extensionalist." In *Future Pasts: The Analytic Tradition in Twentieth-Century Philosophy*, J. Floyd and S. Shieh, eds., New York: Oxford University Press, pp. 215-22.

———. 2008. *Confessions of a Confirmed Extensionalist and Other Essays*. Cambridge, MA: Harvard University Press.

Quine, W. V. O. and Goodman, N. 1947. "Steps Toward a Constructive Nominalism." *Journal of Symbolic Logic* 12, pp. 105-22.

Reisch, G. 2005. *How the Cold War Transformed Philosophy of Science: To the Icy Slopes of Logic*. New York: Cambridge University Press.

Richardson, A. 1992. "Metaphysics and Idealism in the *Aufbau*." *Grazer Philosophische Studien* 43, pp. 45-72.

———. 1998. *Carnap's Construction of the World*. New York: Cambridge University Press.

———. 2003. "Logical Empiricism, American Pragmatism, and the Fate of Scientific Philosophy in North America." In *Logical Empiricism in North America*, G. Hardcastle and A. Richardson, eds., Minneapolis: University of Minnesota Press, vol. XVIII of *Minnesota Studies in the Philosophy of Science*, pp. 1-24.

———. 2004. "Tolerating Semantics: Carnap's Philosophical Point of View." In *Carnap Brought Home: the View from Jena*, S. Awodey and C. Klein, eds., Chicago and La Salle, IL: Open Court, pp. 63-78.

Ricketts, T. 1982. "Rationality, Translation, and Epistemology Naturalized." *Journal of Philosophy* 79, pp. 117-36.

———. 1994. "Carnap's Principle of Tolerance, Empiricism, and Conventionalism." In *Reading Putnam*, P. Clark and B. Hale, eds., Cambridge, MA: Blackwell, pp. 176-200.

Rosen, E. 2002. "Some Aspects of Model Theory and Finite Structures." *Bulletin of Symbolic Logic* 8, pp. 380-403.

Russell, B. 1918. *Mysticism and Logic and Other Essays*. London: Longmans Green.

———. 1918/1956. "The Philosophy of Logical Atomism." In *Logic and Knowledge*, R. C. Marsh, ed., London: Allen and Unwin, pp. 175-282.

———. 1920. *Introduction to Mathematical Philosophy*. London: Allen and Unwin, 2nd edn.

——. 1940. *An Inquiry into Meaning and Truth*. London: Allen and Unwin.

Schlick, M. 1978. *Moritz Schlick: Philosophical Papers*, vol. I. Dordrecht: Reidel.

Searle, J. 1980. "Minds, Brains, and Programs." *Behavioral and Brain Sciences* 3, pp. 417-24.

Simons, P. 1993. "Nominalism in Poland." In *Polish Scientific Philosophy: The Lvov-Warsaw School*, F. Coniglione, R. Poli, and J. Wolenski, eds., Amsterdam: Rodopi, vol. 28 of *Poznan Studies in the Philosophy of the Sciences and the Humanities*, pp. 207-31.

——. 2002. "Reasoning on a Tight Budget: Lesniewski's Nominalistic Metalogic." *Erkenntnis* 56, pp. 99-122.

Sober, E. 2000. "Quine's Two Dogmas." *Proceedings of the Aristotelian Society* 74, pp. 237-80.

Stein, H. 1992. "Was Carnap Entirely Wrong, After All?" *Synthese* 93, pp. 275-95.

Stevens, S. S. 1974. "S. S. Stevens." In *A History of Psychology in Autobiography*, New York: Appleton, Century, Crofts, pp. 395-420.

Suppes, P. 1978. "The Plurality of Science." *Philosophy of Science Association (Proceedings 1978)* 2, pp. 3-16.

Tait, W. W. 1981. "Finitism." *Journal of Philosophy* 78, pp. 524-56.

Tarski, A. 1935. "Einige methodologische Untersuchungen über die Definierbarkeit der Begriffe." *Erkenntnis* 5, pp. 80-100.

——. 1983. *Logic, Semantics, Metamathematics*. Indianapolis: Hackett, 2nd edn.

——. 1986. "What are the Logical Notions?" *History and Philosophy of Logic* 7, pp. 143-54.

Tarski, A. and Lindenbaum, A. 1936. "Über die Beschränktheit der Ausdrucksmittel deductiver Theorien." *Ergebnisse eines Mathematischen Kolloquiums* 7, pp. 15-22.

Tennant, N. 1997. *The Taming of the True*. New York: Oxford University Press.

——. 2008. "Carnap, Gödel, and the Analyticity of Arithmetic." *Philosophia Mathematica* 16, pp. 100-12.

Uebel, T. 2001. "Carnap and Neurath in Exile: Can Their Disputes be Resolved?" *International Studies in the Philosophy of Science* 15, pp. 211-20.

——. 2007. *Empiricism at the Crossroads: The Vienna Circle's Protocol-Sentence Debate Revisited*. Chicago and La Salle, IL: Open Court.

van Fraassen, B. C. 1980. *The Scientific Image*. New York: Oxford University Press.

——. 2002. *The Empirical Stance*. New Haven, CT: Yale University Press.

White, M. 1987. "A Philosophical Letter of Alfred Tarski." *Journal of Philosophy* 84, pp. 28-32.

———. 1999. *A Philosopher's Story*. University Park, PA: Pennsylvania State Press.

Wilson, J. 2000. "Could Experience Disconfirm the Propositions of Arithmetic?" *Canadian Journal of Philosophy* 30, pp. 55-84.

Wittgenstein, L. 1921/1961. *Tractatus Logico-Philosophicus*. Atlantic Highlands, NJ: Humanities Press International.

Wolenski, J. 1993. "Tarski as Philosopher." In *Polish Scientific Philosophy: The Lvov-Warsaw School*, F. Coniglione, R. Poli, and J. Wolenski, eds., Amsterdam: Rodopi, vol. 28 of *Poznan Studies in the Philosophy of the Sciences and the Humanities*, pp. 319-38.

Woodger, J. H. 1937. *The Axiomatic Method in Biology*. Cambridge: Cambridge University Press.

———. 1952. *Biology and Language*. Cambridge: Cambridge University Press.

Index

Λ (empty set), 161, 185, 212, 237
ω, 161, 176, 212, 228
    -rule, 99

a priori, 74, 81, 97, 103, 113, 152-54, 203, 205
abstract, 8-9, 11, 13, 23, 32-34, 40-43, 47-48, 61, 65, 118, 120
accented expression ('), 78, 163, 165-67, 170-75
analyticity, 25, 34, 35, 37, 46, 63, 67, 68, 71, 73-78, 80-116, 139, 140, 144, 145, 155, 156, 182, 183, 185, 188, 191, 192, 196, 207, 234, 237, 238, 240
arithmetic, 7, 8, 10-14, 27, 28, 46-47, 55, 69-70, 72, 74-75, 78-81, 86, 99, 149, 152, 153, 156-58, 162-66, 169, 174-77, 179-80, 183, 185, 189
Aufbau (Carnap), 35, 36, 40, 110, 120, 123-26, 133-34, 151, 202

behaviorism, 86, 87, 97, 103-4, 113, 153, 189, 204, 241
Bernays, Paul, 43-44, 141, 149, 159, 160, 168, 177, 180, 182, 192, 200, 211, 212, 219, 229, 231, 233
Bridgman, Percy, 2, 153, 204

Cantor, Georg, 21
    Cantor's Theorem, 141, 160, 192, 211

Cantorians, 16
choice, Axiom of, 19, 76, 154
Chwistek, Leon, 15-19, 24, 37, 38, 141, 193
class, 4-6, 12, 23, 39, 62, 64, 78, 91-93, 104, 114, 140, 146, 147, 151, 152, 155, 160, 168, 186, 188, 189, 192, 197, 198, 200-4, 206-8, 211-14, 219, 236, 238-42
Klasse, 240
"On the Concept of Truth in Formalized Languages," (Tarski), *see Wahrheitsbegriff*
consequence, logical, 3, 5, 56, 91, 93, 94, 101-2, 149, 152, 183, 188
    "On the Concept of Logical Consequence" (Tarski), 92-96
c-rule, 99, 100
probabilistic, 185-86
constant, 236
    individual, 76, 77, 125, 126, 147, 148, 155, 184, 185
    logical, 4, 76, 91, 96, 139, 144, 145, 147, 156, 170, 171, 184, 195, 196, 221, 222
    non-logical/ descriptive, 4, 78, 93, 122, 152-54, 159, 184, 185, 188
constructivism, 8, 9, 17, 18, 24, 42, 44, 61, 63, 124, 130, 148

253

contradiction, 43, 44, 75, 142, 144, 146, 149, 160, 178, 188, 194
convention, 84, 86, 91, 103, 129
conventionalism, 16, 68, 104, 149
Creath, Richard, 81-82, 84, 97, 100, 114-16

definability, 16, 17, 119, 120, 134, 145, 148, 149, 158, 169, 184
definition, 32, 62, 78, 85, 91, 93, 104-7, 110, 140, 146, 149, 151, 168, 170, 171, 177, 185, 198, 202, 207, 220-22, 228, 236
   contextual, 148, 149, 182, 199, 200, 234
   explicit, 170, 221
   recursive, 58, 75, 157, 164, 166, 167, 170, 176, 177, 179-81, 208, 215, 217, 219, 228, 229, 231-33
derivation (d-rules), *see* proof
designation, 6, 8, 11, 20, 38, 39, 41, 47-48, 59, 62, 63, 76, 78, 79, 92, 108, 111, 120, 140, 141, 143, 145, 161, 177, 185, 187, 192, 239
   rules of, 75, 76, 79

Eddington, Arthur, 14, 190, 242
empiricism, 36, 58, 113, 122, 129, 149
   logical, 113, 137
epistemology, 28, 35-37, 39-42, 57, 81, 149, 201
   of logic, 113, 149, 200
   of mathematics, 23
extensionality, 18, 89, 90, 107-12, 115, 140, 148, 151, 159, 161, 189, 192, 199, 202, 212, 241

Field, Hartry, 12, 48, 49
finitism, 3-4, 6, 8-10, 13-15, 23-25, 27, 28, 42, 45-47, 52, 54, 55, 57, 59-66, 70-71, 141, 147, 150, 153, 156, 161-65, 168, 176, 178-80, 189, 190, 193, 198, 201, 204, 207, 208, 212-17, 219, 227, 230, 232, 241
Foundations of Logic and Mathematics (Carnap), 30, 31, 33, 53, 57, 67, 68, 75, 78, 91, 97, 110, 152, 156
Frege, Gottlob, 8, 70, 71, 79
   -analyticity, 90, 108

geometry, 67-70, 105, 153, 204
Gödel, Kurt, 52, 57-58, 85, 98-102, 105, 149, 157, 165, 182, 183, 190, 200, 233-35, 242
   completeness, 148, 178, 200
   completeness theorem, 230
   incompleteness, 85, 89, 150, 201
   sentence, 100, 208
Goodman, Nelson, 1, 5, 7-9, 21, 25, 27, 34, 41, 43-44, 48, 54, 56, 70, 82, 85, 110, 114, 150-51, 176, 183, 184, 188-90, 202-3, 227, 235, 239, 241, 242

Hahn, Hans, 25, 52
Hempel, Carl, 1, 7, 10, 96, 134, 188-90, 239, 241, 242
Heyting, Arend, 17, 130, 190, 242
Hilbert, David, 4, 45, 57, 60, 177, 178, 182, 229, 230, 233

identity (=), 108, 147-49, 172, 174, 178, 179, 182
   quasi-, 157
indispensibility argument, 48-50, 107
induction, 57, 163, 167, 170, 171, 173, 179-81, 206, 215, 219, 221, 223, 224, 231-33
infinity, 4, 9, 16, 19, 21, 23-25, 42, 45-47, 61-65, 70, 72, 80, 148, 149, 152, 156, 162, 164, 167, 169, 174, 178-80, 188, 189, 199, 200, 203, 208, 214, 215, 220, 225, 230-32, 241
   axiom of, 13, 19, 23, 69, 76, 77, 161, 163, 212, 214, 215
   infinite arithmetic, 7, 28, 157, 158, 176, 177, 208, 209, 228
   potential, 58-60, 72, 157, 208
intelligibility [*Verständlichkeit*], 4-11, 19, 25, 27-38, 44, 49, 53-59, 72, 90, 137, 140, 150, 153, 156-61, 164, 176, 177, 188-90, 242
   of set theory, 58

Index

intensionality, 25, 82, 87, 89, 90, 94, 107, 108, 110, 111, 140, 144, 156, 189, 191, 192, 195, 207, 241
interpretation, 30, 31, 38, 49, 53-55, 67-69, 74-75, 77-78, 100, 105, 122, 140, 152, 155, 166, 178, 187, 190, 192, 207, 238, 239, 242
   of arithmetic, 12, 63, 79, 153, 156, 165, 175
   of modal logic, 82
   partial, 7, 31, 33, 57, 72, 92, 177, 187, 189, 229, 238
Introduction to Semantics (Carnap), 30, 64, 73, 75, 78, 91, 92, 94, 111, 140, 154, 156
intuition, 31
intuitionism, 17, 34, 44, 66, 101, 130, 141, 148, 149, 190, 193, 199, 200, 242

Kant, Immanuel, 31, 74, 132
Kaufmann, Felix, 19
Kokoszynska, Maria, 119
Kotarbiński, Tadeuz, 4, 15, 19-21, 46, 153, 160, 204, 211

L-false, *see* contradiction
L-truth, *see* analyticity
law, 31, 32, 39, 48, 53, 55, 57, 58, 85, 86, 118-19, 122, 134, 150, 169, 201, 206, 220
   of excluded middle, 141
Leśniewski, Stanislaw, 20-22, 160, 211
Logical Syntax of Language (Carnap), 6, 9, 11, 13, 15, 29, 32, 46, 51, 52, 59, 78, 89, 96, 99, 101, 105, 110, 119, 128-30, 157, 167, 208, 219

Mancosu, Paolo, xiv, 2, 3, 9, 15, 41, 57, 69, 86, 93, 114-16, 120, 141, 152
Mathematical Logic (Quine), 1, 109, 148, 149, 160, 183, 185, 199, 200, 211, 234, 236, 237
meaning, 8, 10, 19, 23-25, 31, 32, 35-37, 41, 44, 54-59, 68, 72, 73, 75, 83, 93, 104, 106, 110, 111, 117, 121-23, 125-28, 130-32, 137, 148, 154, 171, 185, 187
metaphysics, 17-18, 22-24, 37-42, 54-57, 59, 74, 103, 117-18, 122-37
modality, 25, 60, 72, 82, 89, 107-8, 111, 112, 140, 156, 191, 207, 208
model, 4, 67, 71, 74, 76, 81, 91-94, 100, 146, 153, 158, 185-87, 189, 197, 205, 210, 236, 238-39, 241
   non-standard, 155, 206
myth, 39, 54, 133, 150, 177, 201, 202, 229

Neumann, John von, 13, 17, 146, 149, 159, 197, 200, 211
Neurath, Otto, 24-25, 29, 33, 37, 38, 118-22, 125, 129, 131-33, 136
nominalism, 2, 5-15, 20, 21, 25, 27-29, 34, 38-45, 47-50, 52, 56, 60-62, 64, 136, 141, 148, 151, 193, 199, 203
   Chwistek's, 15-19
nonsense, 20, 38, 41, 54, 107, 129, *see also* meaning
number, 5, 8-15, 17, 22-23, 44, 47, 48, 52, 57-60, 63-67, 77, 79, 94, 130, 141, 144, 145, 149, 150, 156-57, 162-65, 169, 176-78, 189, 190, *see also* arithmetic
   cardinal, 146, 154, 162
   ordinal, 161

observation, 8-10, 25, 32-33, 51-57, 86, 96, 103, 127-29, 137, 139, 150, 162, 186, *see also* protocol sentence
operator, 58, 145, 147, 157, 172, 173, 176, 180, 182, 196, 198, 208, 209, 224, 232, 234
   existential, 125, 171, 223, 228
   K-, 166, 171, 218, 223, 231
   restricted, 166, 168, 169, 171, 177, 179, 217, 220, 222, 229
   universal, 99, 157, 163, 166, 171, 173, 176, 181, 215, 217, 222, 224, 225, 228, 232
   unrestricted, 15, 141, 171-73, 189, 193, 222-24, 241

order, 130, 160
   ω, 161
   first-, 5, 19, 23, 38, 39, 45, 46, 59, 74, 81
   higher-, 5, 17, 23, 38, 39, 41, 42

paradox, 42-45, 150, 164, 165, 201, 216, *see also* contradiction
   Russell's, 43-44
Peano arithmetic, 11, 13, 55, 69, 72, 74, 78, 79, 99, 152, 154, 163, 176, 203, 206, 214, 228
   non-standard models of, 155
physicalism, 120-22, 131
physics, 8, 9, 33, 44, 46, 54-58, 86, 97, 106, 113, 114, 118, 120, 148, 150, 153, 154, 169, 177, 184, 188, 190, 191, 199, 201, 204, 206, 220, 229, 236, 240-42
Platonism, 4, 5, 15-17, 29, 38-40, 42-44, 52, 54, 69, 130, 141-43, 148, 153, 193-95, 200, 204
Poincaré, Henri, 16-17, 57-58, 66, 74, 141, 193
Popper, Karl, 190, 242
predicativism, 16, 66
Principia Mathematica (Russell and Whitehead), 23, 44, 99, 107, 122, 125, 159-61, 210-12
probability, 2, 25, 147, 185, 186
proof, 4, 5, 8, 14, 24, 29, 30, 44, 62, 67, 68, 70-71, 89, 90, 98-102, 105, 146, 148, 149, 153, 156-62, 165, 169, 174, 178, 183, 184, 197, 200, 207-13, 216, 218, 220, 224, 225, 230, 232, 234-36
property, 20, 28, 76-78, 92, 108, 140, 155, 187
proposition, 17-18, 83, 143-44, 195-96
   pseudo-, 41, *see also* nonsense
protocol sentences, 29, 52, 127, 129, 131, 132
psychology, 29, 104, 118, 119, 121, 124, 133, 142, 150, 154, 190, 194, 202, 205, 242
Putnam, Hilary, 48

quantum mechanics, 31-32, 46, 86, 164

reism, 4, 15, 19-22, 46, 65, 153, 163, 204, 214
relativity, theory of, 97, 106
Russell, Bertrand, 1, 18, 22-24, 36, 38, 41, 73, 77, 79, 84, 114, 141-43, 150, 161, 193-95, 201, 212

Schlick, Moritz, 25, 38, 52, 117, 123
semantics, 7, 20, 25, 28, 36, 71, 90-94, 99, 102, 104, 106, 115, 126-29, 132, 140, 143, 149, 157, 158, 169, 176, 184-87, 191-92, 195, 200, 209, 220, 228, 235-37, 239, 241, *see also* interpretation, *see also* meaning
   Chwistek, 18
   conception of truth, 66
   general, 139, 145-47, 191, 196-99
   of scientific theories, 31-33
   semantic rules, 30, 53, 75-81, 96, 97, 100, 188, 238, 240
sequence, 11-12, 14, 28, 61-65, 78-79, 92, 147, 161, 163-64, 174-75, 184, 185, 187, 188
set, 7, 8, 38-42, 44, 55, 58, 72, 141, 145, 147, 158, 159, 168
Skolem, Thoralf, 153, 158, 204, 210
space, 6, 12, 19, 23, 45-47, 55, 61, 68, 93, 105, 120, 161, 164, 174
state of affairs, 76, 91-94, 107, 108, 147, 164, 186, 188, 189, 239
"Steps Toward a Constructive Nominalism," (Goodman and Quine), 21, 27, 34, 62, 70
synonymy, 34, 82, 87, 90, 92, 104, 106, 108, 112, 155, 207
syntax, 7, 9, 18, 33, 52, 70-71, 78, 104, 105, 126, 132, 140, 145, 147, 148, 158-60, 167, 169, 174, 175, 177, 183, 184, 189, 192, 196, 197, 199, 200, 209, 210, 212, 219, 220, 225, 226, 229, 235, 236, 241
   finitist, 61-65, 161-62, 164-65, 212-13, 215-16
   syntactic view of scientific theories, 32
tautology, 95, 178, 183, 184, 229, 234, 236

"Testability and Meaning," (Carnap), 25, 33, 36, 52, 53, 56-58, 127
theology, 24, 129, 133, 142, 194
theorem, 8, 24, 55, 64, 77, 86, 90, 101, 102, 105, 106, 141, 146, 149, 150, 161, 178, 183, 184, 193, 198, 200, 201, 212, 230, 235, 236
time, 23, 45-47, 61, 76, 120, 162, 164, 214-16
tolerance, principle of, 10, 44, 49, 51-52, 66-68, 95, 96, 128-30
Tractatus Logico-Philosophicus (Wittgenstein), 8, 23, 24, 38, 41, 52, 101, 125, 136
"Truth by Convention (Quine), 81-87, 97, 103, 105, 106, 108, 113, 114
"Two Dogmas of Empiricism," (Quine), 34, 81-84, 86-87, 89, 90, 96, 97, 103, 106, 108-16
type, 15, 38, 44, 141, 145-46, 157, 159-61, 184

understandable, *see* intelligibility
unity of science, 1, 26, 117-33, 136-37
universals, 4, 6, 20, 28, 39, 40, 114, 148, 149, 153

variable, 4-6, 16, 38-41, 43, 58, 59, 65, 72, 76, 114, 141, 144-49, 153, 155-57, 159, 160, 163, 168-72, 176, 179, 182-85, 188, 189, 193, 195-200, 204, 206-11, 214, 215, 220-23, 228, 231, 234-36
verification, 127
  criterion of meaning, 36, 122, 124, 127

Wahrheitsbegriff (Tarski), 17, 42, 75, 90, 92, 109, 135, 141, 145, 146, 160, 197, 211
Weyl, Hermann, 190, 242
White, Morton, 82, 87, 114
Wittgenstein, Ludwig, 8, 18, 24, 37, 41, 125
Woodger, J. H., 49, 114, 115, 121-22
Word and Object (Quine), 62, 81, 86, 90, 103, 104
Wundheiler, Aleksander, 152, 153, 155, 204, 206

Zermelo, Ernst, 13, 141, 145, 146, 150, 159, 161, 192, 197, 201, 211, 212
Zilsel, Edgar, 129

www.ingramcontent.com/pod-product-compliance
Lightning Source LLC
Chambersburg PA
CBHW030109010526
44116CB00005B/164